Freemasons FOR DUMMIES®

2ND EDITION

by Christopher Hodapp

WILEY

John Wiley & Sons, Inc.

Freemasons For Dummies®, 2nd Edition

Published by
John Wiley & Sons, Inc.
111 River St.
Hoboken, NJ 07030-5774
www.wiley.com

For general information on our other products and services, please contact our Customer Care Department within the U.S. at 877-762-2974, outside the U.S. at 317-572-3993, or fax 317-572-4002.

For technical support, please visit www.wiley.com/techsupport.

Wiley publishes in a variety of print and electronic formats and by print-on-demand. Some material included with standard print versions of this book may not be included in e-books or in print-on-demand. If this book refers to media such as a CD or DVD that is not included in the version you purchased, you may download this material at http://booksupport.wiley.com. For more information about Wiley products, visit www.wiley.com.

Library of Congress Control Number: 2012954768

ISBN 978-1-118-41208-4 (pbk); ISBN 978-1-118-41210-7 (ebk); ISBN 978-1-118-41215-2 (ebk); ISBN 978-1-118-41216-9 (ebk)

Manufactured in the United States of America

V10002920_080118

WILEY

About the Author

Christopher Hodapp is the editor of the Journal of the Masonic Society. He has been a Freemason since 1998 and is a Past Master of Broad Ripple Lodge #643 and Lodge Vitruvian #767, Free & Accepted Masons of the State of Indiana. He is an honorary member of African Lodge #459, Prince Hall Affiliation, in Boston, Massachusetts. He is a member of the Royal Arch Masons, Cryptic Masons, the Allied Masonic Degrees, and the Knights Templar. He is a 33° Mason in the Ancient Accepted Scottish Rite, Indianapolis Valley, and he is a member of the Royal Order of Scotland.

He has served on the Masonic Education and Technology Committees of the Grand Lodge of Indiana and is a member of the boards of Indiana Freemasons' Hall and the Grand Lodge of Indiana Library and Museum.

Chris is a Founding Fellow of the Masonic Society. He is a member of the Southern California Research Lodge, the Scottish Rite Research Society, the Philalethes Society, the Phylaxis Society, the Grand College of Rites of the United States of America, and the Quatuor Coronati Correspondence Circle. In 2006, Chris was presented with the Duane E. Anderson Excellence in Masonic Education Award from the Grand Lodge of Minnesota for *Freemasons For Dummies*.

His second book, *Solomon's Builders: Freemasons, Founding Fathers and the Secrets of Washington D.C.* (Ulysses Press), was published in December 2006. He has also co-written *The Templar Code For Dummies* and *Conspiracy Theories & Secret Societies For Dummies* with Alice Von Kannon. He has written numerous articles about Freemasonry for both the Masonic and mainstream press and has appeared in numerous television documentaries about Masonry.

He has spent 25 years as a commercial filmmaker and editor and has written scripts for corporate and nonprofit clients. He and his wife Alice have spent more than 30 years positively besotted with each other, and they live with their very French poodle, Wiley, in Indianapolis.

Dedication

To Alice, to the memory of her father, and to a little group of Texas Freemasons who unknowingly started me on my journey.

Author's Acknowledgments

This is one of those books that I wondered why no one had written over the years, and then I wound up being the guy writing it. I owe profuse and heartfelt thanks to Richard J. Elman, Grand Master of Masons in Indiana during 2004 and 2005, for many reasons too complex to bore you with here, but especially for saying, "I know someone who could write this." I owe an equal debt of gratitude that can never be repaid to Roger S. VanGorden, Grand Master of Masons in Indiana during 2002 and 2003. From my first Internet contact with an Indiana Freemason to his boundless assistance with this book — and everything in between — Roger remains my greatest Masonic mentor, and I am ever grateful for his trust and his friendship.

Thanks to Dr. S. Brent Morris of the Scottish Rite Southern Masonic Jurisdiction and editor of the *Scottish Rite Journal* and Richard Curtis of the Northern Masonic Jurisdiction and former editor of the *Northern Light Magazine* for their assistance in negotiating the shoals and eddies of the Scottish Rite. And special thanks to the late Nelson King, past president of the Philalethes Society and editor of *The Philalethes Magazine*, and to Bud Householder, also of the Philalethes Society, who served as technical editors of this book.

Thanks for the assistance of Brothers Jeff Naylor, Eric Schmitz, Tom Fellows, Timothy Bonney, Jim Dillman, Bill Hosler, Billy Koon, Ed King and Stephen Dafoe; for Worshipful Brother Don Seeley whose example always reminds me to get it right; and for Worshipful Brothers Jerry Cowley and Wilson Lorick, who introduced me to Prince Hall Masonry. And an extraordinary note of thanks goes to my great friend of three decades, Nathan Brindle, who never fails to whisper good counsel in my ear, and was my Brother long before we joined a lodge together.

Thanks to Tracy Boggier at Wiley Publishing, for putting a lot of trust in an unproven author and for teaching me everything I know about raising a puppy, and to my editors Elizabeth Kuball, Vicki Adang, and Caitlin Copple for calmly guiding me through the wilderness.

My deepest gratitude goes to Carolyn Steele, for taking care of business when I couldn't. And finally, to my wife Alice, for her support and her boundless energy, and for more than 30 years of better and worse, richer and poorer, sickness and health. She remains my biggest cheerleader, my greatest research assistant, my dearest friend, the love of my life, and the best writer I personally know.

Publisher's Acknowledgments

We're proud of this book; please send us your comments at http://dummies.custhelp.com. For other comments, please contact our Customer Care Department within the U.S. at 877-762-2974, outside the U.S. at 317-572-3993, or fax 317-572-4002.

Some of the people who helped bring this book to market include the following:

Acquisitions, Editorial, and Vertical Websites

Senior Project Editor: Victoria M. Adang
   (*Previous Edition: Elizabeth Kuball*)

Senior Acquisitions Editor: Tracy Boggier

Copy Editor: Caitlin Copple

Assistant Editor: David Lutton

Editorial Program Coordinator: Joe Niesen

Technical Editor: Bud Householder

Editorial Manager: Michelle Hacker

Editorial Assistants: Rachelle Amick, Alexa Koschier

Cover Photo: © Christopher Hodapp

Cartoons: Rich Tennant (www.the5thwave.com)

Composition Services

Project Coordinator: Katherine Crocker

Layout and Graphics: Jennifer Creasey

Proofreader: Bonnie Mikkelson

Indexer: Potomac Indexing, LLC

Publishing and Editorial for Consumer Dummies

Kathleen Nebenhaus, Vice President and Executive Publisher

David Palmer, Associate Publisher

Kristin Ferguson-Wagstaffe, Product Development Director

Publishing for Technology Dummies

Andy Cummings, Vice President and Publisher

Composition Services

Debbie Stailey, Director of Composition Services

Contents at a Glance

Introduction **1**

Part 1: What Is Freemasonry? **9**

Chapter 1: Lodges, Aprons, and Funny Handshakes: Freemasonry 101 11

Chapter 2: From Cathedrals to Lodge Rooms: A History of the Freemasons 21

Chapter 3: The Philosophy of Freemasonry 55

Chapter 4: Politics, Religion, and Freemasons: They Don't Mix 63

Part 11: The Inner Workings of Freemasonry **89**

Chapter 5: How the Freemasons Are Organized: Who Does What and Why 91

Chapter 6: The Ceremonies of Freemasons 115

Chapter 7: The Symbols of Freemasonry 129

Chapter 8: Myths and Misconceptions about Masons 151

Part 111: When One Lodge Isn't Enough: The Appendant Bodies **163**

Chapter 9: Introducing the Appendant Bodies: Who's Who, and Who Isn't 165

Chapter 10: The York Rite 181

Chapter 11: The Ancient Accepted Scottish Rite 203

Chapter 12: Shriners International 221

Chapter 13: The Extended Masonic Family 231

Part 1V: Freemasonry Today and Tomorrow **249**

Chapter 14: So Is It Still Relevant? 251

Chapter 15: Freemasons and the Future 259

Chapter 16: So You Want to Become a Freemason 267

Part V: The Part of Tens **279**

Chapter 17: Ten Groups of Famous Masons 281

Chapter 18: Ten Amazing Conspiracies, Anti-Masons, and Hoaxes 289

Chapter 19: Ten Cool Masonic Places 301

Part VI: Appendixes **305**
Appendix A: The Regius Manuscript 307
Appendix B: Anderson's Constitutions 329
Appendix C: Finding a Lodge 335

Index **347**

Table of Contents

Introduction 1
About This Book 2
Conventions Used in This Book 2
What You're Not to Read 3
Foolish Assumptions 3
How This Book Is Organized 4
    Part I: What Is Freemasonry? 4
    Part II: The Inner Workings of Freemasonry 4
    Part III: When One Lodge Isn't Enough: The Appendant Bodies 5
    Part IV: Freemasonry Today and Tomorrow 5
    Part V: The Part of Tens 5
    Part VI: Appendixes 6
Icons Used in This Book 6
Where to Go from Here 7

Part 1: What Is Freemasonry? 9

Chapter 1: Lodges, Aprons, and Funny Handshakes:
Freemasonry 101 11
What Is Freemasonry? 13
What Do Masons Do? 14
    Conferring the three degrees 15
    Meeting in lodges, blue lodges, craft lodges, and more 15
    Performing public ceremonies 16
    Wearing aprons (Real men do it!) 17
    Keeping "secrets" 17
    Providing something for everyone 18
Are [Fill in the Blank] Freemasons, Too? 19

Chapter 2: From Cathedrals to Lodge Rooms:
A History of the Freemasons 21
Turning Stonecutters into Gentlemen: Freemasonry before 1700 22
    Operative Masons: The great builders 22
    Speculative Masons and the big change 28
Building Men: The 1700s 31
    Founding the first Grand Lodge 31
    Establishing Masonry in America 38
    Finding favor and persecution during and after the French
        Revolution 41

Growing, Changing, and Branching Out: The 1800s..............................42
    Reuniting Antients and Moderns 43
    Spreading throughout America.......................................44
Surviving and Surging: The 1900s..50
    Relieving social concerns in the early 1900s..................50
    Being cast as villains and heroes in World War II 51
    Growing again post-war 51
    Declining in the '60s..52
Experiencing the New Millennium: More Changes on the Way.............53
    Traditional Observance lodges 53
    The Dan Brown effect..54

Chapter 3: The Philosophy of Freemasonry......................55

Defining What Masons Believe In 56
    Promoting brotherly love, relief, and truth...................56
    Adhering to basic principles 58
Establishing a New World Order?...60
Experiencing Mystic Masonry..61
    Connecting members through a mystic tie 62
    Expressing concepts through symbolism 62

Chapter 4: Politics, Religion, and Freemasons: They Don't Mix.....63

Exploring the History of Religion and the Masons...........................64
    Bringing limited religion into the lodge 64
    Examining the history of Freemasonry and Catholicism....66
    Pairing Freemasons and Protestants peacefully (mostly)...........71
    Bridging great divides: Freemasonry and Judaism 72
    Finding conflict between Freemasonry and Islam
    (where none exists) 75
Refusing to Play Politics 77
    Placing Freemasonry amid the political turmoil
    of 18th-century Europe..77
    Sparking anarchy in French lodges 78
    Surviving the revolution 80
    Enduring the rule of dictators.......................................82
    Continuing to weather distrust.....................................84
    Maintaining Brotherhood during war 85

Part II: The Inner Workings of Freemasonry.................. 89

**Chapter 5: How the Freemasons Are Organized:
Who Does What and Why....................................91**

What's Inside the Lodge?...92
    Examining the lodge room...92
    Meeting and eating at the lodge.....................................94

Who's in Charge around Here? 94
    Officers in the progressive line 95
    Officers not in the progressive line 100
What Makes a Grand Lodge So, Well, Grand? 105
    The Grand Master 105
    The rules 106
What Is a Regular, Recognized Lodge? 108
    Which one's legit? Sorting through multiple Grand Lodges.........108
    Irregular, unrecognized, and all over the place:
        Lodges out of the mainstream...111

Chapter 6: The Ceremonies of Freemasons 115

Understanding Where Masonic Ritual Comes From 116
    The historical medieval guild rituals...................................116
    The written account 119
Performing the Rituals of the Modern Lodge..........................121
    Setting the stage for the ritual..121
    Entered Apprentice: Initiation and youth............................123
    Fellow Craft: Passing through manhood...............................127
    Master Mason: Raising, age, and death...............................127
    Movin' on up!..128

Chapter 7: The Symbols of Freemasonry 129

Symbolizing the Lessons of Freemasonry 130
Deciphering the Key Masonic Ideas 131
    The number three...131
    Tracing boards: 18th-century PowerPoint 132
    Solomon's Temple 134
    Square and compass 136
Explaining More Masonic Symbols 137
    Scythe and hourglass 138
    The 47th Problem of Euclid or the Pythagorean theorem............138
    Jacob's ladder 139
    Anchor and ark...139
    Sun, eye, Moon, and stars...139
    Lamb and lambskin apron 139
    Slipper 140
    Point within a circle and parallel lines...............................140
    Pot of incense 141
    Beehive..141
    Plumb 142
    Level 142
    Letter G..143
    Five-pointed star 145
    Naked heart and sword..145
    Tyler's sword and the Book of Constitutions.......................146
    Trowel 146

Handshake 146
Rough and perfect (or smooth) ashlars 147
Pillars 147
The shovel, setting maul, coffin, and sprig of acacia 148
24-inch gauge and the common gavel 150

Chapter 8: Myths and Misconceptions about Masons **151**
Digging to the Root of Freemasonry Misunderstandings 152
Debunking Common Myths about Freemasonry 152
Riding the lodge goat 153
Keeping an eye on you with the all-seeing eye
and the U.S. $1 bill 153
Reading a Masonic bible 155
Worshipping strange gods 156
Pairing up Pike and Lucifer 159
Taking over the world 161
Breaking the law 162

**Part III: When One Lodge Isn't Enough:
The Appendant Bodies** *163*

**Chapter 9: Introducing the Appendant Bodies:
Who's Who, and Who Isn't** **165**
What Are Appendant Bodies? 167
Concordant bodies 168
Appendant bodies 170
So What about These Other Groups? 172
Animal lodges 172
Service clubs 173
Other unrelated fraternal groups 175
Masonic-sounding groups 177

Chapter 10: The York Rite **181**
The York Rite System 182
Why York? 183
How it's organized 183
Royal Arch Masonry 185
Mark Master 186
Past Master 186
Most Excellent Master 187
Royal Arch 188
The Cryptic Rite 188
Chivalric Masonry and the Knights Templar 190
The chivalric orders 191
A crash course in Templar history 193

Other York Rite Bodies 198
    York Rite College.. 199
    Knight Masons.. 199
    Allied Masonic Degrees.. 199
    Societas Rosicruciana in Civitatibus Foederatis...................... 200
    Rectified Rite or Chevalier Bienfaisant de Cite Saint (CBCS) ...200
    Holy Royal Arch Knight Templar Priests................................ 200
    Knights of the York Cross of Honour 201
    Red Cross of Constantine 201
    St. Thomas of Acon.. 201
    The Operatives... 201
York Rite Charities 202

Chapter 11: The Ancient Accepted Scottish Rite 203
Surveying the Scottish Rite System... 205
    Organization: Meeting the departments that confer degrees 205
    Membership: Earning degrees in the Scottish Rite 206
    Presentation: Raising the curtain and lighting the lights 208
Seeing How the Scottish Rite Started... 208
    France: Freemasonry's foundry furnace.................................. 209
    The Americas: The Scottish Rite's real home 210
Meeting Albert Pike: Sage of the Scottish Rite.......................... 210
    Pike's life outside of Masonry 211
    Discovering Freemasonry.. 211
    Writing and revising rituals, morals, and dogma..................... 213
    Putting Pike in perspective... 215
Listing the Degrees of the Scottish Rite..................................... 215
    The Southern Jurisdiction degrees 216
    The Northern Masonic Jurisdiction degrees............................ 217
Serving Communities through Charitable Work........................... 219

Chapter 12: Shriners International 221
Getting to Know the Shriners.. 222
Tracing the History from Partiers to Philanthropists................... 222
    The Knickerbocker boys start the fun 223
    So why the goofy hats?.. 223
    The first growth of the Shrine 224
    Polio and the first Shrine hospital 224
    Depression and growth... 225
    Greatest philanthropy in the world.. 225
Putting a Little of the Boy Back in the Man............................... 226
    Becoming initiated.. 226
    Gathering at temples 226
    Forming units to suit every Shriner....................................... 227
    Having fun in little cars 228
Considering the Shrine's Place in Freemasonry.......................... 229

Chapter 13: The Extended Masonic Family **231**

Bringing Women into the Lodge 231
The Order of the Eastern Star 232
The Order of the Amaranth..236
The White Shrine of Jerusalem 238
The Social Order of the Beauceant..239
Not Just Kidding Around: The Youth Groups..............................239
DeMolay International for boys 240
The International Order of the Rainbow for Girls 242
Job's Daughters..242
Checking Out Lesser-Known Masonic Groups..............................243
The Mystic Order of the Veiled Prophets of
the Enchanted Realm of North America...........................243
The Ancient Egyptian Order of SCIOTS................................244
The Tall Cedars of Lebanon of North America 244
National Sojourners..245
High Twelve International...246
Investigating Masonic Research Societies 246
Quatuor Coronati Lodge No. 2076 247
Philalethes Society...247
Phylaxis Society 247
Scottish Rite Research Society..248
Lodges of research 248
The Masonic Society 248

Part IV: Freemasonry Today and Tomorrow **249**

Chapter 14: So Is It Still Relevant? **251**

A Breakdown in Community 252
Isolating individuals 252
Disconnecting from each other..253
Getting shortchanged in social capital 254
Where Freemasonry Fits In 254
Making good men better ones...255
Providing something for everybody.......................................255
Supporting brotherly love 256
Involving people in charitable work......................................256
Practicing religious tolerance 257
Giving comfort through constancy...258

Chapter 15: Freemasons and the Future **259**

Speculating on the Future of the Craft...260
One-day classes...261
Advertising...262
Paying your dues 262

Going Back to the Future...263
    Staying small to survive.................................263
    Returning to old ways.....................................265
    Exploring ancient lessons with new technology.........265
Breaking Down Barriers through the Internet.................266

Chapter 16: So You Want to Become a Freemason **267**
Examining Why Men Become Masons 268
    What's in it for you......................................268
    Hearing from Masons themselves 269
    Why I joined...270
To Be One, Ask One......................................272
    Finding a Freemason....................................272
    Finding a lodge 273
Joining a Lodge..273
    Qualifying for membership.............................274
    Petitioning to join the lodge...........................275
    Being investigated......................................275
    Balloting 276
    Scheduling your degree ceremonies 276
    Being welcomed as a Brother..........................278

Part V: The Part of Tens 279

Chapter 17: Ten Groups of Famous Masons **281**
Founding Fathers...281
Explorers and Adventurers...............................282
Pioneers of Science and Medicine........................283
Actors and Entertainers..................................283
Incredible Athletes 284
Military Leaders..285
Significant Businessmen 286
Players in the World of Statecraft 286
U.S. Civil Rights Leaders 287
Men of Arts and Letters 287

Chapter 18: Ten Amazing Conspiracies, Anti-Masons, and Hoaxes. . . **289**
Leo Taxil and the Great Hoax!............................289
The Illuminati! 291
Trilats, CFRs, and Bilderbergers, Oh My! 292
The Secret 33rd Degree!..................................293
Jack the Ripper: A Freemason!............................294
The Italian P2 Lodge Scandal! 295
Washington, D.C., Is Satan's Road Map!...................296
Aleister Crowley, Satanist and Freemason!................297
Freemasons Founded the Nazis!..........................298
Masonic Cops! Masonic Judges! 299

Chapter 19: Ten Cool Masonic Places 301

George Washington Masonic Memorial (Alexandria, Virginia) 301
House of the Temple (Washington, D.C.) 302
Freemason's Hall (Philadelphia) 302
Masonic Temple (Detroit) 302
Grand Lodge of the State of New York (New York City) 303
Scottish Rite Cathedral (Indianapolis) 303
Freemason Hall (London) 303
Templar Church (London) 303
Rosslyn Chapel (Roslin, Scotland) 304
Grande Loge Nationale Française and Other
   Masonic Buildings (Paris) 304

Part VI: Appendixes **305**

Appendix A: The Regius Manuscript 307

A Poem of Moral Duties 307

Appendix B: Anderson's Constitutions 329

The Charges Of A Free Mason 329
   i. Concerning God And Religion 330
   ii. Of The Civil Magistrate Supreme And Subordinate 330
   iii. Of Lodges 330
   iv. Of Masters, Wardens, Fellows, And Apprentices 331
   v. Of The Management Of The Craft In Working 331
   vi. Of Behavior 332

Appendix C: Finding a Lodge 335

Mainstream U.S. Grand Lodges 335
Prince Hall Grand Lodges 340
Canadian Grand Lodges 344

Index *347*

Introduction

● ●

*T*ake a look at the symbol on the cover of this book. Whether you know it or not, you've seen this symbol in many places — on buildings, car bumpers, jewelry, and the Internet. Chances are actually pretty good that every day you drive past a Masonic lodge without even noticing it. Chances are also pretty good that you don't really know what a Freemason is. That's okay. You aren't alone.

A hundred years ago, this book wasn't needed. Back then, 1 out of every 4 American men was a member of some kind of fraternal organization, and 1 out of every 25 men was a Freemason. So many secret handshakes, passwords, lapel pins, and funny hats were going around that it was a challenge for a man just to remember all the groups he belonged to. I'd be willing to bet that your father, grandfather, uncle, or another man in your family was a Freemason.

The Freemasons were the first, the biggest, and the best-known gentlemen's organization in the world. Up until about 1960, if you weren't a Mason, you at least knew what one was. As secret societies go, they were a pretty badly hidden one. If you started looking for Freemasons at your office, factory, school, or family reunion picnic back then, you could throw a stick and whack a sizeable cluster of them. Today, if you go looking for Freemasons in those same places, you'll more than likely be met with the sort of blank stares and lizardlike slow blinks usually reserved for conversations with a tax attorney.

Literally hundreds of books that have been written by Freemasons for Freemasons have been moldy tomes or sensational speculation, filled with a miasma of mythological and metaphysical mumbo jumbo and a minimum of facts. And non-Masons who seem to have their tinfoil hats screwed on a little too snugly have peddled lots of books, accusing Freemasons of conspiracies and lunatic plots so whacked out that even an ardent *X-Files* fan wouldn't fail to snort uncontrollably at them.

What's been missing all along is a basic book by someone armed with the facts, the history, the symbolism, and the, well, real secrets. This is your book, and I'm your guy. I am a Freemason myself, a Past Master of two Masonic lodges, and I'm here to help. Don't get me wrong. As I explain a little later, we do have some secrets that I can't tell you, and I'm no stoolie. But the list of what I'm leaving out is a whole lot smaller than you're probably thinking.

About This Book

Freemasonry is a strange topic. It's not a religion, but it's religious. It's not a political movement, but its members have been some of the greatest political and social reformers of history. It's not a charity or a service club, yet its various organizations operate outstanding charities. Its language comes from the 18th century, yet its lessons apply to the 21st. To really understand it, you need to know a little something about history, religion, politics, philosophy, mythology, language, and symbolism. In this book, I touch on all these topics and more.

So if Freemasonry is a secret society, how can I write a book about it if I'm supposed to keep it all a big secret? Simple. Most of the word on the street about Masonic secrecy is a big misconception, and I can tell you the history and most of the basics of modern Masonry. But as a Mason, there are a few things I'm just not going to tell you. Sorry about that. Them's the rules. Freemasons promise not to write, print, paint, stamp, stain, cut, carve, hew, mark, or engrave any of the secrets of the fraternity so that non-Masons can discover them. The official secrets of Freemasonry are mostly the methods Freemasons use to identify each other (passwords, gestures, and secret handshakes), and a few of the details of the third and final ceremony ritual of the lodge.

Now, anti-Masons, opportunistic ex-members, and other rats have been publishing books with all the secrets of Masonry in them since about ten seconds after the first lodges met. Most libraries and bookstores have them on their shelves, and the Internet puts nearly every Masonic ritual at your fingertips. You just won't find those very few details here. And even if you did, you wouldn't be able to bluff your way into a Masonic lodge. Don't even try it. We guard our doors with sharp, pointy swords, which I tell you all about in Chapter 5.

Conventions Used in This Book

This book doesn't use many unusual conventions — I leave that for the Masons themselves. But whenever I use and define a new term, I put that term in *italic*. And whenever I give you an e-mail address or web address, I put it in monofont so you can easily identify it as such.

What You're Not to Read

Freemasons For Dummies is a reference, which means that you don't have to read it from cover to cover, and you won't be quizzed on what you've read on Friday. You can skip over anything marked with a Technical Stuff icon (more about that in the "Icons Used in This Book" section, later in this Introduction). Those paragraphs likely have way more information than you're interested in knowing — but don't let that stop me from telling you!

You can also skip over the text in sidebars (boxes with gray shading). The information I include there is interesting, and often pretty detailed, but not necessary to your essential understanding of Freemasonry. Feel free to skip the sidebars for now and come back to them when you have the time and interest.

Foolish Assumptions

Freemasons For Dummies is actually written for a pretty wide audience, but I make a few assumptions about you. I assume at least one of the following describes you to a T:

- ✔ **You're Masonically clueless.** If this sounds about right, don't worry. I explain what the square and compass symbol means, where it came from, what it has to do with building buildings and laying bricks, and why so many men have strapped on a little white apron and locked themselves behind the doors of the Masonic lodge. If you found Grandpa's Masonic ring in an old cigar box and you never knew what it was, you'll find the answers here.

- ✔ **You're thinking about becoming a Freemason or you've recently become one.** This book is a pretty concise reference, discussing the origins of the Craft, what it is and what it isn't, what the rituals mean, how lodges are set up, and why Masons do what they do. I also help you make sense of the complex minefield of related Masonic organizations so you can understand why a Shriner is a Mason who might be a Knight Templar but not necessarily a Master of the Royal Secret. Or vice versa.

- ✔ **You're the wife, girlfriend, or relative of someone who's thinking about becoming a Mason or of someone who already is a Mason and you want to know what the heck Freemasonry is all about.**

> ✓ **You're suspicious of Freemasons and you're pretty sure that we're a bizarre cult — but you're open to finding out the truth.** For the curious crowd who has their heads filled with lots of anti-Masonic mush, I spend plenty of time debunking the more common myths, accusations, and urban legends that have been flung at Freemasons over the last 300 years of its modern life. If you picked up this book looking for serious answers, you'll find them here.

How This Book Is Organized

If you perused the table of contents on your way here, you saw that this book is divided into six parts. Feel free to read them in any order you choose. After all, you paid for the privilege. Here's what you'll find.

Part 1: What Is Freemasonry?

This section explains just what Freemasonry is and is not. If you know absolutely nothing about Freemasonry, start with Chapter 1. Chapter 2 is a long one, but it's a crash course in Masonic history from 1000 BC until today. Chapter 3 discusses the basic beliefs and philosophy of the Masonic institution and the messages it tries to communicate to its members. Chapter 4 talks about the two subjects that Freemasons avoid talking about in lodge — politics and religion — and their effects on the development of Masonry.

Part II: The Inner Workings of Freemasonry

This section gets down to the nuts and bolts, or stones and mortar, of what goes on in a Masonic lodge. Chapter 5 identifies all the officers of the lodge and then goes on to explain the governing powers of Grand Lodges, as well as the thorny issues surrounding recognition and regularity of foreign Freemasonry. In Chapter 6, the ceremonies and rituals of Freemasonry are examined and explained, including secret stuff, bloody oaths, and the three essential Masonic degrees. Chapter 7 talks about the many mysterious symbols used by Freemasons, what they mean, and why they're used. And Chapter 8 covers the myths, misconceptions, and party gags about Freemasonry, where they came from, why they keep getting passed around, and why your Masonic ring won't get you out of a speeding ticket.

Part III: When One Lodge Isn't Enough: The Appendant Bodies

Freemasons are big joiners, and becoming a Mason can often be like trying to eat one potato chip. This section shines a light on the many different groups within the Masonic family (known as *appendant bodies*), who joins them, who *can* join them, and what their appeal is. Chapter 9 is an encapsulated overview of the appendant bodies, making the distinction between Masonic organizations and other groups that look and sound similar but aren't. Chapter 10 is an in-depth explanation of the York Rite degrees, including the Royal Arch, Cryptic, and Knights Templar. Chapter 11 concentrates on the 29 additional Scottish Rite degrees, plus the 33rd degree. Chapter 12 covers the Shriners, why they wear those overturned flowerpots on their heads, why they seem to be in love with all things motorized with wheels, and just what they have to do with being a Freemason. Chapter 13 explains the extended Masonic family, including groups for women, children, and party animals.

Part IV: Freemasonry Today and Tomorrow

How does a very old, very private fraternity that pushes faith, morality, harmony, and personal responsibility survive in an age of isolation, indifference, and no "rulz"? Chapter 14 talks about the abrupt and destructive changes to a society that used to crave togetherness but now does everything it can to keep us all strangers, and how Freemasonry holds the potential to help counteract that. Chapter 15 examines what the Masonic world is doing to get men interested again. Some of it is good, some of it isn't, and some changes will be forced on Freemasons whether they like it or not. In Chapter 16, you discover the steps to finding a lodge and becoming a Mason.

Part V: The Part of Tens

This section of the book is a conversation starter. Chapter 17 is a list of famous Freemasons, from founding fathers, civil rights activists, and scientists to musicians, actors, and sports figures. Chapter 18 is a list of ten amazing conspiracies, anti-Masons, and hoaxes, proving that you should never trust the history you get from movies, comic books, or fellow college students while they're drinking. Chapter 19 puts ten cool Masonic places on the map, so whether you're a Mason or just a Masonic groupie, you'll have plenty of sightseeing opportunities to drag your family around to.

Part VI: Appendixes

Just like your second cousin Mort in New Jersey, this book could get along without an appendix, but it wouldn't be a proper reference book without it. So I include the two most important documents from Masonic history: the Regius Manuscript, the first written record of the workings of a Mason's lodge; and the Ancient Charges, the framework for the government of Masonic lodges and the conduct of their members. I also include contact information for the Grand Lodges in the United States and Canada.

Icons Used in This Book

The icons lurking in the margins of this book help you home in on interesting facts as well as give you a little scenery to gaze at.

When a new candidate enters the Masonic lodge for the first time, he is faced with unusual rituals, strange vocabulary, and occasionally obscure traditions. New Masons are always encouraged to ask the Past Masters plenty of questions, because they're sort of the Masonic Yodas of their lodge. They know the rituals, the rules, the right way, and the wrong way to do things. This icon is your personal Past Master. Feel free to pester him.

This icon points out the necessary road trips into history — either an important point in Masonic history or an event in history that had an effect on the fraternity. Sometimes it's blessedly short and to the point. Other trips into the murky mists of time take a little longer to explain and can be skipped over by anyone with a life-threatening allergy to historical subjects. They do give a deeper understanding of why we are who we are and the events that gave birth to modern Freemasonry.

Setting aside all touristy side trips and anecdotes, this icon marks key points that are vital to understanding Freemasonry.

This icon highlights such things as additional data, explanations of obscure rituals and practices, or other information that may interest you but can be ruthlessly skipped over without missing the important themes of the chapter.

Freemasonry is a worldwide fraternity, but it has no international governing body. As a result, there's a lot of variation from one country (and even one state) to the next in customs, ceremonies, and other details. A lot. This book is written from the point of view of Masonry in the United States, but this icon alerts you when there are major or unusual differences in other places to be aware of.

No institution on earth has attracted more lies, half-truths, urban legends, and myths, not to mention fakers, charlatans, con artists, and humbugs, than Freemasonry. This icon takes aim at these myths and misconceptions to reveal the truth about Freemasonry.

Where to Go from Here

If you first came across the Freemasons in Dan Brown's *The Lost Symbol,* you've come to the right place to find the real story. That's fiction. These are the facts. The great news is that this is not a textbook. It's more like a Las Vegas dinner buffet. You can cut in line, go back for an extra chicken leg, or just snag all the chocolate mousse pie, with no haughty maitre d' to look you up and down like you've packed in enough chow for the night.

If all you want to know about is Masonic symbolism, pore over Chapter 7. If you've always heard about 33rd-degree Masons and can't wait patiently to find out what they are, feel free to plow into Chapter 11. Secret Masonic symbols on the back of the dollar bill got you feeling nervous every time you pull out your flash wad to pay for a double cheeseburger? Brazenly saunter into Chapter 8 like you own the joint. You can always go back and read about Masonic aprons or the Shriners some other time.

Part I
What Is Freemasonry?

The 5th Wave   By Rich Tennant

"This is the new Freemason lodge? So much for all that grand architect of the universe business."

In this part . . .

You've seen the symbol on cars, buildings, and jewelry. You've heard Freemasons mentioned in books and movies. Dad or Grandpa may have even been a member. So what is it? What *isn't* it? What's the big secret?

In this part, you get the crash course in Freemasonry — its mythical, legendary, and real history; its basic philosophy; and the lessons it hopes to teach its members.

Chapter 1

Lodges, Aprons, and Funny Handshakes: Freemasonry 101

. . . .

In This Chapter

▶ Defining Freemasonry

▶ Discovering what Freemasons do

▶ Getting the scoop on all those secrets

. . . .

Mystery creates wonder, and wonder is the basis of man's desire to understand.

— Neil Armstrong

Drive through just about any town in America and keep your eyes open. Sooner or later, you'll pass a building or a sign sporting a square and a compass, like the one shown in Figure 1-1. It may be a large, impressive building or a small humble one. It may be marked with a huge sign in the yard or have a simple cornerstone. But it will be there. It is a sign universally recognized throughout the world for centuries as a symbol of truth, morality, and brotherly love. It is the square and compass of Freemasonry.

The greatest lure of Freemasonry is the mystique of a locked door. On the other side of that door are rituals, symbols, and ceremonies known only to its members and Masters, and unwritten secrets that have been passed from mouth to ear for centuries.

Masonic libraries are filled with books of antiquity. Science, philosophy, history, religion, and symbolism all collide in the collected works of Masonic scholars. The literature of the fraternity is strewn with legends, myths, and ancient mysteries.

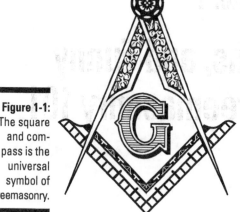

Figure 1-1:
The square
and com-
pass is the
universal
symbol of
Freemasonry.

Image courtesy of Christopher Hodapp

Voltaire, Mozart, George Washington, and Winston Churchill were all members, as were 9 signers of the Declaration of Independence and 14 U.S. presidents. The Founding Fathers of the United States embraced Masonic principles and wrote them into the foundations of U.S. government. But dictators like Adolph Hitler, Joseph Stalin, and Saddam Hussein all outlawed their gatherings. Many religions forbid their members to join the Masons, and terrible accusations have been made against members of the fraternity, charging them with assassinations, conspiracies, attempts at world domination, and other evil crimes. Millions of men the world over have joined the Freemasons, yet even today, some countries threaten Masons with fines, imprisonment, or even death.

Even so, in almost every country of the world, every week hundreds of thousands of men slip on jackets and ties, reverently fasten small, white aprons around their waists, and enter the confines of windowless lodge rooms. There they escape the outside world for a few hours and replace it with the comfort of friendship combined with ritual ceremonies from centuries ago.

What is it about this self-described fraternal and benevolent organization that evokes such opposite reactions? Is Freemasonry a mythic mass of mind-expanding, magical, mystical manifestations? An evil organization for socio-economic pirates? Or just a place for a hot hand of euchre and a fish fry? In this chapter, I give you a brief overview of what Freemasonry really is, what Masons do, and how other organizations are related to Freemasonry.

What Is Freemasonry?

Freemasonry (or just plain Masonry, for short) is a society of gentlemen concerned with moral and spiritual values and is one of the world's oldest and most popular fraternal organizations. It's perhaps the most misunderstood, yet mainstream, "secret society" the world has ever known. It's also the most visible one. Every state in the United States and almost every country in the world has a Grand Lodge of Freemasons, and each has its own website. Masonic buildings are clearly marked, and their addresses and phone numbers are freely available. Freemasons themselves don't hide — they wear rings, jackets, and hats emblazoned with the square and compass. Their cars often have Masonic license plates and bumper stickers. Some Grand Lodges have even started advertising on billboards. If the Freemasons are a secret, they need a refresher course on camouflage.

Freemasons don't always do such a good job of defining just what they are or what they do, but that's often because the answers non-Masons are looking for are really too complicated. No simple, one-line definition satisfactorily describes what Freemasonry is. It is a philosophy and a system of morality and ethics — and a pretty basic one at that. Here are the main points that make Freemasonry different from any other organization:

- Freemasonry is a fraternity of men, bound together by oaths, based on the medieval stonemason craft guilds.

- Masonic laws, rules, legends, and customs are based on the *Ancient Charges,* the rules of those craft guilds (see Appendix B).

- Freemasonry teaches lessons of social and moral virtues based on symbolism of the tools and language of the ancient building trade, using the building of a structure as a symbol for the building of character in men.

- Masons are obliged to practice brotherly love, mutual assistance, equality, secrecy, and trust between each other.

- Masons have secret methods of recognizing each other, such as handshakes, signs, and passwords.

- Masons meet in lodges that are governed by a Master and assisted by Wardens, where petitioners who are found to be morally and mentally qualified are admitted using secret ritual ceremonies based on the legends of the ancient guilds.

- Freemasonry is not a religion, and it has no religious dogma that it forces its members to accept. Masons must simply believe in the existence of a Supreme Being, whatever they conceive that deity to be. Their personal beliefs are just that: personal.

> ✔ Freemasonry is not a science, but it does teach its members to value learning and experience. It encourages Masons to think but does not tell them *what* to think.
>
> ✔ Freemasonry teaches Masons to be tolerant of the beliefs of others and to regard each man as their equal, deserving both their respect and their assistance.

What Do Masons Do?

Lodges have regular meetings throughout the year. Most gather once a month for a business meeting, at which communications are read, bills are paid, new members are voted on, and the members catch up on each other's lives. Often, guest speakers are invited or a member gives a presentation on the ritual, history, philosophy, or symbols of Freemasonry.

Other special meetings are held to initiate new members and perform the various ceremonies to advance them to full membership. And because the primary goal of Freemasonry is fraternalism, a meal is usually served before or after the meeting, either in the lodge building or at a nearby restaurant.

No one "speaks" for Freemasonry

The world outside of Freemasonry is sometimes very confused about who leads the fraternity and what their purpose is. Thousands of books with long names and respected authors propound their theories about the history, philosophy, and symbolism of Freemasonry. And there is no shortage of convoluted-sounding titles for officeholders, especially in some of the other Masonic organizations outside of the Lodge — *Grand* this, and *Supreme* that, and *Most Sovereign* something or other.

But an important thing to understand about Freemasonry is that it has no one, single, worldwide governing body. No one man speaks for Freemasonry, and no one ever has. Not even guys who write *For Dummies* books. That's important to understand whenever you hear criticisms and accusations against Freemasons, especially when they quote "authoritative sources," "supreme leaders," or "unseen superiors."

Every state in the United States, every province in Canada, and nearly every country on earth has a governing Grand Lodge — often more than one. Each Grand Lodge has rules and regulations that govern the lodges within its jurisdiction, and every Grand Lodge has a Grand Master who is essentially the president within that jurisdiction. But Grand Masters wield no power to make rules or decisions outside of their borders. There is no national or international group that controls or directs the Grand Lodges, which makes any diabolical plan for world domination a bit tricky to coordinate.

Modern Freemasonry started out by gathering in taverns over a nice dinner, and Masons have spent 300 years obsessing on the importance of the culinary arts. Their feasts are called *festive boards* (from the days when *board* meant "table"), and a tradition of many of these gatherings is a series of ceremonial toasts.

Still, the mission of the Masonic lodge is to make new Masons, and it's accomplished by conferring degrees.

Conferring the three degrees

The ceremonies a new member must go through are called *degrees*. Masonry has three of them — Entered Apprentice, Fellow Craft, and Master Mason — and they're based on the levels of membership in the old medieval craft guilds. The ceremonies are modeled on rituals used by those guilds centuries ago.

Today, modern Freemasons have retained much of these degree ceremonies, including lots of fancy, old-fashioned language. They share these characteristics:

- ✔ **The degrees are a progression and must take place in proper order.** Each builds on the previous one, and the degrees are connected by the story of the construction of Solomon's Temple.

- ✔ **Each candidate takes an *obligation* (oath) for each degree.** He promises to keep the secrets he is told, to help other Masons and their families, and to obey the rules of the fraternity.

- ✔ **Depending on the lodge, advancing from one degree to the next can take days, weeks, months, or even years.**

- ✔ **A member must prove his proficiency in his degree before moving up.** Proving proficiency is usually accomplished by memorizing a portion of the ritual and reciting it in front of the other members. Some lodges require the member to present an original research paper on a certain topic in order to prove that he has studied the fraternity. Others may require a written quiz.

Meeting in lodges, blue lodges, craft lodges, and more

The *lodge* is the most basic unit of Freemasonry. It is a term used for the individual chapter, for a collected group of Masons who meet together, for the room they meet in, and sometimes even for the building in which they gather.

Several individual lodges can share facilities and meet at different times in the same lodge room. This arrangement is, in fact, the norm in larger cities. In smaller communities, or in the case of a very prosperous lodge, just one lodge may occupy the building.

In this book, I sometimes refer to the *blue lodge.* (I explain why it's "blue" in Chapter 7.) Other terms you'll see are *symbolic lodge, craft lodge,* and *Ancient Craft Masonry.* These various terms all describe the first, most essential starting point in the world of Freemasonry: the local neighborhood lodge that confers the first three degrees of Masonry — the Entered Apprentice, Fellow Craft, and Master Mason degrees.

Masons sometimes refer to Freemasonry as the *Craft,* because its origins are the medieval craft guilds. They most definitely are not referring to witchcraft.

Freemasonry has many different branches of membership and study. These branches or groups are called *appendant* or *concordant bodies,* and I talk a lot more about them in Part III. You may have had a relative or a friend who said he was a 32nd-degree Mason or even a 33rd-degree Mason. Those additional degrees do exist, and they're confusing, so I explain them in Part IV as well. But the truth is that in *Ancient Craft Masonry,* no degree is higher or more important than the three degrees a man receives in a Masonic lodge. These other degrees may have higher numbers than the first three conferred in a lodge, but they're simply different, additional ceremonies, and are in no way meant to be construed as more important or superior to becoming a Master Mason.

Performing public ceremonies

Most of the ceremonies of the Masons go on inside the confines of the lodge, but you may have seen two special Masonic events in public. These public ceremonies are symbolic of beginning and ending.

Cornerstone ceremonies

Because of their heritage as builders of cathedrals and other public structures, the Freemasons have historically performed a special ceremony at the laying of cornerstones for new buildings, upon request. In modern times, these events are barely noticed by the public, but in previous centuries, the laying of a cornerstone for a new building was a very big, festive celebration. In the case of a courthouse, city hall, or other major government building, parades were often held, speeches were given, and the Freemasons would symbolically lay the cornerstone.

In the Masonic cornerstone ceremony, the stone is checked by using ancient tools to be certain it is square, *plumb* (straight), and level, because a building constructed on a poor foundation will not be strong. Next, the cornerstone is consecrated with corn (or grain), wine, and oil — all of which are Masonic symbols of prosperity, health, and peace. Finally, the stone is symbolically tapped in place with a gavel.

Funeral services

The first way many people come into contact with Freemasonry these days is at the funeral of a friend or relative who was a Freemason. Masons perform a solemn memorial service for their members, when the family requests it. The words of the ceremony provide a brief glimpse into the beliefs of the fraternity; it's a moving and deeply meaningful service. Many men, myself included, have sought membership in a lodge after seeing the funeral service performed for a loved one.

Wearing aprons (Real men do it!)

Yes, it's true: Grown men wearing little rectangular aprons are de rigueur fashion for the properly dressed Freemason. The aprons are symbolic of those worn by ancient stonemasons to protect their clothing and to carry their tools. Although aprons worn by many Masons are made of simple white cloth, they're traditionally supposed to be made of white lambskin, an emblem of innocence. Some Masonic aprons are very ornate. They may be decorated to denote an officer's position, a place of honor such as a former Master of a lodge, or just simply a cool design. The Mason's apron is the first gift given to him upon his initiation into the lodge, and it is to be kept clean and spotless throughout the Mason's life as a symbol of the purity of his thoughts and actions.

Masons wear their aprons in a specific manner, according to the degree they have attained. Nobody — with the exception of an uninitiated candidate — gets into a lodge without an apron.

Keeping "secrets"

Masons like to say that Freemasonry is not a secret society; rather, it is a society with secrets. A better way to put it is that what goes on in a lodge room during its ceremonies is private.

For a lot of years, fathers, grandfathers, and neighbors baffled young men who were interested in joining the fraternity by refusing to discuss anything about it, out of a fundamental misunderstanding about Masonic secrecy. They figured they weren't allowed to tell anything about it. "Join and you'll see," was their standard answer. Fortunately, that perception is changing, and Freemasons are not so squeamish these days about talking about Masonry.

"Has he the pass?"

Freemasons who go traveling may visit Masonic lodges all over the world, but not every lodge uses the same methods of recognition. Every Grand Lodge has its own local customs and variations. American lodges issue membership cards, but outside of the United States, most lodges don't have or know about such things. A Mason may be asked many questions before being allowed in if he is not known and "vouched for" by a member of that lodge.

Making matters even more confusing is the fact that one jurisdiction may use different ritual ceremonies, different passwords, and different grips than another. When a language barrier exists, visiting a lodge can be even more challenging. One of my Masonic brothers was traveling in the Philippines while in the Navy, when he and a friend came upon a Masonic lodge that was clearly in session. When they attempted to enter, none of the local brethren spoke English, and there were differences between the local Masonic signs of recognition. While they waited outside, they could hear a terrible commotion inside the lodge room. The door opened, and they were escorted in. What they found were all the furnishings of the lodge piled in the center of the room. To prove they were Masons, they had to put everything back in its proper location. They did, and there was much rejoicing.

The secrets that a Mason may not discuss are the *grips* (handshakes), passwords, and *signs* (gestures) that are modes of recognition, and some details of the Masonic degree ritual ceremonies. Undoubtedly, some old-school Masons out there will read something in this book and believe that I should be driven to the state line in a trunk for daring to talk about it, but they should chat with their Grand Lodge before calling to check my measurements.

Just knowing the modes of recognition won't get you into a Masonic lodge. If you're interested in becoming a Mason, don't let some big mouth in a book or on the Internet ruin the ritual experience for you by blurting out all the surprises. If you aren't interested in joining and you just want to be able to gloat about knowing some secret information, there is no shortage of books and websites that tell them all. You can leap into a gathering of Masons screaming "A-ha!" and blurt out a password if you like, but the *real* secret of Freemasonry has to be experienced, not explained, which is why your little stunt will be ignored.

Providing something for everyone

Masonry is as diverse as its members, so it can seem like something very different depending on whom you talk to or which lodge you visit or join.

Some Masons concentrate on the many charities the fraternity participates in. Some are consumed by the history or the philosophy or the symbolism of the fraternity. Others consider the lodge to be primarily a place to go to play cards or cook a monthly breakfast, in order to be with old friends and make new ones. Still others enjoy performing the ritual ceremonies and make a life-long passion of taking dramatic parts in it.

For men who become lodge officers or members of committees, Masonry is a personal development course that teaches them leadership skills, public speaking, and more. Men from every walk of life have the opportunity to do things in a lodge that their job or their social or economic status rarely offers them. And then some men just like high-sounding titles, badges, ribbons, tuxedos, and spiffy accoutrements. The point is that there is something in Freemasonry for every man, whatever his interests may be.

Are [Fill in the Blank] Freemasons, Too?

Because Freemasons are an eclectic mix of men from all walks of life, other Masonic organizations have developed over the years to expand on the lodge experience. They all require someone to be a member of a lodge as a third-degree Master Mason before that person can join them. They are collectively known as *appendant bodies,* and the list is almost endless.

Following are the three major players:

- **The York Rite:** This body is made up of three different basic groups: Royal Arch Masons, Cryptic Rite Masons, and Knights Templar.

- **The Scottish Rite:** This group confers 29 degrees — the 4th through the 32nd. Additionally, the Supreme Council, the overall governing body of the Rite, can award the 33rd degree to members who have performed outstanding service to the Scottish Rite.

- **The Ancient Arabic Nobles of the Mystic Shrine:** This group is more properly known today as Shriners International. Yes, these are the guys with the funny hats and little cars. The Shrine was created in 1872 by a group of Masons who felt that the lodge had become too serious and too stuffy. The Shriners confer only one degree on their Nobles, and are dedicated to putting a little bit of the boy back into the man. They also operate Shriners Hospitals, which provide free orthopedic and burn care to children.

Many more appendant bodies exist, including the Grotto, the Order of the Eastern Star (a group women may also join), Tall Cedars of Lebanon, the Order of Amaranth, the White Shrine of Jerusalem, DeMolay (for boys), Rainbow and Job's Daughters (both for girls) — the list goes on and on. All these groups grew out of the incredible explosion of interest in fraternal organizations in the 19th-century United States and elsewhere.

I go into loads of detail about all these groups in Part III.

No girlz allowed!

The modern version of Freemasonry that formed in 1717 in London was based on the ancient stonemasons' guilds. The original rules of the guilds were absolutely, 100 percent, dyed-in-the-wool, pig-headedly male only (see Appendix A). Part of the reason is that in most of Europe, women in the early 1700s had the same legal status as minors.

Over the last three centuries, Masonry has remained a fraternity just for men, and the world's vast majority of garden-variety, mainstream Freemasons have taken an oath not to be present at, nor give their consent to, making a woman a Freemason. It isn't done. It's just not kosher. We'll get cooties.

That's the official, mainstream Masonic explanation. But the truth is always more complex. Modern Freemasonry started in Scotland and England, but it quickly spread to the European continent. As early as the 1740s, some French lodges began to initiate women as fellow members. Over the years and almost entirely in Europe, several groups made up of lodges for both men and women (called *co-Masonry*) or for women only have started. These women did not necessarily want to barge into a lodge full of men, but they did want to enjoy the degree ceremonies, symbolism, and philosophy of Freemasonry. In England, these groups include the Order of Women's Free-Masons, founded in 1908; the Honourable Fraternity of Antient Free-Masons, founded in 1913; and the Order of Ancient, Free, and Accepted Masons for Men and Women, founded in 1925. France has several such groups, including Le Droit Humain, a co-Masonic group founded in 1893, and the women's Grande Loge Féminine de France, started in 1945. There are several others.

In the United States, a women's lodge existed in Boston in the 1790s, with Hannah Mather Crocker as its Worshipful Master, but it soon died out. A pseudo-Masonic order, called the Order of the Eastern Star, was created in the mid-1800s. It was carefully designed by its creators so that it did not *actually* confer Masonic degrees on women, in order to stay out of hot water with the mainstream Masons. As a result, it became an accepted member of the family of American Freemasonry, and it still functions today (see Chapter 13).

These days, the Internet is making the world a very small place, and these groups are benefiting from the worldwide and instant exchange of ideas. Female and co-Masonry is expanding in the United States and elsewhere. The American Federation of the Human Rights is headquartered in Washington, D.C., and has several co-Masonic lodges in the United States. There are other co-Masonic bodies, among them George-Washington Union and the Grand Lodge Symbolic of Memphis-Misraïm. The Women's Grand Lodge of Belgium, meanwhile, has chartered at least four lodges in New York; Washington, D.C.; and Los Angeles.

Feminine and co-Masonic groups remain pretty much ignored by the mainstream male lodges, a fact that doesn't cause these female Masons all that many sleepless nights. They know they're Freemasons, even if the boys don't agree.

Meanwhile, mainstream Freemasons are forbidden to visit or "converse Masonically" with either co-Masons or female Masons, on threat of expulsion from the fraternity. Cooties, you know.

Chapter 2

From Cathedrals to Lodge Rooms: A History of the Freemasons

In This Chapter

▶ Understanding what the first Masons were all about

▶ Shifting focus from building cathedrals to building men

▶ Spreading around the world in the 19th century

▶ Growing in the United States before and after WWII

▶ Going through decline and looking to the future

*W*hat the earliest Freemasons did was truly mystical. They went into rock quarries and carved huge stones. They transported gigantic blocks weighing thousands of pounds and raised them high in the air to construct soaring cathedral walls that defied gravity. They could peer at a small drawing and, through the mysterious art of geometry, build monuments to God that have stood for nearly a thousand years. It was wondrous. It was magical. And how they did it was a secret.

So how did a collection of labor leaders and stonecutters in the Middle Ages get transformed into the world's largest philosophical fraternal organization? Theories about the origin of Freemasonry abound. Masonic writers in the 1800s wrote massive books that told lavish histories of Freemasonry, tracing it to ancient Egypt, Biblical Jerusalem, or even the Knights Templar of the 12th century AD. Modern scholarship has pretty much calmed down and made more-reasoned conclusions.

This chapter discusses the medieval guild system of cathedral builders and its evolution into what became modern Freemasonry. Much of the earliest history of the Masons is unknown because of a shortage of written material. And much of what Freemasonry became was due to a variety of influences in society around it.

In this chapter, I concentrate on mainstream Ancient Craft Freemasonry, which is the system of three Masonic degrees conferred in the lodge you're likely to find up the street. Just like the history of literally thousands of different branches and variations of Christianity, the history of Freemasonry could — and has — filled whole library shelves. The variations of Masonry in France alone over a period of 300 years are a huge topic all by themselves. In an effort to keep the confusion and the chaos to a minimum, I explain the most important turning points in the fraternity and how they affected what's most commonly practiced in England and the United States.

Turning Stonecutters into Gentlemen: Freemasonry before 1700

Freemasons today use the terms *operative* and *speculative* to describe the difference between the two types of Freemasonry. *Operative* Masonry refers to the time before 1700 and describes the period when Freemasons were really working with stones, chisels, and hammers. After the operative Masons began to be replaced by "admitted" or "gentleman" Masons, the order changed into a philosophical, fraternal, and charitable organization and became known as *speculative* Freemasonry. As an identifying symbol, speculative Masons adopted the working tools of the operative Masons: the compass and the square.

Operative Masons: The great builders

The *mythical* origins of the fraternity date back to the building of the Temple of King Solomon in Jerusalem, around 1000 BC. King Solomon's Temple was the greatest and most magnificent monument to man's faith in God constructed during the Biblical era. Its innermost sanctuary, the *Sanctum Sanctorum,* was built to hold the Ark of the Covenant, which contained the sacred words of God — the tablets God gave Moses that contained the Ten Commandments. The temple was eventually destroyed (first by the Babylonians, then by the Romans), and little remains of it today except for stone foundations, commonly known in modern Jerusalem as the Wailing Wall.

The generally accepted *historic* origins of modern Freemasonry can be traced to the stonemason guilds that formed during the Middle Ages in Scotland, England, and France. As early as the eighth century, Masons were being organized and instructed by Charles Martel in France. The earliest English documents claim that Athelstan, who was technically the first King of all of England, organized a guild of Masons in York in AD 926.

Like most things in Freemasonry, no one really knows where the term *Freemason* comes from. Some historians say that it refers to the fact that the members of the mason guilds weren't required to stay in a certain city or county, so were free to travel and look for work — thus, *free masons*. The other theory is that it may be a shortening of the term *freestone mason*. Freestone is a soft, fine-grained stone that can be carved, like sandstone or limestone (as opposed to harder rock with heavy grain that has to be split).

The Freemasons knew how to build Gothic cathedrals and castles from massive stones, and they knew the science of geometry. The Masons jealously guarded these trade secrets that could turn a small drawing into an enormous structure — the knowledge wasn't even divulged to the bishops, priests, or kings who employed the Masons. Because this group was indeed a craft guild, its members today sometimes refer to Freemasonry as the *Craft*. They *aren't* talking about witchcraft, but what they accomplished did seem like magic.

Gothic architecture

The Gothic style of architecture lasted from the 1100s until the late 1500s. Gothic cathedrals like Notre Dame in Paris and Westminster Abbey in London are two of the most famous. Before this style was developed, buildings had thick, heavy walls, small windows, and wooden roof supports. The older styles were limited in size and shape by the technology of the period. The Gothic style changed all that.

If you look at the picture of the inside of Notre Dame in Paris, you see walls that almost look like they're made out of stained glass, as is typical of Gothic cathedrals. This is because the high walls are designed to transfer the massive weight of the building and the roof to exterior supports called *flying buttresses,* which makes possible the big expanses of delicate glass (check out the flying buttresses in the second photo). The roofs were constructed with what is called a *ribbed vault,* which more evenly transferred the weight. The flying buttresses keep the whole thing from collapsing outward like a house of cards but allow the heavy support structure to stand outside the building.

During this time, the Catholic Church had become the overwhelming religious influence in Europe, and paganism was suppressed. The cathedrals were designed as symbols of Church power — they were generally the largest buildings around. But they were also designed as places to teach the faithful about their religion. And symbolism was literally *everywhere*. The classic Gothic cathedral floor plans were laid out in the sacred shape of a cross. The buildings were enormous and many stories tall, so the individual felt he was in the presence of an all-powerful God. The common folks couldn't read, so the stained-glass windows, and the often thousands of stone carvings in every nook and cranny of the church, were designed to pictorially tell stories from the Bible.

The designers were often immensely talented and visionary bishops, priests, or abbots, but there were also architects who weren't members of the clergy. Although the whole community pulled together, donating money and labor for years and even decades to build these magnificent churches, skilled laborers were

(continued)

(continued)

needed to do the exacting work of translating the fanciful designs into buildings that would last ten centuries or more. Complex geometry and exact measurement and construction were necessary, and that's where the craft guilds and the Freemasons came in.

Photograph courtesy of Christopher Hodapp

Photograph courtesy of Christopher Hodapp

First written records

The oldest surviving document recording rules of the Freemasons is called the *Regius Manuscript,* and you can find it today in the British Museum in London. An unknown author wrote it in 1390, but most historians agree that it was probably copied from even older documents. (You can read a modern translation of the Regius Manuscript in Appendix A of this book.) It describes in a series of rules the standards of morality and conduct Masons were expected to abide by. It covers standards of workmanship, a moral code, rules for membership, and an especially strong desire for friendship among the members. Although the rules changed a bit through the centuries, the essential structure of government for today's Masonic lodges can be found in this document.

Guilds were developed to train men in the skills needed to construct these magnificent buildings, to enforce a standard of workmanship, and to hold their members to those high standards — as well as to protect their valuable trade secrets. If everybody knew how to do it, it wouldn't be a highly paid job anymore. And if you knew the *right* secrets, you could travel and work all over the country, wherever the guild was working.

Master Masons were in possession of the Master's *word* (password) and *grip* (handshake), secret methods these master workmen used to recognize each other. It was a simple way to quickly identify yourself as a trained member of the guild — especially given that business cards, diplomas, and dues cards hadn't been invented yet. The secret word and grip kept you from having to carve a gargoyle everywhere you went, just to prove to some sharp-eyed foreman that you knew your stuff.

Apprentices began as young as age 12 and were indentured to a Master Mason for seven years. After three years, they went through an initiation ceremony. They were told certain signs of recognition to identify themselves as a Mason's apprentice, and they were granted permission to have their own *mark,* a small symbol they could carve into stone to identify their own work. After they completed their seven years of service, they became a Fellow of the Craft (what unions would today call a *journeyman*), and in time, with more experience, a Master Mason. (For more details about Apprentices, Fellows of the Craft, and Master Masons, see Chapter 6.)

The Renaissance

Renaissance simply means "rebirth." By the 1500s, Europe was dragging itself out of the muck of the Middle Ages, and a great rebirth of science, art, and learning was taking place, thanks in no small part to the invention of the printing press. Suddenly, people could share ideas half a world away, and in bulk.

The Scottish connection

The Masons had a unique position in society. True, they were peasants, but they were darned skilled peasants. Kings and popes and lords and bishops all needed their skills — and needed them in a big way.

Masons were building all over Europe, and they were admired for their skill and their moral code. In Scotland, King James III was so happy with the work of his Master Mason, Robert Cochrane, that he made the lowborn stonemason a noble, declaring him Earl of Mar. This sort of thing was unheard of in Scotland at the time, and the Scottish nobles had a different idea. They hanged this upstart earl in 1482 and locked up the king for daring to water down the importance of nobility. What good was being a nobleman if you couldn't lord it over the peasants?

By the late 1500s, the honor was reciprocated in the opposite (and less argumentative) direction. The Freemasons were admired by society, and suddenly, nobles wanted to join the Scottish Masonic lodges and to bask in some of their reflected glory. They didn't have any real desire to know how to carve stones, but there was a certain prestige to being an honorary member of a group that held sacred knowledge that had been passed down from biblical times, with a legendary connection to Solomon's Temple. And the Masons gladly took them in because it never hurt to have a favored nobleman in your midst.

In the late 1500s, a hot rumor went around that King James VI of Scotland had become a Freemason. Whether or not it was true, it had an incredible recruitment effect on Scottish lodges. Today, it's universally accepted that the oldest surviving Masonic lodge is in Scotland. Kilwinning Lodge has the distinction of the title "Mother Lodge of Scotland" and dates its origins back to 1140. To show that it predates all other lodges, it is denoted as Lodge No. 0.

Things started to change dramatically for the Masons because society changed around them. The common people became better educated across Europe, and the Masonic guilds lost their grip on the big building contracts. All somebody had to do was print instructions on how to build an arch and fit a keystone in the middle of it and suddenly the closed guilds weren't in demand anymore. Plus, the Gothic style of architecture had lost its popularity by the 1600s. Bricks, not stone, became the popular building material. As operative Masons ran out of work, speculative Freemasonry would soon rise to take its place (see "Speculative Masons and the big change," later in this chapter).

With the dawn of the Renaissance, the Catholic Church started down a long road of trouble. Faced with a need for reform on the inside and revolts of the faithful on the outside, Catholicism was losing its once-total grip on the nations of Europe.

Trouble in Christendom

The 1500s and 1600s were marked more than anything else by a long, bloody series of religious wars that affected every country of Europe. After the religious revolts of Martin Luther in Germany and King Henry VIII in England, Catholics and Protestants were squaring off all over Europe, trying to knock off the biggest chunks of real estate for themselves.

Eventually, throughout the 1600s, even the Protestants went to war with each other, with swelling numbers of new sects — High Church Anglicans, Low Church Protestants, Presbyterians, Calvinists, and Lutherans — all generally hating one another. And just when the Treaty of Westphalia in 1648 looked like it might bring a little religious tolerance to the world, the English Civil War erupted, a new and even bloodier episode of "Kill Your Neighbor over God."

It was a frightening and confusing time. An element of fanaticism marked most of these wars, and the loser often found himself not killed honorably in battle but tied to a stake and burned alive. Just as an example, take a look at the land that gave Freemasonry its birth. Picture yourself a simple middle-class tradesman or landowner in England. In that country alone, these two centuries played host to a constant and bloody changing of the guard insofar as the nation's official religion was concerned.

King Henry VIII broke away from the pope and created the Church of England so he could divorce his wife and marry his mistress. He burned or beheaded anyone, including priests and bishops, who got in his way.

After Henry VIII died, his fanatical daughter Queen Mary (lovingly known as Bloody Mary) tried to force everyone back to Catholicism and burned more than 300 devout Protestants at the stake, whether clergy, noble, or commoner. After just five years of inept religious, social, and foreign policy, in a stroke of excellent timing, Mary dropped dead without an heir.

Queen Mary's sister, Queen Elizabeth I, brought back Protestantism with a minimum of bloodshed, but she was barely cold in her grave when the Catholics tried to blow up both king and Parliament in the Gunpowder Plot, naturally starting fresh waves of anti-Catholic rioting, egged on by the new and much more fanatical Protestant sect, the Puritans.

Then along came the angry Puritan Oliver Cromwell, who took over during the English Civil War, beheaded the king, and set up a Puritan government so strict that it banned everything from dancing to Christmas, making life for the average Englishman about as much fun as a visit to the tooth-puller.

After Cromwell came the Restoration. England brought the monarchy back with King Charles II, and back came the Church of England with him, one more time. But the next king in line, James II of England (with the dual position of being James VII of Scotland), was another Catholic, and it was like Bloody Mary all over again when he tried to give the whole country back to the pope. James was deposed by the Protestants in Parliament and fled to France, causing many more decades of attempted takeovers by his Catholic followers. They wanted to finish off all the Protestants in England, both Church of England and Puritan, because to the Catholics, the whole bloody lot of them were heretics.

Whew.

Now, picture yourself as some poor John Doe of a tradesman or farmer. Just what are you supposed to think about all of this? Do you believe in the miracle of the Mass this year, or don't you? Is that treasured Bible you own, the one written in English rather than Latin, kosher now, or is it liable to get you drawn and quartered? Is it all right that you kept your dear grandmother's rosary, or do you need to go back to hiding it underneath the Church of England's Book of Common Prayer? And by the way, you'd better be careful what you say to that new brother-in-law of yours, because you know he's really a Puritan at heart. You heard him say it, just last year, when it was still legal to be one.

These bloody and chaotic events had a deep effect on the new men of science and reason who were waiting in the wings with a novel idea for getting along with one another.

Speculative Masons and the big change

The period after the English Civil War became known as the Age of Reason. It was when the *scientific method* was developed to test new theories. Religious dogma, magic, and superstition were rejected in favor of hypothesis, experimentation, and conclusion. Faith was still important, and the new scientists were religious people — but for the first time, believers acknowledged that the Bible might not have *all* the answers to Life, the Universe, and Everything.

Who let all these "gentlemen" in here?

Beginning in the 1640s, the English lodges, like the Scottish lodges, began to admit members who were not workers in stone. These men were called *admitted* or *accepted* Masons. There's no written record of *why* the English lodges did this, whether it was a deep commitment or simply a new fashion, but several very interesting names pop up in connection with the Masons about this time.

Some of the most respected men of science in the mid-1600s from across Britain had met and formed the College for the Promoting of Physico-Mathematicall Experimentall Learning. That was a mouthful, and in 1663, it was renamed the Royal Society of London for Improving Natural Knowledge (or just Royal Society for short). The Royal Society in London was a place where scientists, philosophers, and scholars could meet and discuss their latest theories. The group was the darling of King Charles II, who thought of himself as something of a scientist.

What makes the Royal Society interesting to Freemasons is that Robert Moray, Elias Ashmole, Dr. Jean T. Desaguliers, and Sir Christopher Wren were all among the first members of the Royal Society. They were also all Freemasons. Speculative Freemasonry became a hothouse for the discussion of the new sciences and philosophies of reason, in a less formal gathering than the stuffy lecture halls.

Building cathedrals in men

By the late 1660s, these new philosophical and scientific Masons saw in Freemasonry the ideal symbolism for building character in men — construction of a strong, well-balanced structure, built with the assistance of many like-minded men, and dedicated to God, much like the cathedrals of old. Suddenly, Freemasonry wasn't just for a bunch of scruffy old rock carvers anymore.

The symbolism of architecture was important to them for another reason. The architect on a medieval cathedral project was a true intellectual. He possessed specialized knowledge that few others had: *scientia.* An architect had to know about mathematics, geometry, physics, art, and even literature. He had to communicate well, because he was verbally passing along plans to his workmen, who couldn't read anyway. He had to be well versed in the Bible, because much of the decoration that was carved in the stone and designed in the stained-glass windows of these cathedrals was meant to tell biblical stories without words.

The architects and cathedral builders of the Middle Ages were really liberal arts majors. So when a group of scientific intellectuals decided to transform the Freemason guilds into something more modern and more symbolic, they figured they were in pretty good company.

The Templar theory

The Knights Templar was an order of warrior monks that formed in 1118, after the First Crusade. Its official name was the Poor Knights of Christ and the Temple of Solomon, and its mission was to protect pilgrims traveling between Europe and the Holy Land. As its name implied, the order was based in Jerusalem, and the members took up residence under the remains of Solomon's Temple. They quickly developed a reputation for being among the fiercest knights in Christendom, but they remained bound by the monastic rules of poverty, chastity, and obedience.

In a remarkably short period of time, the Templars grew in power, prestige, and wealth by creating one of the first international banking systems. When a knight rode off to go slay the infidels, he would deposit gold in a Templar *preceptory* back home. He then carried a letter of credit that allowed him to withdraw money from other Templar posts along the road to Jerusalem. Not exactly an ATM network, but it was the first time anyone had done this on such a large scale.

As quickly as they had grown in power, the Templars were destroyed, and not by any Muslim army. Back in France, King Philip IV was upside down on his wartime loans and had quickly run out of money. Philip, known as Philip the Fair, was no fair-haired boy with the rest of Europe; he had orchestrated the installation of his own handpicked man as the newly elected Pope Clement V in 1305. Philip needed cash — lots of it, and fast — so he went to the Templars to get it, knowing the Paris Preceptory alone had more than what he needed for his immediate troubles. Not surprisingly, the Templars weren't interested in the king's scheme.

Not to be put off, Philip convinced his new pope to excommunicate the entire Templar order; Clement decreed that every Knight Templar in France be arrested on Friday, October 13, 1307. The knights were tried for heresy on a variety of largely trumped-up charges, and many were tortured or burned to death. The pope's orders spread all around Christendom, and any country that refused to arrest any Templar knight was threatened with mass excommunication.

King Robert the Bruce of Scotland wasn't impressed with such ecclesiastical saber rattling because he and the entire country of Scotland were already excommunicated. Word quickly spread to Templars fleeing the pope's edict that Scotland was the place to flee to.

Here is where the legend of the Templars and the Freemasons cross. Author John Robinson, in his book *Born in Blood*, asserted that those Templars hiding out in Scotland actually were the originators of speculative Freemasonry. Robinson wasn't the first to suggest this notion — Chevalier de Ramsay in 18th-century France was a big proponent of this theory.

Robinson's reasoning was that they were on the run and had to hide from loyal Catholics who might otherwise betray them, so they needed to establish secret passwords and other modes of recognition. The Templars considered themselves devout Catholics whom the Church had wrongly declared heretics, so discussion of religion would be forbidden among them — it was enough to say they believed in God. Templars wore a sheepskin "girdle" around their waists as a symbol of chastity, and it may have developed into the aprons Freemasons wear during their meetings. Because the Templars were a French order that spoke French in their daily activities, Robinson gave possible French origins to many of the unusual words associated with Freemasonry. That's not a big stretch, because the French-speaking Normans had conquered England in 1066, but it doesn't prove a Templar connection.

Most historians, Masonic and otherwise, discount Robinson's theory, and even the present-day Knights Templar order of Freemasons doesn't claim a direct link to the original knights. Nevertheless, Robinson brought up some interesting possibilities and more than a few unanswered coincidences. (See Chapter 10 for more about the Templars.)

Building Men: The 1700s

The Great London Fire destroyed much of the city in 1666, and rebuilding it took decades. Freemason Christopher Wren designed an astonishing number of the new buildings, and construction projects were everywhere. One of the biggest was the rebuilding of St. Paul's Cathedral. It started in 1673 and took almost 40 years to complete. Operative Masons came from all over England to work on the project, and many joined the Lodge of St. Paul. By 1710, the great cathedral was complete, and many lodges disbanded as Masons returned to their hometowns. By 1715, just four London city lodges were left.

London had grown at an incredible rate since the Great Fire and had become the largest city in Europe. People had become more mobile, and they were leaving the countryside to come to the big city to make their fortune, or at least find a better paying job than milking a cow. The result was a growing middle class that had never existed in Britain before. European life until the 1700s had a very rigid social structure, and it was unheard of for a peasant to become a nobleman. Now, that peasant could work his way into a better life, and the lines were beginning to blur.

Alehouses and coffeehouses became the natural places for people to gather and socialize, and the social club was a hugely popular concept. Social clubs formed among members who shared an interest in politics, literature, gossip, fine food, or just plain drinking.

Founding the first Grand Lodge

By this time, Masonic lodges also met in coffeehouses or alehouses, and they were generally named after the places they met. In February 1717, the Rummer and Grapes, the Crown, the Apple Tree, and the Goose and Gridiron lodges all gathered at the Apple Tree tavern in Charles Street in the Covent Garden area of London to discuss the future of Masonry in England. Three of the lodges were made up of mostly operative Masons, with a few "accepted" gentlemen members. But the Rummer and Grapes was almost entirely a gentlemen's lodge, with a handful of noblemen thrown in.

They wanted some rules and regulations. They wanted to gather as a big group every year for a celebratory feast. And they wanted to see to it that Masonry increased its membership. The one thing they *didn't* want was for the Freemasons to become just one more eating, drinking, and carousing club, like the many such clubs popping up all over London. To accomplish all this, they decided to form a governing group known as a Grand Lodge.

The lodges met again on June 24, 1717, Saint John the Baptist Day, at the Goose and Gridiron alehouse in Saint Paul's churchyard, under the shadow of the great cathedral. They elected Anthony Sayer, a gentleman member of the Crown Lodge, as the first Grand Master of the Grand Lodge of England. An operative Mason would never be elected as Grand Master. Freemasonry was changed forever.

What made this action so revolutionary was that the new Grand Lodge announced that it alone claimed the right to charter any new lodges of Masons in England. The original lodges were numbered 1 through 4, and new lodges were numbered sequentially as they signed on to the new Grand Lodge of England.

Of course, the lodges of Masons outside of London found this news to be something of a surprise. And the Scottish and Irish lodges were completely unimpressed by such a la-di-da presumption of authority. Up until this point, all that had been needed to start a lodge was for ten Masons to agree to do so, as long as they adhered to the *Ancient Charges,* the old rules set down in works like the Regius Manuscript. This new Grand Lodge had taken a pretty bold step in claiming such sweeping powers. Predictably, it soon caused an argument or two.

One of the first things the new Grand Lodge did was to go after more nobility as members, figuring it would give them greater prestige. The Duke of Montagu became the fourth Grand Master in 1721. Eventually, royalty arrived, in the form of the Duke of Cumberland, brother of King George III; the Duke of Cumberland became Grand Master in 1782.

The surest way to establish itself as being more respectable and noble than the run-of-the-mill social clubs was to prove its ancient pedigree. Freemasonry was no longer for stonemasons, but it was still connected by a legendary trail back to those first Masons' lodges chartered by old King Athelstan back in 10th-century York. Its mythical origins went back to King Solomon, and even before him.

Writing the history: The Book of Constitutions

A Presbyterian minister named James Anderson was directed by the Grand Lodge to write a history of the Craft and outline its rules. First published in 1723, the collected work was known as the *Book of Constitutions* and contained a new and improved version of the Ancient Charges (see Appendix B). Ever since that time, most modern lodges and Grand Lodges have been governed in a general sense by the basic guidelines set down by James Anderson's work.

One of the most important and revolutionary rules is the very first one. It reads, in part,

> . . . *in ancient Times Masons were charged in every Country to be of the Religion of that Country or Nation, whatever it was, yet it is now thought more expedient only to oblige them to that Religion in which all Men agree, leaving their particular Opinions to themselves; that is, to be good Men and true, or Men of Honour and Honesty, by whatever Denominations or Persuasions they may be distinguish'd.*

This policy was truly avant-garde stuff. Freemasons required a belief in God to become a member, but no questions would be asked about the member's personal religion. To further cement this requirement, Masons referred to God in their rituals as the *Grand Architect of the Universe*. From this point on, Catholic, Anglican, Presbyterian, Calvinist, or Puritan believers were all welcome to join, as long as they kept their religious arguments and prejudices to themselves. Even non-Christians were allowed to become Masons, and Jews began to take an interest in the fraternity.

The gentleman

One of the basic ideas of Freemasonry was that all men, whether upper or lower class, met on the same level in the lodge. Given the very rigid class distinctions in 18th-century society, this concept was truly unique and came directly from the history of the fraternity. Noblemen asked to join lodges of skilled laborers who worked with their hands for a living, not the other way around. It was the exact opposite of the way elitism usually worked.

Upper and lower classes and country and city folks were now meeting together and sitting side by side. The concepts of politeness, manners, social graces, better speech, and the value of intellect started to rub off on men who'd never given it much thought before. This was the origin of the notion that Freemasonry's purpose was to take good men and make them better. The concept of gentility began to grow and spread. Being tolerant of a man's views and behavior if you knew him well was one thing, but extending that tolerance to men you'd never met before was an enormous change. As James Anderson stated in the Book of Constitutions, "Masonry becomes the Center of Union, and the Means of conciliating true Friendship among Persons that must have remain'd at a perpetual Distance."

Freemasons were also forbidden to discuss politics in the lodge. The rules specifically required Masons to be good citizens and obedient to the government of their country. No one was going to be able to accuse the Freemasons of being traitors or revolutionaries . . . they hoped.

Pitting London against the rest of Britain

It didn't take long for Freemasons across Britain to question the authority of the new Grand Lodge in London, and many of their objections had to do with the question of antiquity. Lodges across the English, Scottish, and Irish countryside were older than the ones claiming authority in London. Besides, the older lodges had their own ways of doing things, and they didn't care for London's growing desire to standardize ceremonies and practices.

They also didn't care for the way the new Grand Lodge courted nobility and royalty as members. The argument had something of a city mouse/country mouse aspect. The London lodges had started to concentrate on the more learned aspects of the medieval architect in their ritual ceremonies, while the country lodges preferred to stress the honest labors of the men who worked with their hands.

In 1725, lodges in York decided they'd had enough and formed the Grand Lodge of All England at York (or *Totius Angliae* in Latin), which died out by the 1790s. Not to be outmaneuvered, the London-based Grand Lodge of England granted a charter to Irish lodges to form the Grand Lodge of Ireland. But Scotland wasn't about to be told what to do by anybody, so it formed its own Grand Lodge of Saint John of Scotland in 1736. Further turf wars popped up as time passed.

In 1751, a group of London Masons, largely in town from Ireland, formed a competing Antient Grand Lodge, led by Laurence Dermott. In his book *Ahiman Rezon: or A Help to a Brother,* Dermott claimed the Grand Lodge of England had fallen away from the older customs of Freemasonry, and his group was actually preserving them. The new group began to paradoxically refer to itself as being more ancient (or the Old English spelling, *antient*) than the older Grand Lodge of England. Over time, the bickering between the Antient Grand Lodge versus London's Grand Lodge of England became known as the *Antients and the Moderns.* In general, the Antients wanted to perform ceremonies (or rituals) that were closer to the old, operative lodges, whereas the Moderns were making the fraternity a more philosophical organization. The schism between the two sides was eventually healed in 1813 by a merger and the creation of the United Grand Lodge of England.

Fathering new Masonic degrees: Chevalier de Ramsay

In the 1740s, Chevalier Andrew Michael Ramsay, a Scotsman living in France, published a speech that claimed the Freemasons were descended from the

Knights Templar (see the sidebar "The Templar theory," earlier in this chapter). Ramsay's theories became enormously popular in England and France. The Royal Arch, Cryptic, and Christian Chivalric degrees developed quickly, largely growing from his exciting, romantic, and completely imaginary theories. These additional Masonic degrees could only be conferred after a man had become a Master Mason. Suddenly, middle-class tradesmen, shopkeepers, and artists could be granted lavish titles of knighthood and nobility, even if it was only in the confines of Masonic lodges. All these additional degrees would eventually become known in England and the United States as the York Rite, which I discuss in more detail in Chapter 10.

In France (not Scotland), Ramsay's same theories developed into what became the Scottish Rite degrees, which I explain in Chapter 11. Both the York Rite and the Scottish Rite crossed the Atlantic to the United States. In Europe, England favored the York Rite while France developed and expanded the Scottish Rite, but in the United States the York and Scottish rites grew and competed but coexisted side by side.

Jacobites and Freemasonry in France

Cracking open the door on French Freemasonry, even just a little, is a daunting task, because it became so complex and divided in a very short time. To understand the differences in French Freemasonry, you have to go backward in English history a bit. In the 1600s and 1700s, France was literally crawling with Englishmen and Scots. For centuries, France had been the place for Englishmen to flee to when caught on the wrong side of a political war. France was a mostly Catholic country, so it was a haven for English Catholics whenever anti-Catholic sentiment ran high. One fight in England took advantage of this haven more than any other.

The Restoration's King Charles II probably had more illegitimate children than any British monarch before or since, but he had no *legitimate* heir to the throne. He had deep Catholic sympathies, but he was wise enough to keep it under his hat to get back in power — and stay there — with a mostly Protestant Parliament. When

he died, his brother James Stuart became both King James II of England and James VII of Scotland (because Charles and James were both great-grandchildren of Mary Queen of Scots, and legitimately entitled to the thrones of both countries).

The problem was that James, like his great-grandmother, was openly and rabidly Catholic, and he was determined to make England Catholic again, which didn't go over well in a country that was finally settling down as predominantly Protestant. Almost immediately after becoming king, he went on the religious warpath, persecuting Protestants, trying to pack Parliament with his supporters, and engaging in "intrigues" with the King of France. Had he kept his religious views to himself as Charles II had, he might not have gotten into trouble, but Parliament had no intention of having a pro-Vatican "papist" king ever again. James was pitched off the throne in a brief uprising known

(continued)

(continued)

as the Glorious Revolution, and, naturally, fled to — surprise! — France. Meanwhile, his Protestant daughter, Mary, and her husband, William, were installed as joint rulers in 1689.

The men who wanted to put James II (or his offspring after he died) back on the throne were called *Jacobites* (after a Latin version of *James*). France became a haven for them. The Jacobites were a magnet, not just for Catholics or Scots, but for anyone with a gripe against the English crown, and France's kings lapped this up. England and France were constantly at war during this period, and using the Jacobites to annoy the English was a favorite pastime for French kings, more fun than boar hunting in the Loire or shopping for a new mistress.

The large number of Jacobites living in exile in France was one reason why the development of French Freemasonry is so confusing. So many variations of Freemasonry sprang up that cataloging them all is nearly impossible. Some historians claim that the first Freemasons in France were guards of the Stuart family while they were in exile in St. Germain en Laye. No matter how they got there, English and Scottish Freemasons were all over France, and in 1728, they formed a Grand Lodge in Paris. Before long,

a competing English Grand Lodge of France had sprung up. France had so many English Freemasons that the Grand Lodge didn't have a French Grand Master for many years. Other competing Grand Lodges quickly appeared.

Believe it or not, the English Masonic feud between the Antients and the Moderns spread to France, as well. The equivalent of the Antients in France were more Scottish oriented. They wanted to keep the old ways and ceremonies, but they also began to develop new and more numerous Masonic degrees based on old biblical and Templar legends. The French equivalent of the Moderns, on the other hand, became less enchanted with any sort of religious connection to Masonry or higher degrees, and in 1773, they formed the Grand Orient of France, a new governing body. The Grand Orient came to be identified with the French Revolution in 1789 and after. (I cover the involvement of European Masons, revolutions, and politics in Chapter 4.)

By the way, you see both the terms *Jacobins* (bloodthirsty French revolutionaries) and *Jacobites* (bloodthirsty English Catholic rebels) in French politics and history. Confusing. What can I say — it's France.

Going global: The Age of Enlightenment

The Age of Enlightenment was an intellectual, philosophical, and political movement that spread throughout Europe and followed hot on the heels of the Age of Reason. It was characterized by a belief in science and reason over faith and superstition.

Many of the philosophers, scientists, and artists of the Age of Enlightenment were drawn to Freemasonry in the early and mid-1700s, including the French author Voltaire, the German poet Goethe, the English philosopher John Locke, the American statesman and philosopher Benjamin Franklin, and the Austrian composers Haydn and Mozart.

Deism: The natural religion

The religious concept of Deism sprang from scientific thinking during the Enlightenment. The idea was that if the scientific method of investigation worked for natural and technological subjects, then scientific theories might also be applied to society, government, and religion as well.

Not just Catholicism and Protestantism, but Christianity itself and *all* organized religion began to be questioned as a corruption of a *natural* religion. This philosophy, known as *Deism*, taught that although God existed and created the world, He had never revealed himself to man. According to Deism, the Bible contained many important truths and teachings, but God hadn't written it. Nor was Christ the Son of God. Mere faith was no proof of the Almighty. The Deists felt that belief in God had to come from experience. This philosophy wasn't *atheism* (the belief that God doesn't exist), but it was just as heretical to the leaders of every Christian church.

To the Deists, God made the world, and He made it as a perfect, but complicated, machine.

A favorite comparison was that God was like a Divine Watchmaker, and after the earth was created, it needed no further tinkering with. Deists didn't believe in miracles, prophets, revelations, or for that matter, saviors. God was impersonal, but that didn't mean the Deists felt alienated from or ignored by Him. They felt awe and reverence for God because the discovery of His divine plan required personal growth and a constant search for knowledge.

One of the earliest criticisms of fundamentalist Christians about Freemasonry was that it sure walked, swam, and quacked like Deism. They felt that the religious tolerance espoused by Masons was nothing more than a cover for the heretical questioning of Christian beliefs. Thus began a long-standing misunderstanding of what goes on in a Masonic lodge. Religious discussion of any kind is forbidden, but that rule hasn't stopped many outsiders from believing that Masons engage in some sort of peculiar pagan religious worship within their lodge rooms.

Even members of royalty who saw themselves as philosophers and learned men were drawn to the fraternity, such as a long list of members of the English royal family and Frederick the Great of Prussia, who joined in 1738 when he was the crown prince. In fact, the German states (Germany was not a united country yet) often referred to Masonry as the *Royal Art*, because more than half of the early Masonic lodges there were created by royal decrees.

Whether these men — philosophers, artists, royalty — influenced the direction Freemasonry took or whether Freemasonry influenced them has long been a matter of debate. But the popularity of the fraternity first exploded and expanded worldwide during this period of philosophy.

Establishing Masonry in America

Freemasonry appeared in the American colonies soon after the first Grand Lodge of England was organized. The earliest American Masons had been members of English lodges or colonists who joined a lodge while visiting Europe.

Introducing Freemasonry to the colonies

Communicating with London was a long and difficult process, and from the beginning Americans have always been a brash bunch of individualists. Masons in America didn't always wait for permission to start a lodge or a Grand Lodge. By 1730, there were lodges in Philadelphia and Boston. When American colonists discovered that Freemasonry was popular among the fashionable set back in Mother England, lodges began to spread like wildfire. The Grand Lodge in London set up provincial Grand Lodges throughout the colonies, which were empowered to charter new lodges and essentially act as the Grand Lodge's foreign offices.

Lodges also sprang up spontaneously, without the blessing of the Grand Lodge or its provincial officials. Colonists who were members of the Grand Lodge of Scotland, the York-based Grand Lodge of All England, and the Antient Grand Lodge of England opened lodges, so the Antients-versus-Moderns competition went on in the colonies as well. Over time, because the Moderns were very interested in bringing nobility and even royalty into its ranks, the Grand Lodge of England came to be regarded as more pro-British than the Antients when the American Revolution broke out.

Officers and soldiers in the British Army quickly took to the fraternity as well, and military lodges became quite popular. The difference was that a military lodge traveled with a regiment instead of being anchored to one particular place. Irish and Scottish regiments were especially fond of these, and they operated under authority of the Grand Lodges of Ireland and Scotland. As a result, Freemasonry spread around the colonies, with a variety of ceremonies, customs, and traditions, depending upon the Grand Lodge origin of its members. One scholar asserted that receiving a charter from the Grand Lodge of Ireland was more popular with Scottish troops because it was, well, cheaper.

Fighting for a new country: Freemasonry and the American Revolution

The connection between Freemasonry and the Revolution has been exaggerated over the years, but Freemasons were present at many of the turning points that led up to the war with England and the formation of a republican government. In addition, many of the philosophies written into the Declaration of Independence and the U.S. Constitution were talked about and practiced long before in the Masonic lodges.

The Boston Tea Party

The story of the Boston Tea Party describes how a group of men dressed as "Red Indians" dumped crates of tea into Boston Harbor in 1773 to protest British tea taxes. It has long been alleged that the "Indians" were, in fact, members of Boston's St. Andrews Lodge. The lodge met at the Green Dragon Tavern, but so did the Sons of Liberty, a revolutionary political group. The two groups had many members in common — including Paul Revere and John Hancock — but the Tea Party was most definitely not a Masonic outing.

Revolutionary thinking and planning was everywhere leading up to the war, so it's only natural that many Freemasons sought independence from Britain. Nine Freemasons — including John Hancock and Benjamin Franklin — signed the Declaration of Independence, and two of the men who were directed to draft the Declaration — Franklin and Robert Livingston — were not only Masons but also Past Grand Masters in their colonies. When the war ended, 39 men signed the U.S. Constitution, and one-third of them were Masons. Nevertheless, plenty of Freemasons in the American colonies wanted to remain part of England.

Freemasonry became immensely popular with American military officers and soldiers. More than 40 percent of the generals commissioned by the Continental Congress either were or would become Freemasons before the war ended. The wealthiest colonists in America didn't join the army as a rule — they remained loyal to England (they were, after all, British citizens). So unlike the British Army, in which rank was often based on social status, wealth, and nobility, the Continental Army quickly became as democratic as America itself would become. Freemasonry also taught new social manners to rustic men who had gone from farmer to military officer overnight.

The concept of representative democracy was a new invention of the Enlightenment. Even England's Parliament was not as socially equal in its representation of the whole population as the form of government that was created in the new United States. Freemasons had already been practicing true democracy within their lodges by electing new members and officers, and their rituals stressed love and charity for all men as equals. Familiar notions that would become a basic foundation of U.S. government were being taught in Masonic lodges long before the Revolution. In the lodge, all men were created equal. Freedom of religion, of assembly, and of speech were all practiced in the lodge, even in countries that outlawed such things.

ORIGINS

Prince Hall and African American Masonry

A Mason named Prince Hall is considered to be the father of Freemasonry in the African American community. Evidence suggests that he was born in Africa and brought to America as a slave in his early teens. He was freed after 21 years, and he probably took his last name from his Master's household.

Prince Hall and several other black Bostonians were interested in forming a Masonic lodge for other free Negroes. On March 6, 1775, Prince Hall and 14 other black men were initiated into Lodge No. 441, an Irish military lodge attached to the 38th Foot Regiment, garrisoned at Castle William (what is now Fort Independence) in Boston Harbor. The Master of the lodge was Sergeant John Batt, and the lodge conferred the Entered Apprentice, Fellow Craft, and Master Mason degrees on the men in one day and granted them a special dispensation to meet as *African Lodge,* which allowed them to march in processions and perform funeral services, but not to initiate new members. Black men would somehow have to receive their degrees in other lodges before joining African Lodge.

When the Revolutionary War broke out, Prince Hall and many of his brethren enlisted in the Continental Army. Hall himself is believed to have fought at Bunker Hill. African Lodge survived the war and by its end had 33 members. But after the Revolution ended, American Freemasonry was in an organizational turmoil. Because most of the lodges in America had been authorized by English (both Antient and Modern), Irish, or Scottish Grand Lodge warrants, the new states created new Grand Lodges to administer the lodges within their borders. In fact, several states (including Massachusetts) formed two Grand Lodges, continuing the Antients-and-Moderns feud.

But when Prince Hall and African Lodge sought a charter from the new Grand Lodge of Massachusetts, they were turned down. Although Freemasonry's goals of equality were lofty, the white American Masons of the period wouldn't rise above the prejudices of their place and time, and they shunned Hall's requests. Frustrated, in 1784, African Lodge petitioned the Grand Lodge of England for a new charter. It was granted in September but took three years to be delivered to Boston. On May 6, 1787, the lodge officially became Lodge No. 459 of the Grand Lodge of England.

Whether it was out of true Masonic brotherly love and friendship or an opportunity for the Grand Master of England (who just happened to be the brother of King George III) to tweak the nose of white Americans by authorizing a new lodge of black men on American soil is unknown. African Lodge forwarded its annual dues payments to London each year but was ignored for years. In 1792, after being visited by black Freemasons from Pennsylvania and Rhode Island, African Lodge authorized the creation of a lodge in each of those states under authority of its English charter.

African Lodge was stricken from the rolls of the Grand Lodge of England in 1813 after its annual dues payments stopped arriving in London. At this point England and the United States were at war again, and the Grand Lodge of England never sent any correspondence informing them of their administrative fate. The lodge tried one last time in 1824 to request clarification of its status and a renewed charter from London. It, too, was ignored.

So in 1827, African Lodge declared itself to be its own Grand Lodge, just as most of the Grand Lodges in the new United States had done after the Revolution. It and the other two lodges it had chartered became the origin of black Freemasonry in North America. In honor of its founder, it was eventually renamed Prince Hall Grand Lodge, and today more than 250,000 members belong to the 4,000 Prince Hall–affiliated lodges worldwide in 45 independent jurisdictions. Prince Hall Grand Lodge

of Massachusetts remains the only American Masonic body still in possession of its charter from England, and it predates most of the other Grand Lodges in the United States.

Prince Hall was a fascinating man. At various times in his life he was a leather worker, soldier, civic leader, caterer, educator, property owner, and abolitionist. He fought for the establishment of schools for black children in Boston and opened a school in his own home. In 1787, as a registered voter, he successfully petitioned the Massachusetts legislature to protect free Negroes from being kidnapped and sold into slavery. Until the day he died on December 4, 1807, he always referred to himself as an African.

Finding favor and persecution during and after the French Revolution

Freemasonry's popularity in France was exceeded only by its variety. Before and after the chaos of the French Revolution in 1789, the Grand Lodges in France disagreed in philosophies, politics, and rituals, and a dizzying array of Masonic organizations developed: 36 Masonic groups, 26 orders that admitted women, and nearly 1,400 different degree rituals! (Today, at least 14 competing Grand Lodges operate in France, most of them claiming some sort of direct descent from the original body that began back in 1728.)

French Freemasonry divided, merged, closed, reopened, and underwent a mind-boggling series of changes before and after the French Revolution. At first, the public admired the Freemasons and their motto of *"Libertie! Egalitie! Fraternitie!"* (Liberty, Equality, Brotherhood!). But the Revolution quickly degenerated into years of murder and terror, and many people began to identify the Masons with those years of madness. Masonry almost vanished in France until Napoleon's reign returned order to the shattered country. (I cover more about the French Revolution and why politics and Masonry don't mix in Chapter 4.)

The Presidential Bible

George Washington remains the most famous Freemason in U.S. history, and every American Mason proudly feels a connection to him. Washington was initiated as a Mason in 1752, in Fredericksburg, Virginia. He became a Master Mason the following year. Before the War of Independence, Washington had distinguished himself as a British military officer, and he was highly respected and admired when he was picked to lead the new Continental Army. His patriotism, heroism, and visionary leadership during the war are well known.

It is perhaps difficult for modern Americans to understand just how universally beloved Washington became, both during and after the war. He was offered many honors and positions in the wake of this adoration. As the United States' most honored war hero, its first Commander in Chief, first president, and a host of other firsts, he was acutely aware that every action he took would create new traditions and set possibly dangerous precedents for the new country. As a result, he calmly and wisely turned down many offers and honors for the sake of the nation's future.

When Washington was inaugurated as the first president of the United States, the ceremony had obviously never been performed before. Like everything else in the new nation, it needed to be created from scratch. Washington was to be sworn in at a ceremony in New York City on April 30, 1789. The 57-year-old hero set out on horseback from Mount Vernon, and his long trip to New York was filled with celebrations, cannon salutes, fireworks, and feasts.

By the time he got to New York, it was a full-blown party. The ceremony was to take place in Federal Hall, on Wall Street. When the time came, Washington requested a Bible on which to take the oath of office, but no one had thought to bring one for the occasion. Robert Livingston, Grand Master of New York, knew there would be a Bible in nearby St. John's Lodge #1, and sent for it. Washington took the oath of office on the open Bible and then kissed the open book. The page was bookmarked where Washington's hand rested, and the lodge has preserved the Bible for more than 200 years.

At least four other presidents have taken the oath of office on the St. John's Bible: Warren G. Harding, Dwight D. Eisenhower, Jimmy Carter, and George H. W. Bush. But out of the five presidents, only Washington and Harding were Freemasons. George W. Bush requested the Bible in 2001, and the fragile, 10-pound book was hand-carried to Washington, D.C., by members of the lodge. Unfortunately, the rain poured down on inauguration day, which would have put the book in danger. The Bible was placed on display in a museum in New York later that year, just three blocks away from the World Trade Center. In a display case, it survived the horrible destruction of September 11, 2001.

Growing, Changing, and Branching Out: The 1800s

Freemasonry traveled literally around the world throughout the 1800s. European Grand Lodges formed provincial Grand Lodges in Africa, Asia, and South America — everywhere their ships traveled. English, Scottish, and

Irish soldiers carried Freemasonry with them into Africa, Asia, India, and the Middle East. European colonists frequently formed local lodges, and in many countries it became common for tradesmen, members of the military, and government workers to join them as well.

For many years Napoleon Bonaparte was rumored to be a Freemason, but there is no historic proof of it. Still, many of his military officers, members of his Grand Council for the Empire, and 22 of the 30 Marshals of France were. So were his four brothers, three of whom were made kings by Napoleon. The Emperor's wife, Empress Josephine, was even admitted into a French female lodge in 1804. Regardless of whether Napoleon was ever made a Mason, he did adopt the title Protector of Freemasonry, along with the lengthy list of other titles he assumed when he became emperor in 1804. It made the business cards look more impressive.

Belgium became an independent nation in 1830, and King Leopold I was a Freemason. Royalty was often part of Masonry in Scandinavian countries as well. However, some governments didn't believe that Masonry was free of political or religious subversion, and in some countries it wasn't. Separating the beliefs of the fraternity as a whole from the actions of some of its many variations and members was — and still is — difficult. Russia outlawed the fraternity in 1822, and its prohibition continued all the way through the Soviet regime in the 20th century.

Ongoing Vatican disapproval of Freemasonry continued from the 1700s, but Freemasonry became so popular that many Catholics ignored the succession of pronouncements of the popes. Most regarded the anti-Masonic rules of the Church to be political in nature, not a deeply spiritual issue. Masonry spread to the mostly Catholic Central and South American countries, and it became very popular when it was discovered that Simon Bolivar, the renowned liberator of the continent, was a Mason. Benito Juarez, the father of Mexican independence who threw off the French occupation of his country in 1866, was also a Freemason. Again, rightly or wrongly, revolution was seen to be a byproduct of Masonic infiltration in some countries (see Chapter 4).

Reuniting Antients and Moderns

In England, the Antients and the Moderns patched up their fight and signed an agreement of union in 1813, forming the new United Grand Lodge of England. One of the sticking points was that the Moderns felt that Freemasonry should be restricted to only the first three degrees of Entered Apprentice, Fellow Craft, and Master Mason. The Antients felt that the Moderns had left out an important part of the Master Mason degree, so they lobbied for the inclusion of an additional ceremony called the Holy Royal Arch to complete the story told in the third degree.

In a classic case of the double talk of peace treaties, the oddly worded agreement defined Freemasonry as consisting of *only* the first three degrees, *including* the Royal Arch degree. In any other universe, that would be four degrees, but that's diplomacy for you. (See Chapter 10 for more about the Royal Arch degree.) The agreement also refused to require specific, standardized ritual, allowing local lodges to retain their individual customs. This agreement only affected English lodges charted by the two warring factions. The newly established Grand Lodges in the new United States had moved on and developed their own way of doing things.

Spreading throughout America

Freemasonry's greatest and most explosive growth was in the United States in the 1800s. The Rhode Island Freemason and ritualist Thomas Smith Webb published *Freemason's Monitor* in 1797, which had the effect of standardizing Masonic ceremonial degree work for many lodges as well as becoming a handy guidebook for new Masons wanting to learn the ritual. (See Chapter 6 for more about Masonic rituals and how they came about.)

As the United States pushed its borders to the west, Grand Lodges formed in the new states. Freemasonry quickly became associated with the Founding Fathers, and the word spread across the new country.

Earning the "higher" degrees

One of the reasons for Masonry's increasing popularity was the allure of new, additional degrees offered by two rival groups. One system of degrees was offered by the Royal Arch, Cryptic, and Chivalric (especially the Knights Templar) branches of Masonry that became known as the American or York Rite. Thomas Webb was a particularly avid promoter of these degrees (see Chapter 10). The other system of degrees came out of France and was mostly administered by the Supreme Council in Charleston, South Carolina. This system was eventually known as the Scottish Rite (see Chapter 11). The spread of the York Rite dominated the northern states, whereas the Scottish Rite had its greatest early success in the southern states.

These sets of additional degrees were different and mutually exclusive, but both grew from the fanciful ideas of Chevalier de Ramsay. Literally dozens of new additional Masonic ceremonies were being performed and enjoyed in the United States for all the same reasons they had grown in Europe.

For all the American Revolution's rhetoric about equality and casting off the shackles of Britain's monarchy, Americans still loved pomp, pageantry, and really cool titles. The York and Scottish Rite degrees were packed full of them. Each degree told a new symbolic story, had its own dramatic presentation, and often conferred an impressive title on the candidate. Each degree taught a morality lesson and brought biblical and other legendary stories to life, with the individual Mason at the center of the ceremony. They were also often emotionally exciting and a form of frontier theater for entertainment-starved pioneers.

Leaving the taverns for the temples

Masons in the United States needed new, larger buildings to accommodate the expanding numbers of members. They also needed bigger, private spaces in which to perform these new degrees. Putting on a dramatic presentation with an expanding list of secret props, costumes, and visual aids in the room over an alehouse wasn't practical.

After the War of Independence, custom-built Masonic halls started to appear. The new halls made Freemasonry more visible to the public than it had ever been — and they were alluring as well. Lodges often gave over their public rooms for community events, such as dinners and dances to celebrate special events. The Masons helped the community, such as during the War of 1812 in Richmond, when they turned over their hall to be used as a hospital. But no outsider got to see inside the private lodge rooms themselves or see the ceremonies that went on in them. Naturally, that secrecy made it even more popular.

Moving out of the taverns also brought a new level of respect and seriousness to the teachings that went on in the lodge. Masons began to refer to their buildings as *temples,* because they regarded them as sacred places for imparting truth and knowledge, and to make a connection to the Masonic legends of King Solomon's Temple. Of course, all that seriousness was offset by plenty of drinking and eating, too.

Men flocked to the fraternity, and popular political figures were often Freemasons. But with popularity came distrust from social and religious leaders. Christian leaders were especially concerned that Freemasons were teaching Deism to their members. They were also worried that Freemasonry itself might become a substitute for established religion. Plenty of conspiracy theorists were afraid of evil plots that might be hatching among these important men. Here was a secret society that the most respected men in business and government belonged to, and what they did behind its doors was a big mystery. It wasn't long before the anti-Masonic forces got unexpected ammunition with which to attack the fraternity.

Getting a bad reputation: The Morgan Affair

In September 1826, the disappearance of a man in a remote corner of upstate New York set off 25 years of anti-Masonic hysteria. In the little town of Batavia, a disgruntled and down-on-his-luck Mason named William Morgan announced his intentions to write a book exposing all the "secrets" of the Freemasons. Several local Masons decided that Morgan was something of a scoundrel and, by exposing the rituals of the lodge, he was breaking his Masonic vows. They abducted Morgan and carried him off to Fort Niagara on Lake Ontario, along the Canadian border. The conspirators claimed they paid Morgan $500, gave him a horse, pointed him north, and told him never to come back. Whatever the truth may have been, Morgan was never seen again, and some evidence suggested that the men might very well have drowned him in the lake.

Twenty-six men were indicted in connection with his disappearance, but only six were ever tried, and none on murder charges. It was discovered that the prosecutor and many of the jurors were Freemasons, and the trial resulted in very lenient sentences.

The result was a firestorm of protest that quickly spread across New York and then the country. The public believed that the Masons had killed Morgan "according to Masonic ritual" and then cheated justice by receiving short sentences from their Masonic friends who controlled the courts and the government, including Governor and Freemason Dewitt Clinton. What began as a small-town crime became a nationwide outrage, and it certainly sold lots of newspapers. It remains the only authentic case in history of Freemasons seriously accused of murdering a member who had broken his Masonic vows.

Going underground: The anti-Masonic movement

William Morgan's book (see the preceding section) was published after his death, and it was an instant bestseller. One hundred anti-Masonry meetings were held in New York in 1827. On St. John's Day that year, 3,000 protesters marched to the lodge in Batavia, attacked the Masons inside, and looted the building. The next year, a statewide anti-Masonic convention was held in Utica, and over the next five years, the anti-Masonic movement went national.

By 1829, more than 100 anti-Masonic newspapers were being published, mostly in the north. Almost as quickly, anti-Masonic political parties formed in several states, and in 1831, the Anti-Masonic Party became the first third-party movement in the United States, running former Freemason William Wirt for president, carrying the state of Vermont, and receiving 8 percent of the national vote. The party elected governors in Pennsylvania and Vermont as well as a number of U.S. congressmen. Their platform was simple: Masonry was antidemocratic and anti-American, and it opposed Christianity. Therefore, Masonry must be driven out of the country.

The hysteria was so bad that for nearly two decades, a toddler couldn't get sick in the United States without someone claiming the Masons had poisoned the kid's porridge. Lodges went underground or closed all over the country as men renounced their membership, and several Grand Lodges shut down as well. Nationwide, Masonic membership dropped from 100,000 in 1827 to less than 40,000 ten years later.

Adapting to changed times: A slow rebirth

The strong desire in the United States for fraternalism and elaborate ritual ceremonies didn't disappear, it just went elsewhere. Masons fled to other organizations that began to appear, organizations that modeled their structure and ceremonies on the Freemasons and gladly took in the former Masons as members.

U.S. Masons didn't totally vanish, but it took time before they could safely come up for air again. To rebuild their image, in the 1840s, Grand Lodges passed rules removing alcoholic beverages from their buildings and meetings and eliminating the boisterous, freewheeling revelry that used to accompany lodge gatherings.

To root out anti-Masons who had signed up only to spy on the meetings, the long-standing rules that allowed new Entered Apprentices to attend business meetings were revoked, requiring members to be Master Masons before having full membership rights. Money that was saved on liquor could be spent on bigger and better-organized charities as well as on costumes and other increasingly magnificent lodge paraphernalia. As a result, the rituals, especially for the additional degrees, became more and more elaborate, requiring large casts of men to perform.

As other non-Masonic fraternal groups grew in popularity, Freemasonry found itself competing for members. With the alcohol ban came a stronger desire for higher moral standards. Grand Lodges developed highly structured rules for Masonic trials of members accused of un-Masonic conduct. Socializing was rejected in favor of rehearsal and perfection of the performance of the rituals. Masonry became more spiritual in its outlook.

In fact, as more anti-Masons published an increasing number of frequently exaggerated exposés to embarrass the Masons, the real consequences were quite unexpected: More and more curious men wanted to join in order to see these big secret spectacles they'd read so much about. Proving that there's no such thing as bad publicity, the result was a growing number of new members who wanted bigger, better, more elaborate ceremonies. The three basic lodge degrees hadn't changed much since Thomas Smith Webb's *Freemason Monitor* was published in 1797, even though there were wild variations from one state to another and even among lodges. The so-called "higher" degrees of the York and Scottish rites were catching on across the country and motivating the rebirth of the fraternity.

Resurging interest in organizations: Animals, Indians, Knights, and Odd Fellows

After the Civil War, another tidal wave of interest in the fraternal organizations occurred, for many reasons. The many new groups included the Odd Fellows, the Improved Order of Red Men, the Order of the Star-Spangled

Banner, the Sons of Honor, the Order of Good Templars, the Grange, the Ancient Order of Foresters, the Holy and Noble Knights of Labor, the Benevolent and Protective Order of Elks, the Loyal Order of Moose, and literally hundreds of others. It was the Golden Age of Fraternity, and the United States became a nation of joiners. Nearly every group that appeared during this period could trace its initiation ceremonies back to Freemasonry's original designs.

One of the more popular books in the pre–Civil War South was Freemason Sir Walter Scott's *Ivanhoe*. The tale of 13th-century knights in England influenced many of the notions of honor and chivalry, and even the formal language that became so pervasive during and after the Civil War. (It was so influential that Freemason and author Mark Twain went so far as to blame the works of Sir Walter Scott for leading to the war by glorifying an outmoded era of rank, caste, and privilege.) After the war, veterans became infatuated with the pseudomilitary orders like the Knights of Pythias, the Grand Army of the Republic, and the York Rite's Knights Templar, who decorated themselves with ersatz military uniforms, swords, medals, drill teams, and the titles of knighthood. The regalia factories that had provided these items to the military during the Civil War found new life manufacturing them for the fraternal groups.

Meanwhile, women were increasingly unhappy that they went off to church meetings while their husbands went out to the lodges and had fun. As a result, women's groups formed, including the Order of the Eastern Star (see Chapter 13).

Masons had never excluded Catholics, but the Catholic Church had long prohibited its members from becoming Freemasons (see Chapter 4), and the Church was uneasy about the many other similar fraternal groups that were popping up overnight in the United States. To answer the desire, many Catholics had to become part of this fraternal wave, and the Catholic Knights of Columbus was created in 1882.

Gaining appendages: The rise of appendant bodies

American Freemasons weren't going to be left out of this growing wave of fraternal popularity. In 1853, Albert Pike joined the Scottish Rite in Charleston, South Carolina. The degrees he witnessed were interesting to him, but Pike was a devoted scholar of history and world religions. He felt the degrees taught important lessons but could use some improving.

Over the next decade, he rewrote all the 4th- through 32nd-degree rituals and embellished them with lavish tales of kings and knights, of ancient religions and legends (see Chapter 11). Pike's revisions helped to make the Scottish Rite the largest and most popular appendant body of Freemasonry in the world. Its degrees were presented not for one or two initiates in a lodge room but as massive stage productions for hundreds of candidates in specially built auditoriums, using state-of-the-art lighting, scenery, and special effects.

To this day, these Scottish Rite auditoriums, theaters, and cathedrals like the Scottish Rite Cathedral in Indianapolis (see Figure 2-1) remain the largest Masonic buildings ever constructed.

Figure 2-1:
The Scottish Rite Cathedral in Indianapolis, Indiana, was built in 1929 solely for conferring the degrees of the Scottish Rite of Freemasonry.

Photograph courtesy of Christopher Hodapp

The price of being a joiner

To understand just how popular being a member of a fraternal organization in the United States was after the Civil War, looking at a few statistics is useful. By 1899, more than 6 million out of 21 million adult men in the United States were members of one or more of the country's 300 fraternal organizations, which conferred about 1,000 degrees on 200,000 new members a year. The average fraternal lodge member spent $50 a year on dues and insurance, and another $200 on initiation fees, ritualistic paraphernalia, banquets, and travel. Bear in mind that the average factory worker at that time earned just $400 to $500 a year. In 2012, those $50 dues would be equal to $1,330. And that $200 budget for initiation, paraphernalia, banquets, and travel in 1899 would cost $5,321 today, on an adjusted salary of between $10,641 and $13,302 a year. Bottom line: These guys were paying about 50 to 60 percent of their yearly salaries just to be members of fraternal organizations.

Remember that these were the days before HMOs, Medicare, and Social Security, and many of the fraternal groups began to offer inexpensive insurance programs to their members. In fact, many groups existed solely as insurance societies that just happened to have initiation rites! Seen in that light, they were well worth the money, even for men of limited means. A common workingman no longer had to worry about what would happen to his wife and children if something happened to him. His fraternal brothers would take care of his family when he was gone.

Because the U.S. Masonic lodges had driven alcohol and potentially embarrassing behavior out of their buildings after the Morgan Affair (see "Getting a bad reputation: The Morgan Affair," earlier in this chapter), a group of Freemasons in New York decided that Masons needed a place to lighten up from all their serious degree work. They created the Ancient Arabic Nobles of the Mystic Shrine in 1879 as the playground of Masonry. Their initiatory ceremony was based on an Arabic legend, and they adopted the red fez as their identifying headgear (see Chapter 12).

Surviving and Surging: The 1900s

Masons were heroes of World War I. Generals "Blackjack" Pershing and Mason M. Patrick, father of the Air Corps, were Freemasons, as was air ace Eddie Rickenbacker. Of the five U.S. presidents who served between 1897 and 1923, four of them — William McKinley, Theodore Roosevelt, William Taft, and Warren Harding — were Freemasons.

By 1925, 3 million Americans were Freemasons, but a majority of the hundreds of other non-Masonic fraternities died out after the 1929 stock-market crash and the Great Depression. As more civic-minded service groups like Kiwanis, Lions, and Rotary clubs came into being, Freemasonry changed, too. (See Chapter 9 for more about which groups are and are not Masonically related.) Masonry stopped stressing its "ancient" and mythical origins and began to concentrate on expanding its charitable concerns. The Masonic Service Association was created to assist Masonic soldiers during and after World War I.

Relieving social concerns in the early 1900s

Social Security, old age, and disability pensions didn't exist in the United States in the early 1900s and after World War I, the nation witnessed a growth in the numbers of orphaned children. Because no national safety net for the poor and elderly in the United States existed, Grand Lodges began to build Masonic homes for senior citizens, widows, and orphans. They were often magnificent facilities, and many survive today.

Higher education was becoming a reality for more Americans, so Masonic scholarship funds were created. And the Shrine began to construct a number of hospitals dedicated to treating burns and orthopedic problems in children, at no cost.

Being cast as villains and heroes in World War II

When Adolf Hitler came to power in Germany in 1933, he had carefully laid out his beliefs in his book, *Mein Kampf (My Struggle)*. Germany was mired in a horrible economic and psychological depression after World War I, and Hitler's plan to fix his country's problems centered on his belief that Germany's troubles were caused by the Jews. According to Hitler, Freemasonry was just another front for Jewish domination of the world's economic system. Therefore, Germany had to rid itself of these evil men.

Hitler cooked up much of this theory from a book called the *Protocols of the Learned Elders of Zion*. (I talk more about it in Chapter 4.) The *Protocols* had been a propaganda hoax popularized by the czar's secret police in Russia in the late 1800s. In it, a secret group of Jews outlined their plan for world domination, in part by using the Freemasons as their willing servants. It wasn't true, but people believed it.

Many of Hitler's anti-Semitic laws were passed in response to the so-called "Jewish conspiracy" outlined in the *Protocols*. As a result, in addition to the persecution and extermination of Jews in Germany, Freemasons in every country invaded by the Nazis were arrested, sent to concentration camps, and put to death. Lodges were destroyed, and Masonic paraphernalia were put on display in Nazi-occupied cities to show the "evil devices" of the Masons. German Freemasons went underground.

Outside of the Nazi-occupied countries, Masons played a huge role in ending the war and putting an end to Hitler's evil regime. Freemasons Franklin D. Roosevelt, Winston Churchill, and King George VI led the United States and Britain during the war. Other Masons, like Generals Omar Bradley and Douglas MacArthur, fought it on the ground. Another Mason, President Harry S. Truman, Past Grand Master of Missouri, ended the war in Japan. And Freemason George Marshall oversaw the careful and even-handed reconstruction of Europe after the war.

Growing again post-war

After World War II ended, Freemasonry surged again in popularity. The Greatest Generation wanted to celebrate, and the United States had much to celebrate. Military support groups like the Veterans of Foreign Wars (VFW) and the American Legion exploded in popularity, often driven by their social activities. The sons of the Golden Age of Fraternalism became joiners, too, and Americans joined bowling leagues, bridge clubs, country clubs, and fraternal organizations. Lodges crept into popular television shows, like the "Raccoon Lodge" on *The Honeymooners* and the "Water Buffaloes Lodge" on *The Flintstones*.

The Shrine became enormously popular for much the same reason. It was a fun place to go, and its hospital charity was well respected. The national prohibition of alcohol enacted in 1919 had been repealed by the 21st Amendment in 1933. Shriners became known for enjoying their parties, parades, circuses, brass bands, and the occasional drink. All that activity resulted in the expansion of the hospitals to 22 facilities in the United States and Canada. The catch for joining was that a man had to join a Masonic lodge and then complete the degrees of either the York Rite or the Scottish Rite before he could become a Shriner. (See Chapter 12 for more on the Shrine.)

Masonic membership reached an all-time high in 1959, with more than 4 million Masons in the United States alone. It was common for lodges to have hundreds, and sometimes more than a thousand, members.

Declining in the '60s

The Vietnam era brought challenges to Masons in the United States. The gap between the World War II generation and their children couldn't have been wider. Each successive generation of Freemasons had passed along the fraternity to their sons. Masons were the new heroes of the space program: John Glenn, Gus Grissom, and Tom Stafford were all Masons, as was the second man to walk on the moon, Buzz Aldrin. In 1974, Gerald Ford became president and, as of 2012, he was the last Freemason to occupy the Oval Office.

The Vietnam generation wanted nothing to do with the customs and institutions of their fathers. The Baby Boomers as a group turned their backs on the "establishment." As a result, Freemasonry, like almost every other social and civic group established prior to the 1960s, plummeted in popularity.

This group had other distractions, as well. Television became a motivation for staying indoors rather than socializing. Seemingly simple advances like air conditioning let people stay in their houses instead of sitting on the front porch to take the air and to chat with their neighbors. Suburban sprawl meant people no longer walked to jobs that were close to their homes. Neighborhood groups that shared employers, favorite bars and clubs, common hobbies, and other bonds drifted apart, and society became more solitary and individual.

Computers and the Internet only continued this trend. But the wired society suddenly allowed Freemasons all around the world to communicate with each other and easily exchange ideas about different customs and attitudes. In the 1990s, partially encouraged by online discussions, the mainstream and predominantly white Grand Lodges and the mostly black Prince Hall Grand Lodges began to jointly recognize each other after 200 years of mutual silence.

Experiencing the New Millennium: More Changes on the Way

The Internet is fueling something of a rebirth in Freemasonry. On the surface, the membership numbers are dropping today, but only because of the explosive growth of Masonry after World War II. The men who joined in the 1940s and 1950s are dying at an increasing rate, so the overall figures are declining. Today, the group has somewhere between 4 and 5 million members worldwide and just under 2 million in the United States.

Because the Baby Boomers didn't join lodges, their children weren't exposed to Freemasonry. Most young people today have never heard of it, much less know anything about it. Nevertheless, their grandparents were Masons in record numbers, and they're starting to discover Masonry on their own.

The Internet has become a simple place to communicate with Masons around the block or around the world. Popular references have also stirred interest in the fraternity, with graphic novels like *From Hell* and *The League of Extraordinary Gentlemen,* movies like *National Treasure,* Dan Brown's books *The Da Vinci Code* and *The Lost Symbol,* and even ridiculous references like the "Stonecutters Lodge" in *The Simpsons.*

Grand Lodges in the United States are developing new, if controversial, ways to get the message out to young men about the fraternity. Many states have started advertising campaigns and are designing large, one-day ceremonies to reduce the amount of time it takes to receive the three degrees. For the first time in three centuries, the trend has been to promote and demystify the organization.

Curiously, outside the United States, especially in non-English-speaking countries, Masonic organizations that haven't demystified or promoted themselves have been growing. In countries where Freemasonry has remained small and retained its "secret" aura, renewed interest in the fraternity has led to greater growth.

Traditional Observance lodges

In the U.S., a movement known as Traditional Observance or European Concept lodges is gaining popularity. Fueled by the Masonic Restoration

Foundation (http://traditionalobservance.com), these lodges are intentionally small in size and put a greater concentration on rituals and a more spiritual approach to attending lodge without focusing on religion. They are usually more formal, and generally have a strong presentation of Masonic education, followed by a sumptuous meal (known as a festive board), complete with ceremonial toasting.

These types of lodges are gaining popularity, but they are by no means taking over the Masonic world. They remain few in number and act more as an example of a different way to hold a lodge meeting, as opposed to being a silver bullet that will expand the membership numbers. Still, their adherents are enthusiastic and have a strong Internet presence. Almost every state has a TO or EC lodge of some kind.

The Dan Brown effect

Dan Brown's novels — *The Da Vinci Code, Angels and Demons*, and especially *The Lost Symbol* — have had a dramatic effect on Masonic membership. Brown's fascination with all things esoteric led him to portray Freemasonry's rituals and beliefs a little spookier than in real life, but he has mostly been very kind to the fraternity. As a result, the next generation of Masons may join because of what they read in Brown's novels or saw in the movies based on them. It's important to understand that Brown's descriptions of Masonic rituals are based on 19th-century exposés by non-Masons (Brown is not currently a Mason himself) and aren't a correct presentation of what Masons do today. Nevertheless, with millions of books in print and billion-dollar takes at the box office, his stories may be where the next great influx of members get the first inkling of joining.

An explosive growth of Freemasonry — like the booms Freemasonry saw in the late 1800s and the 1950s — probably won't occur anytime soon. Nevertheless, Freemasonry continues to draw new members and is experiencing new interest from younger men. In spite of its long traditions and customs, Freemasonry has always adapted to serve the age in which it has existed, and younger men seem to be in search of the sense of community that no longer exists in modern society. It may very well be that Freemasonry again stands on the doorstep of a new renaissance. (For more on the future of Freemasonry, turn to Chapter 15.)

Chapter 3

The Philosophy of Freemasonry

In This Chapter

▶ Understanding the basic beliefs of Masonry

▶ Uncovering the Masonic plot to take over the world

▶ Reacting to Freemason mysticism and symbols

*A*part from worldwide networks of evil super-criminals run by bald-headed, cat-stroking masterminds found in James Bond movies, most organizations are founded with a certain sense of idealism, optimism, and good intentions. The trick is always whether that optimism can prevail and withstand the test of time without being compromised or torn apart by internal quarrels.

At the opening of the Entered Apprentice degree, the initiatory ritual ceremony of Freemasonry, the question is commonly asked, "What come you here to do?" The answer is, "To learn to subdue my passions and improve myself in Masonry." Freemasonry was designed from the very beginning to survive the pressures that have otherwise derailed churches, clubs, companies, and kingdoms, and it has managed to survive in its modern form for 300 years. Freemasonry is a fraternity, but it also qualifies as a philosophy.

If you look up *philosophy* in the dictionary, you discover that it is the love and pursuit of wisdom by intellectual means and moral self-discipline, and a system of values by which one lives. In fact, the word comes from the Greek term *philosophos,* which means "lover of wisdom." At its most basic level, Masons are taught to be lovers of wisdom, to pursue and value knowledge, and to live by a moral code of self-discipline.

Chapter 2 discusses the history of the fraternity, and Chapter 4 covers the specifics of why certain Masonic rules came about. This chapter talks about the basic beliefs of Freemasonry, and by explaining them, provides some insight as to why it became the world's largest and most respected gentlemen's society.

Defining What Masons Believe In

Freemasonry is a charitable, benevolent, educational, and religious fraternity, and it doesn't hide its principles and beliefs. It's not a secret society. It doesn't hide its locations, and it doesn't require its members to hide their participation.

Masonry does have ceremonies it wants to keep private, along with methods of identification (passwords, handshakes, and others), just as corporations have information they want to keep confidential. But as secret societies go, Masons have done a pretty rotten job of silencing loose lips. Almost immediately after forming the first Grand Lodge in England in 1717, books trumpeting the secrets of the lodge began to arrive on shelves.

No international administration or authority controls Freemasonry. You can't call some office to get the official, worldwide policy position of Freemasons, because no such policy exists. In the United States, each state has its own Grand Lodge. But some basic beliefs are common to all regular, mainstream Masonic organizations.

Promoting brotherly love, relief, and truth

The beliefs of Freemasonry can be boiled down to three simple concepts. Masons are taught to believe in the following tenets:

- ✔ **Brotherly love:** Love for each other and for all mankind
- ✔ **Relief:** Charity for others and mutual aid for fellow Masons
- ✔ **Truth:** The search for answers to the universal questions of morality and the salvation of the soul that only a man's individual faith and his relationship with God can provide

I go into each of these points in greater detail in the following sections.

Brotherly love

Simply put, Masons believe in the golden rule: Treat others the way you want to be treated. The golden rule is part of every major world religion, so it qualifies as the single, unifying theme of all faiths. Its most basic concept is the cornerstone of Freemasonry, no matter how it is phrased:

- ✔ **Buddhism:** "In five ways should a clansman minister to his friends and families; by generosity, courtesy, and benevolence, by treating them as he treats himself, and by being as good as his word."
- ✔ **Christianity:** "Do unto others as you would have them do unto you."
- ✔ **Confucianism:** "What you do not want done to yourself, do not do to others."

> ✔ **Hinduism:** "Men gifted with intelligence . . . should always treat others as they themselves wish to be treated."
>
> ✔ **Islam:** "No one of you is a believer until he loves for his brother what he loves for himself."
>
> ✔ **Judaism:** "Thou shalt love thy neighbor as thyself."
>
> ✔ **Taoism:** "Regard your neighbor's gain as your own gain, and regard your neighbor's loss as your own loss."

Relief

Many people who are familiar with Freemasonry but are not members are aware of some of the fraternity's philanthropic and charitable contributions to society. A common statement is made that, internationally, Freemasons provide $3 million every day to charity — $2 million in the United States alone.

Three centuries of encouraging good works in its members have resulted in large, institutional charities supported by Freemasons. These include scholarships, relief for natural disasters, and donations to schools and to destitute families. Masons have provided retirement homes for their own members as well as schools and homes for orphans, and they participate in a dizzying list of community and social programs. Especially notable are the many medical philanthropies supported by Masons, which range from neuromuscular, dental, and eye care to the world-famous Shriners Hospital program for children (see Chapter 12).

Although these charities make an enormous contribution to and have a tremendous impact on society, Masons don't perform such services to mankind to receive gratitude or recognition. Individual Freemasons are encouraged to participate in all forms of charity and benevolence for society, not just the ones that get on the evening news or in the morning paper. And Masons do not teach, and have never taught, that good works on Earth are a means of salvation in the afterlife. Masonic charity is practiced to improve the lives of men here and now.

Masonic charity doesn't just mean writing a check or throwing coins in a basket. It means giving a part of oneself and one's time — commodities that are always in short supply. By participating in improving the life of a whole community or a single human being, by example, they hope to encourage others to do the same.

Truth

Masonic truth is a little more difficult to explain, because it means something different to every man. When a new initiate enters the lodge, aspects of the ritual ceremony seem unusual. For example, he is blindfolded. Blindfolding is done for a variety of reasons (see Chapter 6), but the primary symbolism of being blindfolded is that the candidate is seeking light. Light in a Masonic lodge is a symbol of spiritual truth and knowledge, and every candidate must discover that light on his own. To be in darkness is to be ignorant and unaware. No lodge ceremony or Masonic lesson can pretend to provide ultimate truth for a Mason, but Masonry seeks to inspire the individual to search for knowledge on his own.

Adhering to basic principles

Freemasons promise never to bring anything offensive or defensive into the lodge with them. That restriction includes swords, knives, spears, guns, and weapons of mass destruction. It also means words, ideas, and actions that can divide and destroy friendships and institutions. All men are mortal and have mortal weaknesses. And all men have ideas and opinions that may offend others. The object of the lodge is to create a place where those divisions are left outside so Masons can engage in activities that unite them instead of separating them.

Morality

Freemasonry is a social organization that brings good men together to study, teach, and practice its lessons. The intention of those lessons is to improve and strengthen the character of individual Masons. By improving men, Freemasonry tries to improve mankind. By taking good men and making better ones, Masonry seeks to improve the community, one person at a time.

Freemasons believe that honor still exists and that a man has a responsibility to behave honorably in everything he does. Masonry teaches its members the principles of personal decency and personal responsibility. It hopes to inspire them to have charity and goodwill toward all mankind and to translate principles and convictions into action.

Charity

Freemasonry is charitable because it's not organized for profit, and none of its income is collected in order to benefit any individual. It is devoted to the promotion of the welfare and happiness of all mankind. Freemasonry teaches its members that unselfishness is a duty and that giving is not only more blessed than receiving but also more rewarding.

Education

Freemasonry teaches a system of morality and brotherhood by the use of symbols and dramatic presentations. It encourages its members to expand their knowledge of the world around them.

As a Freemason advances through the degree rituals, he interprets the symbols and lessons for himself, and they can be interpreted in as many ways as there are Masons. No Freemason may dictate to any other how he should interpret the degree rituals, and no one man may speak for the institution itself.

The president and the gardener

While he was president, Teddy Roosevelt visited his home lodge, Matinecock #806 in New York, in September 1908. Afterward, he spoke of the experience of seeing his own gardener serving as Master of the Lodge that evening while he sat on the sidelines. "Clearly I could not call upon him when I came home. It would have embarrassed him. Neither could he, without embarrassment, call on me. In the lodge it was different. He was over me, though I was president, and it was good for him, and good for me."

In Masonry, all the trappings of status or prestige worn in the outside world are left on the other side of the door of the lodge — even for presidents.

Faith (but not a specific religion)

Freemasons believe in the brotherhood of man, under the fatherhood of God. Freemasonry is not a religion, but it is religious because it requires its members to have faith in a Supreme Being, according to the individual Mason's belief. It's not a sectarian organization and doesn't promote one religion over another. Masonic ceremonies describe a moral code, using basic principles that are common to all religions.

Masons refer to God in their ceremonies as the *Great Architect of the Universe*. This term isn't used because Masonry is a religion with its own name for God. It is simply Masonic language, a shared reference for all Brothers of all faiths, designed not to conflict with the many terms used for God by the world's religions.

Masonry is not, and has never claimed to be, a substitute for religion. A Bible or other Volume of Sacred Law held to be holy by the members of an individual lodge is open on its altar whenever a lodge is in session, as a constant reminder for the individual Mason to look within the pages of the sacred book of his own faith for spiritual guidance. If members of a lodge follow different faiths, multiple holy books are often opened on the altar side by side.

Social responsibility

Freemasonry stands for the reverence of God and the proper place of individual faith in society; for truth and justice; for fraternity and philanthropy; and for orderly civil, religious, and intellectual liberty. It charges each of its members to be true and loyal to the government of the country to which he owes allegiance and to be obedient to the law of any state in which he may reside.

However, Masonry does philosophically oppose tyranny, dictatorship, and any destruction of human dignity, basic human rights, and the free exercise of religion. This philosophy is, in part, where Freemasons have gathered a reputation for being involved in revolutionary politics. But Masonry teaches that the best way to oppose such tyrannies is to lay a strong foundation of principle and morality upon which men of every race, country, sect, and opinion can agree.

Political neutrality

One of the first rules of Freemasonry forbids the discussion in Masonic meetings of religious matters and politics — topics likely to cause personal arguments. The fundamental principles of Freemasonry also forbid Masonic organizations from taking political action or attempting to influence elections or legislation. A Freemason is encouraged to act according to his individual judgment and the dictates of his conscience, not by any opinion imposed on him by the fraternity.

Equality among members

Freemasonry regards no man for his worldly wealth, social status, or outward appearance. Kings, princes, and sultans have been Masons. Doctors, lawyers, captains of business, movie stars, and symphony composers have all been members of the fraternity. So have paperboys, garbage men, factory workers, and fast-food fry cooks.

Establishing a New World Order?

When you become a Mason, are you now a part of the New World Order that has some secret plan to replace all government and religious leaders with Freemasons and rule the world under a kind but stern, watchful, and secret authority?

Right. We'll get around to that world-domination thing just as soon as we decide what date to hold the fish fry.

Oh, there's no question that Masons want to take over the world. If everyone believed in equality, personal liberty, religious freedom, and social responsibility, we could all tear up our membership cards and save a lot of dues money. Those aren't just Masonic ideas; they're noble, common-sense ones, and Masonry has no corner on that market. But no one in a lodge will tell you what to think, how to vote, what church to go to, what to read, who your friends should be, or how to pray. Masonry has no other agenda than to improve the lives of its members and hope that they go on to improve their communities.

If the day ever comes that a Mason truly believes that something in Freemasonry conflicts with his duty to God, his country, his family, his neighbor, or himself, Masonry has no power to keep him "under its spell." He is free to leave. Men become Freemasons because they want to. Men remain Freemasons because it's an important part of their lives.

Experiencing Mystic Masonry

Freemasonry affects men on a deeper level than just simply promising to be good men, good citizens, and good churchgoers, and it is different for everyone who kneels at its altars and receives its degrees. Every man reacts in his own distinctive way to the ceremonies of Freemasonry, and becoming a Master Mason is indeed a memorable and poignant event.

Mysticism, magic, and Masonic mumbo jumbo

If you read enough about Freemasonry, you'll soon come across the writings of Albert Mackey, Manley Hall, Arthur Edward Waite, and Albert Pike. These men and many others have filled reams of paper with scholarly observations of Freemasonry. They eloquently linked the Craft to the ancient Mystery Schools of Egypt and elsewhere. They wrote that Masonry was directly descended from pagan rites and ancient religions. Some wrote that Masonry was the stepchild of *magick*, alchemy, and the shadowy mystics who dabbled in the world of the *Kabbalah* (Jewish mysticism) and in mysterious ancient writings like *Hermes Trismigestes* and the *Key of Solomon*. The works of these men were filled with fabulous tales of beliefs and cultures and cryptic theories of the deepest and earliest origins of Freemasonry.

Guys like Pike and Mackey were incredible scholars and had dazzling intellectual and spiritual knowledge. Their works are both enlightening and frustrating, because they reach into obscure legends and beliefs and drag out what appears to be a lavish and alluring connection over a 3,000-year period to modern Freemasonry. Unfortunately, much of it is metaphysical wishful thinking.

Sadly, they put their own spin on the documented evidence that exists in England and Scotland that really tells the story. Freemasonry descended from the stonemason guilds and was taken over in the late 1600s by philosophers

and men of science and learning. The Masons didn't build cathedrals by using incantations to levitate stones. They didn't cast spells to turn their enemies into stone gargoyles shaped as demons. They didn't transmogrify base metals into gold to pay their wages. As Arthur C. Clarke has said, "Any sufficiently advanced technology is indistinguishable from magic." Geometry was not a sorcerer's art — if it were, no one would be safe from a high-school student with a calculator and a protractor.

Unfortunately, Pike, Mackey, and Hall were prolific. They wrote big, thick books that are in every Masonic library, so people who don't understand their works to be Masonic folklore trot out the writers as experts, "noted" Masonic scholars, and long-dead spokesmen. The problem is that their writings are continually cited as "proof" of an occult connection to Masonry. Worse, their writings are often deliberately altered by the critics of the Craft, and Freemasons have to explain all over again to their relatives and ministers that, no, they aren't reenacting the dismemberment of Osiris, making pagan sacrifices to Lucifer, stirring cauldrons, or worshiping goats (see Chapter 8).

They were all well read on the wide variety of world religions and cultures, and their work on the subjects of symbolism and philosophy can be fascinating. But let's just say their version of the history of modern-day Freemasonry is not always accurate and leave it at that.

Connecting members through a mystic tie

The Scottish poet and Mason Robert Burns described Masonry as a *mystic tie,* and it mythically and symbolically binds its members to millions of brethren around the globe, spanning the centuries.

This bond is what allows two strangers to meet on a street in a foreign land and greet each other as though they've known each other all their lives — something that can unnerve one's spouse the first few times it happens. It is the bond that has seen enemies on battlefields treat each other with respect and dignity when death loomed. It is the bond that has helped and protected Brothers in their times of greatest need.

Expressing concepts through symbolism

A common 19th-century definition of Freemasonry was "a peculiar System of Morality, veiled in Allegory and illustrated by Symbols." An *allegory* is a story that takes a complicated concept and makes it simple to understand, often by making characters or story points represent more-complex issues. Fables and parables commonly do this. Masonic ceremonies use the same method to simplify their lessons.

Symbolism is a little more complex, because symbols are an attempt to represent an idea through something visual. As a result, explanations of symbols can be personal, subjective, and very different, and the exploration of the meaning of symbols can be endlessly debated.

Freemasonry uses symbolism in every lodge degree to illustrate or represent a wide variety of ideas (see Chapter 7). The symbols have been assembled and added to and subtracted from the ceremonies over the years, and Masonic scholars have spent a considerable amount of time pondering them. There is much to study for the Mason inclined to such things.

The degrees themselves represent a journey through the three stages of life in search of the light of knowledge — youth, manhood, and old age. At each step, the Mason learns more and is taught lessons of morality and virtue, wisdom and strength, honor and fortitude.

The very nature of the fraternity is symbolism itself. The individual Mason's life represents a building, constructed with the stones of experience, friendship, and deeds. Like the great cathedrals, this spiritual building is dedicated to God. And when a man has died, the legacy of his life remains as a monument to his achievements.

Chapter 4

Politics, Religion, and Freemasons: They Don't Mix

· ·

In This Chapter

▶ Separating Freemasonry from religion

▶ Resisting revolts, dictators, and tyrannies

· ·

*R*ight-wing Republican and former presidential speechwriter Mary Matalin and left-wing Democratic strategist James Carville are married to each other. You can't find two more polar opposites of the political spectrum than this happy couple of attack dogs. They stay happy and keep from participating in slap-fights and smack-downs on the front lawn every Thanksgiving by following one simple rule at home: No political discussions in the house.

Freemasonry is the same way.

Freemasonry is a fraternity made up of men who come from all different ages, backgrounds, faiths, professions, and political persuasions. Its popularity crosses all social barriers. In most other organizations, this diversity would be a recipe for argument and division. Because of its history and development, Freemasonry found a way to unite its members and to avoid the two most common topics that can destroy any friendship: politics and religion.

In this chapter, I discuss why mainstream Freemasons have officially steered clear of these topics for centuries and how they still manage to get accused of religious and political sabotage on a regular basis.

Exploring the History of Religion and the Masons

Freemasonry has always been shaped by the countries and societies it has existed in, and with literally millions of members, thousands of lodges, and hundreds of associated organizations, generalities are hard to make. Nevertheless, for the most part, since its modern origins in 1717, Ancient Craft Freemasonry has gone out of its way to be *nonsectarian* (never promoting one religious belief over another).

Here are some of the basics to understand about religion and the Masons:

- **A Masonic lodge meeting is not a religious service.** Going to lodge is not like going to church.

- **There is no Masonic religion.** Freemasonry is *not* a religion and has never claimed to be.

- **There is no Masonic god — nor a Masonic devil, for that matter.** Masons don't worship Osiris, sun gods, Baal, or Baphomet. Masons refer to God as the *Grand Architect of the Universe,* a reverent but nonsectarian name that's specifically designed to be all-inclusive.

- **There is no Masonic bible that is revered above any other.**

- **There is no Masonic plan for spiritual salvation.** Masonry does not offer its members a place in heaven in return for doing good works on Earth.

- **Masonry is not occult.** It does not dabble in witchcraft, engage in pagan ceremonies, or encourage worship of idols.

- **Masonry is not a cult.** It does not engage in "mind control," nor does it force members to stay. Anyone who wants to leave a lodge for any reason simply stops attending and ceases paying annual dues.

- **Freemasonry is an invention of man.** It has never claimed anything else. Masons have never pretended that modern Masonic ceremonies originated from the hand of God or are God's divine word.

Having said that, Freemasonry *is* religious. In the following sections I first explain how religion plays a part in Masonry and then explore its history with some of the world's major religions.

Bringing limited religion into the lodge

Atheists may not join Masonic lodges (with the exception of a very few jurisdictions in Europe). As a requirement of membership, every candidate must state that he has a personal belief in a Supreme Being, but every Freemason is encouraged to worship in his own way, according to his private beliefs and convictions. *What* he believes and *how* he worships are his own business.

No regular lodge of Masons may be opened without the Bible or another sacred book holy to its members opened on its altar. Again, like the Grand Architect of the Universe, Masons refer to the book as the *Volume of Sacred Law,* as a nonsectarian reference to the lodge's religious tolerance. Depending on what part of the world you're in and the beliefs of the members, this sacred book could be the King James Bible, the Hebrew Tanach, the Muslim Koran, the Hindu Veda, the Zoroastrian Zend-Avesta, or the Proverbs of Confucius. In certain lodges in Israel, finding three books — a Bible, Tanach, and Koran — all opened together on the same altar, out of respect for the different religions of their members, is common.

Masons require their members to place their hand on the Volume of Sacred Law while taking the obligations of the three degrees for an important reason. If a man does not believe in a power higher than himself, an oath can have little meaning to his conscience.

Freemasonry has never been intended as a substitute for religion. Still, each man interprets Masonic philosophy in his own way, and plenty of Masons have tried to make the lodge their church. Masonry has also attracted many religious people who have tried to impress their own church's dogma onto the lodge. Many men, both friends and foes of the fraternity, have tried to describe Masonry as something it was never intended to be.

In a few parts of the world, mainly the Scandinavian countries, some Grand Lodges have a requirement that members be Christians. In other jurisdictions, like the irregular Grand Orient of France, atheists are permitted to join. These are opposite ends of the extreme and are unusual exceptions. Again, mainstream Ancient Craft Freemasonry, the kind you're most likely to find up the block from your home, is nonsectarian.

Some of the additional York Rite and Scottish Rite degrees that have developed over the years have expressly Christian themes, and the York Rite's Knights Templar Order specifically requires candidates to swear to defend the Christian religion. Nevertheless, although a few of these degrees teach lessons of morality by using events from the New Testament, they do not necessarily require a belief in Christianity. (I discuss these degrees in more detail in Chapters 10 and 11.) For example, many Jewish Masons have been through these degrees and have become officers in the bodies that confer them. When asked how he reconciled the question of defending the Christian religion to his own beliefs, one Brother said, "Of course I'd defend the Christian religion to the death. Just as I believe my Christian Brothers would defend the Jewish religion."

Learning from intolerance

Between the 1500s and the 1800s, different kings and queens of England persecuted, chased, imprisoned, killed, or just plain annoyed Catholics, Anglicans, Methodists, Puritans, Lutherans, Presbyterians, Calvinists, Quakers, and virtually every other Christian variation of their subjects. The differing religious persuasion of each individual monarch had potentially irksome, and occasionally fatal, consequences for their unfortunate subjects who didn't worship at the same altar. A man's brief time on earth was insignificant as compared to his picking the right team to be on in the hereafter, and these were literally matters of more importance than just simple life and death.

The English Civil War is important to Freemasonry for a lot of reasons, even though today most non-English Freemasons know little about it. The war broke out in 1641, after the stubborn and extremely hard-to-like King Charles I got fed up with his battles with members of Parliament over money and religion and literally chained the doors shut on the Parliament building for 11 years. Essentially, it was a fight between King Charles and the nobility on the one side, called the Cavaliers, and Oliver Cromwell and the Protestant Puritans on the other, called the Roundheads. It was a struggle between the established church and the radical Protestants, between the power of the nobility and the desire for self-government of the rising middle class. But worst of all, like the U.S. Civil War, it was a conflict that pitted brother against brother and friend against friend. These terrible aspects of the war affected the future and philosophy of Freemasonry for centuries to come.

The Roundheads took over the government and beheaded King Charles in 1649. Even though he had not been especially liked by anyone, no one particularly wanted to see the symbol of centuries of English power and majesty lopped off at the neck. After the bloody nine-year war ended, it took less than a decade of Cromwell and the Puritans' grim and tyrannical government before England wanted its monarchy back.

King Charles II was crowned in 1661, and unlike his father, he was clearly a lover, not a fighter. He also was far more interested in science and reason than he was in religious persecution. He was truly a man of a new age, an age that would welcome the new principles of speculative Freemasonry.

In 1717, when the first Grand Lodge was formed in London, unusual rules were established. First, discussion of religion was prohibited. Meetings would not be disrupted by arguments between Catholics, Anglicans, Puritans, and Protestants. As long as members believed in God, no one would question anyone's faith. Second, the political battles between Royalists and Parliament supporters that had led to the Civil War would not be tolerated. The Freemasons were determined to survive the issues that had torn the country apart. And no one was going to be able to accuse them of plotting treason or heresy. Instead, the lodges stressed friendship, mutual assistance for their members, and charity for others. And, of course, a good, hearty dinner.

Examining the history of Freemasonry and Catholicism

In Rome, the Pope wasn't especially happy about Freemasonry. It had been created in England, a non-Catholic country, and allowed men of all faiths to join — including an increasing number of Jews. Worse, it made its members take oaths of secrecy.

Catholics had joined lodges — especially in France, Italy, and South America — for years. The lodges welcomed Catholics, but the Vatican wasn't nearly so open minded. In 1738, Pope Clement XII enacted a *papal bull* (edict) threatening any Catholic who became a Freemason with excommunication.

Today, we think of the pope as the head of the Catholic Church, who happens to live in a neighborhood of Rome called the Vatican. But from the late 700s until 1870, the pope was not just the spiritual leader of the Catholic Church. Popes also ruled as kings over a big slice of what is now Italy and, at times, even parts of France. These areas were known as the *Papal States*.

Over those 1,100 years or so, the popes had armies, engaged in commercial trade, and made nonreligious laws — they did everything kings did. Depending on the point in history, the position of pope meant control over the eternal souls of faithful Catholics as well as control over a powerful military and commercial power, smack-dab in the middle of the Mediterranean Sea.

Some popes had more military interests than others. Pope Julius II in the 1500s was especially ambitious. Apart from hiring Michelangelo to paint the ceiling of the Sistine Chapel, Pope Julius's aggressive military exploits may very well have led to the questioning of Catholic doctrine that turned into the rise of Protestantism. The Church was being attacked on all sides, but the very biggest threat of all came from the printing press.

The Catholic Church's official Bible was written in Latin, and only well-educated people could read it. Thanks to the invention of the printing press in the 15th century, along with translations of the Bible into English, French, and German, people now had something to learn to read. If the Bible was the word of God and people actually could read it, then the Church was no longer quite so important as an interpreter between man and God. Improved literacy is partially what led to the rise of the variety of Protestant religions.

Taking on the Masons in a papal bullfight

Along came Freemasonry in the early 1700s with an openly nonsectarian policy. When Pope Clement XII published his bull titled *In Eminenti* in 1730, he accused the Masons of becoming popular (yes, they were), of binding their members to secrecy (yes, they did), and of threatening their members with penalties for breaking their oaths (guilty again). But the pope's threat of excommunication for Catholic Freemasons went largely ignored, a symbol of the Church's growing loss of influence in the world.

Official communications issued by a pope are called *encyclicals* or *bulls*. They're official rulings or simply letters written by the pope to be widely circulated throughout the Catholic community. The term *bull* comes from the official lead seal, called a *bulla*, affixed to the document. The title of a bull or encyclical comes from the opening words used in the document.

In 1739, another papal edict forbade Masonic membership anywhere in the Papal States, under penalty of death. When the papal executioner in Rome couldn't find any Masons, he burned two books by the Scottish Mason Chevalier Andrew Michael Ramsay in a public square. The Inquisition was going on in Spain, Portugal, and Italy well into the late 1700s, and Freemasons were persecuted, imprisoned, and tortured. In Portugal, in 1743, three members of a Lisbon lodge were hanged.

A succession of popes over the next 140 years issued a series of increasingly angry bulls or encyclicals against the Masons. The strongest one came in 1884, issued by Pope Leo XII (see "Hearing about the evils of freedom from Pope Leo XII," later in this chapter).

Throwing the Catholic world into turmoil

We tend to think that the bumper stickers "Question Authority" and "No Rulz" are modern sentiments. Nothing could be farther from the truth. The world was in turmoil in the 1700s and 1800s. Religions, kings, and countries were under attack all over the world by revolutionaries who questioned everything. Under the new way of thinking, kings had no divine right to rule, nobility was earned rather than inherited, and religion was a personal choice.

Pope Pius IX became pontiff in 1846, and he was well aware of the changes happening in the world. At first, he was a reform-minded liberal, who repealed oppressive laws against Jews living in the Papal States and agreed to government reforms. Revolutionaries were growing popular, and the pope had to import French and Austrian troops to help keep the peace in his own territories.

On the spiritual front, Pius IX caused a firestorm of controversy in the Church by announcing in 1854 that Jesus's mother, Mary, had been conceived without original sin, thereby raising her to an equal spiritual status with Christ himself. He truly shocked the religious world in 1870 when the First Vatican Council proclaimed the doctrine of papal infallibility, meaning that when the pope spoke on matters of faith or morality, he was incapable of making an error. Such announcements resulted in huge waves of anti-Catholic sentiment and protest around the world.

In 1848, a revolt led by Italian Freemason Giuseppe Garibaldi led eventually to the loss of every Papal State, except for Rome. In 1870, even Rome was taken, and the Pope's property was reduced to the tiny area known today as Vatican City. Italy was united into one country, but the Church was no longer a world power. Freemason Simon Bolivar liberated South America, and Freemason Benito Juarez liberated Mexico. The Papacy lost dominance in Europe, property in the New World, and especially plantations, gold mines, and silver mines in Mexico and South America. Clearly, the Freemasons were to blame.

The Grand Orient of France

Ancient Craft Freemasonry has never taken anything other than a neutral stand on religious beliefs, but groups of French Freemasons were especially angry over the changes in the Church, especially the shocking announcements of Pope Pius IX on papal infallibility. The French being the French, there had been an endless string of competing Grand Lodges operating in the country since the early 1700s. The Grand Orient of France was one large group that became increasingly distanced from mainstream Masonic beliefs, and its members began to get involved in politics and social movements. In 1877, they shocked the Masonic world by removing the belief in a supreme being as a requirement for membership, and they stopped requiring an open Volume of Sacred Law in lodge meetings. The vast majority of mainstream Grand Lodges around the world declared the Grand Orient of France irregular, and it remains to this day a large and popular but irregular and unrecognized Masonic organization. (See Chapter 5 for more about Masonic regularity and recognition.)

Hearing about the evils of freedom from Pope Leo XII

Pius IX died in 1878 as one of the longest-reigning pontiffs ever. His successor, Pope Leo XII, was understandably frustrated over the very different geography and influence he inherited (as opposed to the huge territory Pius had inherited 32 years before). The Church was under attack everywhere. In 1882, Leo lashed out with a 25-page encyclical titled *Humanum Genus*. He laid it out for the world to see: The world was divided into the Kingdom of God and the Kingdom of Satan, and Freemasonry sat squarely in the middle of Satan's dominion.

Here are some of the Pope's worst accusations against the Freemasons:

> Then come their doctrines of politics, in which the naturalists lay down that all men have the same right, and are in every respect of equal and like condition; that each one is naturally free; that no one has the right to command another; that it is an act of violence to require men to obey any authority other than that which is obtained from themselves. According to this, therefore, all things belong to the free people; power is held by the command or permission of the people, so that, when the popular will changes, rulers may lawfully be deposed and the source of all rights and civil duties is either in the multitude or in the governing authority when this is constituted according to the latest doctrines. It is held also that the State should be without God; that in the various forms of religion there is no reason why one should have precedence of another; and that they are all to occupy the same place.

If this sounds suspiciously like the instruction manual for the U.S. Constitution, you'd be correct. Leo didn't think this was especially admirable. He went on: "Their chief dogmas are so greatly and manifestly at variance with reason that nothing can be more perverse." If these ideas are perverse, then the entire collection of documents that founded the United States is positively pornographic.

Clarifying the modern Church's position on Freemasonry . . . or not

The Catholic Church's ongoing policy has always been to condemn any group that it differs with. In the 1950s, Pope Pius XII issued an encyclical denouncing, among other things, Rotary clubs.

Today, confusion over the Church's position on Freemasonry remains. The Church considers English and American Freemasons to be "inoffensive and well-meaning people" and admits that Freemasonry is "beneficial to the country, or at any rate quite harmless." Still, the solemn oaths of secrecy are objected to, as well as the belief that Freemasonry "tends to undermine belief in Catholic Christianity by substituting for it what is practically a rival religion based on deistic or naturalistic principles."

The Church also objects to the use of the Bible, prayers, candles, and the mention of God in Masonic ceremonies, saying that Masonry clearly masquerades as a religion, no matter how nonsectarian it all may be.

Canon (Catholic) Law was last updated in 1983. The law prior to 1983 still considered Freemasonry to be a politically and religiously subversive group, but the Church seems to at last understand the difference between regular, recognized Freemasonry and irregular groups or individual Masons who have engaged in religious, social, and political struggles. The absence of the mention of Masonry in the 1983 rewrite appears to allow Catholics to join a regular Masonic lodge, but the Office of the Sacred Congregation for the Doctrine of the Faith (the modern-day successor to the office of the Inquisition) led by Cardinal Alois Ratzinger, disagrees. In 1983, Ratzinger, who would become Pope Benedict XVI in 2005, wrote a clarification saying there has been no change, and that Catholics who become Masons are in a state of grave sin and may not receive Communion.

Individual Catholics are clearly confused. Eighty percent of the Freemasons in the Philippines are Catholic, and Masonry thrives in many predominantly Catholic countries, such as Mexico. Obviously, thousands of Catholics are Masons with no crisis of conscience. Active Freemasons know that no conflict exists between their religion and their fraternity. Nevertheless, Catholics interested in joining a lodge are urged to consult their bishop, through their parish priest, to determine the most current views of the Church.

Of course, the Catholic Church has its own fraternal organization for their fun-loving members, the Knights of Columbus, formed in 1882 (see Chapter 9).

Pairing Freemasons and Protestants peacefully (mostly)

Freemasonry in the United States has undoubtedly been seen as a primarily white, Anglo-Saxon, Protestant organization, regardless of its lofty goals of social, religious, and racial toleration. The overwhelming majority of Freemasons over the centuries have been Protestants, especially in English-speaking countries.

Fundamentalists and Freemasons: Like oil and water

Many fundamentalist Christians object to Freemasonry, because some ministries encourage their members to "witness" their faith at all times and in all places. Being told that the Masonic lodge isn't the place to win converts over to their particular version of theology is heresy to believers of a few brands of enthusiastic, evangelical Christianity. But the conflict that some fundamentalist Christians have with Freemasonry goes beyond the inability to preach in a lodge.

Unfortunately, a small industry consisting of anti-Masonic books, tracts, websites, audiotapes, videos, and lectures has developed among opportunistic fundamentalists. The list of ridiculous accusations against Masons is seemingly endless: Masons worship the devil. Masons practice witchcraft. They have their own Masonic bible. Secrets of their world domination with their Satanic religion are hidden from lowly lodge members and are only revealed to 33rd-degree Scottish Rite Masons in a Luciferian ceremony. And the hits just keep on comin'.

Of course, Freemasons shouldn't feel singled out. Many of these same folks lash out against Catholics, Jews, the United Nations, the Federal Reserve, the World Bank, the Council on Foreign Relations, Metallica, and, on occasion, Procter & Gamble.

In free societies, there will always be people who either exist in the lunatic fringes or make their living off of those who do. They continue to peddle known falsehoods about the fraternity, under the guise of Christian salvation. I explore the most common of these myths and lies in greater detail in Chapter 8.

Remember: The truth is that literally millions of men over three centuries have been members of Masonic lodges, and tens of thousands of them have been ministers, deacons, rabbis, bishops, priests, and other theologians. The overwhelming majority of them have never found any of these malicious lies to be true. Masonry encourages its members to be better citizens and to seek answers to their religious needs in their own churches.

Most Protestant denominations have had no organized objection to their members being Freemasons. Still, occasional dust-ups have occurred between Masons and Protestant churches. Recently, the Southern Baptist Convention, the largest association of U.S. Baptists, announced that Freemasonry is inconsistent with its beliefs. The Free Methodist Church was founded in the 1860s specifically because its creators felt that too many Methodists were tainted by their membership in Freemasonry and other secret societies of the period. Many people associate large numbers of Methodists in the fraternity in the 1800s with the rise of a certain stiff-necked piety that resulted in the ban on alcohol in lodges.

Without question, the biggest problem between Masons and Protestants has been from evangelical, fundamentalist denominations (see the nearby sidebar, "Fundamentalists and Freemasons: Like oil and water").

Bridging great divides: Freemasonry and Judaism

Freemasonry has no conflict with Judaism. However, the acceptance of Jews into Masonic lodges has varied over the years, with the local prejudices of time and place.

Living a life apart

When the Freemasons formed the first Grand Lodge in London in 1717, Europe had an established history of persecution of Jews. After the Black Death, the great bubonic plague that wiped out almost a third of Europe's population in the 1300s, the Jews were made a scapegoat for the plague. They had been accused of poisoning wells to kill Christians and were almost completely thrown out of Western Europe. Most fled to Poland, while a large Jewish community survived in Spain by converting to Catholicism. The Spanish Inquisition was started by the Church as a nonviolent investigation to determine whether converted Jews were sincere.

For hundreds of years, Jews were restricted by Christian societies to live in segregated neighborhoods, called *ghettos*. They were prevented from joining craft guilds or participating in skilled labor, so they were reduced to being peddlers or moneylenders (a job Christians were forbidden to have). Because of the few professions they were allowed to pursue, the ghettos became poor, run down, and overcrowded. Their clothing was dictated by their religious requirements, which made them look different from the rest of the society around them.

In the 1600s, Jews began to drift back into Germany, southern France, and Holland. In 1654, England began to allow Jews back into the country. The violent religious wars of Europe were coming to an end, and the Age of Enlightenment philosophies encouraged greater understanding and tolerance of different religions. Even so, as late as the 1800s, they were generally not allowed to have rights of citizenship in many countries, and in the Papal States they were required to frequently listen to conversion sermons. The laws enacted against Jews caused them to be regarded as an alien species in the countries in which they were allowed to live.

Receiving Jews in the lodge

The first Jews began joining London lodges in 1721, and many Jews began to regard lodge membership as a symbol of freedom from the old social and legal restrictions. The lodge was one of the first places where Christians and Jews were able to sit side by side with any measure of equality.

Many Jews came to the American colonies in the 1700s, and they joined some of the very first lodges that opened. Prior to 1800, at least four Grand Masters of U.S. Grand Lodges were Jewish. Still, prejudice against Jews has been a strong force throughout history, and plenty of lodges around the world have officially or unofficially excluded them.

Germany and Russia both were strongly anti-Semitic and anti-Mason throughout the late 1800s and up through World War II. Gradually, Jews and Masons were seen as working together in a secret plot to destroy Christianity and encourage revolutions, especially after the French Revolution. In Germany before World War I, Jews were barred from joining Masonic lodges.

Freemasonry's rituals make use of stories from the Old Testament, the portion of the Bible shared in common between Jews and Christians. In fact, the three lodge degrees draw heavily on the symbolism of the building of the Jewish Temple of Solomon (see Chapter 7). Despite the fact that Masonry grew from an essentially Christian organization into a nondenominational one, that hasn't stopped anti-Semites from claiming that Freemasonry is an evil, power-mad group, presided over by Jews who seek to (or already do) control the world banking system and all world governments. The world has no shortage of bigots, and all the evidence shown to the contrary convinces them that the Jewish and Masonic influence on world events is just that much more secret.

Protocols of the Elders of Zion

In the late 1800s, the *Okhrana,* the Russian czar's secret police, created a notorious piece of propaganda called the *Protocols of the Elders of Zion.* In it was described a secret meeting of a group of Jews who discussed their world-takeover plans, with the Freemasons as their accomplices.

The *Protocols* are the origin of a widely believed conspiracy theory of a secret group of Jewish bankers who control the world. According to the *Protocols,* Jews are behind a plan for world conquest, and they use Freemasons as their willing stooges; Jews and Masons control the press and the courts; Jewish revolutionaries use liberalism to weaken Christianity and the State; Jewish intellectuals confuse the common people, and they replace traditional educational curriculum to discourage independent thinking and encourage immorality among Christian children; Jews use their international banking monopolies and credit to destroy the economy, favoring paper currency not tied to the gold standard; Jews and the Masons control governments from behind the scenes by blackmailing politicians; and during times of great emergencies, Jews suspend civil liberties and then secretly make the measures permanent.

It is ridiculous stuff, inspired by a 1797 anti-Masonic work written by a French Jesuit priest named Augustin Barruel, who blamed the Freemasons for the French Revolution (he was really describing the Illuminati [see "The Illuminati" sidebar, later in this chapter], but French Freemasonry confused him). Throughout the 1800s, various men reintroduced the conspiracy, repeating the same accusations with a different cast of villains. Eventually the Russian secret police picked it up and loved the basic story, and with some creative script-doctoring, made the enemies both the Jews *and* the Masons, but this time it wasn't just Russia they were out to destroy — it was the world.

A Russian monk named Sergei Nilus republished the *Protocols* in 1905, and over the years claimed a wide variety of explanations for its origin, all of them false. He finally announced in 1917 that they were actually part of the minutes of the 1897 Zionist Congress at Basel, Switzerland. Curiously, the meeting had been open to the public and was attended by a number of Christian clergy and political figures, but no one who attended ever remembered seeing or hearing what was described in the document. What was actually discussed at the meeting was the creation of a Jewish organization to purchase land in Palestine for a Jewish homeland. Despite these pesky details of the truth, the Russians ate it up and used the fictional *Protocols* as justification for slaughtering Jews after the Russian Revolution in 1917.

When Adolf Hitler came to power, he used the *Protocols* as justification for his plans to exterminate the Jews. Freemasons were also on his hit list, and they were packed off to concentration camps. One of the many popular slogans of the Nazis was "All Masons Jews — All Jews Masons!"

The *Protocols* have been widely circulated for over a hundred years, and today they can be found all over the Internet, posted by a wide range of conspiracy-believing groups. The *Protocols* remain very popular in some Islamic countries, particularly Egypt and Saudi Arabia, where they are included in official texts for schoolchildren to study and lapped up as absolute truth. Many groups — including the African American Nation of Islam, the white armed patriot militia groups, the Palestinian terrorist group Hamas, and the American Nazi Party — still peddle the *Protocols* as fact. Others simply remove the words *Jew* and *Freemason* from the allegations and substitute words like *neocons* or *international bankers.* The lies remain the same.

Modeling brotherly love in Israeli lodges

Freemasonry has flourished in Israel, and the country has almost 50 lodges. Jewish, Christian, Muslim, and Druse members work together, and the Jewish *Tanach* (the Hebrew Scriptures), the King James Bible, and the Muslim Koran are commonly all opened on the altars side by side. The official seal of the Grand Lodge of Israel includes a Star of David, a Christian cross, and a Muslim crescent, all imposed over the Masonic square and compass. In spite of decades of violence in the Middle East centering around the creation of the state of Israel in 1948, finding a better illustration of true brotherly love would be difficult.

Finding conflict between Freemasonry and Islam (where none exists)

The teachings of Freemasonry and Islam don't conflict. No group owes more to the Middle East for the origin of its symbolism than Freemasonry. Nevertheless, Masonry has been outlawed in all Muslim countries except Morocco, Lebanon, and Turkey.

After Pope Clement XII excommunicated Catholic Freemasons in 1738, Sultan Mahmut I, ruler of the Ottoman Empire, outlawed Freemasonry throughout the entire Middle East and North Africa, under pressure from his Christian subjects and with the approval of his *ulema* (Islamic theologians).

Masonry was popular for a while in Egypt and Algeria in the 1800s, mostly with Europeans living there. After World War I and the breakup of the territory that made up the Ottoman Empire, Freemasonry briefly came back to the Middle East by way of English, Scottish, and French oil industry workers. A few lodges still exist in Muslim countries on U.S. and British military bases, but most Arab Muslims are forbidden to join by their governments. Foreign workers who are Masons in countries like Saudi Arabia are only allowed to hold lodge in their private enclaves specifically for foreigners.

One of the most influential organizations for interpreting Islamic law is the Islamic Jurisdictional College of El-Azhar University in Cairo. In 1978, it issued an opinion concerning "The Freemasons' Organization." Among its findings were the following:

✔ Freemasonry is a clandestine organization, which conceals or reveals its system, depending on the circumstances. Its actual principles are hidden from members, except for chosen members of its higher degrees.

✔ The members of the organization, worldwide, are drawn from men without preference for their religion, faith, or sect.

✔ The organization attracts members on the basis of providing personal benefits. It traps men into being politically active, and its aims are unjust.

✔ New members participate in ceremonies of different names and symbols and are too frightened to disobey its regulations and orders.

✔ Members are free to practice their religion, but only members who are atheists are promoted to its higher degrees, based on how much they're willing to serve its dangerous principles and plans.

✔ It is a political organization. It has served all revolutions, as well as military and political transformations. In all dangerous changes, a relation to this organization appears either exposed or veiled.

✔ It is a Jewish organization in its roots. Its secret higher international administrative board is made up of Jews, and it promotes Zionist (pro-Israel) activities.

✔ Its primary objectives are the distraction of all religions, and it distracts Muslims from Islam.

✔ It tries to recruit influential financial, political, social, or scientific people to utilize them. It does not consider applicants it can't use. It recruits kings, prime ministers, high government officials, and similar individuals.

✔ It has branches under different names as a camouflage so people cannot trace its activities, especially if the name of Freemasonry has opposition. These hidden branches are known as Lions, Rotary, and others. They have wicked principles that completely contradict the rules of Islam.

✔ A clear relationship exists between Freemasonry, Judaism, and international Zionism. It has controlled the activities of high Arab officials in the Palestinian conflict.

✔ Any Muslim who affiliates with it, knowing the truth of its objectives, is an infidel to Islam.

Again, active, practicing Freemasons know these allegations have absolutely no merit. However, many Islamic countries do not believe in the separation of church and state, and are governed by strict Sharia law, based on literal and narrow interpretations of laws from the Koran. As a result, being a Freemason can result in a death sentence in some countries.

Another area of contention between Muslims and Freemasonry concerns something Masons think is harmless but Muslims clearly do not. The Shriners started in the 1870s as the playground of Freemasons (see Chapter 12). The language of its ceremonies, and its costumes and decorations, came straight out of the exotic *Tales of the Arabian Nights*. Shriners called their jurisdictions *oases;* built their buildings to look like mosques, complete with minarets and domes; wore fezzes; and adopted the Arabic phrase *al salam aleikum* ("peace be with you") as a greeting. Unfortunately, many devout Muslims do not think such things are a homage to their culture. Instead, they feel their faith and culture are being mocked.

Refusing to Play Politics

Like religion, the discussion of politics is forbidden in regular, mainstream Masonic lodges. The original book of Constitutions published in England in 1723 states:

> A Mason is a Peaceable Subject to the Civil Powers, wherever he resides or works, and is never to be concern'd in Plots and Conspiracies against the Peace and Welfare of the Nation, nor to behave himself undutifully to inferior Magistrates; for as Masonry hath been always injured by War, Bloodshed and Confusion, so ancient Kings and Princes have been much dispos'd to encourage the Craftsmen, because of the Peaceableness and Loyalty, whereby they practically answer'd the Cavils of their Adversaries, and promoted the Honour of the Fraternity, who ever flourish'd in Times of Peace. So that if a Brother should be Rebel against the State, he is not to be countenanc'd in his Rebellion, however he may be pitied as an unhappy Man; and if Convicted of no other Crime, though the loyal Brotherhood must and ought to disown his Rebellion, and give no Umbrage or Ground of Political Jealousy to the Government for the time being, they can not expel him from the Lodge, and his relation to it remains indefeasible.

In short, Masons are to be good citizens and keep their politics to themselves. Mainstream Grand Lodges have adopted this wording, or something very similar, almost universally. So how is it that Freemasonry got the reputation of being an evil society that caused revolutions and secretly took over governments?

I'll come right out and say it: Blame it on the French. And maybe one German.

Placing Freemasonry amid the political turmoil of 18th-century Europe

Freemasonry spread quickly from England to the European continent after 1717. Because it started as an English organization, some of the kings in Europe were nervous about lodges operating in their countries. Britain had been the land of the bloody revolution in the 1640s, and Englishmen had beheaded one monarch and expelled another one. Worse, the Masons had "secrets" they refused to divulge. Yet many members of royalty in other countries joined the fraternity when they found out that lodges were designed to be apolitical, because they were eager to embrace the new philosophies of the age.

However, in the nervous political climate of Paris, police started raiding Masonic meetings in the 1730s, and the government didn't like what it found.

Noblemen were sitting shoulder to shoulder with decidedly lowborn men. Doctors and lawyers were attending secret meetings with lowly tradesmen and, in one lodge, even a black trumpeter from the king's palace. Worse, the Masons refused to divulge what went on in their meetings — except for one important and frightening detail. When questioned, every Mason freely admitted that their lodges were administered by officers who had been elected by democratic ballot.

It is undeniably true that many Europeans who were interested in casting off monarchies in favor of republican government joined Masonic lodges. The lodges became the popular place to be for men who wanted to discuss the new Age of Enlightenment philosophical subjects of societal change and the rights of man. The old, comfortable order of nations ruled by hereditary kings, with fat nobles at the top and underfed peasants at the bottom, was being questioned all over Europe, and Masonic lodges were sprouting up everywhere. Plenty of nervous men in power saw a connection between the two. Not that Freemasons had a corner on the market for revolutionary thinking.

Sparking anarchy in French lodges

Masonry came to France almost as soon as it began in England, arriving with the many English and Scottish expatriates who were living there (see Chapter 2). The Jacobites (supporters of the deposed English King James II, who was hiding out in France) in particular enjoyed Freemasonry and formed several lodges. Multiple competing Grand Lodges started to form across the country.

In 1737, Chevalier Andrew Michael Ramsay, a Scotsman living in France, published a lecture claiming that Freemasonry had *not* descended from the operative stonemason guilds, but that it had originated in Ancient Egypt and was carried back to Europe by the noble Crusader Knights, victoriously returning from the Holy Land. Ramsay had not been a Mason for very long, and his lecture seems to have been completely sprung from his own feverish imagination. His lecture would turn Freemasonry on its ear, but Ramsay quickly lost interest and never participated in the fraternity after that.

Ramsay vanished, but his little theory lived on. Creative and enthusiastic French Masons loved Ramsay's story and immediately began to invent what would become 1,100 different degrees conferred by 100 different groups, or *rites*. French aristocrats were suddenly attracted to Freemasonry, now that they could receive degrees proclaiming them to be Knights, Perfect Masters, Magi, High Priests, Princes, and Adepts, conferred by the Chivalric, Sublime, Sovereign, Elect, Supreme, Superior, and Eccossais (French for *Scottish*) rites, orders, and lodges. The three simple degrees of the Masonic lodge were nothing compared to all that pomp and circumstance. By 1750, French Freemasonry was in complete and utter chaos.

The Illuminati

Freemasonry in Prussia, Bavaria, and Austria was almost as confusing as it was in France for many of the same reasons. Lots of competing orders and rites were invented, having little or nothing to do with the original notions of English Craft Freemasonry.

Over in Bavaria, a professor of religious law named Adam Weishaupt had a great idea. In 1776, he formed a group called the *Order of Perfectibilists* (Perfectionists), with the notion that, through mutual aid, philosophical discussions, and careful advice, it would improve morality and virtue, oppose evil, improve society, and, thus, reform the world. It sounded Masonic and, in fact, Weishaupt cribbed some of his ceremonies from Masonic ritual.

Wieshaupt was an intellectual. He was born a Jew, baptized as a Catholic, and educated by Jesuits. Now he was looking for new recruits for his group, so he joined a Masonic lodge in 1777. Through his lodge, he interested several fellow Masons who fancied themselves intellectuals, and they quickly changed the name of the new order to *Illuminati* (meaning "intellectually inspired").

At first, he convinced only four others to join him, and they adopted secret names and codes to communicate with each other. Weishaupt in particular had to keep his role a secret, because he was making his living as a professor of Catholic canon law at a Catholic university. Under the pen name Spartacus, Weishaupt outlined a secret plan to infiltrate the Freemasons, overthrow the governments of nations and churches, take over the world, and create a new world order of tolerance and equality.

In a short time, the Illuminati grew to about 2,000 members; they expanded into Belgium, Holland, Denmark, Sweden, Poland, Hungary, Italy, and, of course, France. A friend of Weishaupt's, Baron Adolf Knigge, was a well-known Mason in Bavaria and assisted Weishaupt with developing degree rituals based on Masonic ceremonies. Unfortunately, the Illuminati attracted both the best and the worst of aristocratic society, and its aims began to lead far more to the destroy-governments-and-churches side than to the improve-society side, and Baron Knigge finally had enough. The fight between the men created a split between the two sides.

At the same time, Weishaupt's Catholic students at the University of Ingoldstadt were being increasingly pumped full of his anti-Catholic rhetoric. The Jesuits figured out just who Spartacus was and outed him. As the confessors to the royalty of Europe, they had their own network of spies and infiltrators, and they convinced the Bavarian government to arrest him in 1784. He fled the country but left behind his incriminating papers, outlining the Illuminati's ambitious, if bizarre, plans for world domination. They were widely published all over Europe to expose the Illuminati's secret plans and to flush out other members, many of whom wound up in prison.

The Illuminati was never popular, and the movement died out completely by the end of the century. It was a tiny, insignificant, and largely ridiculous group that had no effect on any society in which it existed. Yet today, conspiracy theorists believe it still survives as the secret, controlling force in Freemasonry and that it is continuing its evil plans for world domination (see Chapter 18).

Surviving the revolution

In both the United States and France, Freemasonry was pointed to as a force for revolution. The main difference was that in the United States it was given the credit and in France it got the blame.

In the case of Freemasonry in France, there is very little truth in such a charge. The wave of bloodthirsty radicalism that swept the country moved too fast for rational thought. First, the king was executed. Then the men who executed him turned on each other. By the time the last of the terrorists had been sent to the guillotine, the French people began looking at the carnage they had inflicted on one another. Dazed and ashamed, they went looking for someone to blame. Freemasonry seemed to be as good a scapegoat as any other. But John Adams once said that facts are stubborn things, and the facts of Freemasonry in France bear little resemblance to some of the hysterical finger-pointing that went on after the bloodbath was over.

The fact is that the Masonic lodges were the natural home of the French thinkers of the Enlightenment. These men were resentful of the power of the Catholic Church that the Revolution would destroy. They had good reason: The Church had a lot of power in France, more than in any other country in Europe.

Muddling up French politics and religion

It's easy to understand why the Enlightenment thinkers wanted to change the situation in France. The Catholic Church was exempt from all taxes. The Catholic clergy was in charge of virtually all forms of public education. About one-fifth of the farmland was in the hands of the Church, and the tenant farmers who worked it paid their feudal dues and taxes to the Church rather than to a noble landowner.

The high churchmen — the archbishops and abbots — lived a very rich lifestyle, whereas the country monks and priests were very poor, even though they still paid *tithes* (church taxes) to their superiors. Not only could the Church collect tithes, but it also was in charge of all wills, often giving dying sinners promissory notes to be collected in heaven in exchange for money they left the Church. The king ruthlessly expelled the *Huguenots* (the French Protestants), and the monarchy allowed no one to question the supremacy of the Catholic Church.

According to Minister of Finance, while the French government was near bankruptcy, the French church was worth about $200 million a year. The rest of the country can probably be forgiven for resenting their taxes, while the upper clergy lived at court like feudal lords of old. A growing feeling among nearly everyone in France was that the king got his marching orders from the pope in Rome, the people were taught only what the Vatican wanted them to know, and the Church had a free ride economically. All this resentment was building as the Revolution neared.

The Masons were not preaching violent social change but rather trying to lead by example. In the French Masonic lodges, unlike French society before the Revolution, the middle class sat side-by-side with the nobles and the clergy in the lodges. Their motto of "Liberty, Equality, and Fraternity" was a heartfelt truth, and the members' personal politics tended to the middle of the road. They looked to England for a working model of a constitutional monarchy, and they longed for a peaceful transfer of power.

Also at least 700 members of the French clergy were Freemasons, 300 in Paris alone, which was another argument against the lodges being a hotbed of violent rebellion against the Catholic Church.

These Masons were a product of the Age of Enlightenment, and they followed the light of what they called *le bien public* ("the public good"). The lodges were not the usual home for the most violent of the agitators. The *Jacobins* (not the Jacobites), the most radical of the revolutionaries, had their own Jacobin clubs where they went to unwind after a long day of clamoring for the king's head on a pole.

Pinning blame on the Illuminati

After the violence started, fears were quickly raised that the Illuminati (a group of intellectuals who were planning world domination) had worked hand in hand with the Freemasons and that this was just Step 1 in their plan to destroy nations and the Church, as well as to rule the world. The truth was that Masonry in France at that time was largely the enjoyment of aristocrats, and an overwhelming majority of their heads rolled into the basket when the Revolution began. And yet, after the bloody and horrifying years of the Revolution, the legend was born that the Masons had been behind it all, attempting to bring down the Church and the government.

It didn't help the French opinions of Freemasons that Dr. Joseph Guillotine, the inventor of the machine that beheaded so many Frenchmen, had been a Mason. Before the Revolution began, he had designed the machine to be a fast and painless method of punishment, to relieve the awful suffering of the condemned that he had seen. Unfortunately, it turned out to be far more efficient than he could have imagined, beheading hundreds of prisoners each day in the Place de la Concorde for the roaring amusement of the crowd.

Masons in France actually suffered in far greater proportions than non-Masons during the Revolution. Aristocrats had absolutely nothing to gain by encouraging a bloody revolt against themselves and their cushy way of life. The Grand Orient of France, one of two major competing Grand Lodges working in the country, was headed by the Duc d'Orleans, a radical member of the French royal family. In an effort to look a little more revolutionary, he renounced being a Freemason and officially changed his name to Phillipe-Égalité (which translates, believe it or not, as "Phil Equality"). The cunning ploy didn't work exactly as he had planned: He was guillotined in 1793. The radicals had begun to kill their own.

Marking Masons as revolutionaries for life

It was unfortunate that the very same motto, "Liberté, Égalité, Fraternité," that was born in French Masonic lodges became the battle cry of the terrorists of the Revolution. Ever since, the library shelves have been riddled with works of both serious historians and fraudulent crackpots, trying to prove that the French Freemasons engineered the Revolution as part of a larger plan to dominate the whole country. It is also often theorized that the Jews were pulling the strings on the Freemasons who were pulling the strings on the Revolution.

Oddly enough, many French people today still believe the same thing, and respectable French newspapers and magazines often feature articles claiming that the Freemasons are in control of every aspect of the government, from all modern French presidents down to the lowliest country bureaucrat. In neither instance does any legitimate evidence sustain these accusations, but a really good conspiracy theory is a hard thing to kill.

After the Revolution, Masonry went underground in France. Eventually Napoleon restored their rights, along with many of the rights of the Church, during the first days of his reign as he attempted to return some order to his shattered country.

Many people have always thought that Freemasons and revolutions go together like meat and potatoes. As I mention earlier in this chapter, Freemason Giuseppe Garibaldi in Italy, Simon Bolivar in South America, and Benito Juarez in Mexico, along with Masons in Hungary, Poland, and the Balkans, were indeed revolutionary leaders in their countries. They obviously did not adhere to the regulations of being "peaceable subjects" to their governments. Still, those examples do not prove that Freemasonry encourages force for revolt. Masonry neither encourages nor prevents men from sometimes doing what is legally wrong to accomplish what they know is right. The tie binding all these men who were Masons is the encouragement of democracy. In every case cited, these men were fighting against undemocratic and often totalitarian regimes.

Enduring the rule of dictators

Although Masons have often been accused of being revolutionaries throughout history, they have seldom been identified as dictators. Socialist, fascist, Islamist, and communist regimes have always outlawed Freemasonry in their countries. Masons have been both feared and despised by dictators the world over. Germany's Adolf Hitler, Italy's Benito Mussolini, Spain's Primo de Rivera and Francisco Franco, Chile's Augusto Pinochet, Portugal's Antonio Salazar, Iraq's Saddam Hussein, Iran's Ayatollah Khomeini, and of course the leaders of the Soviet Union all outlawed Freemasonry almost immediately after coming to power.

Suffering under Hitler and the Nazis

After World War I ended, Germany's General Erich Ludendorff spent years inventing anti-Masonic propaganda, because he blamed the Masons for Germany's treatment after the war. In a pamphlet entitled *Annihilation of Freemasonry through the Revelation of Its Secrets,* he claimed that Freemasonry was a Jewish device to make "artificial Jews." He continued, "It is cheating the people to fight the Jew while allowing his auxiliary troop, Freemasonry . . . to function."

From his earliest writings in *Mein Kampf,* Adolf Hitler made his views about the Masons clear:

> The general pacifistic paralyzation of the national instinct of self-pres-
> ervation, introduced into the circles of the so-called "intelligentsia" by
> Freemasonry, is transmitted to the great masses, but above all to the bour-
> geoisie, by the activity of the great press, which today is always Jewish.

When he came to power, Hitler's policies against the Jews were also directed at people he called "genetic inferiors," such as gypsies and homosexuals. But he considered the Freemasons to be operating hand in hand with Jews, and Freemasons were arrested, imprisoned, and exterminated along with the others. Lodges were destroyed, and anti-Masonic museums were opened to show loyal Germans just how evil the Masons were.

Hitler also saw a dangerous connection in the fact that Franklin D. Roosevelt, Winston Churchill, and a majority of the French cabinet were all Freemasons. When the Nazis invaded France and other European countries, the policies continued. Wherever the Nazis marched, Masons were identified, shot, or sent to concentration camps. Masonry had to be stamped out because of its policies of "humanity, tolerance, and liberalism" and because it was promot-ing "Jewish ideas and objectives."

It is impossible to say exactly how many Freemasons were murdered by the Nazis during the war in all the countries controlled by Hitler's Third Reich. Estimates range anywhere from 80,000 to 200,000.

In 1938, the Nazi's official printing house issued a book entitled *Freemasonry, Its World View, Organization and Policies,* by Dieter Schwarz. In it, Schwarz outlines the official Nazi position on the fraternity:

> In contrast to the anti-racial attitude of the lodges, the Nazi attitude is
> race conscious. . . . Masonic lodges are . . . associations of men who,
> closely bound together in a union employing symbolical usages, repre-
> sent a supra-national spiritual movement, the idea of Humanity . . . a
> general association of mankind, without distinction of races, peoples,
> religions, social and political convictions.

Freemasonry proudly stands guilty as charged.

Encountering persecution under Mussolini

After the dictator Benito Mussolini came to power in Italy, he declared all Freemasons traitors to Fascism. Mussolini didn't bother to use the anti-Semitic rhetoric of Hitler. Several high-ranking government officials resigned instead of renouncing their membership in the fraternity.

In 1925, Domizio Torrigiani, Grand Master of the Grand Orient of Italy, wrote an open letter to the dictator decrying Fascism and standing up for democracy. He and hundreds of other prominent Italian Masons were arrested and exiled to the Lipari Islands. At the peak of the anti-Mason purges between 1925 and 1927, Fascist gangs looted the homes of well-known Freemasons in Milan, Florence, and other cities, killing at least 100 of them.

Fleeing Iran in the 1970s

Freemasonry gained some popularity in Iran under the rule of the shahs, but the last shah of Iran, Mohammed Reza Pahlavi, was not a member. At its height, Iran had 40 lodges and over 1,000 members of the fraternity. When the Islamic revolution, led by Ayatollah Khomeini, swept through the country in 1978, strict Islamic law replaced Iran's existing laws, and Freemasonry was forbidden. More than 200 Freemasons were executed, and many fled the country.

The Grand Lodge of Iran survives today in exile, and its four lodges meet in the United States for exiles, ethnic Iranians, or their descendants.

Continuing to weather distrust

Masons do not need to be living under dictatorships to suffer from hatred and distrust. In the late 1940s, a third of the population of politically neutral Switzerland voted in favor of a constitutional amendment to suppress the fraternity. Even today, fear or hatred of Freemasonry continues on official levels in many countries.

In Great Britain, laws have been recommended ordering police, judges, and other government officials who are Freemasons to publicly identify themselves by registering on official lists. The Home Office conducted inquiries in 1997 and concluded that Masonic membership was not linked to injustices in the criminal justice system — but there was a public perception of it. In spite of no proof of any wrongdoing, the call continues to be made for public registry of Freemasons. Most recently, Members of Parliament have been required to state their membership in the Masons.

France continues its love/hate relationship with Masonry. Membership in the many different Grand Lodges is growing. Yet the covers of popular magazines are often splashed with anti-Masonic headlines, and the head of Vivendi-Universal (the French parent corporation of Universal Studios) at one point blamed the financial losses of his massive, worldwide corporation on a Masonic plot.

Masonry in the former Soviet republics has made a tentative comeback. The Grand Lodge of Russia was formed in 1995, but it has only a dozen lodges, and the government and public still regard them with suspicion. Outside of Russia, a Ukrainian member of parliament introduced proposed amendments to the Ukraine's criminal code, requiring mandatory prison sentences as long as 15 years for anyone convicted of being a Freemason, with the longest sentences being reserved for government officials.

Freemasonry continues to draw men who are attracted to its principles of brotherly love, charity, tolerance, and morality, in spite of ongoing pressure to destroy it. Clearly, its real power lies in the ability to peaceably bring together men of all beliefs and political persuasions in a world determined to stay in conflict, and for a brief moment, provide a safe haven from its ceaseless turmoil.

Maintaining Brotherhood during war

Freemasonry has struggled to remain apolitical, but war has often placed Masonic Brothers on opposite sides of the battle lines. No evidence suggests that Freemasons ever tilted the outcome of a battle to keep from harming a Masonic Brother. But hundreds of stories from conflicts around the world display the Masonic character of extending Brotherly love and honor to fallen enemies who wore the square and compass. I list just a few of the most poignant of them in the following sections.

The American Revolution

In the 1750s, Sir William Johnson was given the job of enlisting American Indians to fight against the French. Johnson made friends with the chief of the Mohawks and started keeping house with the chief's daughter, whom he called Molly. Her younger brother, Thayendangea, was raised by Johnson and Molly, and Johnson gave the boy the English name Joseph Brant.

Brant fought side by side with Johnson in the French and Indian War. By 1774, Brant was a trusted advisor to the British administration in Connecticut. The next year, he went to England and was initiated into a

London lodge. King George III was so proud of Brant that he presented the young man his Masonic apron. Brant returned to Connecticut and became Master of a lodge there, and later, Master of a lodge in Canada.

During the American Revolution, Brant was ordered to incite Native American tribes to fight on the British side against the rebellious colonists. The Mohawks often tortured their prisoners to death, but Brant took his Masonic vows seriously. Captain John McKinstry of the Revolutionary Army was captured during a battle with the tribe and was tied to a tree to be sacrificed by the Mohawks. Joseph Brant came upon the scene, and McKinstry made a Masonic sign of distress. Brant stopped the potential murder of the prisoners and had his fellow Freemason untied and conducted safely to a group of Canadian Freemasons, who saw to it that McKinstry was returned to the Revolutionary Army.

After the war, McKinstry and Brant corresponded, and Brant visited McKinstry's lodge in New York. At least three other stories tell of Brant stopping similar murders of fellow Freemasons during the war. Brant died in Canada in 1850.

Another story from the American Revolution

On the night of July 15, 1779, Americans under General Anthony Wayne successfully stormed Stony Point, on the Hudson River. The British military lodge's papers and equipment fell into the hands of the American General and Freemason Samuel H. Parsons, who had them returned to the British Commander at New York, with the following letter:

> West Jersey Highlands, July 23, 1779.
>
> Brethren: When the ambition of monarchs or jarring interest of contending States, call forth their subjects to war, as Masons we are disarmed of that resentment which stimulates to undistinguished desolation; and however our political sentiments may impel us in the public dispute, we are still Brethren, and (our professional duty apart) ought to promote the happiness and advance the weal of each other. Accept therefore, at the hands of a Brother, the Constitution of the Lodge Unity, No. 18, to be held in the 17th British Regiment, which your late misfortunes have put in my power to restore to you.

The War of 1812

During the War of 1812, the British ship *Shannon* captured the U.S. frigate *Chesapeake*. British Navy lieutenant Lord Provo Wallace boarded the *Chesapeake* to take prisoners and officially take the enemy ship, and he found a U.S. officer kneeling by the wounded body of a dying gunner, holding his hand.

At first, Wallace was surprised that an officer would be so concerned over the death of a common seaman — such was the attitude of the British Navy in those days. But it turned out that both of the Americans were Freemasons. When he was informed that both men were Masonic Brothers, fellow Mason Lord Wallace knelt with the U.S. officer and held the gunner's hand until he died.

The Civil War

Numerous stories tell of Masons on both sides of the U.S. Civil War helping each other limp from the battlefield or making a Brother's life more comfortable in prisoner-of-war camps. One episode in particular affected a man tied to the future of the nation. William McKinley had enlisted in the Ohio infantry as a private when the war began. He saw many battles, including the horrible carnage at Antietam. By the war's end in April 1865, McKinley had risen to the rank of major and was placed in charge of managing and protecting an Army hospital.

One day, while watching the interaction between a Union doctor and Confederate soldiers, he noticed the doctor spent more time with some than with others, and even gave several of the former enemy soldiers money. McKinley asked the doctor why, when he knew he would never be repaid. "Those men are Brother Masons," he was told. The doctor went on to explain the beliefs of the fraternity to the major.

Just three weeks after the end of the war, McKinley petitioned the closest lodge he could find, Hiram Lodge #21 in Winchester, Virginia. The Union Army major's degrees were presided over by a Confederate chaplain acting as Master. McKinley went on to be elected an Ohio congressman and governor; he was elected President of the United States in 1897. He guided the country during the Spanish-American War and is credited with making the United States a 20th-century world power. He was shot by an anarchist in 1901, and died eight days later.

World War II in North Africa

Robert Strader was a U.S. Army sergeant in the 6th Infantry of the First Armored Division during World War II. The 6th slugged its way across Algeria, French Morocco, and Tunisia in 1942 and 1943 against German and Italian forces. After one battle, Strader and the division chaplain drove through the charred wreckage of burning German tanks and came across the dead body of a badly burned Nazi soldier, hanging halfway out of the turret. On the finger of the German was a Masonic ring. Hitler had outlawed the Freemasons eight years before in Germany, and wearing a Masonic ring on the streets of Berlin would have meant prison or even death. But this soldier was far away from Berlin. Adolf Hitler would not help him if he was captured or killed.

"Oh my God, that guy is a Mason," the chaplain exclaimed. He went back to the platoon and returned with three other U.S. soldiers who were Masons. They carefully removed the Nazi soldier from the tank and wrapped his body in a blanket. The little group of Americans who were his enemies performed a Masonic funeral service for their fallen Brother. Strader looked on, astonished by their tenderness and devotion.

After the war, Bob Strader came home and became a Mason, and he never forgot his first real experience with Freemasonry's principles.

Part II
The Inner Workings of Freemasonry

The 5th Wave   By Rich Tennant

In this part . . .

In this part, I get down to the nuts and bolts, er, the
stones and mortar of what Freemasons do, who does
what, and why they do it. I talk about how lodges and
Grand Lodges are set up, what happens at the ritual ceremonies, and what the curious symbolism of the Masons is
all about.

Chapter 5

How the Freemasons Are Organized: Who Does What and Why

In This Chapter

▶ Discovering what a lodge is

▶ Figuring out who does what in the lodge

▶ Understanding the role of the Grand Lodges

▶ Getting hip to the rules of visiting other lodges

*O*ne of the more common myths told about Freemasonry is that it's an evil global organization that secretly rules the world. The truth is that the Freemasons have no international governing body; in the United States, they don't have a national governing body, either. Nearly every foreign country, every U.S. state, and the District of Columbia has its own governing organization, called a *Grand Lodge*.

Just as your city has a municipal government that runs local affairs and a state government that governs on a wider scale, each lodge under the jurisdiction of the Grand Lodge has its own officers, bylaws, and traditions. And the officers and individual Freemasons of those local lodges must keep within the rules of the statewide (or national) Grand Lodge.

In this chapter, I first walk you through what your lodge down the street looks like and how it's set up. Then I introduce you to the officers and their duties. Finally, I discuss the Grand Lodge and its role in governing Freemasonry in your state.

What's Inside the Lodge?

The word *lodge* really has two meanings to a Freemason. It describes both a place where Masonic meetings are held and the members who meet there. So as weird as it sounds, you could say that a lodge meets in a lodge. In fact, many different lodges can meet at different times in the same lodge building. This practice is common in larger cities, where one building may have many rooms for lodge meetings and dozens of lodges that share them. So you could also say lots of lodges are lodged in the lodge. (Nobody really talks like that, but you *could* say it.)

Lodge is a word from the Middle Ages (from the French word *loge,* meaning "cabin") for the temporary building that medieval stonemasons often set up next to their construction sites. This arrangement made a lot of sense for mutual protection and for training and education. In the lodge, masons could eat, sleep, plan their construction project, and even socialize after a hard day's work.

Original founding members name their lodges. They can be named after the town they're in, a historical figure, a famous Mason, or even a symbolic word or phrase. A number always follows the name of the lodge, such as Washington Lodge #13 or Ancient Landmarks Lodge #319. The number is issued by the governing Grand Lodge and designates the order in which lodges have been chartered in that jurisdiction. The older the lodge, the smaller the number.

Examining the lodge room

Many of the details in a lodge room are patterned after aspects of King Solomon's Temple, as described in the Bible, in 1 Kings and 2 Chronicles, and in other historical records. Freemasonry teaches by symbolism, and much of that symbolism is based on the accounts of Solomon's Temple. The Temple was built in the 10th century BC on Mount Moriah in Jerusalem. Solomon built it as a temple to God and to store the sacred Ark of the Covenant, which contained the tablets of the Ten Commandments given by God to Moses. In its time, its magnificence was known all over the ancient world.

Early stonemasons claimed that their guilds originated with the great construction projects of the Bible to give themselves a long, proud, and sacred pedigree. When Freemasonry became a philosophical organization in the 1700s, the Masons who developed the ceremonies and practices of the fraternity seized on the symbolism of Solomon's Temple to help teach moral and spiritual ideas.

Many details of lodge rooms are based on interpretations of descriptions of the Temple. Many variations exist throughout the world, depending on differences in customs, rituals, and rules, but in general, lodge rooms are arranged this way:

- ✔ **The modern Masonic lodge is a rectangular room, with seating around the perimeter.** The ceremonies of the lodge take place in the center of the room so everybody has a good view.

- ✔ **Lodge rooms are usually oriented east to west.** Ancient temples were constructed this way to be aligned with the east-to-west path of the sun. Even if a Masonic building actually faces north and south, when you walk into the lodge room, you're symbolically facing the East.

- ✔ **The room has an altar where the Bible (or other holy book sacred to that lodge's members) is opened.** This book is referred to as the Volume of Sacred Law. In U.S. lodges, the altar is in the center of the room. In other parts of the world, the altar may be directly in front of the Master's chair.

- ✔ **Three candles or lights are placed in a triangular position next to, or surrounding, the altar, to illuminate the Volume of Sacred Law.**

- ✔ **Officers have chairs in specific positions in the room.** The Master is in the east, on a raised platform of three steps. The Senior Warden is in the west on a platform of two steps, and the Junior Warden is in the south on one step. The steps symbolize the progression of life: youth, manhood, and age.

- ✔ **There are two tall pillars with globes on the top, patterned after two bronze columns that were prominent architectural features of Solomon's Temple.** The pillars are usually on either side of the Senior Warden, or sometimes next to a doorway leading into the lodge.

- ✔ **An illuminated letter *G* is suspended over the Master's chair in the east, or sometimes over the altar.** It represents both God and the science of geometry, which was the secret knowledge of the original stonemasons.

All the ceremonies and rituals of *Ancient Craft Freemasonry* (the most basic brand of Masonry practiced in local lodges all over the world) are conducted in rooms similar to this.

Symbolism is everywhere in a Masonic lodge, and I explain lots more about it in Chapter 7.

Lodge buildings can be large or small, and so can lodge rooms. In some parts of the world, lodge rooms typically seat no more than 30 or 40 members, whereas in the United States many lodge rooms were built to hold hundreds of people. Often the difference is whether many small lodges meet in the same building or one large lodge dominates the area. Most buildings generally have a dining room and, perhaps, other social rooms.

Until recently, it was common for a lodge building to be called a *Masonic temple*. Because of a public misunderstanding about the role of religion in Freemasonry, as well as the accusation that Freemasons actually go to their lodges to "worship," many jurisdictions have asked lodges to remove the word *temple* from their buildings.

Meeting and eating at the lodge

Lodges (that is, the members) meet at regular intervals throughout the year. Most assemble once a month for a business meeting, at which communications are read, bills are paid, proposed members are voted on, and the members catch up on each other's lives. Often, guest speakers are invited, or a member will give a presentation on the ritual, history, philosophy, or symbols of Masonry. These regular gatherings are often called *stated meetings* or *stated communications*.

Other special meetings are held to initiate new members and to perform the various ceremonies to advance them to full membership. These ceremonies are called *degrees*.

Because the primary goal of Freemasonry is fellowship, a meal is usually served before or after the meeting, either in the lodge building or at a nearby restaurant. Depending on the traditions, formality, and finances of its members, meals can be as simple as pizza or bologna sandwiches or as sumptuous as a seven-course feast, in the Old English *Festive Board* tradition of a banquet and ceremonial toasting. Masons also gather for the somber purpose of conducting funeral services for their deceased members.

I explain a whole lot more about the ceremonies of Masons in Chapter 6.

Who's in Charge around Here?

The members of the lodge elect officers, although the Worshipful Master appoints a few. In most lodges, the officers serve in their positions for one year. The names and duties of the officers are mostly taken from very old customs practiced by the medieval stonemasons' guilds and English liveries, where Freemasonry originated.

In England in the 1400s, under the reign of King Edward III, local (or what we now call *municipal*) governments grew out of the merchant and craft industries of the towns. The guilds had lots of money and property as well as organizational and administrative experience. Heads of the guilds became heads of town councils, mayors, sheriffs, and more.

One of the ways a local official proclaimed his rank was by wearing a badge of office, or *jewel,* on a chain around his neck. This practice survives today. If you've ever seen a ceremony in England with a mayor or other local official supervising a ribbon-cutting or a tree planting, you probably saw a *lord mayor* (the British equivalent of a plain old mayor in the United States) wearing an ornate necklace and the medallion of his office. Masonic lodges do the same thing to identify their officers, carrying over this old guild tradition. Masonic jewels of office are symbolic (naturally), and I discuss those symbols in greater detail in Chapter 6.

Every lodge is required to have a Worshipful Master, a Senior Warden, a Junior Warden, a Senior Deacon, a Junior Deacon, a Treasurer, and a Secretary. However, Freemasons do not march in lockstep with one another. The names of officers and their duties vary subtly from country to country as well as from state to state. And yet a Mason from Iowa on vacation in Belgium will recognize the same basic framework of Masonic officers that he had at home in Dubuque.

Officers in the progressive line

Masonic officers are generally part of what is called a *progressive line,* also known as "going through the chairs." It is a line of succession that moves up one position at a time from one year to the next. If a man is appointed to the Junior Steward's position, in a perfect set of circumstances, seven years later he will be Worshipful Master. Although this curious plan for leadership has its drawbacks, it was designed based on the philosophy of equality among Masons. The progressive line is most common in the United States, but it exists in many other jurisdictions as well. Obviously, there are usually more new members that join a lodge than there are entry-level officer's positions, so not everyone gets to be an officer.

The progressive line does away with politicking or campaigning for officers' positions. In the ideal lodge situation, each man simply advances each year, learning each position's duties and a portion of the Masonic ceremonies. By the time he becomes Worshipful Master of the lodge, he has sat in every chair (except, perhaps, the Secretary and Treasurer). He has learned public speaking, management of a volunteer organization, decorum, and responsibility. And eliminating the annual popularity contest for election that many groups suffer results in a smoother, friendlier line of succession. Any man, regardless of his social, business, or economic position outside the lodge room, may aspire to be Master of his lodge.

Jurisdictions differ from one another, and many local lodges observe different customs that may slightly alter these duties. In the following sections, I outline the most common officers' positions in the United States.

Worshipful Master

The Worshipful Master sits in the East, symbolic of the rising sun, and presides over the lodge, like a president or chairman. Even if the building faces the wrong direction, the Master is said to be "in the East." While serving his term as Master, his word is final over the actions of the lodge. He is also responsible, as the ritual instructs, for "setting the Craft to work and giving them good and wholesome instruction for their labor." He presides over business meetings and the conferral of degrees.

The Master's jewel of office (shown in Figure 5-1) is the right angle of a square, a stonemason's tool used for checking the angles of cut and smoothed stones. It is not a measuring square like carpenters use. It's used to make certain an angle is "true." It symbolizes virtue.

Figure 5-1: The Master's jewel of office.

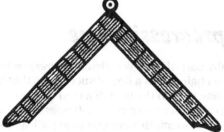

Image courtesy of Christopher Hodapp

Masons call the man in charge of the lodge *Worshipful Master,* but that doesn't mean they worship him. In parts of England, mayors and judges are also called "Worshipful" or "Your Worship." It's a term of honor, from the original intent of the word, meaning "to give respect." French Masons use the word *Venerable* for their Masters.

Senior Warden

The Senior Warden sits in the West, symbolic of the setting sun, and assists the Worshipful Master in opening and closing the lodge. He is the second in command, like a vice-president, and if the Master is unable to attend the meeting, he may open and conduct business. His ancient duties were to pay the Craft their wages and to handle disputes among the workers. These days, he's just a heartbeat away from the East, so his task is to support the Master and to prepare himself for that office for the following year.

The Senior Warden and the Junior Warden (see the following section) often have small wooden columns on the pedestals in front of their positions. When the lodge is *at work* (during a meeting), the Senior Warden's column stands upright and the Junior Warden's column is laid on its side, showing that the Senior Warden is now in charge of the Craftsmen. When the work is concluded and the lodge retires to refreshment, the Junior Warden's column is raised and the Senior Warden's is laid down, showing that the Craftsmen are now under the supervision of the Junior Warden.

The Senior Warden's jewel of office (shown in Figure 5-2) is the level, a stonemason's instrument used to check the level of horizontal surfaces. It symbolizes that all Masons meet on the level, without regard to social, political, or religious status.

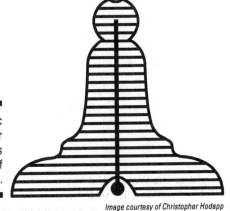

Figure 5-2:
The Senior Warden's jewel of office.

Image courtesy of Christopher Hodapp

Junior Warden

The Junior Warden sits in the South, symbolic of the position of the sun at midday. Because he represents the sun at lunchtime, he metaphorically supervises the Craftsmen when they're at recess, or *refreshment*. He is the number-three officer in the lodge hierarchy, and he also may open the lodge if the Master and Senior Warden are unable to attend the meeting. The Master and the two elected Wardens (the Senior Warden and the Junior Warden) are the only officers who may open a meeting. Only a Grand Lodge officer may override this requirement.

The Junior Warden is often in charge of arranging meals for the lodge, and traditionally the Stewards assist him (see the later section, "Senior Steward and Junior Steward"). One of the Junior Warden's symbolic jobs described in the ritual is to make certain that the members "do not convert (their) refreshment into intemperance or excess." In most U.S. jurisdictions, alcohol is barred from the lodge, but the ceremonial reference to earlier days remains part of the Junior Warden's job description.

The Junior Warden's jewel of office (shown in Figure 5-3) is the plumb, a stonemason's instrument used for checking the alignment of a vertical surface. It symbolizes upright behavior among Masons.

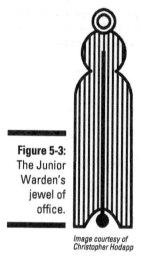

Figure 5-3:
The Junior Warden's jewel of office.

Image courtesy of Christopher Hodapp

Senior Deacon

The Senior Deacon sits to the right of the Worshipful Master. He is the Master's messenger and does lots of walking. He welcomes and escorts both visitors and new candidates into the lodge and usually introduces distinguished visitors. During degree rituals, he is the guide for the new candidate, conducting him around the lodge room. In the opening and closing ceremonies of the lodge, the Senior Deacon opens and closes the Bible and lights or extinguishes the candles at the altar. In many lodges, he also carries the ballot box around the room when new members are voted on.

Both the Senior and Junior Deacon carry long staffs, or *rods*. Because they are messengers of the lodge, the rods they carry are symbolic of the *caduceus,* or wand, that the Roman winged god and messenger Mercury carried. The rods are topped by their jewels of office, to match the ones on their collars.

The Senior Deacon's jewel (shown in Figure 5-4) is a square and compass with a sun in the middle. The sun signifies that his position is in the east, with the Master. (In some parts of the world, the jewel worn on the collar of the Deacons may be a dove, and their rods may be topped by a figure of Mercury or a dove with an olive branch.)

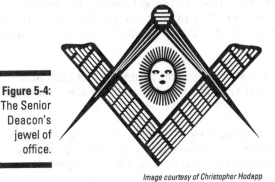

Figure 5-4:
The Senior Deacon's jewel of office.

Image courtesy of Christopher Hodapp

Junior Deacon

The Junior Deacon sits to the right of the Senior Warden, guarding the door to the lodge. He is the messenger of the Senior Warden, as well as the lodge "doorman." His job is to be certain the Tyler (see the "Tyler" section later in this chapter) is guarding the door on the outside, and he allows visitors to enter after they've been properly vouched for. He and the Tyler communicate with each other by knocking back and forth on either side of the closed door.

Some jurisdictions divide this position between a Junior Deacon and an Inner Guard.

The Junior Deacon's jewel of office (shown in Figure 5-5) is the square and compass, like his senior counterpart. The difference is that the Junior Deacon's jewel has a moon in the center, signifying that he is in the West.

Figure 5-5:
The Junior Deacon's jewel of office.

Image courtesy of Christopher Hodapp

Senior Steward and Junior Steward

Because the Stewards are the low guys on the totem pole of the officers' line, they do much of the grunt work. They're the Junior Warden's assistants, and they help to set up the lodge room. They prepare all new candidates before entering the lodge for their degree rituals and escort them to the lodge room, where the Senior Deacon takes over. They may also be the kitchen staff and wait staff of the lodge, which means that they're champing at the bit to move up to the Junior Warden's job.

The Stewards, like the Deacons, also carry rods, in imitation of England's Lord High Steward's rod in the House of Lords. The rods are also topped with the jewels of their offices.

The Stewards' officers jewels (shown in Figure 5-6) are the same: a cornucopia, or "horn of plenty," symbolizing — what else? — lots of food. Masons love to eat and will find any excuse they can to have a breakfast, luncheon, or dinner to commemorate just about anything.

Figure 5-6:
The Senior and Junior Stewards' jewels of office.

Image courtesy of Christopher Hodapp

Officers not in the progressive line

The lodge has several officers who do not usually move in the progressive line, for several reasons. Treasurers and Secretaries often serve for many years. Continuity in those positions is vital for running an efficient lodge. Training them takes time, and having a new one each year would create chaos.

A couple of positions you may hear about but which I don't cover in this chapter are the Marshal and the Director of Ceremonies. The Marshal is generally the officer who conducts visitors into the lodge and introduces them to the members. The Director of Ceremonies position varies widely. He may be in charge of making certain all officers know their required parts in the various ceremonies and rituals of the lodge. He may also be the messenger for the entire lodge. Neither of these officers is common in U.S. lodges.

Treasurer

The Treasurer sits to the right of the Master and behind the Senior Deacon. His duties are pretty obvious, namely to keep track of the lodge's money. He receives all money from the Secretary, keeps a record of it, and pays it out at the order of the Master, with the consent of the lodge.

The jewel of the Treasurer's office (shown in Figure 5-7) is a pair of crossed keys, signifying he's the guy with the keys to the cashbox.

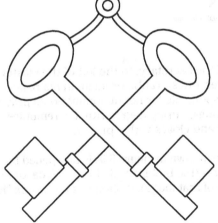

Figure 5-7: The Treasurer's jewel of office.

Image courtesy of Christopher Hodapp

Secretary

The Secretary sits to the left of the Master and, in reality, is the second-most-powerful officer of the lodge, even though the ritual doesn't say so. He keeps the records of the lodge, communicates with other lodges and the Grand Lodge, types the letters, retrieves the mail, takes the minutes of the meeting, and does lots more besides.

Because the Secretary must be well versed in the laws and regulations of his jurisdiction, be familiar with the list of the lodge's members, and help the Master organize his meetings, an experienced member generally occupies this chair. Secretary is truly the office of greatest responsibility in the lodge.

The jewel of the Secretary (shown in Figure 5-8) is a pair of crossed quill pens, even though today he may very well be pounding out the minutes on a laptop computer.

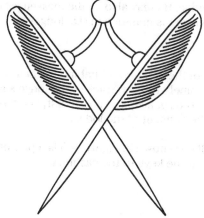

Figure 5-8:
The Secretary's jewel of office.

Image courtesy of Christopher Hodapp

Chaplain

The Chaplain sits in front of the Secretary, to the left of the Master. Although he isn't necessarily a minister, priest, rabbi, or imam in his real-world job, in the lodge the Chaplain is responsible for nondenominational prayers at the opening and closing of meetings, during degree ritual ceremonies, and before meals. Every meeting opens and closes with a prayer.

The Chaplain's jewel of office (shown in Figure 5-9) is an opened book, symbolizing the Volume of Sacred Law (the Bible, Torah, Koran, Veda, or other book held sacred by the members of that lodge). It often has the words "Holy Bible."

Figure 5-9:
The Chaplain's jewel of office.

Image courtesy of Christopher Hodapp

Tyler

The Tyler (sometimes spelled *Tiler*) sits outside the closed door of the lodge room, armed with a sword, guarding the entrance against the approach of "cowans and eavesdroppers." During the Middle Ages, *cowans* were men who built stone walls of poor quality, and they were not initiated or apprenticed as stonemasons. The Tyler's job was to keep these unskilled workmen from listening in on meetings.

After the lodge members are inside, the door closes, and it's up to the Tyler to decide whether late arrivals can come in. He also makes sure that visitors are "properly clothed," meaning that they have on a Masonic apron. Some jurisdictions call this position the Outer Guard.

Many lodges use the Tyler's position as a place of honor for older, retired members. It's kind of a bummer for him, because he's stuck outside and can't hear the business of the lodge. Some lodges have a tradition of paying the Tyler a small salary and making him responsible for setting up the paraphernalia of the lodge room, laundering the aprons, and performing other small tasks.

Other jurisdictions that have very large buildings with many lodges meeting inside on a given night will have one ceremonial Tyler for the whole building.

The Tyler's jewel of office (shown in Figure 5-10) is a sword — sometimes a "wavy" sword, symbolic of the biblical reference in Genesis to the "flaming sword that was placed at the east of the garden of Eden, which turned every way to keep the way of the tree of life." It has no scabbard, because the Tyler's sword should always be drawn and ready for the defense of his post.

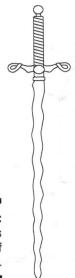

Figure 5-10:
The Tyler's jewel of office.

Image courtesy of Christopher Hodapp

There's no past faster than an old Past Master

After his term of office "in the East," the Worshipful Master is put out to pasture. He goes from having all the power in the lodge to having precisely none. This transition is similar to when the President of the United States leaves office; he becomes just another common citizen again. He may make speeches all over the country, write books, appear on the news more often than when he was running the country, and otherwise bore everyone to distraction. But he has no power, and no one *has* to listen to him. This is the fate of the Past Master.

Nevertheless, his fellow Freemasons look upon a Past Master with great respect. He is honored for the rest of his life by the title *Worshipful Brother* before his name, and the initials *P.M.* after it. Not exactly like having the Secret Service at your beck and call for the rest of your life, but a nice honor anyway.

Some jurisdictions give Past Masters more power than others. A few allow them to vote on legislation at Grand Lodge meetings, and some lodges may have an official position called the Immediate Past Master, someone who acts as a mentor to the Worshipful Master who followed him. Being a Past Master is a special accomplishment, because it represents many years of commitment to Freemasonry and to the lodge. The Past Master knows ritual, rules, history, and customs, and he is a tremendous resource for his lodge. Even though in most cases they hold no office, Past Masters have their own honorary jewel (shown in the figure). In most U.S. jurisdictions, the jewel is an open compass with a sun in the center. At the base of the compass is a curved bar connecting the points, called a *quadrant,* marked in degrees like a protractor, for measuring angles. The sun symbolizes his past position in the east. The quadrant is a tool of complex geometry, symbolizing that the Past Master possesses greater knowledge.

Image courtesy of Christopher Hodapp

Other jurisdictions use a jewel representing the 47th Problem of Euclid (more commonly called the Pythagorean theorem) to symbolize the Past Master's greater knowledge (as shown in the figure). Oh, come on, you remember the Pythagorean theorem for defining the angle of a right triangle: The square of the hypotenuse is equal to the sum of the squares of the other two sides of a right triangle. And you thought you'd never have to know that after high school.

Image courtesy of Christopher Hodapp

What Makes a Grand Lodge So, Well, Grand?

A Grand Lodge is a governing organization that oversees all the local lodges in its jurisdiction. It makes rules governing how lodges conduct their ceremonies, issues warrants (or charters) for new lodges, passes judgment on members who violate the rules of the fraternity, and decides which other Grand Lodge jurisdictions its members may legally visit. These issues have to do with what's called *regularity* and *recognition,* and I cover those terms later in this chapter (see "What Is a Regular, Recognized Lodge?").

The collective group known as a Grand Lodge is generally made up of all the Worshipful Masters from all the lodges in its jurisdiction. The Worshipful Masters meet together, generally once a year, at a *convocation* or *communication,* where they elect Grand officers, vote on new legislation, and address other business.

The rest of the year, Grand Lodges generally don't meet, although this practice may differ in some jurisdictions. Its officers are pretty much a mirror image of the officers' line in a local lodge, except these men are Grand Officers: Grand Master, Senior Grand Warden, Junior Grand Warden, and so on. In addition, Freemasons generally give the Grand Master greater respect by officially calling him *Most Worshipful* Grand Master. A Past Grand Master is often referred to with the respectful prefix of *Right Worshipful.*

Every Grand Lodge does things a little differently, so you may also find positions like Deputy or Provincial Grand Master, District Deputy Grand Master, District or Area Grand Representatives, and many more. These positions were created because the Grand Master is only one man and can't be everywhere at once. Deputy, District, or Provincial Grand Masters have variations of the Grand Master's powers and often act as his proxy around the state or country.

The Grand Master

Because the Grand Lodge generally only meets as a big group once a year, the Grand Master basically acts in place of the entire Grand Lodge for the rest of the time. What that means is that he can issue *warrants,* or charters, to create new lodges, make decisions on rules disputes, suspend or expel members who've broken the rules, and perform other actions. His word is law — at least until the Grand Lodge's convocation is in session. At that time, the members of the Grand Lodge can review and approve or disapprove of his actions.

When the Grand Lodge is actually meeting together, the Grand Master is in charge of the meeting, just like a Master in a local lodge.

In the United Grand Lodge of England, the Grand Master is traditionally a member of the Royal Family (currently, the Duke of Kent), and he holds the position for life, or as long as he wants it. The position is largely a ceremonial and honorary position. In the United States, Grand Masters usually have a one-year term, although some states elect for terms as long as three years.

Depending on the rules of a Grand Lodge, Grand Masters often have special powers for performing certain ceremonial shortcuts. These may include opening or closing a lodge in *ample form* (meaning a shortened version that doesn't require the officers to go through the normal ceremonial opening) or making Masons *at sight* (bestowing the membership of Masonry on a man who has not progressed normally through the three lodge degrees).

Again, the powers of Grand Masters have as many variations as there are Grand Lodges, and they all depend on that jurisdiction's customs and rules.

The rules

Every Grand Lodge has an official published book of constitutions or Masonic law. The rules cover a wide variety of topics, ranging from defining the powers of officers, how elections are held, and how rituals are to be conducted, to the conduct of members toward each other and the penalties for un-Masonic conduct. The rules can be rewritten or amended at the meetings of the Grand Lodge.

Masonic bling: All those aprons, pins, and medals

As I mention in Chapter 1, every Freemason wears a Masonic apron during a lodge meeting, and it's usually plain and white. Historically, Freemasons wear aprons because stonemasons wore them to protect their clothing. Mythologically, it's because Masons wore aprons when King Solomon's Temple was being built. Symbolically, it's an emblem of innocence, to be kept spotless as a representation of purity of life and conduct. (I talk more about the symbolism of aprons in Chapter 7.)

That said, lots of exceptions to that plain-and-white rule exist. In England, aprons are surrounded by a light blue cloth border to symbolize the *Blue Lodge* (a term for the Masonic lodge). Fellow Crafts get two blue rosettes added to the bottom corners, while Master Masons get a third rosette on the triangular flap. The apron also has two vertical bands of cloth, with metallic tassels dangling from the ends. These tassels are an ornamental representation of the old custom of long apron strings that wrapped all the way around the waist and tied under the flap in front, with the ends dangling out from under the flap.

In the United States, officers have special aprons with the jewel of their office embroidered on it to match the jewel on their neck. Past Masters are entitled to wear special aprons denoting their honored status. At the very least, it includes a Past Master's jewel (either the compass with a quadrant or the geometric representation of the Pythagorean theorem, depending on the jurisdiction). Past Masters' aprons are often beautifully embroidered and decorated with various designs. Again, the predominant colors are blue and white.

Grand Lodge officers take apron designs to an elaborate level. They're usually white surrounded by purple (from the old European custom of royalty wearing purple), but lots of gold fringe and stitching are involved. The design often includes a circular badge with the jurisdiction's name and seal in the center.

In Europe, to avoid the societal suspicion of Freemasons, most Masons don't draw attention to themselves by wearing Masonic jewelry. American Masons, on the other hand, are very fond of Masonic jewelry, pins, rings, hats, shirts, jackets, and belt buckles. After you become a Master Mason, you can wear items with a square and compass on them. If you are *not* a Freemason, you shouldn't wear something you aren't entitled to. It's sort of like wearing a policeman's badge or a Purple Heart ribbon if you aren't a cop or a wounded veteran. This rule has a few exceptions; for example, the widow or daughter of a deceased Mason may wear his jewelry.

In the 1800s, large lodges, Grand Lodges, and Masonic conventions commonly created commemorative badges, ribbons, or medals, which have become popular collector's items today. Today, lodges and Grand Lodges often create pins to commemorate a major anniversary or a Grand Master's "year." Again, Masons love these items, and it's not uncommon to see Masonic coat lapels festooned with a handful of shiny, multicolored pins.

The appendant bodies (see Part III of this book), especially the York Rite groups, developed and expanded after the Civil War, and capitalized on the postwar love of military pomp and pageantry. As a result, the appendant bodies often issue military-looking medals for many of the additional degrees they confer.

In the days before wristwatches, Masonic pocket watches were all the rage. Their faces often had Masonic symbols rather than numbers, and the backs or covers were often engraved with symbols as well. William Dudley made the most collectable Masonic watches in the early 1920s. The faces were quite plain, but they contained a Masonic "secret." The back was either clear or removable, and all the inner workings of the watch mechanism were shaped like Masonic symbols — a trowel, square, compass, plumb, level, Bible, and others. Only 4,000 of these watches were ever made, and today they're worth thousands of dollars.

You may have heard that Masons have horrible, bloody penalties for misbehaving members who break their secret rules. The truth is that the only penalties for violating Masonic law are reprimands, temporary suspension of membership, or expulsion from the fraternity.

What Is a Regular, Recognized Lodge?

Regularity and recognition. They're very confusing issues, and I have to warn you right now that this topic may make your eyes glaze over. It's tedious. It's technical. It's also, unfortunately, important to understand. Start gulping down the caffeine and get comfortable.

The words *regular* and *irregular* are official terms used by one Grand Lodge to describe other Grand Lodges and their members. Every single Grand Lodge, according to its own rules and regulations, determines Masonic regularity. Grand Lodges that regard each other as legitimate are said to be *in amity*.

Freemasonry is not a like a corporation or a single, solid, worldwide entity. As a result, no one owns the worldwide trademark to the square and compass logo, and no one can claim to hold the universal copyright on Masonic rituals. It would be like the Methodist Church claiming it holds the universal rights to all trademarks, symbols, and sacred texts of Christianity. The Methodists or Catholics or Baptists can't keep a new Christian group from building a church and placing a cross over its altar, or stop its choir from singing "Onward Christian Soldiers."

Likewise, Grand Lodges can't stop a group of people from obtaining Masonic rituals out of a book, buying a stack of aprons and officers' jewels, and claiming that they have their own Grand Lodge. Like branches of the Christian churches, differing Masonic groups have argued and had schisms over the centuries, and factions of Masons have started their own Grand Lodges.

Which one's legit? Sorting through multiple Grand Lodges

For lack of a better word, I'll refer to the most commonly recognized, regular Grand Lodges in the world as *mainstream*. England, Scotland, and Ireland each have a mainstream Grand Lodge. The six provinces of Australia each have a mainstream Grand Lodge. Canada's provinces are arranged in much the same manner, and the country has ten mainstream Grand Lodges. The United States has 51 mainstream Grand Lodges — one for every state, plus the District of Columbia. Also operating in the United States are 46 Prince Hall Affiliated (PHA) Grand Lodges (see the "Prince Hall recognition" sidebar). Apart from these exceptions, most countries have just one regular Grand Lodge that is considered "recognized" by the mainstream.

Prince Hall recognition

Forty-six Prince Hall Affiliated (PHA) Grand Lodges share territory with the mainstream U.S. Grand Lodges. Several southern states have resisted recognition of the predominantly African American Prince Hall Grand Lodges, but the vast majority of states and international Grand Lodges regard them as regular and have recognized them. They share the same geographic territory with their mainstream counterparts by mutual agreement, basically a Masonic treaty.

The states that do not recognize their Prince Hall counterparts generally insist that it's because they regard the PHA Grand Lodges' Masonic pedigree as suspect. As I discuss in Chapter 2, Prince Hall Grand Lodges do descend from an English charter — which they still physically possess — but the few states that do not officially recognize PHA Grand Lodges officially declare those historic claims to be bogus. With all this obsession on legitimacy and historical justification, you'd think we were discussing the crowning of a pretender to the throne of Freedonia instead of which Masons can visit what lodges.

So who gets to decide what lodges are mainstream or legitimate? Well, in Freemasonry, might makes right in most cases. That sentiment may sound a bit nasty, and it's a pretty tight club. The big group of mainstream Grand Lodges represents the greatest number of Freemasons in the world. As the 800-pound gorillas in the Masonic universe, they get to collectively make rules they all agree to abide by.

To further confuse matters, every Grand Lodge gets to decide what Masonically related, or *appendant*, groups they regard as regular or recognized. So Grand Lodge A may allow its members to visit lodges in Grand Lodge B's jurisdiction but still declare another Masonic group operating in Grand Lodge B's territory (and with Grand Lodge B's full blessing) as irregular and off limits.

Defining regular Freemasonry

Regular Freemasonry is defined by mainstream Masons as lodges and Grand Lodges that follow these general guidelines:

- ✔ **Grand Lodges must have been descended *in some way* from the original Grand Lodges of England, Scotland, or Ireland.** Even if a Grand Lodge is in all other ways "regular," if it can't trace its origins to the original Grand Lodges, it won't be recognized by the mainstream.

- ✔ **Lodges must require a belief in a Supreme Being.** Members must take an oath on, or in view of, an open Bible or other Volume of Sacred Law.

✔ **Lodges must admit only men.** They may not admit women or associate with female or mixed-gender lodges.

✔ **Lodges must not allow discussions of religion or politics during meetings, nor may they allow members to engage in plots or conspiracies against their country.**

✔ **Lodges may confer only the three degrees of Entered Apprentice, Fellow Craft, and Master Mason.** They may not confer any other additional degrees (see Part III for more about appendant bodies and additional Masonic degrees).

✔ **Lodges may only receive visitors from other Grand Lodge jurisdictions that are deemed regular, and recognized as such, by their own Grand Lodge.**

Legitimizing recognized Grand Lodges

Recognition means that one Grand Lodge accepts the legitimacy of another Grand Lodge and its members. Every Grand Lodge is sovereign in its jurisdiction. No other Grand Lodge may tell it what to do or how to do it. Having said that, the system of regularity and recognition is controlled by a simple mechanism.

Grand Lodges that go off and do something the rest of the mainstream disagrees with get stripped of their recognition as a mainstream group. It's very effective. Being declared *irregular* means that members of that Grand Lodge cannot visit in other regular jurisdictions. It means being shunned on a national and international level. Grand Lodges as a rule don't like to do anything that may endanger their recognition status.

How do you know who's off limits?

One of the rules of Freemasonry is that a Mason will not communicate Masonically with a clandestine Mason or visit a lodge of clandestine Masons. So how does a Mason know what lodges he can legally visit?

Every Grand Lodge has a Grand Secretary whose job it is to answer these very questions. Before traveling to another state or country, a Mason wanting to visit a foreign lodge should contact his Grand Secretary, who will determine what lodges may be visited and provide a letter of introduction. Like international diplomacy, there is an official protocol for going visiting. On the other hand, if you meet a Mason on the street and you know he's a member of a jurisdiction in amity with yours, he's welcome to invite you, and you're welcome to accept.

Some lodges are far more formal than others. Just dropping in and expecting admission may be acceptable at one lodge, while another may demand that you follow the official protocol.

For more information regarding the mainstream Grand Lodges, see Appendix C of this book.

Here are some of the guidelines that determine how a Grand Lodge is entitled to have jurisdiction over its particular part of the world.

- **There is one Grand Lodge to a state, province, or country.** The Prince Hall Grand Lodges are the notable exception to this rule. Others exceptions exist, like in Ontario and South Africa, but they're unusual cases. Exceptions are only permitted by agreement between the Grand Lodges involved.

- **A new Grand Lodge may only be created legally by existing lodges and with the agreement of the Grand Lodge it was chartered by.** For example, the Grand Lodge of India was created in 1961 by existing English, Scottish, and Irish lodges working in India, with the mutual agreement of the three original governing bodies.

- **Unless Grand Lodges agree to share a territory by treaty, competing lodges operating in a Grand Lodge's territory are declared irregular, *clandestine* (a generic word meaning irregular and/or unrecognized), or otherwise illegal.**

- **In regions that have no local Grand Lodge, the mainstream Grand Lodges have organized provincial Grand Lodges.** This system is how the Grand Lodges of England and Scotland operate lodges in countries in the Far East and other parts of the world. In an example that's a little closer to home, the Grand Lodge of Massachusetts has chartered a lodge in Guantanamo Bay, Cuba.

Irregular, unrecognized, and all over the place: Lodges out of the mainstream

Outside of the mainstream Grand Lodges, there are Freemasons all over the world who belong to lodges that they consider to be every bit as regular as anybody else. Regularity is in the eye of the beholder, and every individual Freemason considers himself to be a member of a "regular" lodge. Territorial and procedural arguments arise when Masons try to visit lodges that their own considers irregular.

Nevertheless, there are thousands of these so-called *irregular* Masons the world over, happily going about their business, unconcerned by recognition issues. No fewer than 20 Grand Lodges are operating in New York, but only the Grand Lodge of New York and the Prince Hall Grand Lodge of New York are considered regular and recognized by the mainstream. France has at least 13 Grand Lodges, but only the *Grande Loge Nationale Française* is recognized. Italy has no fewer than 22 Grand Lodges in its borders, but only the *Grande Oriente d'Italia* is commonly recognized.

Lady Masons: Sometimes allowed but never mainstream

This may come as a shock to mainstream Freemasons, but yes, Virginia, there *are* female Freemasons. In the United States, Canada, England, France, Belgium, Italy, and many other countries, female and coed Grand Lodges exist. These lodges are considered irregular, but their rituals are almost identical to mainstream Masonry (with women in many cases calling each other "Brother").

Most Grand Lodges the world over reject the notion of initiating women as being in violation of the Ancient Charges, which allow only men. Female Grand Lodges and *co-Masonic* (mixed-gender) Grand Lodges get around this by interpreting the regulation as referring to men as in the generic, *mankind* sense of the word. They've provided examples of female operative stonemasons from medieval history as proof that women should be allowed to join. They've also provided one historic example of a woman being initiated into an Irish Lodge in the 1730s as justification for entry.

The United Grand Lodge of England has recently softened its stance on women's Masonic Grand Lodges by actually admitting the existence of the female-only Honourable Fraternity of Antient Freemasons and its 350 lodges operating in the United Kingdom. Nevertheless, there is no official communication, visitation, or other Masonic contact between them.

The Order of the Eastern Star (OES), which I cover in more detail in Part III of this book, is a Masonically related group, primarily in the United States. Yes, women can join it. But the OES is *not* Freemasonry for women. It is coed, and it does not confer the three degrees of Entered Apprentice, Fellow Craft, and Master Mason. It has its own unique ritual, and it has the blessing of most U.S. Grand Lodges.

If you're a lady inclined to seek out a feminine Masonic organization in the United States, the major groups are the Ancient and Primitive Rite of Memphis-Misraim and the Women's Grand Lodge of Belgium. The largest group of co-Masons in the United States is the American Federation of Human Rights (sometimes referred to by its French name, *Le Droit Humain*).

The Grand Orient of France: Immense but invalid

French Freemasonry is as complicated as French history has been for the last 300 years. At least 13 Grand Lodges operate in France, and probably more.

Proof that the biggest Grand Lodge is not always the mainstream one, the Grand Orient of France claims 41,000 members and 1,000 individual lodges. It is the largest Grand Orient in the world and the largest Masonic organization in France. It's also not recognized by the mainstream groups.

A Grand Orient is different from a Grand Lodge in a couple of ways:

- ✔ **A Grand Orient considers itself to be a federation of different lodges.** The lodges it presides over may have a wide variety of rituals, customs, and practices, and the Grand Orient acts as a simple administrative body with few actual rules for the whole group.

- ✔ **A Grand Orient is comprised of a Grand Master and a council appointed by him.** That council, in return, appoints the Grand Master. It does not have a governing body made up of representatives of the many lodges it oversees. In effect, it is a self-perpetuating, Masonic *oligarchy* (government by the few, in case you didn't recently finish Political Science 101).

Some Grand Orients around the world are recognized by mainstream Grand Lodges. What makes the Grand Orient of France different? Its lack of uniform requirements for all its lodges violates many of the rules of regularity that are accepted by the mainstream. These violations include the following:

- ✔ **It does not require belief in a Supreme Being.** Atheists may join Grand Orient of France lodges.

- ✔ **It does not require obligations on a Bible or other Volume of Sacred Law.** Grand Orient lodges often have no book on their altar, or they may have a blank, white book that substitutes for all sacred texts of all beliefs.

- ✔ **It does not forbid its members from visiting female or coed lodges.** In fact, Grand Orient of France lodges have started to admit women as members.

- ✔ **It has constituted lodges in foreign jurisdictions where there are other established Grand Lodges already in operation.** Washington, D.C., and London are just two examples of cities where Grand Orient of France lodges exist.

Although the Grand Orient of France has a pretty closed governing body, it allows its lodges far greater autonomy than most mainstream Grand Lodges do (that is, lodges are allowed to make their own rules to better suit their local membership). This flexibility is why some of its lodges admit women or atheists and some don't. Some Masons regard this approach as very open-minded; others decry it as chaos.

The mainstream French organization that *is* recognized by mainstream Freemasonry is the *Grande Loge Nationale Française*. It is neither the largest nor the oldest in France, but it is descended from the United Grand Lodge of England and follows the rules of regularity.

Bogus Masonic groups in the black community

Freemasonry has been highly respected in the African American community since colonial times, when Prince Hall and his brethren received their charter from England. Grand Lodges of Prince Hall Affiliation (PHA) in 46 jurisdictions trace their direct lineage back to this original document.

Unfortunately, over the years, more than 200 small groups have popped up, many claiming some kind of connection to the Prince Hall Grand Lodges. They may have had legitimate arguments with their leadership, they may have been started as copycat organizations, or they may have been created simply as fraudulent moneymaking schemes.

For whatever reason, these bogus Grand Lodges exist all over the United States and only confuse men interested in becoming Masons. They have no Masonic legitimacy outside of their own small group, and their members are not regarded as regular in any other lodge but their own.

If you're interested in joining a Prince Hall lodge, do some research and be certain you're joining a lodge under the jurisdiction of a PHA Grand Lodge. The PHA Grand Lodges are listed in Appendix C of this book.

The Phylaxis Society, a research organization dedicated to Prince Hall Masonry, has created a Committee on Bogus Masonic Practices. Its reports can be found at www.thephylaxis.org/bogus/history.php.

Being out of the mainstream

Most people who join a lodge are not aware that there are competing organizations in the world that call themselves Masonic but are not considered to be legitimate by the majority of Freemasons. Only regular, recognized Masons can make regular, recognized Masons. Only regular, recognized Grand Lodges can charter regular, recognized lodges, or agree to cede a territory to a new Grand Lodge.

Over the centuries, disgruntled Masons have started new groups. Some Grand Lodges have changed their rules, and those changes violate the rules of the mainstream. Some enterprising hucksters have created new Masonic degrees or groups, simply for the purpose of making money by trading on the reputation of Freemasonry. Still others have discovered or created new rituals that they purport to be better, more interesting, more enlightening, or more correct. For whatever reason, thousands of group member are regarded as illegitimate Freemasons by the worldwide majority.

None of this is a huge issue to the individual Mason until he starts to travel and visit other lodges or encounters other Masons. An irregular Mason will not be welcomed into a mainstream lodge, and his degrees and documents will not be considered legitimate. He will not be entitled to the honors, benefits, and fraternalism enjoyed by millions in the Masonic world.

This is not to say that unrecognized Masonic groups have nothing to offer. It's simply a warning so you're certain that the lodge you join will provide what you're looking for.

Chapter 6

The Ceremonies of Freemasons

In This Chapter

▶ Tracing the origins of Masonic rituals

▶ Going behind closed doors: The three degrees

*T*he ceremonies Freemasons practice in their lodges are referred to as *rituals.* Rituals aren't peculiar to Freemasonry — they occur all around you in everyday life. Everything from handshakes to applause and graduation ceremonies to singing the national anthem at a baseball game can be considered a ritual. Rituals reinforce spiritual or social bonds through repetition and widespread use. Rituals transmit common experiences across time and connect modern society with the past.

Churches, courtrooms, college fraternities, Boy Scouts, Girl Scouts, weddings, funerals, the Marines — all use rituals that have developed over the years. Freemasonry is no different.

Rituals of initiation, like weddings or baptisms, have an especially powerful effect on people. They imply the beginning of a physical or spiritual journey, as well as the promise of learning secrets that have been kept from us.

In Ancient Craft Freemasonry, the variety of Masonry conducted in your local Masonic lodge, these rituals are called *degrees,* and they progress from the Entered Apprentice to the Fellow Craft and finally to the Master Mason. The degrees connect Freemasons down through the centuries, and knowing that you're going through the same experience that millions of other men around the world have gone through for hundreds of years is an awesome feeling.

I am a Freemason, so you won't catch me breaking my vows here. I won't be putting anything in print that I've promised not to, no matter how much the nice *For Dummies* people pay me. Having said that, just like the 18th-century exposures, the Internet is filled with plenty of websites (hosted almost entirely by anti-Masons) that gleefully show and tell every "secret" we Freemasons have. Libraries and bookstores have plenty of volumes that do the same thing. Anybody who *really* wants to know has been able to find out for nearly 300 years. In this chapter, I discuss the most basic aspects of the degrees of Freemasonry. I leave lots of details out, but the most important thing to remember is that a big part of the reason for Masonic secrecy in the modern age is to keep from spoiling the degree experiences of new candidates. Half the joy of any initiation is the discovery of new experiences.

If you read about the whole thing before you join, you have robbed yourself of enjoyment. So be warned: **This chapter contains some spoilers, starting with the section "Performing the Rituals of the Modern Lodge."** If you have a strong desire to join a lodge, stop reading, go call a Mason, and skip to another chapter instead.

Understanding Where Masonic Ritual Comes From

Lots of different fraternal organizations appeared in the 1800s (see Chapter 2), but the vast majority of them used the degree rituals of Freemasonry as their model. It wasn't just the Knights of Columbus, the Elks, the Odd Fellows, and the Red Men. Literally hundreds of fraternal lodges, conclaves, chapters, and halls full of knights, nobles, chiefs, hierophants, patrons, potentates, and poobahs sprang up, all with ever-more-elaborate ways to induct new members. Everything from the early Ku Klux Klan to the Mormon Church, and even benevolent life-insurance brotherhoods, all patterned their initiation ceremonies on the ones used in Masonic lodges.

Unlike the early Church, which kept a written record of its ceremonies, the nature of early operative Freemasonry was to attempt to keep its rituals a secret. After all, if the craft guild was supposed to be making sure that unqualified workers didn't steal their building and drafting techniques, writing it all down in an easily stolen form would have been dangerous. And don't forget that during the operative Masonry period, most of the world's population was illiterate. Knowledge was passed down "mouth to ear," because most people couldn't read or write.

The historical medieval guild rituals

The earliest record of Masonic ritual is found in a document known as the *Regius Manuscript,* written in about AD 1390. It is written as a long poem and tells a lavish history of Freemasonry dating back to ancient Egypt. It goes on to lay out 15 *articles,* or rules, about who may and may not be made a Mason, how a Mason should conduct himself at work and in private, and the moral duties of a member of the Craft. Even though it was written in the 14th century, it is believed to have been copied down from the oral traditions that had been passed on since approximately the 10th century AD. (You can read the Regius Manuscript in Appendix A of this book.)

The oral tradition continued as the Masonic guilds spread across Europe. Anyone who has whispered a rumor at one end of a dinner table, only to hear it mangled by the time it comes around the other end, knows that stories told over centuries, in different countries and languages, tend to change. A lot.

The Lowly Apprentice

The Regius Manuscript implies that originally, Masons had only one initiation ritual. Apprentices in those early days were one step above slaves and were considered to be the property of their masters until their period of apprenticeship was completed, generally seven years. So the earliest initiation rituals were designed to make a very big deal out of a young man's transformation from apprentice to his new position as a journeyman or Fellow Craft.

The ritual opened with a prayer, followed by the telling of the "ancient" history of the guild. This part of the ceremony was embellished with questionable history to impress everyone that Masonic lineage and authority dated back to biblical times. If the Masons were there at the building of the pyramids, the walls of Jericho, the Tower of Babel and King Solomon's Temple, then they were certainly more knowledgeable than some upstart barrel maker's guild.

Then the new initiate had a Bible opened before him, and he was informed of the laws, rules, and regulations of the guild. He was then required to swear an oath of fidelity to the king, to the Master of the Guild, and to the other members that he wouldn't break the rules.

By the 1500s, the English Parliament passed a series of labor laws that implied that an apprentice wasn't an inanimate piece of property that could be bought and sold after all. Instead, he might actually be a human being. Under the _Statute of Apprenticeship,_ it was unlawful to "exercise any craft, mystery, or occupation" that was being practiced in England without serving an apprenticeship of at least seven years. So by 1550, two degrees were developed by the Masons. The brand-new apprentice was brought in, and apparently a portion of the ceremony was spent trying to scare the bejesus out of the young man. A long series of questions and answers were rehearsed for him to memorize — test questions by which he identified himself as a Mason. He was told certain methods of recognition — a _grip_ (handshake), a _sign_ (hand signal), and a password. He then took an oath vowing to never divulge the information, under pain of terrible torture and an ugly execution. After he had taken the oath, he was known as an Entered Apprentice — a very big step up in the world from being a piece of property.

The mystery plays

By the mid-1200s, merchant and craft guilds began to produce mystery or miracle plays, based on stories of the Bible. Interestingly, the word *mystery* is from the French word *mystere,* which meant any trade or craft during the Middle Ages. The stories depicted generally had something to do with whatever the guild specialized in. The Carpenters might present the story of Noah's Ark. The Fishmongers might tell the story of Jonah and the Whale. The Bakers would present the Last Supper. The Pinners (nail makers) might stage the tale of Jesus's crucifixion. And the Masons often presented the story of the building of King Solomon's Temple.

The plays were performed on holy days in honor of the saints, and the Masons' patron saints were Saint John the Evangelist and Saint John the Baptist. On these festival days, the plays were often presented on giant rolling carts that were decked out as stages, complete with huge set pieces. These carts were called *pageant wagons* and are the origin of our modern-day pageants. The pageants traveled the countryside, and the members of the guilds got to be actors for a while. These members were generally illiterate, so the plays were learned by repeating the parts over and over until they were memorized. (When you're carving a 900-pound rock for a church wall, having something to do to pass the time is fun.)

By the early 1400s, the "professional" actors and musicians in England were fed up with amateurs horning in on their territory, so they formed the Minstrel's Guild to try to corner the market on theater. They had mixed success. The towns still enjoyed the plays of the guilds, and they continued for another two centuries.

As time went on, the degree became longer and more embellished with lectures. It seems more and more older (and long-winded) Masons wanted to teach the young guys a thing or three about the world around them. As the 17th century came to an end, the old reliance on religion as an explanation for everything in the universe was falling apart, in favor of the new fields of science and philosophy. By the time of the early 18th century, the ritual had grown to talk about living a virtuous life, the different styles of architecture, appreciation of arts and sciences, and even the five senses of the body. It was sort of a crash course in the liberal arts, presented in a one-night session.

The Fellow of the Craft

Because apprentices were now being initiated into the guild rather than being treated like dumb kids and left outside, a second degree was designed for the journeyman, who was ready to go out into the world and earn his living. His responsibilities to his fellow guild members were increased, and he was given further test questions and answers, more grips, signs, and finally, the *master's word* (the secret word, combined with a grip that allowed him to travel freely and make himself known as a Master Mason anywhere members of the guild were to be found). He swore a new oath, with a bloodcurdling penalty of torture and execution.

After working and learning as an apprentice for seven years, a Mason was given a choice. He could go to work under contract for the same employer he had apprenticed under, now as a journeyman. In Scotland, he was known as a *Fellow of the Craft*, or simply *Fellow Craft*. Or, he could set up his own business as a Master Mason. Either way, he possessed the same knowledge. The terms were only used to show whether he was an employee or an independent businessman.

The Master Mason

By the time of the changeover from operative to speculative Masonry in 1717 (see Chapter 2), lots of well-educated men were forming new lodges all over England, Scotland, and France.

During the Age of Enlightenment, the term *speculative* meant an exercise of the mind, and not a risky investment in junk bonds.

The idea of this new version of philosophical Freemasonry was catching on fast. But although they liked the idea of basing the fraternity on the craft guilds and their ceremonies, somehow it needed, well, something bigger.

As a result, more than a few men were writing new rituals and ceremonies based on the old ones, with some new twists. A fascination with the old guild, new learning, biblical allegory, the miracle plays, and a little drama led to the creation of a third degree, the Master Mason, in about 1726. First performed as a play by an all-Masonic cast at the *Philo Musicae et Architecturae Societas Apollini* (Apollonian Society for the Lovers of Music and Architecture) in London, it dramatically told two stories: the building of King Solomon's Temple and the death of Noah, and with his death, the loss of his "secret knowledge."

The written account

In 1772, an English Mason named William Preston gave a lecture that he then published as "Illustrations of Freemasonry," which analyzed and explained the ritual and symbolism of the degrees. The book was a huge hit, and Preston published nine editions of it over the next 20 years. It explained the ritual and symbols but left out anything that was considered to be secret.

An American Mason in Rhode Island named Thomas Smith Webb read William Preston's book, but he thought it left out interesting symbols and lectures he had seen in his own Masonic experience. And he had ideas of his own about the best way to present the degrees. So he added to what Preston had done and published his own descriptions of the rituals, called "Freemasons Monitor" in 1797. It became very popular in the new U.S. Grand Lodges, and most U.S. lodges today practice this Preston-Webb version of Masonic ritual.

ORIGINS

Who is Hiram Abiff?

By the 1730s, the two stories of Hiram and Noah had been tinkered with and combined into one dramatic tale, the Masonic legend of Hiram Abiff, the Grand Architect of the Temple.

Two passages of the Bible describe the building of the Temple. The first is 1 Kings 7:13–14:

> And king Solomon sent and fetched Hiram out of Tyre. He was a widow's son of the tribe of Naphtali, and his father was a man of Tyre, a worker in brass: and he was filled with wisdom, and understanding, and cunning to work all works in brass. And he came to king Solomon, and wrought all his work.

The second is 2 Chronicles 2:13–14:

> And now I have sent a skillful man, endued with understanding, of Huram, my father's, the son of a woman of the daughters of Dan, and his father was a man of Tyre, skillful to work in gold and in silver, in bronze, in iron, in stone and in timber, in purple, in blue, and in fine linen, and in crimson; also to engrave any manner of engraving, and to devise every plan which shall be put to him, with thy skillful men and with the skillful men of my lord David thy father.

From these brief passages, along with some errors in translating the original Hebrew, the occasional misspelling and lots of imagination, came the story that formed the basis of the third and last degree of the Masonic lodge. It tells the tale of Hiram Abiff, a widow's son, and the Master Architect of King Solomon's Temple, who as a Master Mason, possessed even greater secrets than the skilled Fellows of the Craft, or journeymen. Here's the way the story goes:

Each day, Hiram enters the temple to pray and to draw his designs for the workmen to accomplish on his *trestle board,* or drawing board. When leaving one day, he is accosted by three of the temple's Fellows of the Craft, who are eager to discover the secrets of the Master Masons. They threaten the Architect and attack him with their tools. The third one delivers the final, deadly blow. Hiram dies without divulging the secrets he has vowed to protect. The secret words of the Master Mason go to the grave with him. The three disgraced workmen bury the body and attempt to escape the country but are brought to justice and executed by the horrible penalties of their Masonic oaths. The decomposed body of Hiram Abiff is found, and after several attempts to lift it from its grave, the strong grip of a Master Mason at last pulls it from its resting place. Hiram's body is carried back to the temple for a proper interment, and a monument is erected to his fidelity, honor, and steadfastness in the face of death.

This story is the central piece of what's called the *Hiramic legend.* The moral is a strong one, teaching men to have faith, to keep to the ideals of morality and virtue, and to stand by their promises. But unlike previous Masonic degrees, this one was now acted out instead of being presented as a mere lecture or monologue.

And so, with the addition of a Master Mason degree, the old degrees were rearranged into their present format. The new Entered Apprentice was simply initiated and sworn to secrecy. The new Fellow Craft was now given the lecture about architecture, science, and the arts. And this brand-new Master Mason degree told the tale of Hiram and the Temple. In an astonishingly short period of time, all these rituals that had taken centuries to develop became the regular practices of a Masonic movement that was quickly going global.

Performing the Rituals of the Modern Lodge

With all this talk about rituals, you'd think this is all that goes on in a lodge. The ritual is what Freemasons use to make new members and teach simple lessons about morality and conduct. Plenty of socializing goes on, too, but learning and teaching the ritual is a big part of the responsibilities of the officers. Outside of the United States, many Grand Lodges allow their members to print their rituals, as long as they leave out the specific "secrets." The officers are then allowed to read their parts.

In most U.S. lodges, these *cipher books* are allowed for studying, but the ceremonies themselves must be memorized and recited without any written aids. If you aren't much of a public speaker when you enter the lodge, you'll get over your fears very quickly, because even the newest Entered Apprentice has a part to learn and play.

Setting the stage for the ritual

Degrees may be performed on a regular business-meeting night, but they're usually done by themselves at a special, or *called,* meeting (a meeting that has been called for a special purpose). Lodges generally confer a degree on only one man per meeting, because it's supposed to be his special event. Some jurisdictions allow several men to go through the degree together. Members who haven't attained the Fellow Craft of Master Mason degrees can't attend these ceremonies.

Some U.S. Grand Lodges have created what is called an "All-Degree Day" to allow men who do not have the time to take the degrees individually a faster way to become Master Masons. In these sessions, dozens, hundreds, or even thousands of men sit in an auditorium and watch all three degrees, while one candidate goes through as the group's metaphorical representative. All the men watching take the obligation for each degree in unison. This practice is controversial outside of the states that allow it, and it's not universally available. In fact, many Grand Lodges have strongly objected to its use, and it is not done outside the United States.

In the United States, the rituals are usually performed from memory and are not read. Each officer has a part in the degrees, and there may be roles for others as well. Most lodges pride themselves on being able to "cast" all the parts required from within their own membership. But it is perfectly acceptable for visiting brethren from other lodges to take on a part. And frequently a close friend or family member will want to personally participate in the degree work of a new Brother by taking an important role.

Freemasons — EXPOSED!

Now, if all this stuff is supposed to be a secret, how do we know about it? Well, as Freemasonry became more and more popular in the early and mid-1700s, a little side business popped up. The surest way to make a lot of easy money in the publishing business in the mid-18th century was to say you were printing a book that exposed the secrets of what was fast becoming the world's most popular "secret society." These *exposures* (or *exposés* in French) may or may not have been entirely factual in telling all the ceremonies going on in the lodges, but they had another interesting side effect. Most of the people who bought them were Freemasons who were trying to learn their ritual and were frustrated by having to learn "mouth to ear." So whether the exposures were accurate or not, they had the effect of helping to standardize the very rituals they were exposing. By "outing" the Masons, these publishers helped to spread Freemasonry around the world with freshly printed handbooks.

In England, an argument broke out in the late 1700s between the Grand Lodge of England and a group of Masons who claimed that too many innovations had been made in the Masonic ceremonies. They called themselves the *Antients,* and the existing Grand Lodge of England came to be called the *Moderns* (for more about this, see Chapter 2). In 1813, they finally ended the feud, merged together, and agreed not to standardize their ritual. As a result, lodges in England are not required to work a specific ritual, although they're all very similar in concept. The difference is in the details.

Like the English, the Americans didn't require their lodges to adopt any one standard ritual. Every local lodge had its own favorite way of doing or explaining things. But as Freemasonry spread all across the United States, the Grand Lodges began to regard diverse developments of ritual as a messy way of doing things. By the 1840s, many states were wrestling with the problem. Most decided on Thomas Webb's book as a guideline, but every state had its own favorite variations. Masonic rules — part of the oath taken by the Entered Apprentice — created the biggest problem. All Masons vowed not to "write, print, paint, stamp, stain, cut, carve, hew, mark, or engrave" any of the secrets of the fraternity. So how do you write down something you promised not to?

To get around the rules, many states printed *cipher rituals* — all the ceremonies reduced to the first letter of each word, with a few extra consonants thrown in to clarify tough ones. For instance, if the ritual was to say, "In whom do you put your trust?" the cipher might appear as "I Wm D Y P Y T?" This is a lot like trying to learn the part of Hamlet by studying 90 pages of capital letters.

Other Grand Lodges went farther, creating a special cipher code. To read it, the Masonic James Bond first had to decipher a double-secret code of squares, lines, and dots in order to figure out the letters. And to this day, there are still almost a dozen U.S. Grand Lodges that forbid their members to even own any sort of written ritual study guide at all, secret codes or not. Nevertheless, by the early 1900s, the individual U.S. lodges were all on the same basic page, in their respective states, and the ritual was at last "carved in stone." Pennsylvania is the one notable exception, and its ritual is completely different from other states'.

With some differences, Masonic ritual quit changing dramatically after that. Today's lodges confer the Entered Apprentice, Fellow Craft, and Master Mason degrees, and the Master Mason ritual is the tale of Hiram Abiff and Solomon's Temple. The language has changed very little since the 1750s.

With some differences around the world, this basic ritual is used to open every lodge meeting:

1. The Tyler sits outside the door, guarding the entrance with a sword.

2. Everyone in the lodge room is examined to be certain he is a Mason, by way of passwords and handshakes, or *grips.*

3. Each officer stands and recites his duties.

4. The Chaplain prays, and the Three Great Lights are displayed — the Bible, or Volume of Sacred Law is opened, and a square and compass are laid on it.

5. The Worshipful Master declares the lodge properly opened, and the degree may begin.

The Masonic ritual is designed around the symbolic story of the building of a great, spiritual temple, as represented by the Temple of Solomon. The Entered Apprentice degree represents the ground floor of the temple; the Fellow Craft is in the middle chamber; and the Master Mason degree takes place in the *sanctum sanctorum,* the "holy of holies."

Symbolically, the temple is built by a group of men all working together, on a design that is a mystery to them individually. Only the architect knows the complete plan and the ultimate use of the temple. Each man must do his best to complete the work set before him — his fellow men depend on him, as he depends on them. He must constantly study the designs and be aware of the proper place of the temple within the world around it. And because the temple is so enormous, he knows the work will take him a lifetime.

To a Freemason, the temple is his own character; the designs are the virtuous and moral lessons most sacred to his own religion, and the architect is the Grand Architect of the Universe.

Entered Apprentice: Initiation and youth

The three Masonic degrees are designed to represent three stages of life: youth, manhood, and age. The Entered Apprentice degree represents youth, because it teaches the most basic lessons of belief in God, the necessity of charity to mankind, the importance of truth, and the value of keeping one's word.

When a newly elected man arrives at the lodge for his first degree, the members greet him. In most lodges, a dinner is served before the degree begins; this is to introduce him informally to the other members and to put him at ease. In other parts of the world, the dinner may come after the degree. Next, the newly elected man is seated outside of the lodge room while the members go in for the ceremonial opening. (Before reading on, you may want to glance over Chapter 5 to familiarize yourself with the names and duties of the lodge officers.)

To be initiated, the candidate must have his clothes arranged in a certain symbolic way. In earlier times, he would simply take off a shoe, roll up his pants leg, and open up his shirt. Most lodges today provide special clothing — a shirt with one sleeve and a slight opening over the breast, and a pair of pants with only one leg — for this ceremony, so he doesn't feel quite so undressed. Next, he has a length of rope, called a *cable-tow,* draped around his neck. Finally, he is blindfolded, or *hoodwinked.*

Although many other fraternities often take the initiation ceremony as an opportunity to embarrass or harass the new candidate, Freemasonry specifically forbids any embarrassment or discomfort for the new man. The candidate is blindfolded here for many reasons. Blindness fuels the imagination and heightens the other senses. He'll focus on the words instead of becoming distracted by the details of the room or the face of a friend who might be doing the talking. But more important, he is symbolically in darkness, seeking the light of knowledge. Until he takes the oath, or *obligation,* he can't receive that knowledge or be allowed to see the lodge room.

Some historians believe the term *cable-tow* comes from an Old English term. Spun yarn, fiber, or string was called *tau* or *taw,* and when it was woven together into a strong rope, it was called a *cabled-taw.* On a medieval worksite, a Mason working on a high wall or roof used a cable-taw to climb and to haul up his tools from the ground. Small holes were cut in the stone walls, and bits of short lumber were stuck in the holes to lash temporary poles together to form a rickety version of scaffolding. Not exactly OSHA approved. The length of a worker's cable-taw represented the height he would safely climb this bundle of sticks and haul tools and mortar. The more daring the climber, the longer the cable-taw. Anything past the length of his cable-taw was considered to be an unreasonable request. That's the legend, anyway.

After the new member has been hoodwinked, he is carefully led to the door of the lodge, where he must knock on the door with his own hand. When he's allowed to enter, the Stewards hand him over to the Senior Deacon, who will act as his guide through the rest of the degree.

What follows is a procession through the lodge, stopping at each of the primary officers, where the new member is questioned and examined by each one. At last, he kneels at the altar, places his hand on the Bible or the Volume of Sacred Law, and takes the *obligation* (oath) of an Entered Apprentice. In that obligation, he promises not to divulge the secrets he is about to receive, nor to write them or print them or in any other way make them known to anyone who is not a Mason.

Circumambulating

As the Senior Deacon leads a candidate around the lodge room, he is said to be *circumambulating*. They walk around the lodge in a clockwise direction, symbolic of the travel of the sun through the sky. But walking around a Masonic lodge has to be done in a specific manner. Walking is always done in a straight line. When a Mason comes to a corner, he stops and turns to the right, making a precise corner, like a square. This is, in fact, called *squaring the lodge*. But why?

Each degree has a series of lectures that take place, describing certain symbols. As the lectures got longer and more complex, some kind of visual aid was needed, both to assist in a new Mason's learning and to jog the memory of the guy giving the lecture. In the days when lodges met in taverns, the lecturer would draw out these symbols on the floor in chalk. At the end of the lodge session, the new member or the Stewards would then be responsible for getting a mop and wiping out any trace of the drawings.

Later, these drawings were painted on large cloths that were rolled out onto the floor. Because they were beautiful, large, and most important, quite valuable, no one was to walk on them. So, anyone walking around the room had to step around the cloth. The fashion quickly became to "square" the corners when walking around the lodge.

Later, these drawings were taken off the floor and made into cards or boards, called *tracing boards* (see Chapter 7). They could more easily be set up on easels or mounted to walls, and they could be very elaborate and beautiful. Today, most lodges rely on slides or even PowerPoint presentations for the visual aids, but the custom of squaring the lodge still persists.

After taking the obligation, the cable-tow is removed from the new member's neck, and the hoodwink is lifted. For the first time he sees the lodge in candlelight and he is welcomed as a Brother. Gradually, the lights are brightened, and he is shown the signs, steps, and handshakes, and given the password of an Entered Apprentice.

He is next presented with the white leather apron, or *lambskin,* and its symbolism is explained, along with the proper ritualistic way to wear it, according to his rank as an apprentice.

In most U.S. lodges, this initiation apron is to be carefully put away and stored, used only during his degree work, and placed in the Mason's coffin when he dies. Its pure white surface is representative of his endeavor for a pure and spotless life. In other jurisdictions, this is the apron he will wear throughout his Masonic career. And in still others, a special apron is provided for each of the three degrees.

Zounds! Bloody oaths!

Freemasons are told during every degree that the obligations they are about to take contain nothing that can conflict with their duty to God, their country, their neighbor, or themselves.

Nevertheless, the obligations taken by Freemasons have been the source of complaints for many years by critics who have taken the "bloody penalties" as a serious threat. But no recorded evidence suggests that any Freemason has ever had his throat slit, his chest torn open, or his body disemboweled for telling a non-Mason how to give the secret handshake.

English mariners took variations of these types of oaths during the 15th century. They were also similar to oaths taken by lawyers admitted to the bar in London during the 16th century. These oaths actually grew out of court-mandated punishments during the Middle Ages and were designed according to the beliefs of the Catholic Church. It was believed that an incomplete body could not rise from the dead, nor could a body buried in unconsecrated ground. Therefore, to be stuck in the ground without all your parts was an awful condemnation to death both on Earth and in the hereafter.

In the Middle Ages, breaking a vow, oath, or what the French called a *parole*, was a far graver offense than modern man can comprehend.

Over the years, critics have objected to such oaths, and different Masonic jurisdictions have answered the criticism in different ways. In England, they have been removed from the obligations altogether. In many U.S. jurisdictions, the oaths have been modified to say they're symbolic only, or that these were the ancient penalties, now no longer enforced. The truth is, they never were. The only penalties in Freemasonry are reprimand, suspension, or expulsion from the fraternity.

Finally, he is taught about charity and the importance of aiding his fellow man and fellow Masons. He is taken back to the preparation room to dress back into his own clothes, and then he returns to the lodge for a series of lectures that explain the symbolism of the ceremony.

As in the earliest days of the craft guild, the Entered Apprentice must memorize a series of questions and answers. This memorization is done for several reasons:

- The Entered Apprentice can demonstrate that he has made a proficient study of the lodge and its workings. If he can't bother to learn this first requirement, he's not serious about moving on.

- If the Entered Apprentice wants to visit another lodge where no one knows him, he can vouch for his own knowledge and prove he is an Entered Apprentice by answering the questions in proper form.

- By learning these questions and answers, he becomes a link in the long chain of millions of men who have passed the ritual down through the centuries, connecting him to the earliest Masons of antiquity.

Fellow Craft: Passing through manhood

The second degree is the Fellow Craft, which represents manhood, the middle period of life. During this degree, the importance of education and work and the awesome power of God are taught to the Mason.

The preparation of the brother is very similar to that of the Entered Apprentice. In fact, the first half of the degree is strikingly parallel. His clothes are prepared, a cable-tow is applied in a different manner, and he is again hoodwinked. He is conducted around the lodge in a similar fashion as before.

The obligation he takes as a Fellow Craft is longer than that of the Entered Apprentice and increases his duties to his brethren. In addition to secrecy, he promises to help his brothers and to obey the rules and laws of the lodge. After taking the obligation, he is again "brought to light" and shown the step, grip, signs, and password of the Fellow Craft degree.

The second section of the Fellow Craft degree is a lengthy lesson taken from the early-18th-century ceremony. The Brother symbolically climbs a winding staircase into the middle chamber of the temple, and each step represents an increase in knowledge. The lecture explains the design of Solomon's Temple, the orders of architecture based on the teachings of the Roman architect Vitruvius, the five senses, and the seven liberal arts and sciences. Although it all may sound a bit quaint and a little dull to modern sensibilities, this degree, more than any other, is a strong connection with an earlier time, when public education did not exist.

Although Masons know the Entered Apprentice degree as *initiation,* the Fellow Craft is said to be *passing.* It is a passage through the adult stage of life, when we learn and experience new things every day.

Master Mason: Raising, age, and death

The Master Mason degree is the third and last degree ritual of the lodge. Although the first half is almost the same as the other two degrees, the second half is very different. The second portion of the degree is the dramatic presentation of the legend of the death of Hiram Abiff (see the "Who is Hiram Abiff?" sidebar, earlier in this chapter). In the course of the degree, the new Master Mason is taught the importance of living a life true to the principles of morality and virtue. Masons refer to it as *raising* because the body of Hiram Abiff is raised out of his grave by the use of the grip and the word of the Master Mason.

Some people believe the story of Hiram is a parallel to resurrection and could be traced back to the Egyptian legends of Osiris who rose from the dead, but the ritual itself does not say that Hiram is brought back to life. His body is simply raised out of its grave, and that event is the point at which the secret word and the grip of a Master Mason are told to the brother.

The Master Mason degree represents age. The brother is encouraged to reflect upon his deeds and make peace with his God, because death is a strong theme during this degree. How a man lives and dies is the most important message the degrees of Masonry teach.

Movin' on up!

Degrees are traditionally given one at a time, with a waiting period between. These waiting periods vary widely from one part of the country or the world to the next. Some Grand Lodges allow degrees to be given to a member one night, one week, or one month apart. In some European countries, it can take a year or more between degrees.

Before moving up to the next degree, a Mason must prove he is proficient. In most lodges, *proficiency* means knowing the password, signs, grips, and other modes of recognition for his degree. A Mason is also commonly required to memorize a series of questions and answers about his degree, called the *catechism,* or simply the *Q & A lecture.* To prove his proficiency, he must answer the questions from memory in a lodge meeting. Other jurisdictions may require him to take an educational course or to write a research paper to show proficiency.

There is no degree in a Masonic Lodge higher than the third degree, the Master Mason. You've probably heard about men who were 32nd- or even 33rd-degree Masons. They exist, but *not* in the Masonic lodge. Additional degrees are conferred by what are called *appendant groups,* such as the York Rite and the Scottish Rite (see Part III of this book). Although those degrees have higher numbers, they don't outrank a Master Mason, nor are they in any way more important than a Master Mason.

Chapter 7

The Symbols of Freemasonry

In This Chapter

▶ Clarifying Masonic symbolism

▶ Understanding the key Masonic symbols

▶ Examining numerous symbols used around the world

Symbolism is a tricky business. Many years ago, my wife and I were visiting the ruins of a Greco-Roman temple in the Italian village of Paestum. In the nearby museum are many artifacts found in the area. As we rounded the corner, there appeared a sculpture from the fifth century BC of a women's headless torso, decorated with large black swastikas.

To anyone who lived during or after World War II, the twisted cross of the swastika is a symbol of the most murderous regime in modern history, Nazi Germany. It is a symbol that represents the deaths of 28 million Europeans, including the genocide and mass murder of more than 20 million civilians, plus hundreds of thousands of Americans. The swastika is today considered so repugnant and so symbolic of evil that the European Union considered passing laws outlawing its public display.

Yet, in 500 BC, the swastika was a pretty cool design to use on Grecian urns and sculptures. In India, China, and Japan, the swastika has been found in its many forms — curved or straight, clockwise or counterclockwise. In the East it was a positive symbol, sometimes associated with Buddhism. It has been found in the ruins of ancient Troy and in the Christian catacombs of Rome. It was a common Celtic symbol and is still used in Nordic countries like Finland. It came to be a symbol for power or energy and was commonly displayed on warning signs for Swedish electric power plants. In other cultures, it's often a symbol of luck or of the positive and negative forces of nature in perfect balance.

A *symbol* is an object or design or other material object that stands in for something abstract or even invisible. In a way, it's shorthand. To a driver, a red octagon-shaped sign means *stop,* even if the letters are worn off. To a Christian, a simple cross stands for an entire religious philosophy. A red circle with a diagonal slash through it has become a universal symbol for *no*, whether it refers to littering, smoking, or turning left. Doves symbolize peace, candles symbolize knowledge, and a circle with an arrow stands for boys, whereas a circle with a cross stands for girls. The list is endless.

For a symbol to truly be universal, everybody has to agree on what it means. And a symbol can be far more complex than it first appears. The U.S. flag, like all national flags, is a symbol that excites patriotism in many of its citizens. But it takes more explanation to understand that it has 13 stripes for the founding 13 colonies, while the stars stand for the current number of states, or that the red stripes stand for the blood shed by its first defenders, the white for purity and freedom, and the blue for truth and fidelity. Symbols need explanation, especially when they're unfamiliar.

In this chapter, I discuss some of the more common symbols of Freemasonry, explaining what they mean to a Mason and where they fit into Masons' rituals.

Symbolizing the Lessons of Freemasonry

Whether you're reading books, surfing the Internet, or walking into a lodge, you'll quickly discover that Masonic symbolism is literally everywhere. You'll see tools, hourglasses, eyes, skulls, columns, stairs, hearts, swords, letters, and numbers. And every one of these symbols has an explanation or use in Masonic ceremonies.

At first, you may glance at them and come to the conclusion that these strange drawings have a vaguely sinister meaning or use. Like those 3,000-year-old swastikas my wife and I found in Paestum, symbols don't always have universal meanings. Many detractors, as well as a few older Masonic scholars, have described some Masonic symbols as occult or magical, or even as pagan symbols. The truth is actually much simpler: Symbols are used in Masonry both as a memory device and to illustrate the lessons of the Craft.

Having said that, the investigation of Masonic symbolism is a fascinating realm of study, because it is highly subjective. Beyond the most basic explanations, the Masonic student has an almost endless array of images and allegories to ponder.

The symbols teach the simple philosophies of Freemasonry, not the other way around. You may be tempted to believe that hidden mysteries and even magic are contained in these curious images when, in fact, they're used to simply imprint on the mind the lessons of the fraternity.

The Blue Lodge

A *Blue Lodge,* though not technically a symbol, is a term used to describe a lodge of Freemasons that confers the Entered Apprentice, Fellow Craft, and Master Mason degrees. Your neighborhood lodge is a Blue Lodge. Depending on local custom or the preference of who's doing the talking, your local lodge may also be called a *Symbolic Lodge* or a *Craft Lodge,* and it practices what is described as *Ancient Craft Masonry.* These lodges are where all candidates begin their Masonic careers. In the United States, the term *Blue Lodge* is most commonly used as a simple term to distinguish it from the York and Scottish rites (see Chapters 10 and 11).

The origin of the term *Blue Lodge* is obscure. The Entered Apprentice degree ritual contains a reference to the star-covered canopy of heaven, so the term may be a reference to the blue of the sky. In fact, many Masonic lodges have a blue painted "sky" for this reason. Blue was also a sacred color in ancient Israel; blue and purple dyes in the ancient world were expensive and exotic mixtures, difficult to find and, consequently, revered. Masonic aprons in the United Kingdom and elsewhere commonly are white with a blue border.

Deciphering the Key Masonic Ideas

Coil's Masonic Encyclopedia claims that more than 90 different symbols are mentioned in the three lodge degrees. That's a few more than this book has the space to cover. Masons have written hundreds of books and easily millions of words about Masonic symbolism, and in the following sections, I briefly touch on some of the basics.

Symbols have different meanings for different people, but in the following sections, I give you the accepted meanings for these symbols in Freemasonry. Each one can be explored, studied, and expanded upon, and it's up to the individual Freemason to interpret them on a deeper level for himself. To someone outside the lodge, a compass, an anchor, or a comet may denote something entirely different. But to some extent, a Freemason's reaction to these symbols, shared with his Brothers the world over, helps to bind him to the group as part of a single fraternity. Even where language is different, this is the universal language of the Craft. And when a Mason finds these symbols in a foreign land, he knows he is among Brothers.

The number three

Everywhere you look in a lodge and among its rituals, you come across the number three. There are three degrees, three principal officers, three candles, three primary orders of architecture, three knocks on the door, three steps leading to the Worshipful Master's chair, three principal tenets, three stages of life — the list goes on and on. In non-English-speaking countries, the universal symbol for the Great Architect of the Universe is an equilateral triangle, often with the all-seeing eye in it.

Plato and Aristotle believed that the number three was a symbol for the Supreme Being. Three contains the first two numbers, and it implies a beginning, middle, and end. Three has been a sacred number for thousands of years. The ancient Egyptians worshiped their gods in groups of three — like Osiris, Isis, and Horus. The Greeks revered Zeus, Poseidon, and Hades. The Romans venerated Jupiter, Neptune, and Pluto. The Norsemen deities were Woden, Friga, and Thor. Christianity worships God the Father, Jesus the Son, and the Holy Spirit. Three also represents father, mother, and child in many cultures.

Because Freemasonry was an outgrowth of Catholic, and later Protestant, beliefs, the imagery of the Holy Trinity was very strong. The number three became a symbol of the ongoing search for perfection.

Tracing boards: 18th-century PowerPoint

In Chapter 6, I discuss the ceremonial rituals of Freemasonry. The first rituals were handed down and tinkered with over centuries. They were expanded and embellished, and as they became longer and more involved, they became something of a challenge for the lecturers and ritualists — as well as the new, eager candidate — to remember. A strict rule forbids Masons from writing down the ritual in any manner that could be deciphered by non-Masons, or *profanes* as they were called. The answer to the problem was symbolism.

In the days when Masons met in taverns, they would draw symbols on the floor in chalk to illustrate the lecture being given that evening. After the lecture, the Stewards or the Entered Apprentice, as a lesson in secrecy, would get a mop and bucket and remove all trace of the drawings. All that sketching became tedious to do every degree night, so eventually a floor cloth was painted with the symbols and simply rolled out for the evening. A different cloth was painted for each of the degrees.

Over time, the cloths were taken off of the floor and hung on an easel, like a drawing board at a building site. These eventually became known as *tracing boards*. These days, the tracing boards have largely been replaced by slide shows or PowerPoint presentations of the symbols, but the purpose is the same: It helps the lecturer remember what comes next, and it helps the candidate associate an image with an idea.

Later in this chapter, I go through the tracing board shown in Figure 7-1 and discuss the symbols in it, so stick a bookmark in this page.

Figure 7-1:
A typical
19th-century
tracingboard,
packed with
Masonic
symbolism.

A tracing board should not be confused with a *trestle board,* which is a table laid flat on top of trestles or sawhorses. The trestle board is also referred to in Masonry as the place that builders draw their designs and often as the lodge's newsletter or calendar.

Solomon's Temple

As I explain in Chapter 6, the Entered Apprentice and especially the Fellow Craft and Master Mason degrees are centered around the symbolism of Solomon's Temple on Mount Moriah in Jerusalem.

Checking out the biblical account

To understand why Masons use Solomon's Temple as a symbol of their teachings, it helps to understand the history of the temple. The primary description of the historic Solomon's Temple appears in the Bible in 1 Kings, Chapters 6 and 7. It also appears in 2 Chronicles, Chapters 3 and 4, although these references were probably just rewritten from 1 Kings. The Jewish historian Flavius Josephus also discusses the temple. It was built between 964 and 956 BC as a sacred resting place for the Ark of the Covenant, the golden box that contained the fragments of the original Ten Commandments given by God to Moses. (If you saw *Raiders of the Lost Ark,* you know some of this stuff.)

Construction

King Solomon was the son of David and was the third king of Israel. Before his death, King David had assembled materials and artifacts for the temple but had been forbidden by God to build it because of the terrible bloodshed he had caused. David was a warrior king, a conqueror who not only united Judah and Israel into one nation but also defeated the Philistines with finality. He extended the borders of his kingdom into the Jewish people's only empire and fought a violent and bloody civil war with his son, Absalom.

David provided Solomon, his successor to the throne, with 100,000 talents (3,000 tons) of gold and 1,000,000 talents (300,000 tons) of silver for the temple. The temple took seven and a half years to construct, and it was erected on the sacred site where Abraham was commanded by God to sacrifice his son Isaac.

Stones were cut and prepared in underground quarries in Jerusalem. (Interestingly, the quarries still exist, and Israeli Masonic lodges occasionally hold special meetings in them today.) Master builders on loan from Hiram I, King of Tyre, oversaw the work. Cedar logs were cut in the forests of Lebanon and floated on rafts to the port city of Joppa, later known as Jaffa and now part of Tel Aviv. From there, they were dragged to Jerusalem.

After its completion, the temple sat unconsecrated and unused for 13 years while Solomon built the rest of the citadel and royal palace. At last, in 943 BC, more than 20 years after it was started, the Ark of the Covenant was placed inside, and a celebration, the Feast of the Tabernacles, lasted for seven days, beginning a new era in Hebrew history.

Design

The temple was designed like Egyptian and Phoenician temples. It had a small outer vestibule or porch. On either side of the *Ulam,* or porch entry, were two bronze pillars called Boaz and Jachin (see the section "Pillars" later in this chapter). Next was a large, middle chamber called the *Hekal* (Holy Place or Greater House), and finally you came to the smaller *Debir,* the *Sanctum Sanctorum,* or Holy of Holies, where the Ark of the Covenant resided, hidden behind linen veils of blue, purple, and crimson, and two golden doors. This inner room was lined with cedar and gold and had no windows. It was the dwelling place of God.

The area outside of this three-part complex is where the common people came to worship. The three chambers of the temple itself were reserved only for holy men.

The temple sat on top of the hill and was surrounded by a huge royal city. The actual temple itself was quite small, 90 feet long, 30 feet wide, and 45 feet tall.

Destruction

In 597 BC, King Nebuchadnezzar II, King of Babylon, conquered Syria and went on to seize Israel. After ten years of dealing with constant revolts, he decided to destroy the temple and Jerusalem itself. He stole most of the artifacts in the temple, burned the building, and dismantled the citadel stone by stone. The king took everything else back to Babylon, but the Ark of the Covenant vanished without a trace. The High Priest never would have allowed Nebuchadnezzar to take it, so it may have been buried deep within the mountain itself or smuggled out of the country. The location of the Ark of the Covenant remains one of the greatest mysteries of the Bible.

Zerubbabel rebuilt the temple when the Jews were allowed to return to Jerusalem after their 50 years of exile in Babylon. The Romans later destroyed the second temple in AD 70. The historian Flavius Josephus was allowed to rescue ancient scrolls from the temple before its destruction, and his history, *The Jewish War,* gives an eyewitness account of the events. The Romans finally got fed up with Jewish rebellions and banished the Jews from Jerusalem and the entire nation of Israel. This expulsion was the beginning of the 2,000-year Jewish Diaspora, the scattering of Jews all over the world.

The site of the temple later became the third holiest place in the Islamic faith. Mount Moriah is where the Prophet Mohammed dreamed he ascended to heaven by climbing a ladder of light that rose up from a sacred stone that had been part of Solomon's Temple. In AD 691, Calif Abdul Malik built the Mosque of Sakhra (Dome of the Rock) next to the original site of Solomon's Temple, just 53 years after the founding of the Islamic religion by Mohammed Ibn Abdullah. Years later, the Al Aksa Mosque was added opposite and equally close to the site of Solomon's Temple.

Identifying the Masonic symbolism

The Apostle Paul said, "Know ye not that ye are the temple of God, and that the Spirit of God dwelleth in you?" This quote is the basis of the Masonic symbolism of King Solomon's Temple.

The temple is a symbol for the individual Mason. It takes many years to build this place suitable for the spirit of God to inhabit, and it's constructed with the hard work of many men. The goal of the builders is perfection of workmanship. When it's finished, all who come into contact with it admire it. When the Hebrews lost their spiritual direction, the temple was destroyed, just as men are destroyed when they lose their spiritual direction. And even when it has disappeared, the memory of it lives on in the hearts and memories of all who have seen it, just as the accomplishments of good men live on long after they have died.

Square and compass

The symbol that has come to represent the fraternity of Freemasons is comprised of two different tools of the building trade: the square and the compass (see Figure 7-2).

Figure 7-2: The square and compass represent Freemasonry.

Image courtesy of Christopher Hodapp

Jeremy Cross: Symbolism illustrated

In 1819, a Masonic lecturer from New Hampshire named Jeremy Cross published *The True Masonic Chart and Hieroglyphic Monitor*. It was largely based on Thomas Smith Webb's ritual monitor, which became a reference book for new Masons, but the big difference was the inclusion of a chart containing most of the Masonic symbols I cover in this chapter. Instead of simply describing the symbolism of the degrees as William Preston in England and Webb in the United States did, Cross actually had his book illustrated by an engraver named Amos Doolittle. The illustrations have been copied, traced, enlarged, reduced, and otherwise reprinted with a wide variety of quality over the years. Today, copies of them are still used as slides, filmstrips, and even PowerPoint visual aids in Masonic lodges.

In Masonic ritual, the Worshipful Master explains that the square is an instrument operative Masons use to square their work, but that speculative Freemasons use it as an instrument of virtue to govern all their actions with mankind. Because the square represents honesty, fairness, and virtue, it's also used as the badge of office of the Worshipful Master.

The compass has a slightly more obscure ritualistic explanation. (The more proper term is *compasses,* but Grand Lodges are divided over whether to use the singular or plural version of the word.) Think of the two points of a compass, spread apart, about to draw a circle. The principal tenets of Freemasonry, which are friendship, morality, and brotherly love, are said to be contained between the two points of the compass. When you use a compass to draw a circle, one point remains in the center of the circle. That point represents the individual Freemason. The circle represents the boundaries of his world and the people he comes into contact with. He is to always live by those principles of friendship, morality, and brotherly love in all his dealings with mankind, and especially with a Brother Mason.

Explaining More Masonic Symbols

Refer to Figure 7-1 and you see many symbols. Charts like that one were used as memory devices, for both giving and learning the various lectures of the degree rituals. Start in the bottom-left corner. In the following sections, I go around the chart in a clockwise direction and discuss some of the pictures you see.

Scythe and hourglass

The scythe is an ancient, sharp tool used for cutting tall grass or harvesting wheat. Mythologically, it is a tool of Father Time or the Grim Reaper, to cut the fragile thread of life. It is to remind Masons of the ever-present danger of death that awaits us all.

Like the scythe, the hourglass is an emblem of mortality. Scarier than a clock, the sands slowly slip away and cannot be put back. It teaches a Mason not to waste his limited time on Earth. The wings in this drawing add the emphasis that time is fleeting.

The 47th Problem of Euclid or the Pythagorean theorem

The most useful mathematical equation for use in the building trade, the Pythagorean theorem says that for a right triangle, the square of the hypotenuse is equal to the sum of the squares of the other two sides. You're probably used to seeing it this way:

$$a^2 + b^2 = c^2$$

Pythagoras was a Greek who lived during the sixth century BC and was a teacher, a philosopher, and a mystic. He was a strong believer in numerology, and the Pythagorean theorem exhibits a basic mathematical truth about the way some pieces of the world fit together.

Euclid of Alexandria came along about three centuries later and wrote what is considered to be the first real geometry textbook, so blame him. He collected 465 equations, postulates, theorems, and axioms in his 13-volume work *Elements,* and the 47th one was the Pythagorean theorem.

Many mathematicians think that the Pythagorean theorem is the most important equation in all of elementary mathematics. Using it, drawings can be enlarged, foundations can be laid, and perfectly square angles can be determined. Ask your geometry teacher — she'll tell you all about it.

Surveyors can use the Pythagorean theorem to determine the height of a mountain. Astronomers can calculate the distance of the Sun, the Moon, and the planets with it. Sailors can use it to calculate latitude, longitude, and true time for navigation. Builders use it to determine that a room or foundation is squared. No wonder it was considered a mystical symbol and its application was one of the biggest secrets of the early stonemasons.

Jacob's ladder

In the book of Genesis 28, Jacob dreamed that he saw a ladder stretching from Earth to heaven and angels climbed up and down it. In Masonry, the ladder is described as having three main rungs, representing faith, hope, and charity (there's that number three again). Other rungs include temperance, fortitude, prudence, and justice. Taken together, they are the guiding virtues of Freemasonry.

Anchor and ark

In the lectures of Masonry, the anchor and the ark are combined as symbols of a well-spent life. The anchor is a symbol of hope, first appearing in the Christian catacombs, and alluding to St. Paul's message in Hebrews 6:19, describing hope as an "anchor of the soul, both sure and steadfast." The ark (like Noah's boat) is an emblem of faith that will "waft us over the sea of troubles."

Sun, eye, Moon, and stars

These images are combined to describe God, whom the Sun, the Moon, and the stars obey. God can see the innermost recesses of the heart, which in some Masonic drawings is shown beneath the eye, star, and letter *G* — all symbols of God. The Sun and Moon are also to remind the officers of the lodge to govern the lodge with regularity.

Lamb and lambskin apron

The symbol of the white leather apron (see Figure 7-3) is the universal badge of a Freemason. Aprons, girdles, or sashes have appeared throughout history as symbols of honor or piety or achievement. They appear in ancient Egyptian images and were symbols of priesthood in India, Persia, and many other cultures.

Figure 7-3:
The lambskin apron is the universal badge of a Freemason.

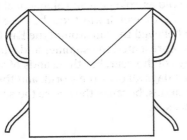

Image courtesy of Christopher Hodapp

Because the lamb has for centuries been considered a symbol of innocence, the apron is traditionally made of lambskin. It is the first gift given to a Freemason, and it is laid to rest with him when he dies. Its pure, spotless surface is intended as a constant reminder to the Freemason of purity of life, conduct, and conscience, and an ever-present symbol of the endless striving for higher thoughts, nobler deeds, and greater achievements.

Differences in customs allow the apron to be decorated in many ways. Officers often have the symbols of their office embroidered on them. Past Masters have their own symbols. Early aprons were often painted with lavish scenes or symbols. But the basic, white lambskin surface is always there, as a reminder of purity of actions and conscience.

Slipper

The slipper is a symbol relating to the way candidates are prepared for the degrees. The Masonic explanation comes from a Hebrew custom of removing one's shoe and giving it to a neighbor to seal an agreement, as a promise of honor and sincerity. Removing both shoes is a way to symbolically enter the *Sanctum Sanctorum* of Solomon's Temple, a place considered to be holy ground by the Hebrews.

Some lodges use the word *slipshod* to describe the way a candidate is prepared. These days, the term means careless work or appearance, but the original meaning was literally to be wearing a slipper or loose shoe, which is how it is used in the lodge.

Point within a circle and parallel lines

This tiny symbol is one of the most confounding images in Freemasonry. It is a circle, with a point in the middle. On top of the circle is a Bible or Volume of Sacred Law. On either side of the circle are two parallel lines. You'll find many conflicting explanations of this symbol, but I give you my own version.

The symbol is actually based on an old astrological and alchemical image. The point in the center represented the Earth, which was thought to be the center of the universe. The heavens were believed to spin around the Earth, represented by the circle. The two lines represented the summer and winter solstices, the longest and shortest days of the year. For thousands of years, these days were celebrated as pagan feast days all over the world, and they were especially important to farming societies, because they were the astronomical methods of determining planting seasons.

In about AD 300, the Catholic Church began to dedicate popular pagan feast days to the saints. June 24, the longest day of the year, was declared St. John the Baptist Day, while December 27, the shortest day, was dedicated to St. John the Evangelist. Collectively, Masons refer to them as the Holy Saints John.

John the Baptist was zealous, while John the Evangelist was learned, and by picking both of them as patron saints, Masons symbolically united both passion and reason.

Freemasonry was first developed when Roman Catholicism was the prevailing religion, and these feast days continued under the Church of England. It was common for guilds and other trade groups to adopt a patron saint or two. The Masons picked both Saints John, and over the centuries Masons commonly celebrate their feast days with banquets. And curiously, even though Freemasonry today is nondenominational and nonsectarian, U.S. Masons have retained these customs of old. Part of the ritual in the United States says that Masons come "from the Holy Saints John of Jerusalem," while in other parts of the world, lodges are dedicated to King Solomon.

The symbol also shows the Volume of Sacred Law at the top. In Masonry, the point represents the individual, and the circle is the boundary of his actions. Taken as a whole, the symbol implies that a Mason should consult the sacred texts of his own religion to achieve the proper balance between passion and intensity on one side, and knowledge and education on the other. In other words, he should balance education, excitement, and faith to effectively subdue his passions. Some scholars have said that the symbol is a graphic representation of the conscience.

Pot of incense

Incense is not typically burned in a Masonic lodge, but the symbol of a pot of incense is used as an allegory for a pure heart (the pot or *censer*) and the prayers that arise from it to heaven, symbolized by the clouds of rising smoke.

Beehive

Bees never quit, as anyone who has ever been chased around his yard after trying to knock a hive out of his garage's eaves will tell you. As a result, bees have long been a symbol of hard work and teamwork. The beehive is especially fascinating, because the honeycomb is a perfect geometric structure. One bee can do nothing; working together, they can achieve a great deal. Men are much the same.

Plumb

The plumb (see Figure 7-4 and the right pillar in Figure 7-1) is a device with a string and a weight at the bottom (called a *plumb bob*) to help a workman determine if a vertical wall or surface is level. Speculative Masons make use of the plumb to remind them to behave in an upright manner in their duty to God and their dealings with their fellow man. The plumb line always points to both the center of the Earth and to the heavens. It is a symbol of justice, rectitude, uprightness, equity, and truth, and in many ways it's similar to the scales of justice, because it must be kept in balance. In the lodge, the plumb is the officer's badge of the Junior Warden.

Figure 7-4:
The plumb is a reminder to Masons to behave in an upright manner.

Image courtesy of Christopher Hodapp

Level

The level (see Figure 7-5 and the right pillar in 7-1) is a building tool similar to the plumb, used to measure the level of horizontal surfaces. Its symbolism to the speculative Freemason is that of equality. It teaches that all Masons meet on the same level, regardless of their social or economic status in the outside world. Additionally, it reminds Masons that they're all living their lives on the level of time, traveling "to that undiscovered country" from which none of us will ever return. The level is also the officer's badge of the Senior Warden.

Image courtesy of Christopher Hodapp

Figure 7-5:
The level
represents
equality.

Letter G

The letter *G* (see Figure 7-6) appears within most North American depictions of the square and compass. It is also prominently displayed in lodges of English-speaking countries, usually over the Worshipful Master's chair. It has two meanings.

First, it is the initial of God, or the Grand Architect of the Universe, and it's an eternal reminder that Freemasonry represents a brotherhood of man under the fatherhood of God. God represents the greatest symbol of all. Everything people can experience, from the universe itself down to the simplest aspects of their own lives, comes from God.

The letter *G* is used to avoid any specific, sectarian representation of a deity, so that all Masons, regardless of their personal religion, may remain reverential to the Grand Architect of the Universe. Men of different faiths have different names and different symbols for God, but within the lodge, the *G* is used to unify, not divide, them. A Jew, a Methodist, and a Buddhist may all stand side by side in a lodge and refer to the Grand Architect of the Universe. In most lodges, the *G* is lit up while the lodge is officially open.

Figure 7-6:
The letter
G stands
for *Grand
Architect of
the Universe*
and
geometry.

Image courtesy of Christopher Hodapp

The letter *G* also stands for geometry, which is the basis of Freemasonry's origins. Through the use of geometry, the earliest Masonic builders could translate small drawings into massive structures, a truly magical talent at the time. Geometry can be used to plot the return of the seasons, determine the orbit of the planets, and otherwise explain and explore the mysteries of the universe. Uniting the concept of God with geometry is a way of connecting the spiritual world to the physical world.

In countries where the language does not begin the word *God* with a G, the All-Seeing Eye is often substituted over the Master's chair, often within a triangle or pyramid. Again, it is simply a nonsectarian representation of a deity.

To *G* or not to *G*

In some parts of the world, the square and compass that represent the universally accepted symbol of Freemasonry are depicted with the letter *G* in the center. However, in most European countries, the letter *G* does not appear between the two tools. More important, in the symbolism of the lodge as explained in Masonic ritual, the square and compass are never associated with the letter *G*. The letter *G* is its own symbol with its own explanation.

The *G* started commonly appearing in U.S. Masonic depictions of the square and compass in about 1850, although there are instances of it before that time. An enterprising jeweler making a ring or a medal most probably added it. It is unknown where the practice originated, but since the Civil War, it has become the accepted form of the symbol in North America.

Meanwhile, jewelry and other insignias made for other Freemasons around the world don't include the *G*. Different languages spell neither *God* nor *geometry* with a *G*, so the practice wouldn't make any sense. And again, because the symbols are actually exclusive of each other in ritual lectures, Masons can make a strong argument that the *G* shouldn't appear with the square and compass at all.

On the other hand, some people think that because the tools represent the Craft and the *G* represents both God and the ancient origins of the fraternity, geometry, the North American version more properly unites the principles of Freemasonry with the spiritual guidance of God and the physical world of geometry in one compact symbol.

Five-pointed star

The five-pointed star is another emblem representative of God, but some jurisdictions also use it as a memory device for a portion of the Master Mason degree called the Five Points of Fellowship. (Sorry, that's one of those secrets, so I can't tell you any more.)

Some call this type of star a *pentalpha*, and it symbolically represents a man with his arms and legs outstretched.

Naked heart and sword

The heart has a sword pointing to it, while the symbols of God look down from above. The heart and the sword symbolize justice. Although what we think, say, and do may be hidden from the eyes of other men, the Grand Architect of the Universe sees what we do, and the sword of justice will sooner or later have its final say over our hearts and our fates.

Tyler's sword and the Book of Constitutions

The Book of Constitutions is the code of Masonic laws that govern the operation of lodges. The Tyler's sword across it is a caution to protect the institution of Freemasonry by guarding against unworthy thoughts, deeds, and words that may bring the fraternity into bad repute.

Trowel

Another tool of the operative Masons, the trowel (see Figure 7-7) is an instrument that is used to spread cement or mortar. That cement makes individual bricks or stones stick together, and when it hardens, those individual stones are interconnected to make a strong, united wall or building. In speculative Freemasonry, the trowel is representative of spreading the "cement" of brotherly love and affection to unite the individual members of a lodge into one unified group of brethren. When joined together by the ceremonies and practices of Masonry, the individuals will work together to help each other and society as a whole.

Figure 7-7:
The trowel is a symbol of the uniting of members into a group of brethren.

Image courtesy of Christopher Hodapp

Handshake

A symbol of two hands shaking is representative of the *grip* or *token* of a Freemason, the way members may recognize each other in silence. Masons really do have a secret handshake to recognize one another silently.

Rough and perfect (or smooth) ashlars

The two brick-shaped stones on either side of the middle candle are ashlars. A *rough ashlar* is a rough, squared stone from the quarry that has been shaped but has not yet been made perfectly smooth. A *perfect* (or smooth) *ashlar* is the completed piece of workmanship, made smooth for the use in a building by a craftsman.

The rough ashlar represents man in his rough, rude, and imperfect state. Masons are taught that by education, culture, discipline, and faith, they can become a more perfect person, like the perfect ashlar, thereby fitting themselves "as living stones for that spiritual house, not made with hands, eternal in the heavens."

Pillars

Pillars are one of the most distinctive symbols found in Masonic artwork (see Figure 7-8). Every lodge has some kind of representation of these two pillars, and they're an important part of the Fellow Craft degree ceremony.

Figure 7-8:
The Pillars
of the
Porch, Boaz
and Jachin.

Image courtesy of Christopher Hodapp

The two pillars represent columns that were erected at the entrance to King Solomon's temple. They were made of bronze and named Jachin and Boaz, as 2 Chronicles 3:15–17 describes:

> Also he made before the house two pillars of thirty and five cubits high, and the chapiter that was on the top of each of them was five cubits.

> And he made chains, as in the oracle, and put them on the heads of the pillars; and made an hundred pomegranates, and put them on the chains.

> And he reared up the pillars before the temple, one on the right hand, and the other on the left; and called the name of that on the right hand Jachin, and the name of that on the left Boaz.

A more detailed description appears in 1 Kings 7. The pillars (or *Pillars of the Porch,* as they are sometimes called) that are found in Masonic lodges also have globes on top of them, representing the Earth (terrestrial) and the heavens (celestial). The real pillars of Solomon's Temple didn't have such globes, and the invention was probably due to an illustration in the Geneva Bible published in 1560 showing bowls that looked in print almost like globes.

In the course of the Fellow Craft degree, the candidate passes between the two pillars on his symbolic way into the Middle Chamber of Solomon's Temple. Individually, they represent strength and establishment, and their descriptions from the biblical accounts are explained at length in the ritual.

The shovel, setting maul, coffin, and sprig of acacia

The four symbols at the bottom of Figure 7-1 are images from the Master Mason degree, so I can't reveal all that they represent. But what I can tell you is that the shovel, setting maul, coffin, and sprig of acacia are reminders that death comes to all men, and Freemasonry was born at a time when men lived shorter lives. The threat of an early death was more prevalent than it is today. Medical care was more luck than science. Families were larger, yet the infant mortality rate was much higher. Childhood diseases as well as adult illnesses were far deadlier than in our own time, and entire families were wiped out by epidemics or wars. As a result, images of death were common and perhaps not so shocking or bizarre as they are for us today. Death is a fact of life, and it's ultimately more ominous than the birds and the bees. In some lodges these symbols are accompanied by a skull and crossbones. We tend to associate skulls and crossbones with pirate movies, Nazi SS uniforms, and rat-poison boxes, but a little over a century ago they were common reminders of the fragility of life itself.

Masonic symbols around the world

The symbols in this chapter are the most commonly used ones in U.S. Freemasonry. But other tools and symbols appear outside the United States, such as in the rituals used in England and Scotland. Some of them include the following images:

✔ **Chisel:** The chisel is a working tool of the Entered Apprentice in rituals in the United Kingdom (although it appears in the U.S. version of the Mark Master degree of the York Rite). It teaches perseverance and that perfection can only be achieved by constant work.

✔ **Skerrit:** A *skerrit* is a reel of string with a rod or pin running through the center. The pin is stuck into the ground, and the string is extended, to either draw a circle or to lay out a straight line, frequently when plotting out a building's foundation. In Scottish and English rituals, the skerrit is a working tool of the Master Mason degree. It points out a straight, undeviating line of conduct and morality.

✔ **Pencil:** The pencil teaches that the Great Architect of the Universe observes and records our thoughts, words, and actions, and that we will someday be held accountable for that record. It's also a working tool of the Master Mason degree in Scottish and English rituals.

The skull in alchemy was called *caput mortuum,* the worthless residue of death, and is a symbol of decline and decay. The alchemists of the Middle Ages sought the secret of *transmuting,* or turning ordinary metal into gold or silver. The first part of the process was called *putrefaction,* when the base metal was heated and decomposed into air, water, and earth. Alchemists called this the *Great Work* — the transformation of common, base metal into gold. Likewise, the transformation of a base, common man into a Master Mason is a similar transformation and the great work of the Masonic lodge.

Like the scythe, the symbols of the grave remind Masons that we shall eventually die and turn to dust. The hearty acacia plant, which thrives in the Holy Land, can often seem to spring back to life from little more than a dead branch, and it reminds us of the hope for immortality that unites all religions.

In some French and Scottish rituals, the lodge in the Master Mason degree is decorated in black and is covered with white or silver tears, representing the sorrow of death.

24-inch gauge and the common gavel

The ruler and hammer hanging on the left-hand pillar in Figure 7-1 are known as the 24-inch gauge (a ruler) and the common gavel (a hammer) and are more tools of the stonemasons. Obviously, the gauge is used to measure work, and the gavel is used to break off the corners and edges of rough stone. Speculative Freemasons use them for more symbolic reasons. The 24-inch gauge is representative of the 24 hours of the day, and Masons are taught to divide their day into three equal parts: 8 hours for work, 8 hours to serve God and their fellow men, and 8 hours for rest and sleep.

The gavel is to remind Masons to endeavor to remove the rough edges from their own character, to become more like the perfect ashlar.

Chapter 8

Myths and Misconceptions about Masons

In This Chapter

▶ Considering why myths about Freemasonry are so common

▶ Dismantling prevalent Masonic myths

*W*hen you drive around with a Freemason symbol on your bumper or wear a Masonic ring, you sometimes become a magnet for strange remarks. My father thought I had to ride a goat to join the lodge. My mother's parish priest sent along his condolences for my soul. Our family doctor's new receptionist held court for ten minutes about Freemasons and their rooster sacrifices and how all the sweet, gray-haired, card-playing ladies in our Eastern Star chapter are worshiping Satan.

Start looking for information about Freemasons on the Internet, and the top sites you'll find are anti-Masonic in nature. Masons are accused of dominating world governments, assassinating non-Masonic leaders, stirring up cauldrons of evil potions, hatching the Antichrist, and building orphanages in order to have an endless supply of tots to use in their pedophilic child sacrifices.

Freemasonry has always advised its members to keep silent when faced with people who know nothing about it. The trouble is, when you don't answer them, the pathological liars and unhinged kooks never get balanced by the truth, leaving the confused bystanders, well, confused.

In this chapter, I explore some of the more common myths, misconceptions, fibs, shams, and five-alarm lies spread about Freemasons over the years.

Digging to the Root of Freemasonry Misunderstandings

For a very long time, Freemasons themselves, members in the rank and file, have misunderstood what is meant by *Masonic secrecy*. Technically, the secrets that Masons are forbidden to discuss with the outside world are the grips, passwords, steps, and signs of the degrees. These are *modes of recognition* that allow one Mason to identify another "in the dark as well as the light."

Unfortunately, generations of Masons have taken their obligation of secrecy to mean that they couldn't discuss the fraternity outside of the lodge room. Undoubtedly, some Masons will want me thrown out of the fraternity just for writing this book, despite the fact that I'm not revealing any of those grips, words, steps, and signs.

Part of the reason Freemasons don't fight back is that they're frankly astonished that so many people around the world could have twisted their benevolent, fraternal, charitable organization that seeks to improve society by improving men into fodder for ridicule, hatred, or fear. We just don't get it.

Meanwhile, the rest of the world just can't understand how a bunch of grown men, sworn to secrecy, who meet behind locked doors, guarded by a guy with a sword, can be up to anything good. *They* just don't get it.

The problem is that, in a vacuum of information, people can easily fill in the holes with wrong information — or just plain lies, if you're out to sell books or videos or push your website. The lies get compounded as they're repeated, and modern anti-Masons continue to use misquotes, invented rituals, false sources, and total fabrications from previous centuries. And they're rarely shy about making up new ones. (For much more on this subject, see *Conspiracy Theories & Secret Societies For Dummies* [Wiley], which I coauthored with Alice Von Kannon.)

Debunking Common Myths about Freemasonry

Modern Freemasonry has officially been around since 1717. The first concocted untruths about the Order appeared in print at almost the same time. The United States was consumed by anti-Masonic hysteria in the late 1820s, and Europe has made Mason bashing a popular sport for two centuries, often tying it to anti-Semitic propaganda. The Internet has only served to resurrect these myths, dragging them out and repeating them all over again. In this section I discuss some of the most common ones.

Riding the lodge goat

Let me dispense with this one right off the bat. Freemasons do not ride a goat in their lodges. It's a joke, perpetrated often by Masons themselves on nervous initiates.

Since at least the Middle Ages, the goat has been symbolic of the devil, and stories were circulated then of witches who called forth Satan, who came riding into town on a goat to take part in their blasphemous orgies. Then as the Freemasons gained popularity, detractors accused them of witchcraft, which is probably where the notion of initiates riding a goat came from.

Adding fuel to the myth is the fact that some early ritual books from the fraternity referred to God as *God of All Things* and abbreviated it as G.O.A.T. That expression wasn't used for long, and Masons now refer to God by the acronym G.A.O.T.U., for *Grand Architect of the Universe*.

Old catalogs from fraternal supply companies in the late 1800s actually offered mechanical goats for use in other fraternal organizations and "fun" degrees. As the golden age of fraternalism resulted in literally hundreds of other groups popping up in competition with the Masons, some were obviously less serious than others. Such items only served to perpetuate the myth that Masons and other fraternities required a goat-ride ritual for their initiations. Freemasonry never has.

Rest assured: There is no lodge goat. The degrees of Masonry are serious business to Freemasons, and there is no horseplay (or goatplay).

Keeping an eye on you with the all-seeing eye and the U.S. $1 bill

If you saw the movie *National Treasure* or read Dan Brown's *The Lost Symbol*, you know all about this one. The back of the U.S. $1 bill contains Masonic imagery of the all-seeing eye over an Egyptian pyramid (see Figure 8-1). And everybody knows that's a Masonic symbol, right?

Figure 8-1:
The Great
Seal of
the United
States.

Image courtesy of Christopher Hodapp

Well, not really. The eye and the pyramid are actually part of the Great Seal of the United States, which was put on the back of the $1 bill in 1935. There is indeed an all-seeing eye floating over an unfinished pyramid, with the words *Annuit Coeptis* (Latin for "He [God] has favored our undertakings").

Beneath it are the words *Novus Ordo Seclorum,* which translate as "A new order of the ages." It does *not* mean "a new world order," as has been alleged, which is just one more reason to lament that high schools don't teach Latin classes anymore. ("New world order" would be written as *Novus Ordo Mundi.* So there. Now go conjugate ten irregular verbs.)

A committee of four men, including Benjamin Franklin (the only Freemason in the bunch), designed the Great Seal of the United States in 1776. The only artist among them, Pierre du Simitiere — who was not a Freemason, suggested the image of the eye within a triangle to represent God. And two other committees tinkered with the design before it was approved. Francis Hopkinson (another non-Mason) suggested the unfinished pyramid, and none of the final designers was a Mason.

The eye within a triangle to represent God appears throughout the Renaissance, long before speculative Freemasonry arrived on the scene. The three-sided triangle represents the Christian belief in the Trinity of God — Father, Son, and Holy Spirit. No records associate Freemasonry with the symbol before 1797, nor is the symbol in any way related to the Bavarian Illuminati (see Chapter 2).

As for the unfinished pyramid, it represents the strong, new nation of the United States, destined to stand for centuries, just as the famous pyramids have stood in Egypt. It has 13 rows of stones, representing the 13 original colonies, with the image of God watching over them.

Many Masonic lodges, especially in Europe, display the all-seeing eye just as it is used on the $1 bill — as a nondenominational representation of God. There is nothing sinister or occult about it, and it appears in numerous instances of Christian art from the 1600s onward.

Reading a Masonic bible

Masons have been accused of using their own, presumably Satanic, bible in their ceremonies. Many people have seen Masonic bibles for sale on eBay and elsewhere and clearly believe that Masons don't use the Christian Bible.

This myth is actually a two-part one. A common custom of lodges in predominantly Christian communities is to present the new Master Mason with a commemorative heirloom Bible. In the United States, the most common one is the 1611 translation of the King James version, published especially for Masonic lodges by Heirloom Bible Publishers of Wichita, Kansas. It contains an area in the front for the Mason to commemorate important dates in his degree work, places for his brethren to sign the record of his degrees, and a 94-page glossary of biblical references relating to Masonic ceremonies, along with essays about Masonry and some common questions and answers. The rest of it is the entire King James version of the Old and New Testament that is available in any bookstore.

The second part of this myth has to do with the use of the Volume of Sacred Law in a Masonic lodge. All regular, well-governed lodges must have a book considered sacred to its members open on the lodge altar during meetings. Depending on what part of the world the lodge is in and the beliefs of the lodge's members, this sacred book could be the Bible, the Hebrew Tanach, the Muslim Koran, the Hindu Veda, the Zoroastrian Zend-Avesta, or the Proverbs of Confucius. It's simply referred to as the *Volume of Sacred Law* as a nonsectarian term.

No strange Masonic bibles are used in lodges. In my own lodge, we open a Tanach, a Koran, and a Bible out of respect for the various beliefs of our members.

Some people have alleged that Albert Pike's book, *Morals and Dogma,* is, in fact, the "Masonic bible" that is used as the Volume of Sacred Law. I fill you in on Albert Pike later in this chapter, but here I'll simply say, no, it is not. No regular, recognized, mainstream Masonic lodge or appendant body — not even the Scottish Rite, where Pike is especially admired — would ever use his book as a Volume of Sacred Law.

In the lodges that operate within the Grand Orient of France, atheists are allowed to join. The Grand Orient believes that a man's religious beliefs — or lack of them — are his own business and that lodges would be improper to require him to believe in anything. Furthermore, instead of filling up their altars with many sacred books to satisfy members of many faiths, their lodges are allowed to substitute a book with blank pages as their Volume of Sacred Law, so as not to force any religious beliefs on any of their members. *Remember:* The Grand Orient of France is considered irregular and is unrecognized by mainstream Grand Lodges around the world. Even so, a blank book is no Masonic bible either.

Worshipping strange gods

A Masonic meeting is not an act of worship. A lodge is not a church. And Freemasonry is not a religion. Freemasons use prayers to open and close their meetings, but so do Congress and Parliament. Freemasons take oaths (or *obligations*) on a Bible or other book sacred to the faith of the individual candidate, but so do Supreme Court justices, the President of the United States, police officers, courtroom witnesses, and even Boy Scouts.

Some people have the misconception that Masonic meetings are some sort of bizarre, secret worship service, offered up to a pagan god. Or goddess. Or goat. Or Satan himself. At any rate, no, the meetings are not religious ceremonies. So where did this ridiculous notion come from? Well, it's a long story. . . .

Tracing the hubbub back to Albert Pike

You find references to Albert Pike all through this book. Born in 1809, he can rightly be classified as a genius by anyone's standards. I talk about him at length in Chapter 11; he is a huge figure in the history of U.S. Freemasonry.

In his day, Pike was regarded as the greatest of Masonic scholars and authors. Many of his opinions about the origins of Freemasonry and its ceremonies have since been discounted as provably false, but at the time, Pike was the Mr. Know-It-All of the Craft.

His most famous Masonic feat was the rewriting of the laws, rituals, and lectures of all 33 degrees of the Ancient Accepted Scottish Rite, starting just four years after becoming a Mason in 1850. Pike's commentaries on the degrees were set down in an 860-page tome called *Morals and Dogma,* published in 1871. Most Masonic scholars today agree that *Morals and Dogma* is big, impressive, obscure — and wrong about many of its conclusions.

Pike got some of the material for the book from works by an unreliable French mystic named Eliphas Levi. The occult was a very popular topic in the 1860s, and by the 1890s it was an absolute mania. Levi was an incredibly prolific writer about mystical topics (mostly because what he didn't know, he made up), and Pike took him at his word. Levi claimed that Freemasonry came from ancient pagan mysteries, alchemy, Egyptian mysticism, Kabbalism, Gnosticism, Zoroastrianism, Brahmanism, and a raft of other *–isms,* and Albert Pike believed most of it. (Don't get fidgety; I'm coming to the Satanism part.)

Introducing the beast Baphomet

Levi's 1855 book *Dogme et Rituel de la Haute Magie* (literally, Dogma and Ritual of High Magic) discussed the character of Baphomet. Levi's now-classic drawing shows a creature with the bearded head and horns of a goat, female breasts, cloven hooves, wings, and an upright pentagram on his forehead. One feminine hand points up to the sun, and the masculine hand points down to the darkened moon, an illustration of the Hermetic saying "As above, so below," and a symbol of both good and evil. The perky, snake-wrapped rod rising from his lap is a symbol of eternal life. Baphomet also contains the ancient alchemical elements of earth (it's sits on a globe), fire (flames of intelligence burn on its head), air (it has wings on its back), and water (scales cover its body).

Figure 8-2 shows Baphomet in all its glory. Take a good look at the image here — you won't find it in a Masonic lodge.

The name *Baphomet* came from the trials of the Knights Templar during the early 1300s, in which they were accused of worshipping this demonic creature (see Chapter 10 for a history of the Knights Templar). Levi found gargoyles on Templar buildings on which he based his drawing, and he believed these gargoyles knew mystical secrets of the universe. But Levi didn't regard Baphomet as Satan.

Figure 8-2:
Baphomet, as it appeared on the cover of Eliphas Levi's book.

Illustration courtesy of Christopher Hodapp

Levi described this peculiar entity as the illustrated embodiment of all the forces in the universe, and you can see it's a densely packed little conceptual drawing. Unfortunately for Levi, most people glance at it and say, "Satan!" Face it — it *looks* like what we all figure Satan to look like. It didn't help that Baphomet popped up as the most popular illustration for the Devil in tarot card decks, either.

So what does this have to do with Freemasonry? In reality, absolutely nothing, but that never stopped a good urban legend. Enter Leo Taxil.

Revealing the whoppers of Leo Taxil

Leo Taxil was one of the greatest purveyors of Masonic lies of all times. That's not my estimation, it was his own — and he gleefully admitted it after duping the Western world for years with one increasingly ridiculous anti-Masonic book after another.

He was born as Gabriel Jogand-Pagès in 1854 in France. After a stint at writing Victorian-era porn, followed by making a paltry living at authoring anti-Catholic tracts, he turned on the Freemasons. Unlike the Church, here was a group he could write almost anything about and get away with it because the Masons wouldn't fight back. And his ultimate goal was to create a hoax so ridiculous that it would make Catholics who believed in it look like fools.

In 1889, Taxil invented an elaborate and completely fictitious, supersecret order of Freemasonry called the *Palladium,* which supposedly admitted women, conducted sexual orgies, performed ritual murder, and most important, worshipped a demon called Baphomet. Albert Pike was the alleged head of the organization. Taxil perpetrated the following story:

> On July 14, 1889, Albert Pike, Sovereign Pontiff of Universal Freemasonry, addressed to the 23 Supreme Confederated Councils of the world the following instructions. . . .
>
> *That which we must say to a crowd is — We worship a God, but it is the God that one adores without superstition. To you, Sovereign Grand Inspectors General, we say this, that you may repeat it to the Brethren of the 32nd, 31st, and 30th degrees — The Masonic Religion should be by all of us initiates of the high degrees, maintained in the purity of the Luciferian Doctrine.*
>
> *If Lucifer were not God, would Adonay whose deeds prove his cruelty, perfidy, and hatred of man, barbarism and repulsion for science, would Adonay and his priests, calumniate him? Yes, Lucifer is God, and unfortunately Adonay is also god. For the eternal law is that there is no light without shade, no beauty without ugliness, no white without black, for the absolute can only exist as two gods; darkness being necessary to the statue, and the brake to the locomotive.*

Thus, the doctrine of Satanism is a heresy; and the true and pure philosophical religion is the belief in Lucifer, the equal of Adonay; but Lucifer, God of Light and God of Good, is struggling for humanity against Adonay, the God of Darkness and Evil.

To add the one-two punch to all this drivel, the cover of the book containing this story included an illustration of a woman outside of a Palladium meeting, holding a severed head of a victim, as Baphomet sits in the background, surrounded by enthusiastic Masonic worshippers.

Scary stuff. And not one word of it is true. Pike never said it. Pike never wrote it. Pike was never Sovereign Pontiff of Universal Freemasonry, nor was anyone else for that matter — the job never existed. There were no Supreme Confederated Councils. There is no Masonic Religion. And Freemasons never have been taught a Luciferian Doctrine, whatever that is.

Other parts don't make sense, either. In the United States, Masons who join the Scottish Rite go through the degrees at different times, but virtually all of them receive the 32nd degree very quickly after joining, even if they don't receive many of the others at the same time. So by limiting a super-duper secret to the 30th-degree, 31st-degree, and 32nd-degree members, 99 percent of the members would be included anyway.

Besides, Pike was dead by this time. It's always safe to slander a dead man from across the sea.

Taxil went on in 1897 to publicly admit his lies, while making merciless fun of anyone who had believed them. He was especially gleeful that he had duped the Catholic Church, all the way up to the pope, into issuing anti-Masonic statements.

Nevertheless, anti-Masonic authors continue to drag out this bilge with great regularity and claim Masons worship Satan. Because of Taxil, unfortunately, the Freemasons, Albert Pike, and the great horned demon Baphomet are forever intertwined. For more about Taxil, see Chapter 18.

Pairing up Pike and Lucifer

As I mention earlier in this chapter, Albert Pike's *Morals and Dogma* is a very long book. He was a student of world religions, world civilizations, and philosophies. He had a voracious mind that constantly sought new knowledge. His personal library, preserved today in the Scottish Rite's House of the Temple in Washington, D.C., was enormous in its scope. *Morals and Dogma* is literally a textbook in comparative religious studies. In it, he explains what ancient and foreign cultures have believed and how it affected their religions.

Buried in the book is a sentence that has been quoted time and again as proof that Albert Pike was a Satanist and that he wrote secret Satan worship into the degrees of the Scottish Rite. It says, "*Lucifer, the Son of the Morning! Is it he who bears the Light, and with its splendors intolerable blinds feeble, sensual, or selfish Souls? Doubt it not!*"

Go ahead, say it. A-ha! There it is! Satan worship just as plain as day! Because everybody knows that Lucifer is Satan. There is, however, a problem with flogging Pike over talking about Lucifer, and it got lost in translation.

Spotting Lucifer in the King James Bible

Lucifer shows up in the Old Testament in Isaiah 14:12: "How art thou fallen from heaven, O Lucifer, son of the morning! How art thou cut down to the ground, which didst weaken the nations!" That's the only reference to Lucifer in the King James Bible, and it's a Latin name, not a Hebrew one.

According to biblical scholars, the original text of the 14th chapter of Isaiah is *not* about a fallen angel, but about a fallen Babylonian king who had persecuted the Israelites. Satan is never mentioned in the chapter, by name or by inference. In fact, if you read all of Isaiah 14, and not just one selected sentence, you'll see that he clearly refers to the subject of his writing as an evil king, and most definitely a man. The Hebrew texts referred to the king by his ceremonial title, *Helal, son of Shahar,* which is translated to mean "Day Star, son of the Dawn."

In Latin, Lucifer is the name given by Roman astronomers to the Morning Star, the bright planet seen in the dawn sky. We know it as Venus. Lucifer actually comes from the Latin term *lucem ferre,* meaning "the bearer of light," and the star was called this because it appeared in the sky just before the sun. The symbolism was that the star called Lucifer was the herald that announced the arrival of the sun in the morning.

Unfortunately, scholars mistranslated the king's flowery title "Day Star, son of the Dawn," into the Roman word *Lucifer.* Lucifer the morning star was transformed by the error in translation by careless readers into a disobedient angel, cast out of heaven to rule eternally in hell. The translators didn't understand that the term was actually describing the king's position, or that he had fallen from it. Instead, it remained and appears to be a name, not a state of being.

We have John Milton's 1667 book *Paradise Lost* to thank for branding Lucifer in the Western mind as a proper name for Satan. Theologians, writers, poets, and the occasional mystic have compounded the error far beyond anything in the single reference in Isaiah, and Lucifer has become just another moniker for Satan, the devil, and paradoxically, the Prince of Darkness.

Just as a side note, the New English Bible translates Isaiah 14:12 as: "How you have fallen from heaven, bright morning star. . . ." Lucifer is nowhere to be found. And to get *really* obscure, the original Latin Vulgate texts used the term *Lucifer* many times to describe the morning star, or the "bearer of light," including descriptions of Jesus himself (II Peter 1:19 and Apocalypse 22:1). No matter what your Sunday school teacher told you, no matter what they told you at vacation Bible school, no matter what Milton wrote in *Paradise Lost,* the Lucifer referred to in Isaiah 14 — the only reference to Lucifer in the King James Bible — is *not* Satan.

Getting at Pike's intention

Okay, so if this Lucifer stuff is so obscure, why did Pike put it in his book, knowing full well that most Christians believe that Lucifer *is* Satan anyway? As Pike's passage goes on, he is plainly saying how odd it is that the Prince of Darkness is called by a name that means "bearer of light." Again, *Morals and Dogma* is a massive book that is very concerned with tracing where cultural and religious ideas came from. Pike was trying to tell a rough, and not especially well-educated, population to search for the origins of customs and rituals, because he truly felt that a deeper understanding of what came before made a man more religious and contemplative.

And honestly, there was a certain amount of intellectual showing off going on, too. If there wasn't, his book would be about one-third of its length and weight.

Just so you know, the terms *Lucifer* and *Luciferian* do not appear in any recognized ritual or lecture of Freemasonry, including the Scottish Rite rituals written by Albert Pike. He was a devout Christian, and his own beliefs would certainly classify him today in the born-again category of Christianity — the very people who frequently accuse him of being a Satan worshipper.

Taking over the world

The actor Howard Da Silva often told a story about a friend who was called before the House Un-American Activities Committee during the very nervous 1950s Cold War. When Da Silva's friend was asked if he was a communist, his snappy comeback was, "We're not allowed to tell." Most people figure that Freemasonry is the same way.

Masons are forbidden to discuss politics in the lodge. Finalizing world-takeover plans is tough if you have to disguise it as discussion about Saturday's fish fry or who's supposed to cut the lodge lawn. Lodge rituals differ from one jurisdiction to another. Grand Lodges disagree on a wide variety of issues. And no cohesive, international governing body runs the Masons. For a bunch of guys who are taking over the world, we're mighty disorganized.

Regular, recognized, mainstream Freemasonry does not now, nor has it ever, aspired to be a world-dominating, secret empire. Nor does it aspire to be the controlling gray eminences behind the thrones, another common charge. Freemasonry is a fraternal organization that simply seeks to improve men so they may, in turn, improve society around them. It doesn't tell them how to do that, nor does it give them political, commercial, or religious marching orders. Some 18th- and 19th-century kings and religious leaders distrusted Freemasonry because it encouraged freedom of thought, freedom of religion, and freedom of expression, the very antithesis of what most conspiracy theorists accuse it of.

Have some Freemasons, or men who called themselves Freemasons, used the basic organization and ceremonies of the Craft to create their own secret societies with less-than-virtuous goals? Certainly — and they were driven from the ranks of the fraternity when their activities were discovered. Moreover, the Grand Master, the leading officer in a Grand Lodge, has the supreme power during his term of office to suspend Masons accused of wrongdoing, and even to suspend entire lodges if their membership engages in un-Masonic or illegal conduct.

Still, this idea that Masons want to rule the world remains one of the most common misconceptions about the Craft. Yes, I know, if I were involved in a secret, worldwide conspiracy, of course I'd tell you it didn't exist. That's just what you'd expect me to say, right?

Breaking the law

Having a Masonic license plate or bumper sticker on your car will not get you out of a traffic ticket, so don't try it. Brother judges and police officers don't stop upholding the law just because a Mason gives them a secret handshake.

For lovers of conspiracies, secret societies make great targets. The truth is that Freemasonry, as an institution, has no power to control its members, privately or professionally. Non-Masons commonly believe that Freemasons swear to protect each other and keep each other's secrets, but Masons aren't sworn to keep quiet about treason, murder, or other criminal acts. A Mason's obligation is to uphold the laws of the country in which he resides, and his obligations to his God, his country, and his own family take precedence over his obligations to his Brother Masons. Further, Masons who engage in illegal behavior are subject to the bringing of Masonic charges, a legal action within the fraternity, and to be tried and reprimanded or suspended if found guilty.

Part III

When One Lodge Isn't Enough: The Appendant Bodies

The 5th Wave   By Rich Tennant

"Yes, I recently joined the Mystic Order of the Noble Yam. How'd you know?"

In this part . . .

Masons quickly figured out that if three degrees were enlightening and fun, then more degrees could be even *more* enlightening and even *more* fun. Freemasonry offers something for everybody, and in this part I prove it. I talk about the different branches of Freemasonry and the many organizations that Masons and their whole families can join.

Chapter 9

Introducing the Appendant Bodies: Who's Who, and Who Isn't

In This Chapter

▶ Defining appendant and concordant bodies

▶ Identifying non-Masonic groups

T he three Masonic degrees of Ancient Craft Freemasonry are fun, interesting, and enlightening. The study of their history, philosophy, symbolism, and ritual can consume a lifetime of research and practice. But after the formation of the Grand Lodge of England in 1717, Masons couldn't resist tinkering with things. If three degrees were enlightening and fun, Masons quickly decided more degrees could be even more enlightening and even more fun! Thus were born the *appendant bodies* of Freemasonry.

At first, these appendant bodies were attempts to embellish the story told by the first three degrees. They filled in more of the story of the building of Solomon's Temple in Jerusalem. Then they branched out to dramatize more lessons of morality and virtue.

These new degrees first developed in individual lodges, and other Masons saw them or heard about them. Grand Lodges quickly established rules that said a lodge could only present the first three degrees of Masonry — not any of the new degrees. The result: These increasingly popular new degrees were orphaned and needed to be presented by some group other than the individual neighborhood lodges. As more degree rituals were written, they often called for more theatrical presentations, with props and costumes, portrayed on stages rather than in lodge rooms. Eventually many of these widely disparate, unrelated degrees were gathered together to be presented by larger, cohesive, governing organizations.

In this part of the book, I give you a look at these many groups and explain them in more depth. This particular chapter provides a brief overview of the overall organization of the Masonic community, who can join these additional bodies, and why anyone would. Here I also tell you about some of the groups who *aren't* Freemasons, just to help you keep things straight about who is and who isn't.

Figure 9-1 is a chart you'll want to refer back to as you read this chapter; it outlines the different appendant bodies, along with their symbols, so you can see how they relate to one another.

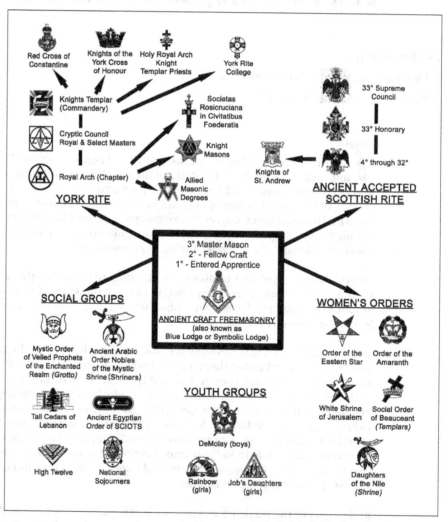

Figure 9-1: The appendant bodies of Freemasonry.

Illustration by Wiley, Composition Services Graphics

What Are Appendant Bodies?

Appendant means just what it sounds like — appendages, or things attached to something else. The word is used to describe groups that require you to be a Master Mason (or to have a relationship to a Mason) as a prerequisite for joining.

Keep in mind that every regular and recognized Grand Lodge has the sole authority in its jurisdiction to confer the three lodge degrees of Entered Apprentice, Fellow Craft, and Master Mason. *No other appendant body is allowed to confer the three degrees.* Any group that claims otherwise is in violation of accepted Masonic law. Every Grand Lodge, in every state or country, has its own rules about what other Masonic groups its members may join, and each and every Grand Lodge decides what other groups operating in its territory are compatible with its own Masonic laws.

Depending on the terminology preferred by the local Grand Lodge, you may hear these groups described as either *appendant* or *concordant.* Technically, a *concordant* group confers additional Masonic degrees that are considered to be a continuation of the basic three lodge degrees. These groups normally are the York Rite (see Chapter 10) and the Ancient Accepted Scottish Rite (see Chapter 11). Jurisdictions that make a distinction between *concordant* and *appendant* regard any other group that requires Masonic membership or relation to a Mason as *appendant.* Confused? Don't let it worry you. If you refer to any of these groups as *appendant,* most Masons will know what you're talking about.

The appendant/concordant bodies developed over the years to address different interests of Masons. The York and Scottish Rite degrees grew in England and France during the late 1700s and early 1800s out of a literary mania for writing rituals based on biblical and legendary sources. Women's groups came about in the mid-1800s to blunt anti-Masonic criticism and to cater to the new women's suffragette movement. The fun-loving, freewheeling party groups started in the 1870s as a reaction against alcohol prohibition, stern ceremonial obsession, and grim seriousness in the Masonic lodges. The Knights Templar started their marching drill teams after the Civil War, as veterans' groups and others cultivated a national obsession with parades and military regalia. The youth groups came about after World War I, as interest in scouting among children and teens became a worldwide phenomenon.

Concordant bodies

The concordant bodies confer additional Masonic degrees that enlarge and expand on the three degrees of the Masonic lodge. You must already be a Master Mason before you can join these groups.

Until 2000, the Shriners, a popular social branch of U.S. Freemasonry, required Masons to be members of a Masonic lodge and complete the degrees of the York Rite or the Scottish Rite before being allowed to join in its fun. One effect of the old requirement was to lead some new Masons to believe that the Shrine was the pinnacle of Masonic achievement. This requirement has since been dropped, and the Shrine now accepts all Master Masons. This change has forced the U.S. York and Scottish rites to reinvigorate themselves on their own merits, instead of relying on a stream of new candidates every year just passing through on their way to becoming Shriners. Outside the United States, the Shrine is largely unheard of, and the two Rites have always been seen as more serious endeavors, rather than as simply a steppingstone to another group.

York Rite

York Rite is a term used to describe a system of degrees that developed over many years, mostly in England.

Some scholars dispute the term *York Rite,* preferring the terms *Capitular, Cryptic,* and *Chivalric* systems. Outside of the U.S., it's referred to as the *American Rite.*

In the United States, the York Rite is divided into three smaller, cooperating groups that confer ten degrees: Three or four Royal Arch degrees, depending on the jurisdiction; three Cryptic Mason degrees; and three Chivalric Orders of Christian Knighthood (culminating in the Knights Templar Order). The Royal Arch and Cryptic degrees don't require a belief in Christianity, but the Templar Order is most decidedly Christian based. York Rite degrees are usually conferred in a lodgelike setting with candidates participating in the ceremonies.

The York Rite is extremely complex because it developed over a long period of time in a pretty chaotic manner. The U.S. York Rite degrees are organized differently from the Rite degrees in Canada, the United Kingdom, and elsewhere. Additional groups operate within the York Rite, including the Allied Masonic Degrees, Knight Masons, York Rite College, Holy Royal Arch Knight Templar Priests, Knights of the York Cross of Honor, the Red Cross of Constantine, and more. These groups offer further degrees and honors to York Rite Masons after they've completed the ten basic ones. After you start joining these groups, it's like eating potato chips — you can't stop.

I go into much more detail about the York Rite in Chapter 10.

Laboring in the obscure

Since Freemasonry's modern beginnings in 1717, literally thousands of degrees, systems, orders, and rites claiming to be Masonic have been written, performed, and conferred with widely varying measures of popularity and success. Some were written by true scholars and legitimately provide philosophical and practical knowledge and benefits to their recipients, in keeping with the ideology of Freemasonry. Others were simply designed as get-rich-quick schemes, providing grandiose titles in nonexistent lodges with fabulous-looking degree certificates for a group that existed only on paper, in a post office box, or in the fertile mind of its inventor. And many others fell somewhere in the vast chasm between intellectual enlightenment and utter crap.

The decision of which Masonic bodies became accepted as legitimate and which were cast into the abyss of obscurity, scorn, or ridicule was often mercurial. History books and rule books are generally written by the winners, and a degree, or system of degrees, was usually accepted as regular and recognized after it became popular within the ranks of a Grand Lodge. The York Rite and the Scottish Rite are the two primary groups of such degrees in the United States and generally throughout the rest of the world, with some local differences.

The Grand College of Rites of the United States of America is a regular Masonic body open to any Master Mason. It was established in 1932 to study the history and ritual of all rites, systems, and orders of Freemasonry not under the current control of any existing, regular, and recognized Grand Lodge or other Masonic body. Its primary goal is the collection and preservation of rituals of various rites, orders, and systems of Freemasonry that would otherwise not be available to Masonic historians.

One of the other purposes of the Grand College of Rites is the prevention of any efforts to resuscitate or perpetuate these old rites, systems, and orders in the United States. It does this by scouring the world for copies of obscure rites and degrees, publishing them in its annual *Collectanea,* and thus copyrighting and controlling them. The Grand College of Rites performs a service for Grand Lodges by preventing upstarts from digging up some moldy old French degree ritual, sticking a flag in the ground, and claiming to be regular Freemasons. The Grand College of Rites hasn't always been entirely successful, but it has cut down on the spread of irregular, unrecognized Freemasonry, especially in the United States.

Ancient Accepted Scottish Rite

You may have heard of 32nd-degree and 33rd-degree Masons before. Technically, they are 32nd-degree and 33rd-degree *Scottish Rite* Masons.

The Scottish Rite did not come from Scotland. Its origins are actually French, and it came to America in the 1700s. The first Scottish Rite Supreme Council was founded in Charleston, South Carolina, in 1801. Today, there are two national governing bodies in the United States:

✔ The **Northern Masonic Jurisdiction (NMJ)** was formed in 1867 and includes the 15 states east of the Mississippi River and north of the Mason-Dixon Line and the Ohio River.

✔ The **Southern Jurisdiction (SJ)** covers the 35 remaining states, the District of Columbia, and other U.S. territories and possessions.

Outside the United States, the governing structures and divisions of the Scottish Rite are very different, and each jurisdiction has its own way of dealing with these additional degrees.

The Scottish Rite confers degrees 4 through 32, and degrees are generally presented as theatrical plays, with costumes, props, sets, and special effects. Unlike the York Rite, candidates generally view the plays from the audience, and because of the elaborate and expensive nature of such productions, they're put on only a few times a year. There are substantial differences between the degrees in the Northern and Southern jurisdictions, but both groups recognize each other as regular.

In addition, the 33rd degree is an honorary degree awarded by each Supreme Council for outstanding service to the Rite, Freemasonry, or humanity. I go into much more detail about the Scottish Rite in Chapter 11.

Appendant bodies

Masons needed to let their hair down sometimes. Thus, the social groups were born. Meanwhile, the family got tired of being left at home by Dad every night of the week as his busy lodge schedule kept him away more and more. New groups were created for wives and children so they could share in Dad's new friendships and life at the lodge.

The rest of the groups I briefly list in the following sections don't confer Masonic degrees, and most Grand Lodges don't regard them as "Masonic organizations." They're simply groups that require members to be a Master Mason or the relative of a Master Mason. They're often referred to as being part of the "Family of Freemasonry." I discuss these groups in greater detail in Chapters 12 and 13.

The social groups

A variety of social groups for Masons concentrate on fun and social activities. They include the following:

✔ Ancient Arabic Nobles of the Mystic Shrine (now officially known as the Shriners; see Chapter 12)

✔ Mystic Order of the Veiled Prophets of the Enchanted Realm (the Grotto; see Chapter 13)

"Dues card and a pin? I'm in!"

At the height of Masonic popularity in the 1950s, it was very common for a Mason and his family to belong to every concordant group and appendant body in Masonry. Collecting degrees, membership cards, commemorative lapel pins, honorary medals, and funny hats became a fun, if expensive, hobby for many Masons. There was something Masonic to do every night of the week for the man of the house, as well as for everyone in the family, plus state and national conventions to attend.

One of the side effects of this trend was that, although Masonry was a great place to forge new friendships, the Masonic lodge became little more than an introductory step to the larger, complex world of the extended Masonic family. Lodges were strongly pressured to keep their dues costs artificially low because Masons just had so many other groups to pay dues to. The new Mason rarely had the opportunity to study the ceremonies and symbolism of the first three degrees because his friends often immediately pressured him to join the Rites, and then the Shrine, and then get himself (and his wife) into the Eastern Star. Masonry of the 1950s and 1960s became a colossal social event.

Many lodges today are suffering from this legacy of cheap dues and a dizzying array of other opportunities for Masons to join and frolic in. They're also facing significant maintenance costs for the elaborate buildings that were constructed during the heyday of Freemasonry. As financial reality sets in, some lodges will undoubtedly have to shrink, merge, or close. The appendant bodies face an even tougher time as younger men are discovering Freemasonry but shunning the other groups. Time will tell which of these appendant groups will remain strong. Some will reinvent themselves, while others will no doubt fail.

- Tall Cedars of Lebanon (see Chapter 13)
- Ancient Egyptian Order of SCIOTS (see Chapter 13)
- National Sojourners (a Masonic veterans organization; see Chapter 13)
- High Twelve International (see Chapter 13)

Androgynous groups

I'm not talking about David Bowie, Tilda Swinton, or Adam Lambert. Androgynous groups in the Masonic sense are open to Master Masons as well as their wives, daughters, and other female relations. Bear in mind that these groups don't have degrees of Freemasonry for women. They're simply groups made up of women who have a connection to members of the Masonic fraternity.

- Order of the Eastern Star
- Order of the Amaranth
- White Shrine of Jerusalem
- Daughters of the Nile (a Shrine organization)
- Social Order of the Beauceant (a Templar organization)

For more information on androgynous groups, see Chapter 13.

The youth groups

These groups are for children of Masons or are operated by Masons for children in the community (whether the children's fathers are Masons or not):

- ✔ DeMolay International (for boys)
- ✔ Job's Daughters International (for girls)
- ✔ International Order of the Rainbow (for girls)

For more information on youth groups, see Chapter 13.

So What about These Other Groups?

So far, this chapter has addressed the many groups that have some kind of Masonic affiliation. Now I want to fill you in on some other groups that sound similar but are *not* made up of Freemasons. Masons can and do join some of them, but the groups have no Masonic connection.

I include them here because knowing who is *not* connected to Freemasonry, in spite of many similarities, is useful. What's important to know is that Masonry was the first fraternal organization in the world and remains the largest and oldest.

Knowing about these groups is also useful, not only for their past and present service to society and their millions of members, but also to help you identify that old sash, sword, or lapel pin of Grandpa's you found in the attic. The following sections describe the common groups that survive today. I mention others that have not survived into the 21st century in Chapter 2.

Animal lodges

I refer to these as the animal lodges, because there was a common trend in the late 1800s of naming fraternities after a wide menagerie of critters.

Loyal Order of Moose

In 1888, Dr. John Henry Wilson started the Loyal Order of Moose (www.moose intl.org) in Louisville, Kentucky, as a men's social club. After a small growth into Ohio, Indiana, and Missouri, it languished and all but disappeared until 1906, when James J. Davis, a Welsh immigrant in Indiana, joined a local Moose lodge and completely transformed it. Davis helped to convert Moose into an insurance-benefit organization for working-class people. In just six years, it grew from 2 lodges and 247 members to 100 lodges of 500,000 members. Today, it operates Mooseheart, an Illinois home for destitute children, and Moosehaven, a retirement home in Florida. It is an international organization with 1.5 million members, concentrating on service to the community.

Benevolent and Protective Order of Elks

In 1868, Charles Vivian and a group of fellow English and American theatrical performers living in New York City formed the Benevolent and Protective Order of Elks (www.elks.org) as a drinking club called the Jolly Corks. Vivian's friends wanted a more noble organization dedicated to fraternalism, and they patterned it after an English fraternal group, the Royal Antediluvian Order of Buffaloes. They replaced the buffaloes with the American elk, it being "fleet of foot, timorous of doing wrong, but ever ready to combat in defense of self or of the female of the species." Today, the order is a fraternal, charitable, and service organization with more than 1 million members.

Fraternal Order of Eagles

The Fraternal Order of Eagles (www.foe.com) began as the Order of Good Things in Seattle, Washington, in 1898. Six competing theater owners started it while they commiserated with each other over a musicians' strike and enjoyed a drink or three. After a few weeks, others joined them in the entertainment business. They adopted the bald eagle as their mascot and officially dubbed themselves the Fraternal Order of Eagles. They refer to their local groups not as lodges but as *aeries,* a word meaning "eagles' nests."

In the beginning, they were primarily made up of entertainers, stagehands, musicians, and other theater people. As shows traveled the United States and Canada, the fraternity grew rapidly, and the Eagles were among the first fraternal groups to offer medical care and other health and insurance benefits to their members. They also became active in lobbying for fair labor laws, workmen's compensation, Social Security, and other retirement- and labor-related issues. Today, the Eagles operate a retirement home and are involved in social and patriotic issues.

Service clubs

The international service clubs all began in a similar fashion over a period of 15 years. All were started as business-oriented groups and quickly changed their mission to a more charitable one, helping their communities. These four are the most prominent and best-known service clubs.

Rotary International

In 1905, Paul P. Harris started Rotary International (www.rotary.org) in Chicago as a social and professional club to promote high ethical standards among business leaders. It has become famous for its "Four-Way Test" of ethics:

- ✔ Is it the truth?
- ✔ Is it fair to all concerned?
- ✔ Will it build goodwill and better friendships?
- ✔ Will it be beneficial to all concerned?

After World War II, Rotary became actively involved in United Nations programs. Today, it promotes international cultural and educational exchanges. Rotary is a strong advocate of volunteerism among its 1.2 million members worldwide.

Lions Clubs International

Chicago businessman Melvin Jones started Lions Club International (www.lionsclubs.org) in 1917. Jones's dream was a business organization that had unselfish community service as its mission. In 1925, Helen Keller addressed the Lions national convention and encouraged the club to help her in the fight against blindness. Since that time, its primary charity has been sight-related programs. It also worked with the United Nations to develop the role of nongovernment organizations around the world. Lions have 1.4 million members worldwide.

Note: In case you're wondering, I don't group the Lions with the other animal groups because its mission from the beginning was very different from the animal fraternities.

Kiwanis International

Kiwanis International (www.kiwanis.org) was formed in Detroit in 1915 as a way to foster business contacts. Within four years, its mission evolved into being more community-service oriented, and its primary charities help children. The name *Kiwanis* supposedly comes from a Native American expression, *Nunc Kee-wanis,* meaning, "we trade" or "we have a good time." Kiwanis has 300,000 members in 96 countries.

Sertoma

Sertoma (www.sertoma.org) was created in Kansas City, Missouri, as the Co-Operative Club in 1912. The term *Sertoma* was coined in 1949 from its slogan "SERvice TO MAnkind." Its programs include community-service matching grants, youth programs, and grants for deaf and hard-of-hearing students as well as graduate students studying audiology and speech pathology. Sertoma has 20,000 members in the United States, Canada, Mexico, and Puerto Rico.

Other unrelated fraternal groups

The United States in the 1800s was fertile ground for fraternal organizations that seemed to mostly be carbon copies of Freemasonry. Many lifted the organizational structure and terminology of Masonry directly and simply substituted their own ceremonial rituals. During the anti-Masonic period between the 1820s and the 1850s, these competing groups popped up everywhere (see Chapter 2 for more details).

Here are the primary surviving groups that, on the surface, may appear to be Masonic, but are, in fact, their own unique organizations.

Independent Order of Odd Fellows

The fraternity with perhaps the funniest of names began in London in the 1740s. The term *odd fellow* is thought to have been used to describe members of professions that had no trade guild or union of their own. In many ways, its organization into lodges and grand lodges (accompanied by schisms between competing grand lodges) mirrored the development of the Freemasons during almost exactly the same time period.

The Odd Fellows (www.ioof.org) came to the United States in 1806, and in 1834 the Independent Order of Odd Fellows separated from its English counterpart. Its symbol is made up of three links of a chain, which stand for friendship, love, and truth. Odd Fellows are taught that they all have a duty to visit the sick, relieve the distressed, bury their dead, and educate the orphan.

Many similarities exist between Odd Fellows and Freemasonry in ritual, beliefs, and organization. Like Masonry, the group requires a belief in a Supreme Being, and it forbids religious and political discussion in the lodge. It has affiliated women's groups (called Rebekahs), youth groups, a military unit similar to the Masonic Knights Templar called the Patriarchs Militant, retirement homes, and orphanages.

At the end of the 19th century, the Odd Fellows held a slight edge over Freemasonry in terms of membership numbers. The 20th century was not as kind to the Independent Order of Odd Fellows, and it has suffered tremendous membership losses. Nevertheless, it remains the largest international fraternal organization in the world governed by one central authority.

Improved Order of Red Men

The Improved Order of Red Men (www.redmen.org) claims to have been formed in 1765 as the Sons of Liberty. Yep, the ones you read about in U.S. History 101 who dressed up as Indians and dumped all that tea into Boston Harbor. Doubtful, but a colorful story.

The current Improved Order of Red Men was formed in 1847 in Baltimore and patterned its ceremonies and organization on Iroquois tribal traditions.

Local lodges are called *tribes*. The Red Men have a strong patriotic heritage, and their public programs often center on flag ceremonies. They erected a chapel at Valley Forge to commemorate the bitter winter encampment of Washington and his troops during the Revolutionary War, and they conduct services at Arlington National Cemetery. They have a women's group (Pocahontas), and youth groups (Hiawatha for boys and Anona for girls). Today the group has about 38,000 members.

Order of the Knights of Pythias

Formed in 1864 by Justus H. Rathbone in Washington, D.C., the Order of the Knights of Pythias (www.pythias.org) was the first fraternal organization to be chartered by the U.S. Congress. Its formation was, in fact, encouraged by President Abraham Lincoln to help heal the wounds of the Civil War by teaching brotherly love and friendship. Its name and ritual ceremonies are based on the ancient Greek story of Damon and Pythias, which was dramatized into a very popular play in 1821 by an Irish author named John Banim.

In the Banim play, Damon and Pythias are two friends in the school of the Greek philosopher Pythagoras. When Damon is imprisoned and condemned to death for speaking against the king of Syracuse, his friend Pythias agrees to be a hostage so that Damon can be allowed to leave prison and say farewell to his wife and child. Damon's return is delayed, and Pythias is to be executed in his place. At the final moment before being beheaded, Damon returns, pushes Pythias out of the way and tells the king to spare his friend and to carry out his own death sentence. The king is so moved by the honesty, brotherly love, and devotion of the two men that they are both spared and made royal advisors.

Like Masonry, Pythianism is religious but nonsectarian.

Knights of Columbus

Catholics have been forbidden by the Vatican from joining the Freemasons since 1738, but that doesn't mean Catholics don't want to engage in fraternal fun. In 1882, Father Michael McGivney, a priest in New Haven, Connecticut, started the Knights of Columbus (www.kofc.org). A strong wave of anti-Catholic sentiment affected the United States at that time, so Father McGivney's Order of Knights gave Catholics their own fraternity and a sense of public pride in their religion. It was named after Christopher Columbus, the Catholic discoverer of America, and the group's mission was clearly designed to compete with other popular fraternities. It vowed to assist widows and orphans of members, along with providing insurance plans.

The Knights offer four ceremonial degrees, dealing with charity, unity, fraternity, and patriotism. It has military drill teams called the Fourth Degree Color Corps. In fact, when the Masonic Knights Templar, the Odd Fellows' Patriarchs Militant, the Knights of Columbus's Color Corps, and many others all marched in parades, these very similar-looking military drill team orders were the proud public faces of these fraternities.

The Knights of Columbus is the world's largest Catholic family fraternal service organization, with 11,000 councils and nearly 1.6 million members. Members are involved in volunteer service programs for the Catholic Church, their communities, their families, young people, and each other. Unlike the Freemasons, the Knights of Columbus takes strong positions on social issues in line with Catholic doctrine. All members must be of the Catholic faith.

In recent years, Masonic groups and the Knights of Columbus have engaged in joint activities such as fundraisers and fellowship breakfasts to spread the friendship of fraternalism and breach disagreements from long ago.

Woodmen of the World

Woodmen of the World (www.woodmen.com) was started in 1883 in Omaha, Nebraska, by Joseph Cullen Root as a fraternal benefit society. Originally called the Modern Woodmen of America, Root had been inspired by a minister's sermon that talked about "the work of the pioneer woodmen clearing away the forest." Root liked the analogy of clearing a member's financial burden to provide for his family, along with the nice tie-in with his own name and tree-root symbolism. Essentially, the Woodmen became an insurance company with an initiation ritual.

They became known for providing members' widows with $100 and a free headstone for their deceased Brother, in the shape of a tree stump, with the group's logo on it. After a schism within the organization, it became the Woodmen of the World, and today it's the largest fraternal insurance and financial benefit organization in the world. The Woodmen have 2,000 lodges and more than 80,000 members.

Masonic-sounding groups

Lots of groups sound like they *might* be Masons, even though they aren't. Masons who got impatient, put off, or just plain thrown out started some of them. A few grew out of authentic Masonic philosophy. Others are no more than blatant rip-offs of Freemasonry.

Ordo Templi Orientis (Order of Oriental Templars)

Ordo Templi Orientis is a pseudo-Masonic group popularized by the famous magician, mystic, adventurer, con artist, and all around professional British pervert Aleister Crowley. The group was originally started in about 1901 as an unrecognized, irregular, mystical variation of Masonry by Theodor Reuss, a German con man who designed it as a rip-off of Masonry with "sexual magic" thrown into its ceremonies. Crowley joined later and added his own sexual kinks and Satan-worship details. Eventually, Crowley took over as head of the order, making the *Ordo Templi Orientis* a handmaiden of his own invented religion, Thelema, as well as a private playground for his occult and bizarre sexual interests.

British and U.S. variations of *Ordo Templi Orientis* exist, and it has gained renewed popularity in recent years. The *caliph* (leader) of the California group goes by the name of Hymenaeus Beta (slightly more impressive than his birth name, William Breeze). It teaches the practice of sexual and occult "magick," and has its own religion, *Ecclesia Gnostica Catholica* (Gnostic Catholic Church). Its 61 degrees sound exactly like Freemasonry, and its lodges use Masonic regalia, officers' titles, and rituals from old Masonic exposés. Some lodges even teach their members how to "infiltrate" regular Masonic lodges. But *Ordo Templi Orientis* is most definitely *not* regular or recognized Freemasonry, and regular Masons need to be aware of them.

Hermetic Order of the Golden Dawn

The Hermetic Order of the Golden Dawn is a mystical fraternity formed in London in 1888 by A. F. A. Woodford and other Freemasons. Woodford found an "ancient" ciphered manuscript dealing with Kabbalah and tarot in a London bookshop. A note was attached directing anyone who deciphered the manuscript to contact Fraulein Ann Sprengel in Germany. Woodford, along with S. L. MacGregor Mathers and William Wynn Westcott, did exactly that, and their reward was permission from their mysterious German contact to start a Rosicrucian society in England.

The fraternity was popular for a time, attracting occultist and Masonic author Arthur Edward Waite (who popularized tarot cards in the 20th century), poet William Butler Yeats, authors H. Rider Haggard and Bram Stoker, playwright August Strindberg, artist Edward Munch (painter of the famous *The Scream*), Aleister Crowley, and many other famous personalities of the period.

The Golden Dawn splintered into various factions when it was revealed that the manuscript that the Order was based upon was a hoax and the fictitious Fraulein Sprengel was nowhere to be found. Golden Dawn teaches occult, spiritual, and psychic philosophy, as well as astral projection, and what they call "practical applications of magic" (as opposed to "impractical" applications of magic, I suppose). At least half a dozen groups all claim to be authentic descendants of the original Order, which is the origin of most of the ritual magic concepts flourishing in the modern occult market.

Skull and Bones and the Knights of Eulogia

Skull and Bones is the oldest fraternity at Yale University. Founded in 1832 by William Huntington Russell because he couldn't get into Phi Beta Kappa, it was originally called the Eulogian Club and was a U.S. chapter of a German student organization. The club met in a campus chapel, and the members posted the symbol of the fraternity — the skull and crossbones — on the door while their meetings were in session. The club's name came from Eulogia, Greek goddess of eloquence who ascended into the heavens in 322 BC, and the "Bonesmen" refer to themselves as the Knights of Eulogia. The number 322 appears on their letterhead.

In 1856, the fraternity moved into its present, imposing, windowless building on the Yale campus, where it is known as the *Tomb*. Its ceremonies are closely guarded secrets, and as a result there is no end to lurid speculation as to what goes on in the Tomb. Bonesmen no doubt revel in this sort of infamy, as most college students would. There have been recent break-ins and clandestine video-tapings of the Tomb's interior, showing it to be little more than a run-of-the-mill college frat house, albeit with its share of peculiar décor.

Because Skull and Bones has an impressive list of famous and powerful members, past and present, conspiracy theories have grown up around the fraternity, alleging that it is a supersecret branch of Freemasonry and the Illuminati (see Chapter 4). Bonesmen are accused of slipping into international positions of power and controlling world commerce and governments, and it is true that they represent the elite of Yale's graduates. Only 15 seniors are initiated each year, and the list includes a wide array of business and government leaders and opinion makers. President George W. Bush, his presidential father, and his grandfather were all Bonesmen. So was Senator John Kerry, who ran against George W. Bush in the 2004 presidential election. Henry Luce, founder of *Time* magazine was a Bonesman, as was William F. Buckley, founder of *National Review*. Although conspiracy theorists claim that membership rosters are kept secret, they have actually been listed in the annual Yale archives since their beginning. Skull and Bones has recently started to admit "Boneswomen."

As you probably guessed from its nickname, Bonesmen seem to have an obsession with images of bones, coffins, and mortality. Although symbols of skulls, crossbones, and coffins do exist in some portions of Freemasonry (most notably in the York Rite's Knights Templar Order, as well as some jurisdictions' depiction of the Master Mason degree), the purpose of the symbolism seems to be the same message in both groups: Time on Earth is short for each man, and he should live each day as though it may be his last, contributing as much as he can to the world. Death imagery was very commonplace in the 1800s and was more of a reminder of the shortness of life in an age of high mortality than it was occult symbolism.

The Skull and Bones founder, Russell, may have been familiar with German Masonic rituals and even those of the defunct Bavarian Illuminati from his studies in Germany. But the group has no connection to Freemasonry, apart from what Russell may have borrowed.

Irregular Masonic groups

For decades, the African American Masonic community has been plagued with unrecognized, irregular groups claiming to be Freemasons. Prince Hall Grand Lodges (see Chapter 2) have fought the problem, but like some exasperating game of whack-a-mole, you knock them down, and they pop up again somewhere else. These include the King Solomon Grand Lodge, the Order of King David Hebrew Grand Lodge, the International Modern Free and Accepted Masons, Empire State Twin Towers Grand Lodge, Mystic Tie Grand Lodge, and literally hundreds of others.

Masonry at the fringe

Fringe groups that call themselves Freemasons, but really aren't, are a problem. Stories come up from time to time that wind up tarring regular, recognized, mainstream Freemasonry with the dirty brush of bogus groups. Tales of Masonic sex parties, lurid Satanic ceremonies, or members being fleeced for ever-increasing amounts of cash to advance higher in the organization look and sound sensational in print and on the Web, but these stories have nothing to do with the authentic practice of Freemasonry.

Unfortunately, when bad things happen and the Masonic label is on them, explaining the long story of why some group isn't *really* Masonic can become difficult. The explanation winds up sounding evasive or just plain lame. The confusing and often tedious explanation doesn't fit into a short sound bite, and most people think

that Freemasonry is one, big, happy, homogeneous bunch of boys.

Again, no single, international group governs worldwide Freemasonry. Mainstream, regular, recognized Masonic organizations have little legal authority to stop anyone from claiming to be a Mason, any more than the National Council of Churches can prevent me from claiming to be the Messiah and that the world will end next Wednesday.

I list the regular, recognized Grand Lodges in the United States and Canada in Appendix C. Legitimate, regular Masonic lodges are affiliated with these Grand Lodges and will have a charter or warrant hanging on the wall of their lodge room proclaiming that affiliation. If in doubt, ask to see its charter, or call the governing Grand Lodge and ask if the lodge in question is legit.

Periodically, new groups form by using old Masonic rituals, claiming they have the "authentic" or secret teachings of Freemasonry and that the rest of the regular Masonic world has it all wrong. These organizations are sometimes hopeful wannabes or disaffected Freemasons trying to stake out a little piece of the Masonic world for themselves. They're sometimes also swindlers selling memberships in groups that exist only on paper.

The Internet makes scams easier than ever because anyone can put up an impressive website and sound authentic. And most bookstores sell copies of old Masonic rituals. Nobody owns the name *Freemason,* so it can be used and abused by anyone.

Before joining a Masonic lodge, do some research and be certain of who and what you're joining. Ask about its history and its Grand Lodge's pedigree. For your reference, Appendix C lists regular, recognized mainstream and Prince Hall Grand Lodges. The Grand Lodges will assist you in finding local lodges in their jurisdictions.

Chapter 10

The York Rite

In This Chapter

▶ Getting to know the York Rite system

▶ Introducing the Royal Arch, Cryptic, and Chivalric degrees

▶ Discovering the history of the original Knights Templar

▶ Understanding the invitational York Rite bodies and charities

The first three degrees of Masonry (and the only ones conferred in the Masonic lodge) are the Entered Apprentice, Fellow Craft, and Master Mason. By the 1730s, these degrees were uniformly declared to be the basic cornerstone of Freemasonry, and every regular and recognized Grand Lodge in the world exclusively administers these degrees in the lodges of its jurisdiction.

But just because Grand Lodges stopped with the first three degrees doesn't mean that creative Freemasons stopped writing ritual ceremonies. It was fun. It was interesting. And every new book that came out with stories about ancient civilizations or little-known religions resulted in a feverish attempt to write a new Masonic ritual about it. In England and France especially, the development of new and more-involved ceremonies continued at a hot pace throughout the 1700s and 1800s. One popular group of additional French degrees eventually came together as the Scottish Rite (see Chapter 11). The additional English degrees became known in the United States as the *York Rite*, named after the city in England where operative Masonry was first chartered by royal decree.

In this chapter, I discuss the degrees of the York Rite and how the various organizations that confer them are organized. I also fill you in on some of the other groups of honorary and research branches that generally get classified with the York Rite.

The York Rite System

York Rite is actually a descriptive term used for three cooperative groups that confer a total of ten degrees in the United States. There are four Royal Arch degrees, three Cryptic Mason degrees, and three Chivalric orders (culminating in the Knights Templar Order). The degrees making up the York Rite are considered *concordant* to the first three Masonic degrees, meaning that they confer additional Masonic degrees that enlarge and expand on the first three lodge degrees. You must already be a Master Mason before you can join the York Rite.

Some differences exist between the American York Rite and the way the Rite degrees are organized in Canada, the United Kingdom, and elsewhere. In some areas, you'll hear about *Capitular, Cryptic,* and *Chivalric* systems. Some of the degrees worked in the United States are not used in other jurisdictions, and vice versa.

York Rite degrees are usually conferred in a lodge-like setting, with candidates participating in the ceremonies. The Royal Arch and Cryptic Mason degrees don't require a belief in Christianity, but the Chivalric orders, especially the Knights of Malta and the Knights Templar, are most decidedly Christian based. All the Chivalric degrees are based on the Old and New Testaments of the Bible, which is one of the primary reasons that these degrees, like the Scottish Rite degrees, are considered entirely optional and appendant to the three lodge degrees. They were partially created by Masons who wanted to have a more Christianized organization after the first anti-Masonic edicts were passed by the Catholic popes in the 1700s.

Other organizations operate as subgroups within the York Rite system. Most are honorary or invitational groups, offering more degrees and honors to York Rite Masons, and each has its own rules and requirements for membership. Outside of the United States, some of these may be stand-alone organizations or classified as belonging to different governing bodies. I talk more about them later in this chapter.

I say this elsewhere, and it bears repeating: The York Rite — like the Scottish Rite — offers additional degrees to Freemasons. They are *not* more important than the three degrees of the Masonic lodge. They add more knowledge, teach more lessons, and provide more opportunities for friendships and participation outside the lodge. But a Mason who has a chest full of medals from the York Rite, carries a gold sword in the Knights Templar, or wears a white 33rd-degree hat in the Scottish Rite is no better than the newest Master Mason in a rural lodge. Masons aren't required — or expected — to advance to these additional degrees. Many never do.

Why York?

It is generally accepted that York, in the north of England, is the origin of what became modern Freemasonry. The first guilds of stonemasons were organized here, possibly as early as AD 600, and good old King Athelstan, Alfred the Great's grandson and the acknowledged first king of "all England," chartered the first Grand Lodge of Masons at York in AD 926.

When the Antient and the Modern Grand Lodges in England were duking it out over who would ultimately govern English Masonry in the 1700s (see Chapter 2), the Antients proclaimed that York was the ancient seat of the Craft because of its long heritage and association, and that London was a gaggle of mere modern upstarts. "Who's been around the longest?" was almost always the big deal in early Masonry, which is why you see the word *ancient* applied to so many things, even things that had just been invented.

Although London's lodges were conferring just the three degrees of Entered Apprentice, Fellow Craft, and Master Mason, by the last half of the 1700s the lodge at York conferred a total of five: the first three, plus the Royal Arch and the Knight Templar degrees. Higher degrees started popping up after about 1737, to continue the story of Solomon's Temple and more.

Interestingly, the U.S. system and rituals today are actually closer to their York originals than what is currently worked in England, because of many compromises made to reunify the English Grand Lodges in 1813. Also of note is that stories told in the Scottish Rite and some of the York Rite degrees have many similarities (see Chapter 11). Because the higher degrees had their origin in France, many parallel concepts occur between them. The three separate groups of degrees that came to be called the York Rite were imported to England and developed their own customs.

Another reason the term *York Rite* was coined was because of areas where the Ancient Accepted Scottish Rite offered a different system of higher degrees. Lumping the three separate groups together under one banner of York Rite became a simpler way of referring to them. It made an otherwise confusing conversation a bit clearer.

All Royal Arch, Cryptic, and Knights Templar members are Freemasons. But these are optional degrees, and not all Masons join these other organizations.

How it's organized

Every state in the U.S. has its own Grand Lodge to govern its individual Masonic lodges. In Canada and Australia, the provinces have their own Grand Lodges as well. As a general rule, most of the rest of the world has one regular, recognized governing Grand Lodge for each country.

3 + 1 = 3?

The Royal Arch degree was one of the major sticking points of the argument between the competing Antient and Modern Grand Lodges in England in the late 1700s and early 1800s (see Chapter 2). The Antients considered the Royal Arch the completion of the Master Mason degree and included it in their lodge ceremonies. The Moderns thought the Royal Arch should be its own separate degree, governed not by the Grand Lodge but by a separate Grand Chapter. When the two sides finally buried the hatchet in 1813, the compromise was one of the most confusing agreements ever arrived at. The Act of Union states

It is declared and pronounced that pure Ancient Masonry consists of three degrees, and no more; viz: Those of the Entered Apprentice, the Fellow Craft and the Master Mason, including the Supreme Order of the Royal Arch.

Anyone who could count to four was very confused. Still, the agreement meant that lodges were allowed to form Royal Arch chapters and go on conferring the additional degrees with the blessing — and without the control — of the Grand Lodge. In many English lodges, you're philosophically not considered to be a *true* Master Mason until you've received the Royal Arch degree.

In the U.S. and Canada, the York Rite has three separate governing bodies. Rather than a single national or international administration, the York Rite is made up of three distinct organizations, one for each degree group, and each with its own local, state, and national structure. Nevertheless, the groups all work closely together and cooperate on policies, requirements, degree work, and scheduling. In ascending order, they are

- ✔ **The Royal Arch:** The Royal Arch has individual chapters that function as lodges do, with members and officers who confer degrees. The chapters are overseen by state- and province-wide Grand Chapters, and a national General Grand Chapter for the United States is above them. Statewide meetings of the chapters and Grand Chapter are called *convocations*. The nationwide General Grand Chapter meets every three years at a *triennial convocation* to elect officers and set national policy.

- ✔ **The Cryptic Rite:** The Cryptic Rite is organized into local Councils of Royal and Select Masters, and the primary officer is the Illustrious Master. There are statewide Grand Councils and a national General Grand Council, although a handful of states don't participate in this national group.

- ✔ **Chivalric Masonry:** Chivalric Masonry is organized into local Knight Templar commanderies. The primary officer of a commandery is the Eminent Commander. The statewide bodies are known as Grand Commanderies, and the national body is called the Grand Encampment, Knights Templar Order. The Grand Encampment meets every three years at a triennial conclave and is actually a legislative body made up of representatives of the state Grand Commanderies.

Templar commanderies also frequently have *drill teams* — units that function separately from the degree work of the commandery. They are the public face of Templary, and they participate in parades and act as honor and color guards at public Masonic ceremonies.

One very confusing aspect of the higher degree systems is that the rituals themselves are generally not presented in a proper, logical, chronological order. Although they build and enlarge on the theme and story of the three lodge degrees, some York Rite degrees take place before the events in the earlier ones, and other degrees come after. The degrees are arranged in the order of importance of the messages they tell, *not* according to a timeline of described events. Each degree should be looked at as an individual lesson and not as part of one long, linear story being told.

Royal Arch Masonry

The four degrees of the Royal Arch are the first steps within the York Rite. *Capstones* (or *copestones*) are the row of stones that are the cap of a wall, and these degrees, especially the Royal Arch degree, are described as the capstone of the three degrees conferred in the Masonic lodge. Therefore, in other parts of the world, these degrees are described as the *capitular degrees*.

Figure 10-1 shows the symbol of the Royal Arch, composed of a circle, a triangle, and three Greek *taus,* which signify the "true" name of God.

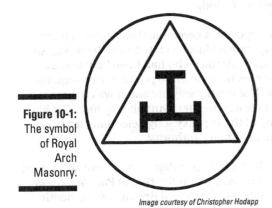

Figure 10-1:
The symbol
of Royal
Arch
Masonry.

Image courtesy of Christopher Hodapp

The Royal Arch has four degrees, and I cover them in the following sections.

Mark Master

The stonemasons who built the great cathedrals and other buildings of the Middle Ages left behind a tiny record of their individual workmanship. They chiseled what are called *Mason's marks* into the stones they worked on to identify their work. Each Mason had his own individual mark that acted as a signature, at a time when most people were illiterate. A stonemason was classified by the quality of his work, and as Ford Motor Company's old advertising line said, "Quality goes in before the name goes on."

The Mark Master degree first appeared in England in 1769 and is probably older. It concerns the workmen building King Solomon's Temple. The degree of Mark Master teaches the candidate the value of workmanship, honesty, and charity. Like the old stonemasons, modern Mark Masters devise their own individual Mason's mark that each chapter keeps on file in a Book of Marks.

Past Master

The Past Master degree goes by a couple of names, depending on the jurisdiction. It's also called the *Virtual Past Master* or the *Installed Master* degree. The confusion comes from the fact that many jurisdictions confer some kind of ceremony that is similarly named on members who are installed as the Worshipful Master of their Masonic lodge. A Mason who has served as Worshipful Master of a lodge is entitled to the title of Past Master. Yet in the York Rite system, the Past Master is a symbolic degree, and the candidate isn't actually installed as the Master of a lodge.

The Past Master degree was developed as a ceremonial loophole. A much older rule from the last days of operative Masons stated that the Royal Arch degree could only be conferred upon Masons who had been installed as Worshipful Masters. As these degrees became more popular, this requirement became somewhat limiting. The sneaky way around it was to create a Virtual Past Master by making a new degree that symbolically installed him as Worshipful Master without any of those pesky lodge elections, and certainly without actually giving him any ruling authority.

Masons who have only received the Past Master degree and have not served as an actual Worshipful Master aren't entitled to the title of Past Master in common usage and aren't referred to as Worshipful Brother, as authentic Past Masters are.

This degree is not worked in Pennsylvania or England.

A lodge or not a lodge?

In the early days of the use of these degrees — especially the Royal Arch and Knight Templar degrees — a regular Masonic lodge would confer them, just as they conferred the first three. They simply opened the meeting by using the proper opening ritual for that degree and proceeded with the ceremony. Later, lodges were restricted to opening and conferring just the Entered Apprentice, Fellow Craft, and Master Mason degrees. The Royal Arch degrees fell under the control of governing bodies called Royal Arch chapters, sort of a lodge within the lodge. This was also true with the Knight Templar degree. They could still be conferred in the lodge room. It's just that a group other than the Masonic lodge officers had to do it.

Over the years, it became more practical — logistically and financially — for the degrees of the York Rite to cooperate. Many of the same Masons who were working the Royal Arch degrees were also in the Cryptic and Templar groups, but not every lodge had the manpower, the time, or the space to put on these additional degrees. They require more people to memorize many more speaking roles than the three lodge degrees, and the ceremonies, when done properly, are quite involved productions.

Staging requirements were also built into the rituals that made conferring them in a lodge room less effective than if they were done in a space specifically designed for them. The Templars, in particular, added marching, flag presentations, and sword drills that are tough to pull off in a narrow room with an 8-foot ceiling.

Plus, not everyone who joined a lodge wanted to belong to these other groups. Being active in the Templar commandery was — and is — an expensive proposition, because of the uniform and other regalia required. Picking a large central or popular location and setting up a group of York Rite bodies that could draw members from several surrounding Masonic lodges made more sense. As a result, some states have hundreds of Masonic lodges, dozens of Royal Arch chapters and Cryptic councils, and perhaps just a handful of Templar commanderies.

Nevertheless, because many British Masons do not consider the degrees of the lodge complete until a Mason has received the Royal Arch, it is much more common for an English lodge to have a Royal Arch chapter attached to it than it is in the United States.

Most Excellent Master

The Most Excellent Master degree deals with the completion of Solomon's Temple. Its U.S. version was possibly cobbled together by Thomas Smith Webb and is similar to one that was worked in Scotland in the 1700s that is known there and in England as the *Super Excellent Master*. And if that isn't impressive, I don't know what is. In England, this degree is actually worked as part of the Cryptic degrees (see "The Cryptic Rite," later in this chapter).

Royal Arch

Depending on the part of the world you're in, the Royal Arch degree is also referred to as the *Holy Royal Arch* degree. It's an old degree that first appears in records in York in 1744. It shows up in Boston, Massachusetts, in 1769, along with the Past Master and Most Excellent Master degrees.

The story of the degree occurs after the destruction of Solomon's Temple, beginning with the discovery of a hidden crypt under the ruins and the secrets found within it. It is the completion of the story started in the first three lodge degrees about the search for secrets that were once lost.

The Cryptic Rite

In the United States, the Council of Royal and Select Masters, or Cryptic Council, usually confers three degrees. Figure 10-2 shows the symbol of the Cryptic Rite, which includes a broken triangle, a trowel, and a sword.

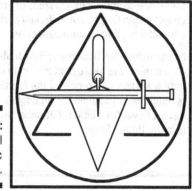

Figure 10-2:
The symbol of Cryptic Masonry.

Image courtesy of Christopher Hodapp

The term *cryptic* in Freemasonry doesn't mean creepy, occult, or obscure. It simply refers to the crypt at the bottom of the ninth vault that contained the ineffable name of God.

The Royal Master and Select Master degrees of this rite are based on the legend of Enoch the Patriarch, the great-grandfather of Noah. Enoch excavated nine underground vaults, one below the other, beneath Mount Moriah in Jerusalem where Solomon's Temple was eventually constructed. Each vault contained secrets, and at the bottom of the ninth vault was the greatest secret of all: the ineffable, unspeakable name of God, represented by the *Tetragrammaton* (see Figure 10-3). The Tetragrammaton is made up of the Hebrew letters (from left to right) *Yod, He, Waw,* and *He.*

Figure 10-3:
The Tetra-
grammaton,
representing
the unspeak-
able or true
name of God.

Image courtesy of Christopher Hodapp

The four Hebrew letters of the Tetragrammaton correspond to the letters YHWH, or IHWH, and are pronounced as either *Yahweh* or *Jehovah*. It comes from the Hebrew meaning "I am." Jewish law and tradition held that saying the true name of God was blasphemous, and when the name of God appeared in the scripture, it was usually translated into the substitute words *Adonoi* or *Lord*. Neither Biblical Hebrew nor Arabic has vowel sounds and, in fact, vowel marks were added to Hebrew biblical texts in the Middle Ages to assist in pronunciation. The truth is that no one really knows precisely how to pronounce the Tetragrammaton. Today, some rabbis say that the commandment given to Moses is explicit — "You shall not take the name of YHVH your God in vain" — and that *any* pronunciation of the Tetragrammaton is blasphemous. When it appears in scripture or prayer, they substitute *Adonoi* or *Ha Shem*, meaning simply "the Name." The Tetragrammaton plays a central role in the study of Kabbalah.

The Cryptic Rite presents three degrees, and some U.S. jurisdictions present one additional degree, for a total of four:

- **Royal Master:** The Royal Master degree returns to the days before Solomon's Temple was completed, and it gives more information about Hiram Abiff, Grand Architect of the Temple, and his successor, Adoniram.

- **Select Master:** The Select Master degree partially concerns the deposit of the secrets of the Temple into their hidden location in the crypt and describes the period of time between the first and second half of the Royal Master degree.

- **Super-Excellent Master:** The Super-Excellent Master degree concerns the period long after the destruction of Solomon's Temple and the exodus of the Hebrews.

- **Thrice Illustrious Master:** When the primary officer of a Cryptic Council is installed in his elected position, some U.S. jurisdictions confer upon him the degree of Thrice Illustrious Master, sometimes referred to as the *Order of the Silver Trowel*. This practice isn't universal.

The Cryptic Rite degrees seem to have appeared between 1760 and the 1780s and are among the most instructive and well written in Freemasonry.

Chivalric Masonry and the Knights Templar

The three Christian chivalric degrees (or *orders,* as they're more properly called) are conferred in the United States by a Knights Templar commandery. The three orders are the Illustrious Order of the Red Cross, the Order of Malta, and the Order of the Temple. The last two in particular are based on the traditions of chivalric orders of knighthood in the Middle Ages.

The chivalric orders are also expressly Christian in nature. This doesn't mean that non-Christians can't take them; it simply means that, unlike most of the other degrees of Freemasonry, they aren't nondenominational. A candidate for the Masonic Order of Knights Templar is asked if he will be willing to defend the Christian faith; many non-Christians have no problem answering yes.

You can see one of the symbols of the Knights Templar in Figure 10-4. Most of the symbols contain a red cross and crown. The Latin motto *In Hoc Signo Vinces* means "By this sign thou shalt conquer."

Figure 10-4:
A symbol of the Knights Templar.

Image courtesy of Christopher Hodapp

Freemasonry contained absolutely no reference to knights of any kind until the Scotsman Chevalier Andrew Ramsay's highly creative — and completely incorrect — assertion in the 1730s that Masonry had spread to Europe from the Middle East by way of returning crusading knights during the Middle Ages (see Chapter 2). This story was exciting and thrilling and romantic — as well as utter hogwash — but the Masons in France and England ate it up anyway, resulting in a rapidly expanding list of new degrees based on knightly legends.

The chivalric orders

The orders of chivalry conferred in a Knights Templar Commandery are fascinating, affecting, and beautiful ceremonies, but given the individual orders and the reality of history, it's a slightly bizarre mix. These orders have little to do with the real orders of knighthood of the same names that have existed throughout history, and there is most definitely no bona fide historical connection between the Knights Templar of the Crusades and those in Freemasonry.

The room in which a commandery meets and the orders are conferred is referred to as an *asylum*, meaning a sanctuary or place of refuge from the outside world.

The Illustrious Order of the Red Cross

The story told in the ritual for the Red Cross acts as a link between the Cryptic degrees and the ones that follow, and it bridges the period between the Old and New Testaments. This degree has a name similar to ones that appear in other branches of Masonry, and it is not conferred within the British Templar system (which only confers the following two orders).

Order of Malta

The story of this order begins by making the candidate a Knight of St. Paul or the Mediterranean Pass, which acts as a prerequisite needed within the ceremony to become a Knight of Malta. For lovers of titles, this order in particular makes the Mason a Knight Hospitaller of St. John of Jerusalem, Palestine, Rhodes, and Malta.

History buffs will find the inclusion of these titles, bundled together with the Knights Templar, to be historical heresy. Nevertheless, it, like the Templar order that follows it, is among the most affecting of the Masonic higher degrees.

Order of the Temple

The last order is the one that dubs the Mason a Knight Templar, and most Masons who have been through it will describe the ceremony as one of the most memorable, thought provoking, and impressive they have ever witnessed. It is truly unique among the degrees of Freemasonry.

Skull and crossbones!

The skull and crossed bones were adopted as an emblem of the Knights Templar between the third and fourth Crusade. According to a strange legend, a wicked Templar and Lord of Sidon broke his vows and fell in love with a beautiful Armenian noblewoman who died very young. The knight couldn't endure to be separated from her, so he exhumed her body and had intercourse with the corpse. He reburied her body and returned home, but a voice came to him in a dream and told him to come back in nine months, and he would find a son. When he returned, he found only a skull and two crossed leg bones in the grave. The voice spoke to him again and told him to guard and keep them always, and he would be successful in all his undertakings. The knight prospered and defeated all his enemies, often by simply showing them the magical head.

Okay, so it's a grisly little legend. How sweet can a story about skulls, bones, and necrophilia really get?

The skull and bones were supposedly passed on to the Templars when the wicked Templar died, and the remains were credited with their rise to affluence and power. The legend was actually created in the 1100s and was not at first even connected to the Templars. But if you're a group of warrior monks trying to keep your infidel enemies afraid of you, you'll claim anything that works to your advantage.

Unfortunately, when the Templars were arrested and charged with heresy, legends of sleeping with dead women and using magical heads from unholy unions worked to their disadvantage. The tale of the Skull of Sidon was not only believed by the Church Inquisitors, it was also used to link the Templars to a sect of Gnostics known as the Cathars, who were branded as heretics by the Church.

The battle flag of the Templars, called the *beauseant,* was black and white, signifying favor to the friends and followers of Christ and death to His enemies. Many people believe that the Templars used the white skull and crossbones on a black field as the flag for their navy. It was later used, as anyone who has ever been to Disneyland knows, as the flag of pirates. (The term Jolly Roger, in case you were wondering, actually comes from a term used for a French naval flag, known as the *drapeau jolie rouge,* meaning "pretty red flag.")

When the Masonic Knights Templar were formed, their early aprons contained the skull and crossbones symbolism (see the figure), as does their ritual. It's used as it is in the Master Mason degree symbolism simply as a reminder of mortality. The apron was shaped like a black velvet triangle. A smaller top triangular flap was perforated with 12 holes. In the center of the flap were two crossed swords while the center of the apron contained a skull and crossbones. This design is obsolete today.

Image courtesy of Christopher Hodapp

A crash course in Templar history

I discuss the Templars briefly in Chapter 2, because some people still believe Chevalier Ramsay's contention that the Templars were the original Freemasons. Most serious scholars don't buy this theory, although there's no shortage of recent books making thought-provoking connections between them. But because of the Templar order that is a part of the York Rite, knowing a little more about them is important. Read on for your crash course. For much more about the medieval and modern Knights Templar, see *The Templar Code For Dummies* (Wiley) by Chris Hodapp and Alice Von Kannon.

Origin

In AD 1099, Jerusalem fell to the warriors of the Crusade, armies of Christian knights who traveled from Europe to the Holy Land to drive the Muslims out. The 500 or so knights who did not return to their homes began to set up independent states in the area, and pilgrims began to make the long and dangerous trip to visit the sacred landmarks of Christianity.

In those days, as with Muslims today who travel to Mecca for the *hajj,* a pilgrimage to the Holy Land was the ultimate act of Christian piety. In fact, sometimes knights and lords who had been excommunicated were sentenced to the difficult and dangerous journey as penance. Popes regularly remitted the sins of criminals willing to go to war against the Infidels.

In 1115, Hugues de Payens and eight other knights from northern France escorted pilgrims from Jerusalem to Jericho and then to Jordan, where Jesus had been baptized. Three years later, the knights took oaths of poverty, chastity, and obedience, along with military vows, and became a small band of something that no one had ever seen before: warrior monks. They called themselves the Poor Fellow Knights of Christ, and their symbol became the image of two poor knights sharing a horse.

In 1124, Hugues de Payens traveled to France and received the official endorsement of the Catholic Church at the Council of Troyes. With the all-important blessing of the pope, along with several influential patrons like St. Bernard de Clairvaux, donations of money, land, and honors suddenly began to rush in, and the Templars quickly became the talk of Christendom. They took up residence in the palace near the former site of Solomon's Temple and were rechristened as the Poor Fellow Soldiers of Christ and the Temple of Solomon.

Growth of the Templars

In 1139, Pope Innocent II granted the Templars powers unknown to any other order. They became answerable only to the pope himself, and no other churchman could question their authority. They were allowed to keep all booty captured from the Muslims, and they were making money from the land and buildings granted to them as donations. In fact, in 1131, they and the Knights Hospitaller and the Church of the Holy Sepulchre had been jointly granted the lands of the kingdom of Aragon in Spain to defend, with its wealth in return.

As their holdings in Europe grew, the Templars constructed fortified outposts called *commanderies* or *preceptories*. These often included churches built in an unusual and very distinctive round shape (see Figure 10-5). With increasing numbers of pilgrims headed for the Holy Land, the Templars started the first system of international banking. A traveler could deposit money into the Temple in London, Paris, or Rome, or a local preceptory, and was given what amounted to letters of credit that he could cash when he got to Jerusalem.

Figure 10-5:
The Templar
Church in
London,
built in the
distinctive
circular
shape.

Photograph courtesy of Christopher Hodapp

If you couldn't afford that trip to Palestine, relax. Your friendly Templar preceptory would be glad to take land or possessions in trade for some of its ready cash. The Templars were a great public-image campaign for the Church and the Crusades. They were warriors, travel agents, translators, bankers, and E-Z credit counselors. Becoming a Templar was a very cool thing for a nobleman. Templars were instrumental in opening the road to trade and commerce with the Middle East.

By the end of the 1100s, the Templars had become the greatest landowners in Syria and Palestine, and their military prowess was world renowned. It was a common legend that they wouldn't retreat unless they found themselves outnumbered three to one, and their military vows included the promise never to surrender to unbelieving infidels. They were the first on the battlefield and the last to leave. The Templars also developed a powerful navy, used to transport pilgrims across the Mediterranean Sea and to harass Muslim shipping.

Defeat

In 1291, the castle at Acre, near Haifa, was besieged by a Muslim army of 160,000 and a bewildering array of catapults and siege engines (dramatized in the 2005 film, *Kingdom of Heaven*). Although both the Templars and the Hospitallers fought bravely to the bitter end, the city towers were breached, and the Christians were driven from the Holy Land. Those who had fought the hardest under terrible odds were blamed for losing Palestine to the Infidels.

Envy

After a brief time on the island of Cyprus, the Templars consolidated their holdings in Europe and settled into a life of banking. The Hospitallers and the Templars had been rivals in the Holy Land, and now that it was lost, many in the Church saw no reason to have any more warrior monks hanging around Europe than were really needed. A new sentiment was growing among jealous Church officials in favor of merging the Hospitallers and the Templars. Their status as the Untouchables of the Catholic Church had done little to endear them to the nobility of Europe, especially kings who needed extensive loans to finance their own military actions.

King Philip IV of France was one such king. Known as Philip the Fair, the king was in serious financial trouble after debasing the French currency, trying to kidnap Pope Boniface VIII, expelling all the Jews in the kingdom and confiscating their property in 1306, and picking a fight with a band of Italian bankers in 1311 so he could steal their assets. During an especially ugly riot in Paris in 1306, Phil hid out in the Templars' Paris preceptory; he never could shake the image of the wealth stored there and of himself getting his royal mitts on it.

A renegade Templar named Esquiu de Floyrian came to Philip alleging that the Templars were engaging in blasphemy, idolatry, and sodomy. When a new pope was elected in November 1305, the French king saw a chance to be rid of the Templars and snatch their wealth in France at the same time.

The cardinals had taken a full year to elect the brand-new Pope Clement V, and Clement had prearranged a deal with Philip that after his installation as the Holy Father, he would eliminate Vatican laws that had been passed against France by his predecessor. In fact, in 1309, Clement V moved the administration of the Catholic Church from Rome to Avignon, right on King Philip's back porch. This move began a long period of chaos within the

Church, known to Catholics as the *Babylonian Captivity*. From the get-go, the new pope was Philip's willing stooge.

Arrest

Philip put growing pressure on the pope to charge the Templars with crimes against the Church, and on Friday, October 13, 1307, all Templars in France (somewhere between 2,000 and 15,000 in number) were arrested simultaneously and charged with heresy, including their aged Grand Master, Jacques de Molay. Philip confiscated their holdings in France, and Clement ordered the knights arrested in all other Catholic countries, something that most of the other kings of Europe weren't in any big hurry to do.

Robert the Bruce, King of Scotland, was already excommunicated — and by association, so was his kingdom. As a result, tweaking the nose of the pope was an added bonus when he quietly made it known that Scotland could be a refuge for Templars fleeing arrest. In Portugal, the Templars merely changed their name to the Order of Christ, where they contributed to the great naval discoveries of Henry the Navigator, who headed the order until his death.

Charges of heresy

De Molay and the Templars spent more than a year in French dungeons, being tortured into confessing to denying Christ, spitting on the cross, engaging in acts of homosexuality, and worshipping idols, including a mysterious deity called *Baphomet*.

Clearly their exposure to the influences of other faiths — Islam, Catharism, and other "dangerous" Eastern philosophies — had left them wide open to the charges of heresy. Although the Templars admitted to a wide variety of crimes, they did suffer terrible torture at the hands of the Inquisitors. One of the knights later said he would have admitted to killing God himself to stop his tormentors. Most of the Templars who were arrested outside of France and avoided torture vehemently denied all the crimes.

Trial and death

When Jacques de Molay appeared before a papal committee in 1308, he and the other knights recanted their confessions. Of course, recanting a confession was an act of heresy punishable by death, and on May 11, 1308, 54 Templars were burned at the stake.

In 1314, after seven long years of prison, torture, confessions, trials, and papal commissions, the end of the Templars finally came. De Molay, now 70, along with three of his senior officers, was held on a platform outside of Notre Dame Cathedral in Paris, where they were sentenced to "perpetual imprisonment." De Molay could stand no more, and he and his friend Geoffri de Charney shouted that they and the entire order were innocent of any wrongdoing, further recanting any and all confessions they and the order had made under torture.

The Templars and Baphomet

The term *Baphomet* turns up in more than a few of the Templar confessions, so we know that the Templars commonly venerated something called by that name. Many scholars believe the name Baphomet was simply a variation of the Latin word *Mahomet,* a medieval European version of Muhammad, the name of the Prophet of Islam. Others believe the word actually comes from the Arabic *abufihamet,* pronounced in Spanish as *bufihimat.* In Arabic it can mean "father of understanding" or "source of wisdom."

The word was often used in reference to a "bearded head" that was supposedly revered by the Templars. Theories have been suggested about the head, but no one really knows the truth. It may have been the legendary head of John the Baptist, and there was a religious sect (called *Johannites* or *Mandaeans*) during the period that believed Jesus was an imposter and that John was the authentic Savior. The father of understanding may also have been the severed head of the order's founder, Hugues de Payen. And then, or course, there's the myth about the skull of Sidon, discussed earlier in this chapter.

Four hundred years after the Templar trials, the French mystic Eliphas Levi clearly believed that the Baphomet referred to in the Templar confessions was indeed the Source of Wisdom, mysterious knowledge discovered by the Knights. Levi believed that the Templars had created secret societies that held this mystical knowledge and that the Freemasons were their descendants who had simply lost or forgotten these supernatural powers. For more about Levi and Baphomet, see Chapter 8.

That evening, the two men were led to the end of a small island in the River Seine, the Ile-des-Javiaux, and lashed to wooden stakes. The old Grand Master asked to be faced toward Notre Dame and for his hands to be unbound so he could die in prayer. As the flames were lit and rose around them, de Molay continually shouted out the innocence of the order and called on both King Philip and Pope Clement to meet him in front of God before the year was out. Clement died the next month, and Philip followed him seven months later.

Secret pardon

The Catholic Church has long held that the Templars were innocent of any wrongdoing and that Clement had been threatened into knuckling under to King Philip. There may be much to this theory after all. In 2001, Dr. Barbara Frale discovered a document in the Vatican Archives called the *Chinon Parchment,* after the castle in France where Jacques de Molay was imprisoned. It states that Pope Clement V actually pardoned any wrongdoing of the Templars in 1314, just before he died.

Mysteries of the Templars

Part of the reason that everyone from the Freemasons to Aleister Crowley to Dan Brown has been interested in the Templars has to do with the mysteries and legends that have come along after their suppression. The Templars excavated around the site of King Solomon's Temple the entire time they were in Jerusalem, and it's possible they found buried treasure there, including sacred relics dating back to Solomon. That said, it's doubtful that the Templars found any such thing, because Jerusalem had been looted, sacked, robbed, and otherwise pretty well gone over for almost 2,000 years between the time the temple was built and the arrival of the Templars. But still, it could have happened. The Templars' find is the legendary treasure described in the opening scenes of the 2004 film *National Treasure*.

When King Philip's troops arrested the Paris Templars, they were shocked to discover that someone had tipped off the knights and that the vast bulk of the treasure the king had seen in the temple was nowhere to be found. To this day, no one knows where the greatest amount of the Templar wealth went. The day of the mass arrests in France, a Templar fleet sailed from La Rochelle, its contents and destination a mystery. Many people believe the fleet set sail for Scotland.

Both Prince Henry the Navigator of Portugal and Christopher Columbus's father-in-law were members of the Order of Christ, the Templars operating in Portugal after the 1307 arrests. Columbus's navigators were of the same order, and his ships' sails curiously were painted with the distinctive red cross of the Templars. Some say that the Templars placed their treasure on ships and sent it to the New World, possibly from Scotland in 1398 with Henry Sinclair, whose family built the famous and mysterious Rosslyn Chapel that plays a role in Dan Brown's book *The Da Vinci Code*. And many claim that the clan Sinclair became Templars themselves, using Templar rituals and organizational structures to create what eventually became modern Freemasonry.

An island in Nova Scotia called Oak Island has hidden a mystery that no one has been able to crack. An enormous pit was discovered in the late 1700s, containing stone and oak platforms, an obvious evidence of man-made excavation. For 200 years, numerous attempts have been made to explore the "money pit," and many believe it was built by the Templars to hide their elusive treasure. A mysterious, round tower in Newport, Rhode Island, is built in a style similar to both Portuguese and Templar design, and many believe it is a Templar building as well.

The Templars have also been tied to legends that they discovered the Ark of the Covenant, containing the pieces of the tablets of the Ten Commandments, and even the Holy Grail. None of these mysteries has ever been proved, yet it's easy to see why any brotherhood with a hint of mystery surrounding it would relish being tied to the Knights Templar.

Other York Rite Bodies

As I mention at the beginning of this chapter, the York Rite isn't governed or organized by any one central authority. It's a loose term used to describe a collection of several groups. As a result, what is considered a York Rite body in one country may not be part of the York Rite in another. In the sections that follow are a few other organizations grouped in the United States under the York Rite banner. Almost all of them are by invitation only, open only to Freemasons who have received the Chapter, Council, and Templar degrees of the York Rite.

York Rite College

Created in Detroit, Michigan, in 1957, the York Rite College (www.yrscna.org) is an invitational organization for members of all three branches of the York Rite. Close to 200 individual colleges are in the United States, governed by the York Rite Sovereign College of North America. They promote education and ritual excellence in the different bodies of the Rite.

The College confers the Order of the Purple Cross, an award given to members who have distinguished themselves in service to the Rite or to the community.

Knight Masons

The Knight Masons (www.yorkrite.com/knightmasons) is an invitational York Rite body that presents degrees that developed in Ireland in the early 1700s. The Knight of the Sword, Knight of the East, and Knight of the East and West are known as the *Green degrees* because of their Irish origin. They're similar to some of the Scottish Rite degrees. Until the mid-1800s, they were worked in Irish Royal Arch chapters and then in Templar commanderies.

In 1923, a Grand Council of Knight Masons was formed in Dublin, Ireland, and they came to the United States in 1936. Today, there are about 70 U.S. Councils of Knight Masons, with approximately 7,000 members.

Allied Masonic Degrees

The Allied Masonic Degrees (www.alliedmasonicdegrees.org) is a scholarly research organization, dedicated to preserving outdated York Rite Masonic rituals that would otherwise have vanished into obscurity. They meet much like a Masonic lodge, but Masonic research papers and presentations are strongly encouraged.

The Allied Masonic Degrees (AMD) are degrees that at one time formed part of the somewhat loosely governed Masonic period of the 1700s. Many of these detached degrees vanished in some places. In time, the better of these degrees were grouped together in an organized body under the title of Allied Masonic Degrees.

Membership is by invitation only and is open to *Companions* (members of a Royal Arch chapter) who have completed the York Rite Royal Arch chapter degrees. The local bodies are called *councils*, and the maximum number of active members of any council is limited to 27.

The AMD is one of the fastest growing Masonic groups in the United States, which is a sign of the increasing interest in the history and symbolism of Freemasonry. Also, because councils are limited to just 27 members, the groups remain small and intimate, made up of active Masons, not simply joiners in search of a new membership card in their wallet. Meetings are short, papers or guest speakers are presented, and, generally, a dinner follows the meeting.

Societas Rosicruciana in Civitatibus Foederatis

Originally founded in 1880 as the *Societas Rosicruciana Republicae Americae,* many Masons classify this as a York Rite body, but technically its only requirement is for members to be Master Masons and Christians. It is also an invitational body. The SRICF (www.yorkrite.org/sricf) is a very small group made up of 31 *colleges* (local chapters) in the United States and Canada, and no more than 72 members may be in a college.

Rectified Rite or Chevalier Bienfaisant de Cite Saint (CBCS)

The Rectified Rite (www.knightstemplar.org/rer) is a Templar Order that was formed in 1782 in France and moved to Switzerland. Today it's an invitational order that confers six degrees, one of which is the Knight Beneficent of the Holy City. It is considered to be the oldest continuously operating Christian chivalric Masonic Order in the world, tracing its roots back to Baron Karl Gotthelf von Hund's "Rite of Strict Observance" in Germany in the 1750s. In 2010, the Grand Encampment of Knights Templar in the United States reestablished this order in the U.S. under its authority with a French charter, after it had devolved into little more than a dinner club. Today, it is growing steadily.

Holy Royal Arch Knight Templar Priests

The Holy Royal Arch Knight Templar Priests (www.hraktp.org) is a body made up of Commanders and Past Commanders of Knight Templar commanderies. Membership is by invitation only. The group meets in regional *tabernacles*, and membership of each tabernacle is limited to 33.

Knights of the York Cross of Honour

Another invitational body, the Order of Knights of the York Cross of Honour (www.k-ych.org) is conferred on York Rite Masons who have served as the Master of a Masonic Lodge, the High Priest of a Royal Arch chapter, the Master of a Cryptic Council, *and* the Commander or Preceptor of a Knight Templar commandery or preceptory. It represents great and dedicated service to the fraternity and is, thus, a very elite group.

The KYCH presents an impressive jewel to its members, and as they serve the York Rite on a statewide and national basis in their grand bodies, quadrants of different colors are added to the jewel. Holders of all four quadrants are often referred to as *four-star generals*.

Red Cross of Constantine

The Order of the Red Cross of Constantine (www.redcrossconstantine. org) is an invitational organization and is considered by many to be the highest honor that can be awarded within York Rite Masonry. It dates to 1865 in England and 1869 in the United States, but its legendary origin is an order founded by Constantine the Great after the Battle of Saxa Rubra in AD 312, when he converted to Christianity.

St. Thomas of Acon

The Commemorative Order of St. Thomas of Acon (www.stthomasofacon.org) is an invitational body, requiring members to be Masonic Knights Templar in good standing. Its rituals and teachings are based on nearly 20 years' study by John E. N. Walker in London's Guildhall Library, and the Order was established in England in 1974. There are 80 meeting groups, called Chapels, in England, Wales, Spain, Canada, the United States, Australia, and New Zealand. The U.S. Chapel was established in 2005.

The Operatives

More correctly known as the *Worshipful Society of Free Masons, Rough Masons, Wallers, Slaters, Paviors, Plaisterers and Bricklayers,* the much easier term for this group is the Operatives (www.operatives.org.uk). The Society exists to perpetuate or preserve a memorial of the practices of operative Free Masons existing prior to, or continuing independently of, modern speculative Freemasonry.

The founder of what is now the Operatives was Clement Edwin Stretton, an English civil engineer in the 1860s. As part of his training, Stretton was sent to a quarry in Derbyshire as a month-long crash course in learning something of how the building trade worked from the stone quarry to the job site. In those days, the operative stonemasons' guilds were dwindling in size and influence, but were still in existence. Although he was treated with indifference at first, his application to join the guild masons opened up a whole new world to him. The guild still conferred a series of seven operative degrees on its stone-working members, and its traditions long predated the formation of speculative Freemasonry.

Stretton became a Freemason in 1871, but was struck by the many differences between the two organizations. He believed the alterations and innovations made by the premiere Grand Lodge in London had diluted the philosophy and teachings of the original guild masons. Even though he went on to serve in many active officer positions in Craft and Royal Arch Freemasonry, he believed that the Master Mason degree that the Grand Lodge added in the 1720s was based on inadequate knowledge of the Operatives' Annual Festival that commemorated the slaying of Hiram Abiff. So Stretton dedicated his later life to preserving the Operative degrees. Today, the Society has more than 2,000 members worldwide.

York Rite Charities

Each of the three primary bodies of the York Rite has its own national charities in the United States:

- The General Grand Chapter of Royal Arch Masons supports an endowment fund for DeMolay International for Boys, a Masonic youth group (see Chapter 13). Additionally, the Royal Arch Research Assistance Program was established in 1974 to support research into treating hearing disabilities.

- The General Grand Council of Royal and Select Masters (the Cryptic Rite) supports a foundation for research and the treatment of arteriosclerosis.

- The Grand Encampment of the Knights Templar established a scholarship loan program in 1922 for needy college students. In 1955, the Knights Templar Eye Foundation was created and has contributed millions of dollars for ophthalmology research and prevention of eye diseases. Additionally, local Templar commanderies often support youth activities and sponsor trips by local ministers to the Holy Land.

Chapter 11

The Ancient Accepted Scottish Rite

In This Chapter

▶ Introducing the Scottish Rite

▶ Explaining its structure and organization

▶ Identifying the North and the South

▶ Getting acquainted with Albert Pike

▶ Understanding the degrees of the Scottish Rite

The Ancient Accepted Scottish Rite (or *the Scottish Rite,* for short) is perhaps the most visible and least understood appendant body of Freemasonry. It isn't particularly ancient, and it didn't come from Scotland. Non-Masons (and even a few Masons) believe that its 32nd degree is the highest "rank" of Masonry, topped only by its extra-double-secret 33rd degree. The 33rd degree, in particular, has attracted an entire branch of anti-Masonic hysteria that insists it is a small group of "unseen superiors" who know the real secrets of Freemasonry, which are deliberately kept hidden from the lowly membership at large.

Meanwhile, the Scottish Rite's greatest champion and sage, Albert Pike, is a lightning rod of criticism, distrust, and hatred by Masonry's critics. He is perhaps the most misquoted author in modern history.

The organization frequently has enormous auditoriums that are landmarks in major cities. Confused citizens rarely know what *Scottish Rite* means, much less that they are part of the Masonic fraternity. Yet, in the years leading up to 1920, the Scottish Rite became the fastest growing fraternity in the United States. Its membership rolls swelled, and Freemasonry enjoyed a huge surge of expansion, because to join the Rite, you had to join a lodge first.

Wings down? Wings up?

If you trawl around the Internet looking at Scottish Rite websites, you'll come across its primary symbol: the double-headed eagle. You're also likely to find it portrayed sometimes with the wings down (see the figure) and sometimes with the wings up. This is one of those gripping dilemmas that has plagued Scottish Rite Masons since their first trip to the jewelry shop to buy a Scottish Rite ring. So what's the difference between double eagles with wings up and double eagles with wings down?

The official adopted logo of the Southern Jurisdiction (SJ) is wings down. As far as the SJ Supreme Council is concerned, anything that is "wings up" is purely an artistic license and has no official symbolism.

In the Northern Masonic Jurisdiction (NMJ), wings down is also the Supreme Council's official logo. However, the wings-up version is used in the NMJ to distinguish its 50 or so active 33rd-degree members (the equivalent of board members), and no one else.

Other Ancient Accepted Scottish Rite (AASR) jurisdictions use wings up as their official logo, including some Prince Hall AASRs as well as more than a few unrecognized, clandestine ones. Some non-U.S. jurisdictions, including Canada, use the wings-up version as well. But in the United States, the symbol is primarily wings down.

Illustration courtesy of Christopher Hodapp

In this chapter, I attempt to simplify the complex story of the development and growth of the Scottish Rite, its expansion in the United States, and its place in the family of Freemasonry. I also discuss Albert Pike and why he is so important to the Rite. Finally, I briefly outline the bewildering lineup of Scottish Rite degrees and why you may address me as "Prince." Kindly keep your head down and back out of the room in my presence.

Surveying the Scottish Rite System

The Ancient Accepted Scottish Rite is an appendant body of Freemasonry, and, like the York Rite (Chapter 10), it's considered entirely optional for Masons to join. It's technically a *concordant* body, because some of its degrees continue the story of the building of Solomon's Temple that is started in the first three lodge degrees. (For more on appendant and concordant bodies, see Chapter 9.)

The Scottish Rite regularly confers degrees 4 through 32 on its candidates. Additionally, the Rite also bestows the 33rd degree on certain members. The 33rd degree is a degree for special service to Freemasonry or the community.

These higher degree numbers should not be considered higher ranks. The 3rd degree, the Master Mason, is the most important and highest degree in Freemasonry, and any other degrees are considered simply extensions of being a Master Mason.

Organization: Meeting the departments that confer degrees

In the United States, the Scottish Rite is divided into two geographical territories: the Northern Masonic Jurisdiction (NMJ) and the Southern Jurisdiction (SJ). Each territory is governed by its own Supreme Council. The local chapters of the Rite are called *valleys*.

Within each valley, the degrees that are conferred are actually divided among what amounts to several internal departments. Each one is in charge of presenting its particular degrees, and each one has its own officers and meetings. They're sort of like in-house lodges within each Scottish Rite valley, and there are differences between the Northern and Southern jurisdictions in the way they divide up these "departments." They are as follows:

- **Lodge of Perfection:** The 4th through the 14th degrees are presided over by the Lodge of Perfection. These degrees are considered to be the *ineffable degrees* and concern further stories of King Solomon's Temple and the search for the ineffable, unspoken, unknown name of God. (These degrees are very similar in theme to the Royal Arch degrees of the York Rite; see Chapter 10 for more about Hebrew beliefs concerning the name of God.)

- **Council Princes of Jerusalem:** In the NMJ, the Council Princes of Jerusalem presides over the 15th and 16th degrees. This division does not exist in the SJ. These degrees concern the rebuilding of the Temple after the Babylon captivity.

- **Chapter of the Rose Croix:** In the NMJ, the Chapter of the Rose Croix presides over the 17th and 18th degrees, whereas in the SJ the chapter is responsible for the 15th through 18th degrees.

- **Council of Kadosh:** The SJ classifies the 19th through 30th degrees as part of the Council of Kadosh. The NMJ does not have this council.

- **Consistory:** The NMJ puts the 19th through 32nd degrees under the authority of the Consistory, but the SJ only places the 31st and 32nd degrees in this group.

The Scottish Rite confers the 33rd degree as a position for members who have performed great service to Freemasonry, the Scottish Rite, or the community. Recipients are given a special medal or jewel and are referred to as an "Illustrious Brother." They may sign *33°* after their name. The Supreme Council's Board of Directors is made up of 33rd-degree members, and a distinction is often made between honorary 33rds and *active 33rds* (those serving on the board of directors).

Membership: Earning degrees in the Scottish Rite

Let me clear up a few popular misconceptions. To be a Scottish Rite Mason, you don't have to be *from* Scotland or go *to* Scotland (you'd be amazed how many people ask). You need only be a Master Mason in good standing with your lodge. In the United States, to be a Scottish Rite 32nd-degree Mason doesn't mean that you have to have every degree from the 4th through the 32nd conferred on you. Nor do you have to experience the degrees in order — they're self-contained lessons. Some are considered more essential than others to have a basic understanding of the philosophy of the Rite, but if you experience the 32nd degree, you're a 32nd-degree Mason. Degrees other than the 32nd are presented in Scottish Rite valleys throughout the year, and members may travel to other areas to attend degrees they haven't seen in their home valleys. Still, experiencing all the degrees of the Scottish Rite can take many years.

Rules vary from one country to the next, and some jurisdictions do require a Mason to progress in order up through the degrees, starting at the 4th and ending at the 32nd. In some countries, joining the Scottish Rite is by invitation only, and getting to the 32nd degree can take years. Progressing in order is not required in the United States, where Master Masons petition the Rite for the degrees and, at the very least, the 32nd degree will be conferred on them.

There is a certain amount of humor in the fact that many anti-Masons believe that the 32nd degree means that anyone holding such a high-ranking degree and title has received certain dark, mysterious, and potentially evil knowledge denied to everyone from the 31st degree on down. The truth is in the United States anyway, being a member of the Scottish Rite means that you are a 32nd-degree Mason, even if you have not had degrees 4 through 31 conferred upon you.

Later in the chapter, I list the different degrees. Many of the names will sound similar to some of the York Rite degrees (see Chapter 10). Bear in mind that both the York and Scottish rites developed as separate branches but grew from the same tree trunk. And that tree trunk first sprouted in France.

North and South

The territory of the Northern Masonic Jurisdiction (NMJ) includes the 15 states east of the Mississippi River and north of the Mason-Dixon Line and the Ohio River (Connecticut, Delaware, Illinois, Indiana, Maine, Massachusetts, Michigan, New Hampshire, New Jersey, New York, Ohio, Pennsylvania, Rhode Island, Vermont, and Wisconsin). Its headquarters are in Lexington, Massachusetts.

The Southern Jurisdiction (SJ) encompasses the 35 remaining states, the District of Columbia and all U.S. territories and possessions. Its headquarters are in Washington, D.C. The SJ got the lion's share of the country because

dividing lines were drawn pretty equally when the country was much smaller. The better-organized SJ retained the right to expand into any new states and U.S. territories, and as a result, as the country grew, the SJ dramatically expanded.

The two groups do not infringe on each other's territory, and they are solely responsible for conferring Scottish Rite degrees on Freemasons. They don't confer the Entered Apprentice, Fellow Craft, or Master Mason degrees, which are reserved only for lodges administered by Grand Lodges.

Presentation: Raising the curtain and lighting the lights

Like the York Rite, the Scottish Rite degrees should be thought of as a continuing-education course in Masonry. Each degree is presented to teach a moral or philosophical lesson. But unlike the York Rite, the presentation of the degrees is handled in a very different way.

The York Rite degrees were designed to be presented in a Masonic lodge room, but the Scottish Rite developed into something more complex. In the United States, the Scottish Rite presents its ritual ceremonies in an auditorium to multiple candidates. The ceremonies are dramatically staged as short plays, generally complete with sets, scenery, makeup, lighting, sound effects, music, and costumes. York Rite bodies may have several different chapters, councils, and commanderies around the state, but there are comparatively few Scottish Rite chapters, which are called *valleys*. Most states have no more than two or three, and degree conferrals (called *ceremonials* or *reunions*) are done only once or twice a year because the presentation of these ritual plays is a major production involving a large volunteer cast and technical crew.

The conferring of Scottish Rite degrees on many candidates at once is done by presenting the dramatic portion of the degree ceremony, often with one member of the audience brought onstage to act as a stand-in, or *exemplar,* for the rest of the group. Each degree has its own *obligation* (oath) and identifying *sign* (gesture). At the proper moment in each ceremony, the audience rises and, in unison, gives the sign and recites the obligation. In the United States, most members see or experience the Scottish Rite degrees in this manner.

Other countries vary in the way they confer the Scottish Rite degrees. The massive ceremonials with dozens, hundreds, and even thousands of candidates are largely unknown outside of the United States. Many differences also exist in the wording and presentation of the degrees themselves. What they have in common are the basic moral lessons imparted by the individual degrees, regardless of the story used to tell each lesson.

Seeing How the Scottish Rite Started

As odd as it sounds, much of what became the Scottish Rite didn't come from Scotland, although some of the legends that were used to create the degrees certainly did. The real source of the majority of the Scottish Rite degrees came from France, possibly from Scottish expatriates living there. The following sections explain how the Scottish Rite took hold and grew.

France: Freemasonry's foundry furnace

Nobody took to Freemasonry like the French. For 150 years, French Masons formed Grand Lodges, councils, chapters, and orders, then got mad at each other, split off, and re-formed them all over again, only to create new alliances with some but not others. Their bewildering politics are just the same.

In the midst of all this Masonic confusion came a declaration from Chevalier Andrew Michael Ramsay of Scotland that Freemasonry was descended from ancient orders and mystical religions and brought to Europe by the crusading knights during the Middle Ages. When he put that idea in the minds of these inventive folks, there was no holding them back.

Throughout France's history, more than 1,100 degrees have been conferred by 26 different orders that admitted men, women, or both, plus more than 30 more pseudo-Masonic groups. Most of the groups that popped up after 1737 were based largely on the suggestion of Ramsay's theory of knights and chivalry, probably made popular by the fact that middle-class shopkeepers could now be dubbed with titles and honors every bit as impressive as the plump aristocratic ponce who lived in the big fat castle down the street.

Ramsay claimed that crusading knights brought Freemasonry to France (many assumed that he meant the Knights Templar) and that it had leapt across the Channel to Scotland in the 1300s, where it hid out for 400 years. In fact, Scottish Jacobites living in France while they waited for the Stuart kings to get back on England's throne had a large role in creating these degrees, which became known as the *Ecossais* (French for "Scottish") degrees. The degrees came from different places, but some became more popular than others and spread. Today the French refer to these sometimes as *Hauts Grades,* meaning "High Grades."

In 1758, a very impressive-sounding Grand Council of Emperors of the East and West organized the Rite of Perfection, consisting of 25 degrees. The 25th and highest degree was the Sublime Prince of the Royal Secret. By 1760, the Grand Lodge of France took the Rite under its wing, but arguments repeatedly broke out over who had the right to organize and administer the degrees. Thus the Scottish Rite began under confused and tumultuous conditions.

The Americas: The Scottish Rite's real home

In 1761, Etienne Morin was appointed as "Grand Inspector to all parts of the New World." He was sent forth to spread the degrees around. In 1763, Morin formed a 25-degree Rite of Perfection in St. Domingo in the West Indies, and it was from here that Scottish Rite Masonry truly began to spread around the world. Four years later, Morin's friend Henry Francken of Jamaica exported the degrees to New York, and in 1783, Isaac De Costa started a Rite of Perfection in Charleston, South Carolina.

I skip the truly sleep-inducing details of who started what first and had proper permission to do it — Masonic historians have argued about it for years. Instead, I just generalize and say that in 1801, a document appeared, backdated to 1786 and supposedly under the royal authority of King Frederick the Great in Berlin, granting the bearer the right to organize new chapters. This constitution added another eight degrees to those already used in the Rite of Perfection and referred to the entire system as the "Ancient and Accepted Scottish Rite." The two guys who rode into Charleston with it were John Mitchell and Dr. Frederick Dalco, and they announced themselves as Sovereign Grand Inspectors General. It clearly impressed a whole lot of somebodies, and on May 31, 1801, they officially formed the Mother Supreme Council 33°, Ancient and Accepted Scottish Rite.

The York Rite was already the dominant group conferring its own additional degrees in the North, so the Scottish Rite was slower to expand there. The Scottish Rite group in Charleston, on the other hand, spread rapidly through-out the South. Still, there were Scottish Rite groups operating in the North that had been formed by Henry Francken, along with several unauthorized rogue groups. One such irregular group was organized by Joseph Cerneau, who caused something of a major turf war in the Northern states for many years. The Northern groups wandered in the wilderness until 1867, when the Northern Masonic Jurisdiction (NMJ) was formed, with the authority to confer the Scottish Rite degrees in 15 states.

Meeting Albert Pike: Sage of the Scottish Rite

Albert Pike is important because of his enormous impact on the Scottish Rite Southern Jurisdiction (SJ) and the sheer volume of his Masonic writings. *Genius* is a word that's overused a lot these days, such as "The musical genius of Lady Gaga!" But Albert Pike was indeed a genius. Even without his Masonic contributions, his life was truly astonishing. That said, he remains Freemasonry's most misquoted author, and many of his rambling passages are fraudulently used as a stick with which to beat Freemasonry over the head. So understanding who he was and what he did is important.

Pike's life outside of Masonry

At the age of 15, Pike passed the entrance exam of Harvard. He completed a two-year program in one year, but he couldn't afford the remaining two years needed to graduate. He left college and educated himself in junior- and senior-year subjects while teaching to make money. At 22, he set off to explore the West, where he encountered Indian tribes and became interested in their cultures. Eventually, he settled in Arkansas, first as a publisher and then as a self-educated lawyer.

Pike was a man of many gifts, and in his remarkable life he became a state Supreme Court justice, a newspaper editor, a commander in the war with Mexico, a Confederate brigadier general in the Civil War, and a diplomat to the Indian nations.

An adopted Confederate from a Yankee upbringing, Pike, like many other Americans, lost everything in the war. He eventually began his life again in Washington, D.C., as a lawyer. Pike lived there the rest of his life. He went on to argue several cases before the U.S. Supreme Court.

Discovering Freemasonry

In 1850, Pike joined Western Star Lodge #2 in Little Rock, Arkansas. He became fascinated with Freemasonry and quickly took part in everything he could find. In 1852, he and 16 others founded Magnolia Lodge #60, and Pike was its Master in 1853 and 1854. He took the ten degrees of the York Rite and became active in the Grand Lodge of Arkansas and the Royal Arch Grand Chapter of Arkansas. Before 1853, Pike had never even heard of the Scottish Rite, but in March of that year he traveled to Charleston, South Carolina, and took the 4th through 32nd degrees. It has been estimated that over his lifetime, Pike had 130 different Mason-related degrees conferred on him.

In 1853, the year that he joined the Scottish Rite, Pike was appointed as Deputy Inspector of Arkansas for the Scottish Rite. Intrigued with but unsatisfied by the degrees as they had been presented, Pike hand-copied all the Masonic degrees on file at the Supreme Council library and started the task he became most famous for in the Masonic world. In 1855, he was appointed to a committee charged with preparing new and improved versions of the degree rituals. Like most committees, the youngest guy with the least experience wound up running with the ball. Eventually, he rewrote them all.

After just six years as a member of the Scottish Rite, Pike was elected and installed as Grand Commander of the Supreme Council for the Southern Jurisdiction in January 1859. He held that office until his death in 1891.

You say Cabala, I say Kabbalah

This little sidebar is potentially brain numbing, so feel free to skip over it if you like. But if you do any looking into esoteric, hermetic, or otherwise mystical subjects in books or on the Internet, you'll generally find mention of something called the *Kabbalah* (or Cabala, or Kabala, or Qabalah, or even Cabbalah — all spellings are used). Much of what is found in Albert Pike's writings on the Scottish Rite degrees was influenced by his study of the Kabbalah.

The Kabbalah is an extraordinarily complex and mystical Jewish course of biblical study. Its various spellings are something of a tiny taste of the mind-boggling complexities of Kabbalah, which is variously translated as "received" or "tradition" (meaning the oral tradition of mystical formulas received by initiates from the learned Kabbalah adepts). For centuries, it was passed down from mouth to ear by these scholars, and a student had to be over 40 years of age to be considered worthy enough to even hear about it. Kabbalah had its written, formalized beginnings in the 12th century, although the tradition of Jewish mysticism stretches back at least to the 6th century BC.

The essential purpose of Kabbalah is to find the hidden faces of God and to understand the origins and operations of the universe. As in traditional Judaism, its holiest book is the Torah, which is made up of the first five books of the

Bible (or the *Pentateuch*) and the collection of commentaries on those five books, a body of Jewish literature and law that was, at one time, strictly an oral tradition. Kabbalah employs the constant metaphor of the Tree of Life, which has ten branches emanating from the *sephiroth,* the ten sacred Hebrew numbers, with the whole tree representing a progressive path to enlightenment and knowledge of God.

There are two main types of Kabbalah: the speculative or philosophical variety, and the practical (or to our Western eyes, the magical) Kabbalah. A staggering amount of written material exists in Kabbalah, but the two principal works are the *Sefer Yetsirah* (Book of Creation) and the *Sefer Zohar* (Book of Splendor). Early practitioners were called *Merkabah riders,* men who put themselves into an ecstatic, trancelike state through fasting and prayer in order to ride the *Merkabah* (Chariot of God) passing through the *hekhaloth* (Seven Halls of Heaven) that led to the Throne of God. The riders carried with them the lengthy secret spells or physical talismans that would protect them from the demons guarding each portal, an idea startlingly similar to aspects of ancient Egyptian mysticism related to the story of Isis and Osiris.

The *Sefer Zohar* said that Kabbalah illuminates *dualism,* the idea that Good and Evil are locked in mortal combat throughout the universe, and it called this supernatural, evil force the *Sitra Ahra* ("the other side"). Don't think that George Lucas hadn't read a little Kabbalah before making Darth Vader and Obi Wan Kenobi opposite sides of the Force. But the Sitra Ahra exists not to fight God; it was created by God to give man the free will to choose between good and evil.

The far more famous aspects of Kabbalah are in the practical, or magical, tradition. The best known of these is the *Gematria,* or the mystical practice of numerology. In the Hebrew language, every letter has a numerical equivalent, and Kabbalists believed that the endless and intricate reweaving of the letters in the holy books could discover hidden truths and prophecies in the Torah, resulting in everything from simple anagrams to complex geometric computations.

An *anagram* is simply a word or phrase formed out of the rearranged letters of another word or phrase. A very simple example of this can be found in an early Christian anagram (yes, there were Christian Kabbalists, but that detail only further complicates matters, so I won't go there). One of the earliest Christian symbols was a fish, because the Greek word for fish, *ichthus,* was used as an anagram for the first letters of the phrase "Jesus Christ, the Son of God, the Savior." In Hebrew, the most well known of

these is the Tetragrammaton, the four-letter name of God, YHVH, or sometimes IHVH, translated as *Jehovah* or *Yahweh.* The four letters are an anagram for God's biblical statement of his identity to Moses: "I am that I am." For the Jews, it stood for the great and unspeakable name of God, too holy to be spoken out loud. This famous anagram can be found here and there in Masonic ceremonies, especially in the Royal and Select Master degrees of the York Rite (see Chapter 10).

Because of the complex manipulation of language, like some sort of cosmic taffy pull, truly understanding Kabbalah without understanding the Hebrew language is nearly impossible. Yet, it's important to have a nodding acquaintance with Kabbalah, because there is virtually no secret brotherhood or occult organization, whether of serious adepts or starry-eyed goofballs, that doesn't adapt, borrow, or steal from it.

Its most recent popular incarnation has been the Kabbalah Centers in Los Angeles and New York, operated by Philip Berg. This version of Kabbalah has loads of celebrity fans (most notably Madonna) as well as plenty of detractors who call it a cult, and some religious scholars are simply aghast over Berg's pop interpretation. It seems that everything old is new again.

Writing and revising rituals, morals, and dogma

Pike finally finished the rewrite of the rituals in 1868. In addition to the 4th through 33rd degrees, he also wrote a ceremony to constitute a new chapter, a funeral service, a memorial lodge ceremony called a Lodge of Sorrow, and even rituals for a women's group, called a Lodge of Adoption.

Albert Pike, racist?

Allegations of racism have often been made about Pike over the years, yet he was a personal friend of Thornton A. Jackson, Supreme Grand Commander of the Prince Hall Southern Jurisdiction's Supreme Council. In fact, Pike presented Jackson with a complete set of his rituals for use by the Prince Hall Scottish Rite. Pike had no problem with blacks having their own "separate but equal" Masonic organization.

Pike was a man of his era. He spent years living in the South and was a Civil War general on the Confederate side. He owned several household slaves in Little Rock, but he personally disliked the institution of slavery. The separation of the races was a way of life in the North and the South, and the concept of parallel groups for blacks and whites was the accepted norm before and after the Civil War. Pike had no interest in integrating Freemasonry, but he had no qualms about sharing Masonic knowledge with black Masons.

Many anti-Masons have attempted to connect Pike with the early days of the Ku Klux Klan. However, no authentic evidence links Pike with the KKK.

Pike also produced what were supposed to be additional lectures to further explain the degrees. He published them as the massive *Morals and Dogma*. The book didn't really follow the degrees, or even illustrate them very well, but it's an enormous volume that explores philosophy and religion as well as foreign and ancient cultures. It was intended to give candidates the information needed to understand the origins and backgrounds of each degree. Pike leaned a lot on fanciful writings of earlier Masonic and mystical authors; he truly believed that Freemasonry, especially the Scottish Rite degrees, had descended from ancient Egypt, Greece, and elsewhere.

The Scottish Rite degrees had originally come out of creative authors in France who relished telling stories and embellishing myths. That Freemasonry grew out of alchemy, Rosicrucianism, mysticism, ancient Egypt, and other ancient pagan mysteries has never been proved. Those influences were certainly in the French *haute* degrees, but they were there because the Masons who wrote them put them there out of imitation, fascination, or simply wishful thinking. No serious Masonic researcher today believes that modern Freemasonry descended directly from those earlier sources.

But Pike sure did. He drew heavily on a particular book by French occultist Eliphas Levi (see Chapter 8). Levi's *Dogme et Rituel de la Haute Magie* ("Dogma and Ritual of High Magic") was published in 1855, and although it was poorly researched and loaded with errors and invention, Pike believed it. Whole passages of Levi's book made it into Pike's. In later years, when he was clearly shown evidence that Levi's book was flawed, Pike had little interest in the daunting task of revising his *Morals and Dogma.*

Putting Pike in perspective

Anti-Masons have used Pike's writings in *Morals and Dogma* almost from the beginning as something with which to beat Freemasons over the head, always plucking isolated passages from it and selectively leaving out critical words and even whole sentences from quotes. (I discuss many of these instances in Chapters 4, 8, and 18.) Misunderstanding *Morals and Dogma* is easy to do; not many people have actually read it all.

Albert Pike was, and remains, hugely important within the Scottish Rite Southern Jurisdiction. He was the Grand Commander of the SJ for 32 years. His knowledge and achievements are regularly praised in the Masonic world. Nevertheless, neither the Northern Masonic Jurisdiction nor by the rest of the Scottish Rite world outside of the United States uniformly adopted his works. He didn't have any effect on regular, recognized Blue Lodge Masonry. He only had authority over the states and other territories of the SJ. Although *Morals and Dogma* was given to all SJ 32nd-degree members until 1974, most used it as a doorstop and never read it. Outside of the SJ, it was rarely even heard of. Some tend to regard Pike as the most important Masonic leader in history. He was, indeed, a genius, and there is scarcely a subject about Freemasonry on which he did not have, and write down, an opinion. But his influence needs to be kept in proper perspective.

Listing the Degrees of the Scottish Rite

Unlike the ten degrees of the York Rite (see Chapter 10), the Scottish Rite's chaotic development has made a simple listing and explanation of its degrees a task far too complex for this book. Not many Scottish Rite Masons know them all, and few have even seen them all performed.

Each of the Supreme Councils (one for the Northern Masonic Jurisdiction and another for the Southern Jurisdiction) is the owner and custodian of the official ritual scripts, and a Ritual Committee is given the power to make changes in the degrees. Such changes are never made lightly, yet both jurisdictions have made major modifications since 2000.

The Southern Jurisdiction degrees

The SJ of the Scottish Rite essentially uses the same rituals that were written by Albert Pike in the 1860s, with some slight updating of dated vocabulary and the removal of long and elaborate staging directions. Pike wrote in Victorian times and liberally included Hebrew, Greek, and Roman mythology as well as Greek and Latin phrases and biblical references that were readily understood in those days. Victorian-era schools concentrated heavily on those subjects, but any modern high-school student today would be as unable to pass an 1870s graduation exam (just as an 1870s student would be unable to score well on the SAT). It was a different time, and the common knowledge of that era isn't as common today. As a result, Pike's work has left many modern Scottish Rite Masons baffled.

The SJ rituals went through a revision starting in 1995 and finishing in 2000, but it was mostly done to eliminate repetition of lines, needlessly obscure references, and unnecessarily drawn-out ceremonies. A few were also rearranged to put them in proper chronological order. Each degree can now be presented in about an hour, and the degrees were standardized so all Scottish Rite valleys can use the same presentation materials. They retain the language and settings of Pike's originals and are referred to as the *Revised Standard Pike Ritual.*

I list the degrees of the SJ in Table 11-1.

Table 11-1	The Southern Jurisdiction Degrees	
Division	**Degree Number**	**Degree Title**
Lodge of Perfection	4	Secret Master
	5	Perfect Master
	6	Intimate Secretary
	7	Provost and Judge
	8	Intendant of the Building
	9	Elu of the Nine
	10	Elu of the Fifteen
	11	Elu of the Twelve
	12	Grand Master Architect
	13	Royal Arch of Solomon (Knight of the Ninth Arch)

Division	Degree Number	Degree Title
	14	Perfect Elu (Grand Elect, Perfect and Sublime Mason)
Rose Croix	15	Knight of the East, of the Sword, or the Eagle
	16	Prince of Jerusalem
	17	Knight of the East and West
	18	Knight of the Rose Croix
Council of Kadosh	19	Grand Pontiff
	20	Master of the Symbolic Lodge
	21	Noachite, or Prussian Knight
	22	Knight of the Royal Axe (Prince of Libanus)
	23	Chief of the Tabernacle
	24	Prince of the Tabernacle
	25	Knight of the Brazen Serpent
	26	Prince of Mercy
	27	Knight of the Sun (formerly the 28th degree)
	28	Knight Commander of the Temple (formerly the 27th degree)
	29	Scottish Knight of St. Andrew
	30	Knight Kadosh
Consistory	31	Inspector Inquisitor
	32	Master of the Royal Secret
Supreme Council	33	Inspector General

The Northern Masonic Jurisdiction degrees

Albert Pike's rituals were never adopted by the NMJ. Although the SJ has stayed pretty much with Pike's original structure and wording, the NMJ has felt freer to tinker with and update the degrees. As a result, the 20th degree, Master Ad Vitam, tells a story about George Washington, and the 25th degree, Master of Achievement, is about Benjamin Franklin. The NMJ believes that the degrees make a bigger impact if some of them tell age-old morals and truths, using references more familiar to modern Freemasons. The SJ tends to sniff with a little derision that it has the more "authentic" rituals, as if they were passed from God's lips directly to Albert Pike's pen. They're older, perhaps, but truth is where you find it. Both systems teach similar lessons, and both have merit.

In 2004, the NMJ rewrote and reorganized its degrees, and it continues to revise them. Table 11-2 lists the latest lineup.

Table 11-2	The Northern Masonic Jurisdiction Degrees	
Division	*Degree Number*	*Degree Title*
Lodge of Perfection	4	Master Traveler
	5	Perfect Master (formerly part of the 23rd degree)
	6	Master of the Brazen Serpent
	7	Provost and Judge
	8	Intendant of the Building
	9	Master of the Temple (formerly part of the 23rd degree)
	10	Master Elect
	11	Sublime Master Elected
	12	Grand Master Architect (formerly the 26th degree)
	13	Master of the Ninth Arch
	14	Grand Elect Mason
Council Princes of Jerusalem	15	Knight of the East or Sword
	16	Prince of Jerusalem
Chapter Rose Croix	17	Knight of the East and West
	18	Knight of the Rose Croix de Heredon Council of Kadosh
Consistory	19	Grand Pontiff
	20	Master Ad Vitam (George Washington)
	21	Patriarch Noachite
	22	Prince of Libanus
	23	Chief of the Tabernacle
	24	Brother of the Forest
	25	Master of Achievement (Benjamin Franklin)
	26	Friend and Brother Eternal (formerly Prince of Mercy)
	27	Knight of Jerusalem
	28	Knight of the Sun or Prince Adept
	29	Knight of St. Andrew

Division	Degree Number	Degree Title
	30	Grand Inspector (formerly the 31st degree)
	31	Knight Aspirant (formerly Part 1 of the 32nd degree)
	32	Sublime Prince of the Royal Secret
Supreme Council	33	Inspector General

Serving Communities through Charitable Work

The Scottish Rite bodies sponsor a variety of charities. The NMJ sponsors learning centers for dyslexic children and funds research into the treatment of schizophrenia. It also operates the National Heritage Museum in Lexington, Massachusetts (www.monh.org).

The SJ operates 165 RiteCare clinics and programs for children with learning disabilities and language disorders. In Dallas, it operates the Texas Scottish Rite Hospital for Children (www.tsrhc.org). In addition, the House of the Temple, its Washington, D.C., headquarters, is a magnificent landmark containing the massive personal library of Albert Pike, a museum, and one of the world's largest collections of books and periodicals about U.S. and international Freemasonry.

Knights of St. Andrew

One of the newest Masonic groups to be created is the Knights of St. Andrew, a service organization developed for 32nd-degree Scottish Rite Masons. The individual chapters are under the immediate supervision of their Scottish Rite Consistory, and they essentially provide services wherever they're needed. Members act as greeters, escort dignitaries at special events, serve as guides, assist in Scottish Rite degree work, and much more.

Each member of the Knights of St. Andrew wears a tartan badge with an emblem attached to it. Some chapters wear kilts, *sporrans* (pouches), and other Scottish accessories to complement the formal attire.

Every chapter has its own charter, bylaws, initiation, and opening and closing rituals. Weldon J. Good founded the first Chapter of the Knights in 1993 in Tulsa, Oklahoma. Since then, it has spread across both the Northern and Southern AASR jurisdictions with great enthusiasm.

Chapter 12

Shriners International

In This Chapter

▶ Making the Shriner-Masonic connection

▶ Understanding the Arabic-themed origin

▶ Helping kids and having fun

You've probably seen parades with grown men driving little cars, or playing bagpipes, or doing close-order doughnuts on motorcycles, most of them wearing hats that look like overturned red flowerpots. Look a little closer at those hats and you see strange, vaguely Middle Eastern–sounding names like *Mizpah, Zoran, Hadji, El Bekel, Syria, Ben Ali,* and *Abdallah,* spelled out in glittering rhinestones. If you live in a moderate-size town, you may have seen the Shrine Circus. If you're a football fan, you've probably watched the East-West Shrine Game. Driving down the interstate, you may have passed a semi with an ad on the back, depicting a man carrying a young girl in one hand and her crutches in the other.

All these images come from one source: the Ancient Arabic Order of the Nobles of the Mystic Shrine (or Shriners International, for short). The Shriners own and operate 22 hospitals across North America, providing no-cost burn, spinal cord, and orthopedic care to children. What you may not know is that each and every one of those Shriners is also a Freemason.

The Shrine is another appendant body of Freemasonry (for more on appendant bodies, see Chapter 9), and it's arguably the most popular. Its mission is very simple: to have fun and help kids. In this chapter, I explain a little bit about where the Shrine came from, how it became one of the largest philanthropic organizations in the world, and what the Shrine has to do with Freemasonry. I also tell you all about those little hats and what that pseudo-Arabic hoodoo is about.

Getting to Know the Shriners

The Shrine has often been called the "playground of Freemasonry." Before a man can become a Shriner, he must become a Freemason. In fact, if you look carefully at the original name — Ancient Arabic Order of the Nobles of the Mystic Shrine — you can rearrange the letters A.A.O.N.M.S. and spell "A MASON."

All Shriners are Freemasons, but not all Freemasons become Shriners. In fact, the Shrine is largely unheard of outside of North America and Panama, except for a few clubs of American Shriners living overseas. Even so, the Shrine now has close to 500,000 members among 191 Shrine *centers,* or chapters, in the United States, Canada, Mexico, and Panama. The most populous Shrine center is Murat Shrine in Indianapolis, with almost 10,000 members.

Until the late 1990s, before being allowed to join the Shrine, Masons were required to join a local lodge, receive their three lodge degrees, and also join either the Scottish Rite or the York Rite and complete their degree work. That policy has changed: Today, candidates for the Shrine are required only to be a Master Mason.

Even though Shriners are Masons, the Shrine is *not* a Masonic organization — it doesn't confer any degree that continues or enlarges on the Masonic degrees. It's simply an organization that requires Masonic lodge membership as a prerequisite for joining.

Tracing the History from Partiers to Philanthropists

In Chapter 2, I discuss the gradual removal of intoxicating liquor from U.S. Masonic lodges in the mid-1800s. Even though the fraternity of Freemasonry had begun in taverns and alehouses, by the 1850s, most Grand Lodges had outlawed booze in the lodges. The local lodges, as well as the York and Scottish Rite commanderies and temples, had become dry establishments, concentrating more on the conferral of degrees and the development of ritual and symbolism than on convivial brotherhood and fun. Masonic halls became solemn places of introspection. Masons had to go to the local bar, restaurant, or private club for their old-style feasts and toasting. One such regular gathering became the root of Shriners International.

The Knickerbocker boys start the fun

In 1870, a group of New York City Masons met regularly for lunch at the Knickerbocker Cottage, a restaurant on Sixth Avenue. They had a regular table and had a reputation for being an especially boisterous group of men. They felt that the lodge had become too stodgy and too wrapped up in ritual and had lost a lot of the fun and fellowship Masonry once had. Dr. Walter Fleming and a traveling actor named Billy Florence decided to do something about it.

Florence had traveled the world, and one night after a performance in Marseilles, France, for an Ottoman diplomat, the post-theater entertainment was an elaborate musical comedy about an ancient, secret society, filled with Arab costumes and a storyline from the Middle East. At the end of the show, the guests were all sworn in as members of this fictional, fun "society."

Florence described the show to Dr. Fleming in New York, and provided details and drawings after seeing it performed again in Cairo and Algiers. Fleming loved it, and he and the Knickerbocker boys added to the concept. Charles McClenachan and William Sleigh Paterson were experts on Masonic ritual, while Albert L. Rawson was a prominent scholar on the Middle East who provided more background and Arabic vocabulary. They wrote up an initiation ritual, devised exotic titles for the officers' positions, and came up with the greeting phrase of the Order based on an Arabic saying, *Es Selamu Aleikum!,* which means, "Peace be with you!"

In 1872, the little group of friends declared themselves to be the charter members of the Mecca Temple of the Ancient Arabic Order of the Nobles of the Mystic Shrine, and Dr. Fleming was elected as the Potentate.

So why the goofy hats?

No self-respecting fraternal group of the 1800s could be without appropriate accessories. The Scottish Rite, the Tall Cedars, and the Knights Templar all had special hats. For their official headgear, the Shriners adopted the red felt fez (named after the 14th-century Moroccan city of Fez where it was first created to replace the pesky and hard-to-wrap turban). Attached to it is a long, black tassel (see Figure 12-1). Shriners wear their fez during all official functions.

In the middle of the fez is a distinctive, crescent-shaped jewel. The crescent represents the claws of a Bengal tiger. In the center is the head of a sphinx. The crescent hangs under a curved *scimitar* (sword), and a five-pointed star hangs beneath the head of the sphinx.

Figure 12-1:
A typical
Shriner's
fez.

Photograph courtesy of Christopher Hodapp

The first growth of the Shrine

At first, the Shrine remained a mostly New York City group. Another temple was chartered in Rochester, New York, but after four years, it had just 43 *nobles* (the Shrine's term for members). In 1876, the group made changes, enlarged the initiation ceremony, and invented an elaborate "history." They established an Imperial Grand Council and started on a nationwide public relations push to grow the new group. It caught on, and by 1890, there were 50 Shrine temples in the United States and Canada, with almost 7,500 members. By 1900, the membership swelled to 50,000 in 79 Shrine temples. America was apparently full of thirsty Masons.

Polio and the first Shrine hospital

An outbreak of polio struck the United States in 1919. We don't think of polio much today, because the last three generations of Americans have been vaccinated against the virus. But in 1919, it killed 6,000 people in the United States and left 27,000 paralyzed. In its aftermath, a huge part of the population, many of them children, needed orthopedic care. In 1920, the Shrine's Imperial Session voted to assess members $2 a year to build the first Shriners Hospital for Crippled Children in Shreveport, Louisiana.

The rules were simple. Care was provided at no cost for any child under 14 (and later, 18) whose family was unable to pay. It had no restriction based on race, religion, color, or national origin — the only requirement was that there had to be a chance of being able to improve the child's condition.

The editorial without words

The drawing that graces billboards, trucks, and other signs for the Shriners Hospitals is known by its members as "the editorial without words," because the story it tells needs no explanation. It depicts a Shriner, wearing his fez, carrying a little girl in one hand and her crutches in the other.

Its origin is a real photograph taken in 1970 at an amusement park in Evansville, Indiana. The little girl in the photo is Bobbi Jo Wright, who was born with cerebral palsy. Her orthopedic problems were treated at St. Louis Shriners Hospital, and Bobbi Jo went on to graduate from Anderson University in Indiana.

The Shriner carrying Bobbi Jo is Al Hortman, who became a Mason and a Shriner after his own daughter was treated at the St. Louis hospital. The image that was photographed almost by accident by a local newspaper photographer has been reproduced on pins, patches, shirts, hats, and even stained-glass windows. A full-size statue of the image stands outside the Shrine's headquarters in Tampa, Florida, as well as at many Shrine centers around the country.

Depression and growth

Fourteen Shriners Hospitals were built in the United States and Canada between 1922 and 1927. The Great Depression struck in 1929, and the Shrine, like other fraternal organizations, fell on hard times. Many other groups didn't survive. Still, the Shriners and its separate hospital corporation managed to invest more than $1 billion in government bonds during the four years of World War II. After the war, a new explosion of fraternalism brought new members in record numbers, and the construction resumed with a new hospital in Mexico City in 1945.

Greatest philanthropy in the world

Since 1920, a total of 22 Shriners Hospitals have been built, all retaining the same criteria for admission and still with no charge to the family for care. The orthopedic care was increased over the years, and in 1962, the system expanded to treat severe burns. In 1980, it was expanded again to provide spinal-cord rehabilitation. Shriners Hospitals have been at the forefront in research for this kind of care and have developed new methods of treatment, as well as made advances in the development of artificial limbs and other prosthetics. The research costs alone come to $25 million a year, and Shriners spend $1.6 million a day on the hospitals. All the money comes from donations by Shriners.

In 1996, because of the expanding range of services and treatments, the Shrine officially changed the name of the system to Shriners Hospitals for Children, dropping the term "Crippled." It is referred to today as the "greatest philanthropy in the world."

Putting a Little of the Boy Back in the Man

From the beginning, the Shrine was intentionally designed to be fun — actually, even a bit juvenile. Freemasons looking for deep, intellectual symbolism and knowledge won't find it in the Shrine. What they will find is old-fashioned, back-slapping, glass-raising, cigar-puffing, high-volume socializing. The group's history is filled with tales of the antics of Shriners, especially when collected together at their annual conventions. Perhaps riding horses through hotel lobbies that wouldn't open the bar early enough would result in a lawsuit or two today, but it's the stuff of legend that gave them their well-earned reputation as America's premiere party animals.

Becoming initiated

Most Shrines conduct a two-part initiation ceremony. The first section is a dramatic enactment of a morality story, much like those done in the Scottish Rite. The candidates sit in the audience, and when the time comes for them to take the obligation of the Shrine, the candidates do it in unison.

The second section is traditionally referred to as *Hot Sands,* and initiates must symbolically cross the "hot sands of the desert" to complete the ceremony. Some Shrines have removed or altered this portion of the initiation or have made it optional. The Shrine has only one "degree," and members are referred to as *nobles.*

Gathering at temples

Shrine temples (or *centers,* as more of them are referred to these days) are often very large. Because most states have only a few, each temple draws on dozens or even hundreds of Masonic lodges for its membership. Shrine temples often have thousands of members.

The Shrine built its own dedicated buildings during prosperous times, and they were generally designed with Middle Eastern architectural details (see Figure 12-2). Shrine buildings look strangely incongruous plopped down in the middle of American cities, with their tall minarets and domed roofs. In keeping with the functions of the Shrine, they often have large auditoriums, plus social rooms, dance halls, restaurants, and bars. With 6,300 seats, the Al Malaikah Shrine Auditorium in Los Angeles is the largest theater in the world. It has been the home of the Academy Awards, the Grammy Awards, and the American Music Awards.

Forming units to suit every Shriner

Most Shrine Temples are divided up into clubs or units. Clowns, motorcycle groups, horse patrols, marching bands, railroad clubs, bagpipers, classic-car owners — the variety is endless. Because the Shrine is intended to be more socially involving, members are encouraged to find a unit that appeals to their interests or hobbies.

Figure 12-2: The Al Malaikah Shrine Auditorium in Los Angeles was built in 1926.

Photograph courtesy of Christopher Hodapp

Some of the units are designed to handle transportation of children and their families to the Shriners Hospitals, and temples often have a small fleet of cars or vans driven by volunteers. Other temples may even have units for private airplane owners who volunteer to fly patients to hospitals across the country.

The Daughters of the Nile is a ladies group for wives and daughters of Shriners. Founded in 1913, over the years it has contributed nearly $40 million to the Shriners Hospitals.

Having fun in little cars

Shriners hold fundraising events to support both themselves and the hospitals. One of the most visible is the Shrine Circus, which is a good, old-fashioned, three-ring, big top, traveling circus that tours the U.S. and Canada. Any event that is designated as a hospital fundraiser sends 100 percent of the proceeds to Shriners Hospitals.

A tradition has developed over the years between Shriners and parades. Shriners enjoy participating in parades to promote a positive image in their communities and pride themselves on their marching bands and wild costumes. As a way to become more distinctive, Shriners began introducing cars, motorcycles, minibikes, go-karts, and tiny cars into the parades. It seems Shriners took to anything with wheels.

One group of Shriners in Omaha, Nebraska, was famous for traveling to Detroit every year and taking delivery of the first 23 Chrysler Imperial convertibles that rolled off the assembly line. Known as the Imps of Omaha, they preordered the cars in matching color schemes.

Humor, homage, or mockery?

Although the Shrine considers its ceremonies, decorations, and traditions to be all in good fun, many Muslims and Arabs do not. Fundamentalist Muslims and some mainstream Muslims feel that the Shrine makes a mockery of their religion and customs. Some Shrine temples are named after real Arabic and Persian locations (like Syria, Tehran, and Mecca), but others have obviously ridiculous names like Moolah. Solemn references to Allah were included in the ceremonies of the Shrine in the 1870s to make it feel more exotic and unlike any other fraternity at that time. Some of these references have been removed from the Shrine's ceremonies over the years, but the complaints remain.

Fundamentalist Muslims who believe that the Freemasons are partners in a Jewish-Zionist plot to take over the Middle East and the rest of the world are particularly infuriated that Masons would use their own culture to mock them. I talk more about Islam and Freemasonry in Chapter 4.

Considering the Shrine's Place in Freemasonry

In the past few years, society has caught up with the Shrine, and perhaps even passed it by, turning its back on some of its activities. What goes on in the Shrine seems like a college fraternity for adults. The concentration on drinking, smoking, carousing, partying, or hazing new initiates seems out of place in an ever-more politically correct and "nanny-ish" society that enacts ever-more stringent laws against such things. Shriners have also been bitten by lawsuits over some of their more frolicsome stunts that got out of hand. Maybe the Shrine is out of place these days. Or it could just be that society needs to lighten up.

The Shrine and the Freemasons have always had an uneasy alliance, and some members on both sides of the fence have called to sever any connection between them. Some feel that Masonry still needs a place to let down its hair and have a noisy bit of fun. Others think some Shrine activity is 180 degrees in opposition to the moral teachings of Masonry. Still more believe that the Shrine's hospital philanthropy is a shining example of Masonic charity's greatest achievement.

When the Shrine and Freemasonry were both at their peak of membership in the 1950s, there was always the question of which dog wagged which tail. Was the Shrine more popular, and so men joined Masonic lodges in droves just to get to the Shrine? Or was the Shrine simply seen as the crowning achievement of Masonry, the fun reward for passing through the many degrees of the lodge and the York or Scottish Rites? It's difficult to say today, but both groups have certainly benefited mutually from the association. In 2008, the organization shucked off its ancient-sounding name and officially became Shriners International to reflect its more commonly known nickname and to emphasize its connection with Shriners Hospitals for Children.

Chapter 13

The Extended Masonic Family

In This Chapter

▶ Bringing Freemasonry to the whole family

▶ Getting to know the more obscure groups

▶ Finding Masonic research groups

The York Rite, the Scottish Rite, and the Shrine are three of the most popular appendant bodies of Freemasonry, but they aren't the only ones. Beginning in the mid-1800s, Freemasons wanted more and more groups to join, including more ways to involve their families. Some groups developed to confer more-involved, Masonic-style degrees. Others satisfied the desire for military-style drill teams. Still others were created to allow wives and children to take part in the lodge experience.

At the height of fraternalism in the United States — in both the late 1800s and again in the 1950s — the lodge became an important part of life for millions of men and their families. Some people were so involved that they could attend some sort of degree, ceremony, dinner, dance, fundraiser, or outing almost every day of the week. The lodge became a social center for the entire family, a place where lasting friendships were made, not just between Masonic Brothers but also between wives, parents, sons, and daughters.

This chapter discusses some of the more common of these other Masonic groups, where they came from, and how they fit in with the adult-male world of Freemasonry. It also introduces some of the lesser-known groups with a Masonic connection. It concludes with several Masonic research societies for Freemasons more interested in the academic and esoteric than the social aspects of the Craft.

Bringing Women into the Lodge

Almost immediately after Freemasonry arrived in France in the early 1700s, Masonic-style organizations popped up that allowed women to join them. England and its colonies weren't so open minded.

One of the unshakable tenets of regular, recognized Freemasonry is that it's an organization for men only. The problem was that wives wanted to know what their husbands were doing all those long nights at the lodge, and many of them began voicing a desire to have something like Masonry for themselves.

Beginning in the mid-1800s, as the anti-Masonic movement began to settle down, several groups for women related to Freemasons were created, with varying degrees of success. The Martha Washington Degree, the Heroines of Jericho, the Good Samaritans, the True Kindred, the Rite of Adoption, the Order of Amaranth, and several others developed throughout the 19th century, but most of them didn't survive. I describe the most popular and lasting of them in this section.

The Order of the Eastern Star

The Order of the Eastern Star (OES) was created to be a Masonic-style organization open to women, without simply being a copy, parody, or rip-off of the Masonic degrees. Dr. Rob Morris, a Boston lawyer and teacher, created the ritual for the Order of the Eastern Star in about 1849. Morris had a boundless love of Masonic ceremonies, and he envisioned the OES as a female branch of Masonry. He strongly felt that the whole family should be able to share in the benefits and inspiration of Freemasonry. Unfortunately, the initial reception given to his idea was unremittingly hostile. Masons didn't especially want a bunch of women in their lodge halls, and Morris wasn't exactly praised.

Morris kept at it, encouraged by his wife, Charlotte. His ritual told stories of the famous heroines of the Bible, both Old and New Testament: Adah, Ruth, Esther, Martha, and the "elect lady" referred to in the second book of St. John the Evangelist, whom Morris named Electa. The trouble was that Morris loved pageantry, and he made his ceremonies so involved and so complex that presenting his vision properly took no small amount of time, effort, practice, expensive scenery, and props, not to mention warm bodies.

In 1860, he simplified the ritual and designed a national governing system of statewide groups called *constellations* and local groups called *stars*. Over the next ten years, he issued charters to more than 100 stars.

In 1867, Morris got involved with Robert McCoy, a Masonic publisher who liked the idea behind the OES. McCoy tinkered with the idea and published a new ritual, which started to catch on. By 1868, the stars-and-constellations idea was scrapped, and a nationwide General Grand Chapter was created at a meeting in Indianapolis, Indiana, in 1876. Local groups are now called *chapters,* and states are governed by Grand Chapters.

The ritual of the OES is moving and instructive. It's similar in structure to the ceremonies of the Masonic lodge yet different enough that it can't be called a rip-off or a simple rewrite. A candidate is simply initiated into the Order — there is only one degree. New initiates take an *obligation,* or oath, to the Order and are taught signs of recognition and passwords.

Joining up

The Order of the Eastern Star is open to men who are Master Masons and to female relatives, spouses, and descendants of Master Masons. The Order's teachings use characters from both the Old and New Testaments, and it's essentially a Christian-based organization, although non-Christians are certainly welcome to join. Like Freemasonry, only a belief in a Supreme Being is required.

Times were different in the United States when Morris and McCoy designed the Order of the Eastern Star. In those days, women didn't go out without a male escort, and unescorted women had little social life outside of church. Places of business often posted signs saying, "Unescorted ladies not welcome." The Eastern Star was set up so that two Master Masons were present at all their meetings. No Mason, no meeting. Women would be under the protection and supervision of at least two trusted Masons. The arrangement protected their reputations as well as their physical safety.

In addition, Masons needed to be involved with the group so there would be no objection to the Order using the traditionally men-only lodge rooms. It was a way to get the Grand Lodges around the country to see the Eastern Star not as a threat to these bastions of male power but as a helpmate. Just like at home, the lodges needed someone to cook and clean and take out the garbage for them, and the ladies jumped right in. The Eastern Star quickly took up the support position for the lodge by cooking meals for Masonic meeting and degree nights, decorating the common areas, organizing bake sales, sponsoring Christmas parties, and directing other fundraising events.

The Eastern Star's fortunes rose and fell with the waves of fraternalism. Over time, membership in the Eastern Star commonly became a "political" requirement for male officers wanting to advance in the lodge. If you wanted to become Master of the lodge one day, you and your wife had better count on joining the Star chapter. This situation isn't so commonplace these days because the Eastern Star has dwindled in popularity.

Explaining symbolism and the star points

The Order of the Eastern Star's principal symbol is the inverted five-pointed star (see Figure 13-1). The star itself is said to represent the Star of Bethlehem in the East that led the wise men to Christ's birthplace. (It is upside down because the bottom point of the star was said to point down to Bethlehem.) The initials FATAL found on some versions of the emblem stand for the phrase *Fairest Among Thousands, Altogether Lovely.*

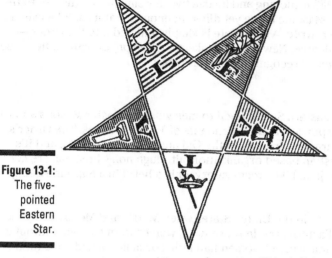

Image courtesy of Christopher Hodapp

Figure 13-1:
The five-
pointed
Eastern
Star.

Each star point represents a different heroine of the Bible and part of the degree of the Order, which each represent a different virtue. I outline them in the following sections.

Adah

Adah, daughter of Jephthah, is the first point; its color is blue, and its symbols are the sword and veil. (It points toward 1 o'clock.)

Jephthah, a judge of Israel, vowed to God that if he achieved victory over the Ammonites, he would be willing to sacrifice the first member of his household to greet him on his return. His daughter greeted him, and Adah willingly accepted her fate. Though she has no name in the Book of Judges other than the daughter of Jephthah, she is known as Adah from long Masonic tradition. She represents obedience and self-sacrifice.

Ruth

Ruth is the second point (moving clockwise); its color is yellow, and its symbol is a sheaf of wheat.

Ruth was the daughter-in-law of Naomi. Naomi and her family were Jews who had fled ancient Judah because of famine, finding a home in Moab (present-day Jordan). Both of Naomi's sons wed Moabite women. When Naomi was widowed and her sons were killed, she instructed her daughters-in-law to stay behind in their homeland, when she returned to Judah. But Ruth, though not a Jew, vowed to stay by her side, as outlined in one of the Bible's loveliest passages: "Whither thou goest, I will go; and whither thou lodgest, I will lodge; thy people shall be my people, and thy God, my God." Together the two women survived hunger and hardship, and Ruth eventually married

Naomi's kinsman Boaz and gave birth to the line of King David. She represents the ideals of loyalty and friendship.

Esther

Esther, the wife and queen of Ahasuerus (Xerxes, of ravening hoards fame), is the third star point; the color is white, and the symbol is a crown and scepter.

Esther is very important in the Jewish faith, and both the Fast of Esther and *Purim,* the Jewish feast day that follows it, celebrate her story. She was a Hebrew captive of King Ahasuerus of Babylon in Persia; through a twist of fate and a beauty contest, she was chosen to be the king's wife. Her Jewish heritage was kept a secret. When the king's evil advisor Haman plotted to annihilate the Jews in Persia, Esther bravely revealed her faith and outfoxed the evil Haman, saving her people. Thus she represents honor and courage.

Martha

Martha, sister of Lazarus, is the fourth point; the color is green, and the emblem is a broken column.

The Book of John tells that Martha prepared to receive Jesus as a visitor in her home. By the time Jesus arrived, Martha had to tell him that her brother Lazarus was dead, saying that if Jesus had been present, her brother surely would have been cured. Jesus asked for and received Martha's absolute faith, famously telling her, "I am the resurrection and the life; he that believeth in me, though he were dead, yet shall he live." Martha agreed to roll away the gravestone, and Lazarus emerged after having been dead four days. Martha represents devotion to the home as well as a belief in the immortality of the soul.

Electa

The fifth star point is *Electa,* named for the *eklekte kuria,* "the elect lady" of the Apostle John's Second Epistle. The color is red, and the symbol is a cup.

Electa's story isn't biblical, but it's a story woven out of myth and Masonic tradition. During the darkest days of Rome's persecution of the Christians, Electa and her family lived in the city of Ephesus, in modern-day Turkey. When ordered by a soldier to trample on the cross, the standard practice for smoking out secret Christians, she instead kissed it and professed her love and loyalty to Christ's teachings. She was imprisoned, scourged, and eventually crucified with her entire family, but she would not deny her belief. In the OES, Electa represents the ideals of fervent love and faith.

Considering the modern Order of the Eastern Star

The Order of the Eastern Star remains the largest fraternal organization in the world that is open to both men and women, with more than 1 million members and 9,000 chapters in 20 countries. The Grand Chapter, headquartered in a beautifully preserved mansion in Washington, D.C., is the international governing body. Curiously, New York and New Jersey's OES are not a part of this system. They have their own rules, rituals, and governing system, but they enjoy a harmonious relationship with the Grand Chapter.

Members refer to each other as Sisters and Brothers. The local chapter's primary officers are the Worthy Matron (the female equivalent of the lodge's Worshipful Master) and the Worthy Patron (a male Master Mason).

The Prince Hall Grand Lodges of Freemasons around the country, which predominantly have black members, are generally affiliated with an Eastern Star organization as well. The first Eastern Star chapter made up of black women was started in Washington, D.C., in 1874. The OES Grand Chapter doesn't govern the Prince Hall Eastern Star groups; they have their own administrative structure.

The Eastern Star supports the Masonic youth groups — DeMolay (for boys), Rainbow and Job's Daughters (both for girls) — which are discussed later in this chapter. They also support a wide variety of charities, generally decided on a state-by-state basis. They're often big supporters of Masonic retirement communities in the states that have them.

For more information on the OES, you can visit its website at http://www.easternstar.org.

The Order of the Amaranth

A second group for both Masons and their spouses and female relatives is the Order of the Amaranth. Although it was never as popular as the Order of the Eastern Star, the groups were connected for a time, and Rob Morris and Robert McCoy were both involved in the Order of the Amaranth as well.

The symbol of the Order is an amaranth wreath with a crown and sword in the center. The amaranth is a broad-leafed plant with many seeds and can be woven, like a laurel or olive wreath. The leaves can also be eaten like spinach. Amaranth was a sacred grain to the ancient Aztecs and is enjoying a new popularity the world over for being a nutritious grain that's easy to grow. Amaranth can withstand drought and is considered to be a symbol of immortality.

From Sweden with love

In 1860, about the same time that Rob Morris was developing the Order of the Eastern Star, James B. Taylor from Newark, New Jersey, was hard at work on a new Masonic society that would admit women. He learned that in 1653, Queen Kristina of Sweden had combined a group of Sir Knights and Ladies together as an excuse to throw huge parties. The chivalric Order of the Amarantha was designed for her royal court, and it was dedicated to the legendary character Lady Amarantha, who was considered to be a beautiful, virtuous, and talented woman. The order still exists today in the Royal Court of Sweden.

The original Order of Amarantha had nothing to do with Freemasonry, but Taylor was so impressed with what he read that he copied many of the symbols and terms he found — even the name.

Rite of Adoption

In 1870, Robert McCoy was tinkering with Rob Morris's rituals for the Order of the Eastern Star. He heard James Taylor's Amaranth ritual and believed it could complement the OES in the same way that the Scottish Rite and the York Rite complemented Freemasonry. McCoy envisioned the Order of the Eastern Star as the initiatory (first) degree, followed by the Queen of the South degree, and finally the Order of the Amaranth as the final degree. An overall governing group known as the Rite of Adoption would oversee these degrees. Morris eagerly agreed.

In 1873, the new and improved ritual system was formed with Robert McCoy as the first Supreme Royal Patron and Rob Morris as the first Supreme Recorder. The organization was known as the Rite of Adoption of the World, consisting of the degrees of the Eastern Star, the Queen of the South, and the Amaranth. From 1873 until 1921, all members of the Order of the Amaranth were required to join the Order of the Eastern Star first and to maintain this membership in order to stay members of the Amaranth.

After Morris and McCoy died, the Grand Chapter of the Order of the Eastern Star decided that it didn't much care for the idea that it was just a stepping stone to the "higher" degrees of the Adoptive Rite and decided to opt out of the system. In 1921, the Rite of Adoption was dissolved, and OES and the Order of the Amaranth are now completely separate organizations. Membership in the OES is no longer a requirement for joining the Order of the Amaranth.

Amaranth today

Although its ceremonies contain some specifically Christian aspects, the Order of the Amaranth is open to all faiths. Like the Order of the Eastern Star, its guidelines are Masonic in nature — a belief in a Supreme Being is required, but it's open to all faiths. A Supreme Council and statewide Grand Courts govern the Order of the Amaranth, and local groups are known as *courts*.

Since 1979, the Order has taken pride in raising funds for diabetes research. It has contributed more than $7 million to the American Diabetes Association, as well as funding five ongoing diabetes research grants. For more information, you can visit its website at www.amaranth.org.

The White Shrine of Jerusalem

Despite its name, the International Order of the White Shrine of Jerusalem isn't a whites-only group, nor is it affiliated with the Shriners. It's a completely independent group. Like the Order of the Eastern Star and the Order of the Amaranth, it's open to Master Masons and their female relatives. Unlike the other two, it is an overtly Christian organization, and members must profess a belief in Christianity and a willingness to defend it.

Charles D. Magee founded the White Shrine of Jerusalem in Chicago in 1894. A group of men and women who were Eastern Star members had discussed the idea that the story of the birth of Christ and the coming of the *Magi* (the three wise men who followed the Star of Bethlehem to Jesus's birthplace) would be a wonderful basis for a Masonic-like ritual and a perfect follow-up degree to the Eastern Star initiation.

In the beginning, the White Shrine required all male and female members to first be members of the Order of the Eastern Star. The OES was already unhappy with its position in the Rites of Adoption as merely the first of several degrees, and when the White Shrine came along with the same kind of requirement, the OES fought back. The White Shrine was put in the sticky situation of requiring membership in a group that refused to recognize or associate with it.

The group was confined to Illinois and Michigan for many years. In 1911, changes took place that allowed it to grow substantially until the Great Depression. After World War II, the White Shrine finally dropped its requirement of membership in the Order of the Eastern Star, and growth was again fast and prosperous.

Its fortunes and failures have followed the membership trends of Masonry, and declines have continued since the 1980s. Today, the White Shrine has 335 local groups in 40 states and Canada. Membership is close to 60,000.

The White Shrine operates a benevolent program called Material Objective to assist those in need, regardless of race, creed, sect, or age, and it isn't confined to its own membership. The program is financed by voluntary contributions and an endowment fund from which each Shrine may provide assistance to five cases a year (up to $5,000 per case). Collectively, the Shrines provide approximately $375,000 per year in financial assistance to people in need.

The White Shrine's symbol is a star, a shepherd's crook, and a cross, with the Latin motto, *In Hoc Signo Spes Mea* ("In This Sign Is My Hope"). Members refer to each other as *Sojourners*.

You can find information on the White Shrine of Jerusalem by going to its website, www.calodges.org/no194/WSJ93/Flyer/Flyer.htm.

The Social Order of the Beauceant

The Social Order of the Beauceant (pronounced *bo*-see-ont) is unusual in American Masonry because it doesn't require or even admit men. It's an organization of women limited to the wives and widows of Knights Templar. It was founded in Denver, Colorado, in 1890 as a support group for the local Templar commandery, which was planning to host a national gathering of the order (called a *conclave*). The relatively small group of Templars was so overwhelmed by the work of hosting the conclave that they appealed to their wives for help.

The wives organized a group called the Some of Our Business Society (SOOB) and even wrote up a short initiation ritual. After the end of the conclave, the ladies never disbanded; instead they continued to meet to help their husbands and just to enjoy each other's company. In 1913, they decided to change the name to something more templary and settled on the Social Order of the Beauceant, using the same initials.

Beauceant is a French term for the banner carried by groups of medieval knights.

The order is comprised of local assemblies, and its emblem is a red cross surrounded by a crown. Today, the SOOB has approximately 6,800 members in 114 assemblies in 35 states. Members of each assembly throughout the country work for charities, including the Knights Templar Eye Foundation. Since 1957, it has donated over $1.5 million to the charity.

You can find more information on the Social Order of the Beauceant at its website (www.yorkrite.com/SOOB.htm).

Not Just Kidding Around: The Youth Groups

Beginning just after World War I, interest grew in providing youth groups for the children of Freemasons. Both the Boy Scouts of America and the Camp Fire Girls had been started in 1910, and the Girl Scouts came along in 1912. A national movement called for programs for kids, supervised by adults, to teach some of the skills that schools weren't offering and to provide closer, meaningful friendships. In a very short period of time, the Freemasons created their own youth programs: DeMolay for boys and both Rainbow and Job's Daughters for girls.

DeMolay International for boys

Frank S. Land was a Mason who was very concerned about boys who had lost their fathers during World War I. In 1919, 17-year-old Louis Lower and eight other boys gathered together in Kansas City, Missouri, to create an after-school club. Lower had recently lost his father, and Frank Land liked the boy and wanted to help. He suggested the boys meet in the local Scottish Rite temple building. (Land was a member of the heroically named Ivanhoe Lodge #446 in Kansas City.)

The boys were looking for inspiration for a name and structure for the club. Land was an officer in the local Knights Templar commandery and told the boys the story of Jacques de Molay, last Grand Master of the original Knights Templar who had been imprisoned, falsely accused of heresy, tortured, and finally burned alive in 1314. (I give you more info on Jacques de Molay and the Templars in Chapter 10.)

The nine boys were enthused by the story of de Molay's bravery and sacrifice, and they decided to name the club DeMolay. By the second meeting, the group included 31 boys. "Dad" Land, as he came to be known, contacted a Masonic Brother named Frank Marshall and asked him to write an initiation ritual for them.

DeMolay spread like wildfire across the country. Marshall was careful not to make his degrees too close to those of Freemasonry, lest he be accused of trying to create Freemasonry for kids. DeMolay confers initiation and knighthood on boys, followed by awards of merit, such as Legion of Honor, Chevalier, Blue Honor awards, and Merit Medals. Its members hold office and conduct the ritual and business of the chapter, teaching boys leadership skills, financial responsibility, civic awareness, and public speaking. Like Masonry, it requires belief in a Supreme Being but not in any specific religion. Today, membership is open to boys between the ages of 12 and 21.

A more recent addition to DeMolay allows boys as young as 10 years old to become a Squire of the Round Table and attend DeMolay meetings and functions. It eliminates the pressure of learning ritual and softens the big age differences that can often intimidate a young boy in a group of older ones. A regular DeMolay member, who acts as the Squire Manor's "big brother," mentors the younger boys. As in the regular DeMolay meetings, an adult (known as a *Dad*) is always present.

Today, there are 1,000 DeMolay chapters in the United States and eight foreign countries, serving almost 20,000 young men. DeMolay alumni include Walt Disney, John Wayne, Walter Cronkite, football great Fran Tarkenton, newscaster David Goodnow, and former U.S. president Bill Clinton.

You can find more information on its website at http://www.demolay.org.

Scouting and the Freemasons

The scouting craze took the world by storm, largely due to the efforts of Robert Baden-Powell in England. Powell had been a British Army colonel in the Boer War in South Africa and had written a short manual called *Aids to Scouting,* designed to train new, young military recruits. He described methods he had developed to recruit native African boys as army scouts during the war against the Zulus — successful methods that taught the young boys initiative, independent thinking, and wilderness survival.

When he returned to England, he discovered that *Aids to Scouting* had become a runaway bestseller. Teachers and youth organizations had seized on its methods of instruction, and scout troops popped up around England spontaneously. In 1908, he published a revision of the book, based on his successes with a small, experimental scouting camp for boys from a wide variety of social backgrounds. The world went wild over it, and scouting for both boys and girls became an international movement. By 1922, there were 1 million scouts in 32 countries.

Baden-Powell was never a Freemason, but curiously several Masonic lodges are named after him, all in Australia. Some of his ideas when he created the Cub Scouts were shaped by the writings of his friend, Rudyard Kipling, who was a devoted Freemason (see Chapter 17).

Freemasonry's relationship with the Boy Scouts in the United States started with a Mason named Daniel Carter Beard. In the late 1800s, Beard founded a boys' program called the Society of the Sons of Daniel Boone, which would later become the Boy Pioneers. Baden-Powell read of Beard's American program and clearly borrowed some of his concepts for his book's revision.

In 1910, Beard merged his group into the Boy Scouts of America and became its first national commissioner. He developed the elements of the Scout badge and the Scout uniform and wrote several early publications of the Boy Scouts of America. Although he didn't overtly pattern the Boy Scouts after the lodge, he was certainly influenced by Masonic ideals.

Boy Scouts today encounter more than a few Masonic-style influences in the Order of the Arrow (OA), created in 1915 by two Scottish Rite Masons named E. Urner Goodman and Carroll A. Edson at Treasure Island, a Pennsylvania summer camp. By 1922, a Grand Lodge of the OA was formed, and ten OA lodges existed. By 1934, there were 45 active OA lodges, and the Boy Scouts of America officially approved the OA ritual for nationwide use.

The Order of the Arrow consists of three honors — Ordeal, Brotherhood, and Vigil Honor — like the three Masonic degrees of Entered Apprentice, Fellow Craft, and Master Mason. In the OA, each honor has its own handshake, hailing sign, and password. Each honor also has its own obligation and ritual, just as in Freemasonry. Candidates are conducted by Kichkinet, who symbolically binds them with a rope and leads them around the campfire to the stations of the guide, Nutiket; the medicine man, Meteu; and finally the great chief, Allowat Sakima. In Masonry, the candidate has a rope (called a *cable-tow*) around his neck. He is similarly conducted by the Senior Deacon to the Junior Warden, Senior Warden, and Worshipful Master. After the OA initiate takes his obligation, he is presented with a white sash, just as the Mason is presented with an apron.

There are many other similarities, and, in fact, the original ceremonies were much closer to Masonic practices than today's. Part of the Boy Scouts' agreement for approving the OA in 1934 was that much of the overtly Masonic content be removed to avoid its being labeled a Masonic organization.

The International Order of the Rainbow for Girls

William Mark Sexson, a Christian minister and active member of a Masonic lodge, started the International Order of the Rainbow for Girls in Oklahoma in 1922. The Reverend Sexson had spent his life dedicated to both fraternal organizations and his ministry, and he noticed a need for a youth organization for young women who were from a Masonic or Eastern Star home. Although its teachings are based on Christian writings, the order is open to children of all religions. It doesn't seek to convert children to Christianity; the Christian lessons are simply used to show basic values that are integral to many religions.

The Rainbow ritual is based on the story from Genesis of Noah and the Great Flood. After the waters receded, God made a promise that He would never again destroy the Earth by flood. As a sign of that promise, He placed a rainbow in the heavens. The rainbow and its colors are the basis for the teachings of the Order: Red stands for love; orange for religion; yellow for nature; green for immortality; blue for fidelity; indigo for patriotism; and violet for service.

Membership is open to girls between the ages of 11 and 20. A girl is recommended by another member, by a member of a Masonic lodge, or by a member of the Order of the Eastern Star or the Order of the Amaranth. Being related to a Freemason isn't a requirement for membership (unlike the International Order of Job's Daughters; see the following section). Parents are invited and encouraged to attend meetings and activities. Rainbow Girls conduct all business and plan all activities for their local assembly, giving many girls their first taste of responsibility. Service to the community is stressed.

Rainbow chapters exist in 46 states and 8 foreign countries. You can find more on the International Order of the Rainbow for Girls by going to its website at www.gorainbow.org.

Job's Daughters

Mrs. Ethel T. Wead Mick founded the International Order of Job's Daughters in 1920. The purpose of the order was to band together young girls with a Masonic relationship for character building through moral and spiritual development, teaching a greater reverence for God and the Bible, patriotism, and respect for parents. The organization was named Job's Daughters after the three daughters of Job in the Bible and was founded on Job 42:15: "In all the land were no women found so fair as the daughters of Job; and their father gave them inheritance among their brethren."

Job's Daughters must be between the ages of 11 and 20, and each member must be a direct descendant of a Master Mason (unlike Rainbow; see the preceding section). Again, like most Masonic groups, a belief in a Supreme Being is required. Although the ritual is based on biblical accounts, membership is open to girls of all religions. The local chapters, which you can find in the United States, Canada, Australia, the Philippines, and Brazil, are called *bethels*. Meetings are formal and help to teach poise, respect, and confidence. Officers of the bethel wear traditional Greek robes, symbols of democracy and equality. Girls are elected as officers of each bethel, giving them their first glimpse of parliamentary procedure.

You can find more information on Job's Daughters at its website (www.jobsdaughtersinternational.org).

Checking Out Lesser-Known Masonic Groups

In addition to the groups described earlier in this chapter, many smaller, lesser-known Masonic groups provide fun or service to the Masonic family. The following sections detail just a few of them.

The Mystic Order of the Veiled Prophets of the Enchanted Realm of North America

No kidding. Most of its members can scarcely remember its official name, and the group is more simply and affectionately known as the Grotto. Over the years, the Grotto has unfairly earned the unflattering nickname "the poor man's Shrine," but the groups do indeed have similarities, and it's true that the Grotto never achieved the popular and financial success of its more prosperous cousin.

In 1889, a group of Masons in Hamilton, New York, met to hold informal meetings and have some good-natured fun. The primary mover and shaker of the group was Leroy Fairchild, and for a while, the group was known as the Fairchild Deviltry Committee. Like the Masons who organized the Shrine, Fairchild believed the lodges had become too serious and that men would be better Masons if the solemn teachings from the lodge could be interspersed with a little socializing and fun.

The idea caught on. In 1890, Fairchild organized a Supreme Council for the MOVPER, and the concept quickly spread. Again, like the Shrine, it's not technically a Masonic organization but a group that requires its members to be Master Masons. It also has an Arabic/Persian motif in its ceremonies and local Grotto names. Members wear black fezzes with long red tassels and refer to each other as *Prophets*. The highest-ranking officer is the Potent Monarch. I'm only reporting it.

Unlike the Shrine, the Grotto didn't branch out into building hospitals. It does direct the Humanitarian Foundation of the Supreme Council, MOVPER, which operates the Cerebral Palsy Child, a charitable trust. Funds are given annually to the United Cerebral Palsy Research and Educational Foundation as well as to the Dentistry for the Handicapped program. Many millions have been contributed by the Grottoes for cerebral palsy research along with other philanthropic charities, projects, and organizations.

You can find more information on the Grotto at its website (www.scgrotto.com).

The Ancient Egyptian Order of SCIOTS

Another of the social, fez-wearing orders is the Ancient Egyptian Order of SCIOTS. Started in 1905 in San Francisco, its motto is "Boost One Another." It's dedicated to social activities and helping each other in their personal and business lives.

The organization was originally called the Boosters, but due to its rapid popularity, other groups adopted similar, copycat names. In 1910, the name was officially changed, and the group adopted Egyptian terms with members wearing Middle Eastern fezes. Local chapters are called *pyramids*. It's largely unknown outside of California, although new pyramids have opened as recently as 2003 in New Jersey and Illinois.

Its ceremonies are based on the democracy of the ancient Greeks on the island of Scio and the legend of the island's inhabitants. According to the organization's ritual, the Sciots traveled to bring democracy to the Pharaoh of Egypt in about 1124 BC, some 60 years after the fall of Troy.

You can find more on the SCIOTS at its website (www.sciots.com).

The Tall Cedars of Lebanon of North America

In 1843, a degree was developed in Pennsylvania and New Jersey called the Ancient and Honorable Rite of Humility. It was more along the lines of good-natured candidate hazing than a Masonic ritual. It became known more simply as the Tall Cedar Degree (the reference is to the trees brought from Lebanon to be used in the building of Solomon's Temple). The degree rattled around New Jersey and Pennsylvania for more than 60 years and became a popular event whenever it was conferred.

In 1902, a group met to officially organize the Tall Cedars of Lebanon as its own fraternal organization, to promote "fun, frolic, and friendship," and to standardize its ritual. Local chapters are called *forests,* and members are called *tall cedars.* Its adopted headgear is a pyramid-shaped hat with a tassel.

The degree is purely for fun. The group is mostly concentrated on the East Coast of the United States. Since 1933, its primary charitable concern has been muscular dystrophy, and it provides money to the Muscular Dystrophy Association (MDA). It also operates the Jerry Lewis Tall Cedar Day Camp for children with the disease.

You can find more on the Tall Cedars at its website (www.tallcedars.org).

National Sojourners

The National Sojourners started as a club in Chicago after World War I. In 1917, 15 Masons met to design a group that would serve the needs of Masonic Brothers from all over the country who had been thrown together for military duty. In just ten years, the first 15 men grew into a national organization of almost 20,000.

National Sojourners is a Masonic club for warranted, commissioned, and senior noncommissioned officers of the United States armed forces. Unlike the common practice in Britain during the 1700s of chartering military lodges that traveled with a regiment, U.S. Grand Lodges rarely authorize such gatherings. The Sojourners act as a link between the local lodges and military personnel who want to join them.

It also has many programs to promote patriotism. They include traveling presentations about the origin of the American flag; the National Anthem Project, which aims to educate all Americans about the "Star-Spangled Banner"; historical reenactments; and a side degree, called Heroes of 76, first created in 1876 to celebrate the centennial of the founding of the United States.

In 1976, the National Sojourners established a library, museum, and national headquarters in a stately home in Collingwood, Virginia. It sits on a portion of land that was once a part of George Washington's River Farm on the banks of the Potomac River.

For more information on the National Sojourners, visit its website (www.nationalsojourners.org).

High Twelve International

High Twelve was started in 1921 by E. C. Wolcott in Sioux City, Iowa, as a luncheon club for Master Masons. Today, they generally meet for an hour once a week to enjoy fellowship and to support Masonic and patriotic causes. Guest speakers are encouraged from the worlds of business, education, and government, and not just to speak on Masonic topics. High Twelve's purpose is to encourage the participation of Freemasons in their own communities.

Today, more than 300 active High Twelve clubs exist in the United States, Canada, and other countries, with about 25,000 members. Local clubs are simple to form, requiring only 15 members to receive a charter, and dues are minimal. Groups generally meet in a local restaurant.

High Twelve's Wolcott Foundation, Inc., provides scholarships for graduate students of government service at George Washington University, in Washington, D.C. Dues, gifts, memorials, and bequests support the foundation. High Twelve is also one of the largest sponsors of DeMolay leadership training conferences. You can find more on High Twelve at its website (www. high12.org).

Investigating Masonic Research Societies

No matter the topic, opinions in Freemasonry are like armpits — everybody has at least two of them. Few subjects apart from religion and political punditry have motivated so many people to write as much as has been written about Freemasonry. Its rituals and practices vary from one country or state to the next. Its symbolism is wide open to interpretation. Detractors can make up nonsense out of thin air because Grand Lodge spokesmen rarely, if ever, officially denounce them.

Because there are so few "official" reference materials published by Grand Lodges, individual authors have stepped up to the plate to weigh in on the topic. And because no one can officially speak for Freemasonry, lots of individuals try it on their own — myself included.

Although they aren't technically appendant bodies, research groups provide Masons with some of the most up-to-date academic studies on Freemasonry. Several Masonic research societies encourage scholarly work and original study of Masonic subjects. The ones I cover in the following sections are the most prominent ones in Britain and North America.

Quatuor Coronati Lodge No. 2076

Chartered by the Grand Lodge of England, *Quatuor Coronati* ("Four Crowns") in London is considered to be the preeminent Masonic research group in the world. It was established in 1886 and publishes a collection of papers each year called *Ars Quatuor Coronatorum*. It functions as a regular Masonic Lodge, and full membership is limited to just 40. However, individual Masons and lodges can join its Correspondence Circle and receive its publications. Its website is www.quatuorcoronati.com.

Philalethes Society

The Philalethes (meaning "lovers of truth") was started in 1928 and is the oldest and largest international Masonic research society in the world. Its membership is open to all "regular" Freemasons, and its purpose is to exchange ideas, research problems confronting Freemasonry, and pass these topics to the Masonic world. Through the Philalethes, many North American Masons have been introduced to topics they had never encountered, such as Prince Hall recognition and differences in foreign Masonic customs.

Of the members, 40 are chosen as Fellows of the Society for their special service, and many Fellows have been prominent Masonic authors. The Philalethes was also among the first Masonic groups to pioneer the use of e-mail and Internet discussion groups to exchange ideas across international borders.

The Philalethes Society publishes a quarterly magazine and holds an annual meeting. Local chapters of the society meet across the United States. Its website is www.freemasonry.org.

Phylaxis Society

The Phylaxis Society (www.thephylaxis.org) is specifically dedicated to the research of international, historical, and literary aspects of predominantly black Prince Hall Freemasonry. It was created in 1973 by a handful of active-duty and retired military personnel. The society publishes a magazine of research papers and also provides instructional workshops around the United States. Although it's based in Louisiana, it has local chapters all around the country.

Scottish Rite Research Society

Started in 1991, the Scottish Rite Research Society (http://scottishrite.org/about/masonic-education/srrs) is based at the headquarters of the Scottish Rite Southern Masonic Jurisdiction (SMJ) in Washington, D.C. Although its emphasis is on the practices, rituals, and history of the SMJ, it publishes papers on a wide range of Masonic topics in its annual collection of papers, *Heredom.* Because of its affiliation with the SMJ's House of the Temple facility, its frequent contributors have easy access to one of the largest collections of Masonic books and periodicals on Earth.

Lodges of research

Many Grand Lodges also have research lodges to encourage the study of Masonic topics in their jurisdictions. One of the more notable is the Southern California Research Lodge (SCRL), which publishes a monthly collection of articles gleaned from a wide variety of Masonic publications around the world. The SCRL also provides an introductory book program for new members of the fraternity. Membership isn't limited to California Masons. Its website is www.theresearchlodge.org.

Many other sorts of research lodges exist around the world. A dedicated Washington, D.C., Freemason named Paul M. Bessel has posted links to most of them on his extensive website, http://bessel.org/resldgs.htm. Brother Bessel has devoted untold hours to collecting Masonic statistics, history, practices, customs, rules, trivia, and literally hundreds of other topics. He is his own one-man research society.

The Masonic Society

The Masonic Society was formed in 2008 specifically for regular, recognized Freemasons. As the new kid on the block, it has a younger, brasher feel than the other groups. Its international membership is limited to Masons of mainstream and Prince Hall grand lodges that are either part of the Conference of Grand Masters of North America or that are recognized by them. The society publishes an impressive quarterly magazine, the *Journal of the Masonic Society,* and holds social and instructional meetings throughout the year. Members participate in an annual conference of Masonic organizations in the Washington, D.C., area, known collectively as "Masonic Week." It also has chapters in each state and Canadian province as well as in countries around the world. The website is www.themasonicsociety.com.

Part IV

Freemasonry Today and Tomorrow

The 5th Wave   By Rich Tennant

EDWARD SCISSORHANDS FREEMASON

"Okay, let's work on the handshake again."

In this part . . .

*F*reemasonry is an ancient organization in a new world, and sometimes even secret societies have to blow the dust off of themselves. In this part, I talk about how a 300-year-old fraternal organization remains important to men in the 21st century. I discuss some of the changes that are happening within the fraternity, both good and bad, and I even tell you how to join a lodge, if you're so inclined.

Chapter 14

So Is It Still Relevant?

In This Chapter

▶ Living in a new, solitary society

▶ Reconnecting with the community through Masonry

*F*reemasonry has been around for a long time. At one point, almost one-fourth of American men were part of Masonry or other fraternal organizations. Well, everybody used to ride horses to the frontier Walmart, too, but society has changed.

The rituals and ceremonies of the fraternity developed largely in the 1700s and 1800s, and apart from small changes in the occasional term or practice, they have remained very close to their original language and intent. In fact, Freemasons often recoil in horror at the very notion of tinkering with anything in their degree rituals or rules.

The symbolism used in Masonic lodges grew out of ancient and biblical sources, and the methods used to teach their meanings have progressed little from the days of drawing them on the tavern floor in chalk. Modern men don't have much time or patience for hearing about the details of an architectural column or explanations of the five senses.

Television, especially the changes brought by cable, DVDs, video games, on-demand programs, and DVRs, has eroded the pool of potential new members, who work long or odd hours with less free time but have more control than ever over their entertainment. Increasing amounts of time spent on their children's after-school activities, especially sports programs, have overwhelmed parents. And the home computer seems to take an even greater share of what's left of leisure moments.

The situation sounds pretty bleak for the Masons. So how does an ancient, "secret" society take its place in a modern world? In this chapter, I discuss why Freemasonry remains relevant to a progressive society and why an increasing number of young men still join it.

A Breakdown in Community

The late 1960s was a time of terrible turbulence in American society. The children of the World War II veterans questioned — and rejected — most of the social conventions, customs, and institutions of their fathers. Although racial desegregation, women's rights, and greater freedom of expression were the admirable achievements of that rebellious period, society lost some of the glue that held it together when most of its established institutions became legitimate targets. The pre-1960s manners, morals, and personal faith were all consigned to the figurative dumpster because they were seen as repressive. The result has been three generations of psychoanalysis, personality-enhancing pharmaceuticals, social problems unlike anything that came before, and an explosion of interest in alternative, non-Western religions, beliefs, and customs. Clearly something has been lost, and people are searching anew for something to fill the void.

Another, more troubling change has been the replacement of those manners, morals, and personal faith with legal substitutes such as government legislation or lawsuits. People no longer control their behavior simply because it's the decent thing to do; now laws and government intervention dictate what people can and cannot do.

Several years ago, my local drugstore installed signs and foot-shaped stickers on the floor to tell me how far away to stand from fellow shoppers so as not to infringe on their privacy. Not all that long ago, people simply had manners that kept them from breathing down the necks of fellow patrons. Now the outlines on the floor, like the lines a coroner draws around a corpse, show where our manners died.

Isolating individuals

Today's society is marked by its isolation. People are more solitary than they have ever been. In offices, they e-mail instead of talking to co-workers sitting 10 feet away. If you telecommute to work, the farthest you have to walk in the morning is from the bedroom to the computer to log on. Aside from going out for food when delivered pizza gets too repetitive, you may rarely leave the house or deal with anyone face to face. Grocery stores have installed self-serve checkouts, avoiding any idle chit-chat with the cashier. ATMs have replaced human tellers at the bank. The gas station lets you pay at the pump. And heaven help you if you actually need to speak to a live human being at the water company. For a list of ways technology has *not* improved society, please press 3.

Having more friends from Facebook than you have from real life is a distinct possibility. The success of reality-based TV shows is symptomatic of an almost creepy desire to watch total strangers go to the hardware store, eat dinner, and fight with their kids instead of living our own lives.

Harvard researcher Robert Putnam's landmark study, *Bowling Alone*, talks at length about the result this solitude has had on society. The title refers to the hugely popular bowling leagues of the 1950s and 1960s that have vanished. But the loss goes far beyond bowling leagues, bridge and poker clubs, block parties, and Moose lodges.

Disconnecting from each other

Society is more mobile than it's ever been, and families are more widely scattered than at any time in history. People have lost the support of their extended family members who used to live within close proximity. Meanwhile, many people live in a house or apartment for years and never know their neighbors. People used to sit on their front porches and interact with other folks walking down the block. These days, people don't build houses with front porches, and backyards are surrounded with 6-foot privacy fences. Air conditioning and improved lighting means you can stay in the house all day and night. And most people certainly don't walk anywhere anymore. Even dry cleaners and pharmacies have drive-thru windows so you can stay safely wrapped in the cocoon of your own climate-controlled car.

All the incredibly diverse forms of entertainment people have available to them have killed off the old ritual of standing around the water cooler or sitting around at lunch discussing the same radio show, television program, or movie they all saw the previous night. People can't even agree on a common cellphone technology, HDTV format, MP3 player, or computer operating system.

Circulation of local newspapers has shrunk, and local TV news programs have lost ratings, replaced by Internet news sources and 24-hour cable news channels. National companies have consolidated local radio stations, and little local news content can be found there. Satellite radio only takes audiences farther away from local information. Because of the endless obsession with 24-hour news, people often feel a deeper personal connection with a crime committed eight states away than with what goes on down the block or in city hall. You may not even know what goes on in your state and municipal government.

The result is that most people don't participate in their own local governments. They don't count on their families or neighbors for support. They've lost common experiences. They've become more than a little lumpy around the middle. Americans overwhelmingly believe that their culture has become coarse and uncivil. They have more freedoms and liberties than any society since man crawled out of the slime, and they don't pester each other very much. But they don't connect with each other anymore, either.

Getting shortchanged in social capital

Just since 1980, 58 percent fewer people attend some kind of club meeting, 45 percent fewer people say they invite friends over to their homes, and an incredible 33 percent fewer people say they have family dinners together. Robert Putnam calls these connections *social capital,* and he argues that social capital is every bit as important as the monetary kind. It's important to the community and to the individual to interconnect, communicate, and participate with each other. Study after study shows that communities that fail to interconnect have higher crime rates, worse drug abuse, poorer health, and more suicides.

Business types are fond of the term *networking,* as if friendships only exist for business purposes, and whether they come right out and say it or not, networking comes down to believing that someone you *actually* know might *actually* do you a favor. Or as Yogi Berra once said, "If you don't go to somebody's funeral, they won't come to yours."

Networks you may not think about — like sports clubs, neighborhood associations, political action groups, or just a friendship with another couple — are all essential types of social capital, and the fewer of these connections, the less likely it is that members of a community will cooperate and work for their mutual well-being. Friends and family cheer you up, bring you chicken soup when you're sick, help you find jobs when you're laid off, baby-sit the kids for you when you're away, buy you a drink at the bar, loan you $20 when you're broke, and remember your birthday. And you do it for them in return. Life without these connections is pretty bleak, and believe it or not, having fewer of these connections actually reduces your life expectancy.

Where Freemasonry Fits In

The *bad* thing about the basic tenets of Freemasonry is that they don't change very much. And the *good* thing about the basic tenets of Freemasonry is that they don't change very much. Freemasonry was developed during a time of massive upheavals in society. England had been entangled in centuries of political and religious turmoil. Masonry's greatest expansions in the United States came after the Revolutionary War, after the Civil War, and after World War II. It always seems to grow when society is at a point of chaos or major change, when people long for a sense of unity — which is what makes it curious that Masonry didn't expand in the 1960s. Instead, it became just one more established institution to reject.

Still, the simple concepts and goals of Freemasonry apply as much to today's world as they did to our grandparents', and they're certainly needed every bit as much now as they ever were.

Putnam and many other sociologists have long contended that joining active, local, engaged groups is vital to a progressive and growing society. But is becoming a Mason, or a member of any other group, like being forced to eat Brussels sprouts — good for you but tough to choke down?

Making good men better ones

Freemasonry was never intended as a refuge for fallen men in need of reformation. It doesn't save souls, cure alcoholism, reform straying husbands, or put chiseling CEOs back on the road to honesty. In fact, its rules and customs are specifically designed to keep such men *out*. Freemasonry has always had standards of conduct for members and hopefuls. Like the Marines, it's looking for a few good men.

In a time of changing standards of morality and behavior, Masonry raises the bar. Its principles are designed to encourage its members to be better fathers, sons, husbands, and neighbors, while not forcing any particular religious or political agenda upon them.

Only about a third of Americans think their fellow man can be trusted, down from more than 50 percent of Americans who were trusting 40 years ago. There has been an equal decline since the 1950s in the belief that Americans are as honest and moral as they once were. Freemasons, on the other hand, encourage each other to be moral and upright, and every Mason is under an obligation to help, aid, and assist Brother Masons and their families. That sense of honesty and responsibility extends to the whole community.

People throughout history have accused Masonry and other "secret societies" of being elite. *Elitism* is defined as belonging to a small group that has more power, social standing, wealth, or talent than the rest of society. Freemasonry doesn't exclude men from its ranks because of their social, racial, and economic status. But it *does* expect them, after they're members, to be the very best workers, parents, and citizens they can possibly be. Beyond that, Masonry binds its members to the concepts of honor, duty, and humanitarianism. If these standards are elitism, most men would benefit from it, and society would certainly benefit if more men had those qualities.

Providing something for everybody

Freemasonry is diverse. It offers fun, interesting, and beneficial activities to interest anyone, including the following:

- Hanging out at the lodge lets you bond with a small group of men from all walks of life and get to know them on an individual basis.

- Performing the ritual ceremonies gives you confidence and experience speaking in public.

✔ Taking part in ceremonies and learning the history connects you to traditions that go back a thousand years.

✔ Participating in special projects gives you an opportunity to cook dinners, run charities, and enjoy a limitless variety of other groups within the family of the fraternity.

If a Mason wants to participate, he can find something Masonic to do almost every day of the week. If he simply wants to sit on the sidelines or have dinner and enjoy the company of his fellow members, no one forces him to do otherwise. Because of the comfort of brotherhood, the unlikeliest of men are often brought out of their bashful or self-conscious shells.

Freemasonry is tailor-made to increase *social capital*, the personal and societal benefits of being connected to other people. Unlike a country club or social group, participants don't have to hurdle any financial or class barriers. Unlike a political group, Freemasonry has no cause to rally around, no single objective that wears blinders to every other viewpoint. Unlike a religious group, it isn't solely focused on the spiritual aspects of life. Instead, it helps to build the whole community, one man at a time. And believe it or not, according to Robert Putnam's study, joining just one active group is as beneficial to your health as quitting smoking.

Supporting brotherly love

Freemasonry's ceremonies join men from diverse backgrounds and from all over the world through common experiences shared in the lodge room. Meeting a Brother Mason on the streets of Paris or London or Cancun or Hong Kong and having an immediate bond is a good feeling. Freemasonry brings together men who may otherwise never have met, and it cuts across all social, economic, racial, religious, and political lines.

Involving people in charitable work

Anyone can write a check to a big, faceless institutional charity or group. The United Way can tackle a much bigger job to help the community than the little neighborhood Masonic lodge, if all you do is look at a problem from a financial point of view.

However, Freemasonry encourages its members to take a greater part in the community. It inspires Masons to volunteer, to donate, and to become engaged in their neighborhoods, places of worship, and governments. Although the many organizations within the fraternity have dozens of official charities, foundations, and grants, its greatest successes lie in the individual acts of kindness and generosity performed by its members.

Freemasonry and racism

The history of the United States has been a segregated one. Slavery was a legal institution in the United States until 1863. Segregation legally lasted for another century, and not just between blacks and whites. At varying times in the United States, Jewish, Catholic, Italian, Irish, German, Romanian, Asian, and many other ethnic groups have been legally or surreptitiously discriminated against with varying degrees of severity. As a result, few organizations that have existed for three centuries cannot be accused of discriminating at some point in their history.

The development of "separate but equal" institutions happened in schools, churches, and social clubs for many years. Despite the attempts by government to force a legal end to such practices, people are stubborn in their private social activities. Freemasonry has had its share of wrestling with the issue.

Prince Hall Freemasonry, made up primarily of African Americans, came about before the Revolutionary War because white Masons didn't want to associate with black Masons, in spite of their fraternal obligations. Since that time, two parallel Masonic Grand Lodge systems developed side by side in this country, and for 200 years, they've mostly ignored each other. Each one knew the other group existed, and in fact, Albert Pike even gave a complete copy of the Scottish Rite rituals to Prince Hall leaders in order to assist them in the formation of their own Scottish Rite organization. But no intervisitation, cooperation, or recognition of each other as legitimate Masonic groups took place.

Beginning in the 1980s, mainstream Grand Lodges and Prince Hall Grand Lodges in the United States slowly began granting recognition to each other, and today joint activities commonly occur between lodges of both systems. But in several states, this interaction hasn't taken place, and an unfortunate number of Masons on both sides of the color divide regard their lodges as a private bastion of racial exclusivity. The complexities and the glacial pace of Masonic government and legislation further suit the prejudices of such advocates of separation, but their numbers are shrinking fast.

A more-complex issue has to do with the customs and traditions of more than 200 years of two groups operating in isolation from each other. No one on either side wants the much smaller Prince Hall groups to be swallowed up by the larger mainstream Grand Lodges. Many Prince Hall Masons believe they would lose their long, proud heritage and the legacy and achievements of their own organization, which actually predate many mainstream Grand Lodges. In some states, the Prince Hall Grand Lodges have not sought joint recognition. As a result, a merger between the two is unlikely in the near future. However, joint recognition and cooperation continues to grow. The mainstream lodges have many black members, and the Prince Hall lodges have many white members, because men often petition the lodges their friends belong to. As society becomes more tolerant and colorblind, the choice will eventually be between two different flavors of Masonry, not two different colors.

Practicing religious tolerance

Personal faith is just that: personal. Masonry doesn't teach any specific religion. Lodges aren't places of worship, and lodge meetings and rituals aren't intended as a substitute for going to church, temple, or mosque. Freemasonry *does* encourage its members to take more-active roles in their religious communities.

The framers of the U.S. Constitution and the Bill of Rights outlined the freedom of religion. The concepts of religious toleration were sentiments strongly expressed in the Masonic lodges of the period. Freemasonry today remains a strong advocate of religious tolerance.

Giving comfort through constancy

The principles of Masonry are timeless, which is how it has endured through centuries and adversity. Just as important, the principles are simple. Reduced to their most basic level, Masonry provides its members with a place to go for a while to escape the strife and struggle of the outside world, leaving the most contentious topics between men outside its lodge-room doors.

There is no question that Freemasonry is still needed and still important in the world. The world may have forgotten about it for a while, but Freemasonry has survived and waited patiently to be rediscovered.

The fraternity has always changed to accommodate the needs of its members throughout its history, while retaining its character, forms, and overall philosophy. (See Chapter 15 for more on how Freemasonry is adapting some of its 18th-century practices for its 21st-century members.)

Masonry reemerges

When the Soviet Union fell on Christmas Day 1991, Freemasonry had been outlawed in Russia for more than 70 years. Just three years later, a new Grand Lodge of Russia was formed. Its Grand Master openly declared his Masonic membership, and he even ran for president.

Masonry, like religion, has slowly come back to life in Ukraine, Hungary, Moldova, Romania, Bulgaria, Armenia, Georgia, Azerbaijan, and other parts of Eastern Europe and the former Soviet nations. In strife-ridden countries, no greater symbol of tolerance can exist than the formation of Masonic lodges.

The former Soviet bloc is a part of the world where the State was designed to control and provide for the day-to-day needs of society,

and the notion of volunteerism became extinct. Freemasonry is helping to bring back the idea of neighbor helping neighbor.

Sadly, Freemasonry isn't without its enemies. The Ukrainian Parliament, for example, nearly adopted laws that would sentence any government official who became a Freemason to up to seven years in prison; the sentence would have been three years for private citizens.

Meanwhile, Russian society is still suspicious of Freemasonry, almost entirely because of the fictitious propaganda known as the Protocols of the Elders of Zion (see Chapter 4). Nevertheless, Masonry continues to expand as freedom grows throughout this part of the world.

Chapter 15

Freemasons and the Future

In This Chapter

▶ Reviving Freemasonry

▶ Reinventing the future by drawing on the past

▶ Realizing universal brotherhood

*F*reemasonry has had a long and varied past and has recently faced an uncertain future as membership declined and the Internet spread misconceptions and perceptions of the fraternity. But Masonry's future is now a little more certain as the membership numbers are leveling out and popular culture seems to be getting the truth out at last about Freemasonry's rituals, history, and role in society. Modern Freemasonry owes a lot to Dan Brown and the History Channel.

Brown's books *The Da Vinci Code, Angels & Demons,* and *The Lost Symbol* stirred new interest in Freemasonry and other so-called secret societies. Brown includes Freemasons, Templars, the Illuminati, the Priory of Sion, Opus Dei, and a host of other groups in his works.

The 2004 film *National Treasure* was a unique creation in modern media — a movie that actually treated Freemasons with some respect, interwoven with an exciting (if unbelievable) story. In its aftermath, Grand Lodges noted an uptick in interest from audiences that had seen the symbol and heard the name but didn't know what Freemasonry was about. Another increase occurred after the release of *The Lost Symbol.*

"Secret societies" began to go out of fashion after World War II, and the ones that survived concentrated on becoming social clubs or service organizations. Freemasonry itself began to play down its esoteric aspects and play up its fish fries, bake sales, bean suppers, and card nights, and lodges became little more than welcome mats for members who *really* wanted to become Shriners. Somewhere in the transformation, some of the mystique was lost in favor of openness, practicality, and serving up a really good bowl of chili. Even Freemasonry's nemesis, the Catholic Church, while still forbidding parishioners from becoming Masons, admitted in recent opinions that the garden variety of Freemasonry practiced in the United States was mostly harmless.

Masonic bad guys

National Treasure is pretty much alone among movies in its flattering references to Freemasonry. Alan Moore's graphic novels *From Hell* and *League of Extraordinary Gentlemen,* as well as the films based on them, weave in allegations of Masonic involvement in the Jack the Ripper murders and (naturally) a world domination plot by a supercriminal. The 1979 film *Murder by Decree* also explored the Jack the Ripper/Masonic theory, using Sherlock Holmes as the vehicle. In the 1970s, the wonderful adventure yarn *The Man Who Would Be King,* based on a Rudyard Kipling story, told the tale of two British soldiers and Freemasons who set off to become kings in a foreign land. But on the way, they engaged in some decidedly un-Masonic behavior.

Perhaps the best-known pseudo-Masonic reference in pop culture is the spoof of Freemasons and Shriners in *The Simpsons* "Homer the Great" episode. Homer longs to join the local lodge of "Stonecutters," which grants its members perks like comfier office chairs and better parking spaces. Their lodge song has become something of a modern Masonic classic. You can find recordings of the song on YouTube.

The public spotlight from popular references and the Internet has started to shine a little stronger on Freemasonry. Giant membership growth in the 1950s has also meant a giant loss in the 21st century as those older members die, but those numbers have stabilized. A new generation of men is joining the fraternity, but what they are finding in most lodges isn't the Masonry they studied about before joining. Some walk away. Others are staying behind and making changes to see to it that Freemasonry remains the biggest, best, and oldest fraternity of gentlemen.

In this chapter, I do the most dangerous thing any author can do: I blow the dust off of my old Magic 8 Ball and do a little predicting of what the future holds for Freemasonry.

Speculating on the Future of the Craft

Freemasonry has been shrinking for a while, and lodges have been panicking. Massive buildings that were built during the boom years now are in danger of closing, and lodges that have been around for a hundred years or more are merging or simply dying. The big membership boom of the 1950s was also a curse, because the big swell of new Masons then has meant the unfortunate deaths of record numbers of those same men now. And the Baby Boomers didn't join.

No shortage of long-faced, sour-pussed articles about Masonry's impending death march to the tar pits has been making the rounds of the Internet for a decade. The good news is that Freemasonry isn't dead. It just smells funny.

About the mid-1990s, local lodges began shrieking for help. Something had to be done, even if they didn't know what exactly that "something" should be. So Grand Lodges stepped up to the plate with some controversial answers. If numbers were the problem, they had ways to get potential members in the door.

One-day classes

Taking a cue from the way the degrees of the Scottish Rite are conferred on many candidates sitting in an auditorium, some Grand Lodges in the United States began to permit the Entered Apprentice, Fellow Craft, and Master Mason degrees to be conferred on a large scale to many men at one time, in a single day. An *exemplar candidate* went through the ritual ceremonies on stage, while the rest of the candidates watched.

In an effort to make them even more popular, some Grand Lodges cooperated with the Scottish Rite and Shrine groups in their jurisdictions, making it possible for a man to walk into the auditorium at sunrise as a non-Mason and become a 3rd-degree Master Mason, a 32nd-degree Scottish Rite Mason, and a Shriner by sunset. These "All the Way in One Day" or "Sidewalk to Shrine" events have been controversial, to say the least. Many members believe they are an appalling development, and they frequently complain of these events cranking out One-Day Wonders or McMasons. Many foreign jurisdictions are outraged by the practice, and rumblings have gone around about the possibility of suspending recognition of Grand Lodges that allow it.

From a practicality standpoint, these events, often held in multiple locations on a statewide basis, have provided thousands of new members overnight. From a bottom-line point of view, they're a big success. They allow men who may not have the time it takes to go through the lodge degrees one at a time, over a period of weeks or months, the chance to become Masons in a day. They also help lodges that may not have a strong lineup of degree ritualists under their roofs who can present the degrees with the proper dignity and impact. In addition, study after study has shown that these "One-Day Wonders" are every bit as likely to remain committed Masons, return to their lodge, become officers, and participate regularly as men are who receive the degrees in the traditional, one-at-a-time method. I myself benefited from such an event, and I'm not exactly a stay-at-home Masonic wallflower.

The flip side is that a vast majority of these new members are disappointed by the big group-degree experience. The result is that these new Masons return to their lodges and insist on learning the ritual and presenting it properly, one man at a time, precisely because of the one-day classes.

My prediction: The one-day classes will burn themselves out. In fact, this burnout is already happening. These massive initiations can only bring in so many men, and then the well runs dry. States that have tried them have seen a diminishing return on their experiment in a few short years. As a result, I believe the internal hand-wringing, as well as the international criticism, will quickly go away on its own.

Advertising

Going hand in hand with the one-day classes have frequently been new advertising campaigns. Freemasons have been slow to seek new members by advertising, because most jurisdictions have rules forbidding asking anyone to become a Mason. The age-old custom has been that a man must ask to become a Freemason, not the other way around.

Billboards, radio ads, and television commercials are controversial developments. Because Freemasonry has been largely invisible to society for almost 30 years, something needs to be done to remind the world that it's still alive. Unfortunately, many of these campaigns have taken the misguided approach of promoting the fraternity's institutional charities as the big reason for Masonic membership. Young men have no shortage of effective charitable organizations to send their money to, without having to go through the extra bother of showing up for lodge meetings and going through initiation ceremonies. Men don't join a Masonic lodge because it gives money to charity.

Paying your dues

One of the results of the popularity of the appendant bodies of Freemasonry was always the growing list of groups with their hands out for a piece of the Mason's wallet, as well as his time. Bigger groups like the Scottish Rite and the Shrine have enormous buildings to maintain and charities to support, and even though they have many more members among whom to spread the costs than the local lodge has, everyone's membership dues have gone up over the years — except, in an unbelievable number of cases, the lowly Masonic lodge. The lodges were often pressured into keeping their dues and initiation fees ridiculously low, partially by all the organizations Masons belonged to. The result was that the local lodge, where every Freemason began his Masonic career, was starving to death because of the success of other groups.

Masonic lodges have come a little late to the table, but they're slowly realizing that low dues have been suicidal. Besides the monetary consideration, low dues generally translate into low emotional commitment by their members. A club that costs $40 a year is simply not perceived as much of a commitment, compared to one that costs its members $200 a year. The argument has been endlessly made that higher dues will make Masonry more elite and snobbier, but lodges finally seem to be coming to their senses financially. After all, truly destitute Brothers can always request help from their lodges. But modern Masons are paying far less in dues, adjusted for inflation, than their grandfathers and great-grandfathers did, and it's time they understood it.

In many European jurisdictions, annual dues cost hundreds of dollars, with fewer meetings a year. Rather than openness and demystification, they stress the mystery and secrecy of the organization. Yet their membership numbers are on the rise. Clearly cost isn't preventing potential new members from joining, and the secret society image is a selling point. There's a lesson for U.S. Masons in that.

Going Back to the Future

Young men are starting to rediscover Freemasonry. This new generation of Masons wants to associate with

- Something ancient, something mythical, something legendary
- A group that has been the fraternity of the greatest of men for three centuries
- A fraternity that is worldwide in its scope and universal in its welcoming of all faiths and all races
- A local lodge that helps the family next door and the school down the street
- A group that once was at the forefront of issues that shaped this country and, arguably, was the crucible that gave birth to the revolution, because they were men of action and social conscience
- A fraternity that claims as its members the most imaginative minds and the most successful of men

Often, the image of what they're looking for doesn't match what they find in the lodge down the street, and some people may argue that such an idealistic institution never really existed. But rather than leaving, these men are staying and starting to build the Masonry that suits their needs, just as their grandfathers did in the 1950s.

One interesting development is that although the Baby Boomers stayed away from Masonry in droves, their sons and grandsons are joining in far greater numbers and are bringing their Boomer dads and grandpas into the lodge after them. This situation is totally opposite of the way things have been for nearly 300 years.

Staying small to survive

Masons in the United States are gradually realizing that they don't have too many lodges, they just have too many *buildings*. Every little town in the United States has its own lodge building, usually inhabited by just one lodge that meets in it. Metropolitan areas are often worse — every major suburb often has its own lodge building. As an example, I live within a 15-minute drive of more than a dozen lodge buildings in the Indianapolis area.

Not every building is a masterpiece or a historic landmark. Many a building was erected at a time when its lodge had 300, 500, or even 1,000 members, but those numbers have plummeted, and reduced memberships can't hold on to every big, beautiful building.

The answer will have to be greater use of fewer buildings by more and smaller lodges. Lodges outside of the United States operate this way, with many lodges using fewer buildings that have very small lodge rooms holding no more than 50 people. Large, grand rooms are reserved for special events, not monthly business meetings and typical degree ceremonies.

A new wave of interest has grown steadily in the United States over what is sometimes called the *Traditional Observance lodge* or *European Concept lodge*. U.S. lodges are frequently bogged down by long business meetings, little Masonic education, and, worst of all, lousy food. The European Concept lodge includes

- A limited number of members (generally no more than 50)
- Excellence in ritual degree work, done by the lodge, without relying on others for help
- A Masonic education program for the advancement of candidates, including the requirement of original research papers
- A *festive board* (dinner) at a local restaurant following meetings
- A dignified dress code
- Required attendance, within reason
- Appropriately priced dues so the lodge may be self-sufficient

Outside of Europe, Lodge Epicurean #906 in Australia pioneered this formula, and it has started to gain popularity in the United States. The Masonic Restoration Foundation (http://traditionalobservance.com) has been formed to share these ideas with interested Masons.

Although U.S. Grand Lodges have seen a decline in membership, Grand Lodges in non-English-speaking countries have witnessed a strong increase in new members. They stress the more intellectual aspects of Freemasonry, take much more time between degrees, and don't have such a fascination with appendant bodies outside the lodge. The Traditional Observance and European Concept lodges are attempting to emulate their success.

Returning to old ways

After the mid-1840s, most U.S. Grand Lodges required the business of the lodges to be conducted with only Master Masons present. Entered Apprentices and Fellows of the Craft couldn't attend business meetings. This was done to prevent some ne'er-do-well from joining a lodge, going through the first degree, and blabbing all the secrets of the lodge to the neighbors. The result was that the slow, methodical, and careful advancement between degrees was sped up to make new members Master Masons as fast as possible.

Today, nearly one-third of U.S. Grand Lodges have returned the right of their Entered Apprentice and Fellow Craft members to attend business meetings, which is the way the rest of the Masonic world operates. This trend will undoubtedly continue.

To curry favor with the growing temperance movements in the 1800s, U.S. Grand Lodges turned their collective backs on Freemasonry's tavern and ale house origins and booted out the booze. Liquor was forbidden in lodge buildings, and many Grand Lodges even refused to initiate men who were bartenders, brewers, or otherwise connected with the liquor trade. The result was the formation of groups like the Shrine (see Chapter 12) and the Grotto (see Chapter 13), organizations made up of Masons, but unrestrained by the stern, sober, spinster aunt that Freemasonry had come to resemble.

Outside of the United States, such appendant bodies were unnecessary, because those Grand Lodges never were bitten by the temperance bug the way their U.S. brethren were.

Today, many U.S. Grand Lodges are softening this stance and are at last beginning to allow lodges to drink the 300-year-old ceremonial toasts with something a little more adult than Brother Cletus's Peach 'n' Persimmon Pucker-Up Punch.

Exploring ancient lessons with new technology

Masons have always used the technology of the period to teach their lessons. Chalk drawings on tavern floors gave way to floor cloths, tracing boards, "magic lanterns," filmstrips, and slide projectors. The Scottish Rite became the most popular fraternal organization of the turn of the last century by using the latest in theatrical scenery, lighting, and special effects. PowerPoint presentations are the latest way to show Masonic symbols and teach the lessons of the lodge. The next wave will undoubtedly be 3-D texture mapping of Solomon's Temple and interactive Middle Chamber lectures.

Some Grand Lodge jurisdictions have tackled the challenges of lodge leadership by adopting existing business leadership courses for the training of Masonic officers. The next generation of these programs will be specifically designed courses in Masonic history, rules, and symbolism, along with leadership skills needed to operate volunteer organizations.

Breaking Down Barriers through the Internet

Grand Lodges tend to move like oil tankers through ice floes. They're slow to respond, difficult to turn, and almost impossible to stop after they set out on a course. Conservative Masons believe this characteristic is a blessing, because it prevents brief outbursts from turning into legally entrenched dumb ideas. Revolutionary Masons believe this slowness is unfair, because it prevents them from acting on every new scheme that comes down the pike. The truth lies somewhere in between.

The open structure of the Internet is frightening to a conservative organization like Freemasonry. Discussion forums or Facebook pages can become hotbeds of dissent or, even scarier, incubators of great ideas. For the first time in history, Freemasons from every corner of the globe can converse and share ideas. The problem for regular, mainstream Freemasonry is that there are an awful lot of other Masons in the world who are *not* part of the mainstream.

The ideas of Masonic regularity and recognition — policies about who can legally talk and visit with each other — are starting to erode. The first step was the large-scale recognition of Prince Hall Grand Lodges, which opened the door to the coexistence of multiple Grand Lodges in the same geographical area. This was a situation that didn't exist prior to 1990. Now the Internet allows other Masons to get to know each other, whether their Grand Lodges recognize each other or not. And they're beginning to ask why they don't recognize each other.

The instant communication of the wired world may at last realize the idealistic philosophy that lies at the very core of Freemasonry: the idea of universal brotherhood. Political squabbles, local differences, and competing groups of leaders erected the walls between certain Grand Lodges long ago. The Internet and the simple communication between Brothers will tear them down.

The 21st century will undoubtedly bring changes just as the 20th did. Masonry has always adapted. The lure of Freemasonry remains the mystery of the closed door, and men will always want to know what's on the other side. Young men will always be drawn to the core ideas of Freemasonry, which remain true and timeless.

Chapter 16

So You Want to Become a Freemason

In This Chapter

▶ Understanding why men join

▶ Getting acquainted with Masons and a lodge

▶ Becoming a Freemason

Since time immemorial, Freemasons have had a rule of never inviting anyone to join the fraternity. Many fathers carried petitions folded up in their wallets for years, waiting for the day their sons would ask to become Masons — and never did. Meanwhile, many of those same sons wondered all their lives why their fathers never asked them to join.

Other Masons had a terrible misunderstanding concerning what they could and could not say about the fraternity. Rather than risk violating their obligation, they thought it best to never tell anyone anything about the fraternity: "It's a big secret, you know."

The problem with being a member of a "secret society" is that you're never really certain just how secret it's supposed to be. Many years ago, some clever Freemason cooked up the phrase, "2B1, ASK1." The trouble was that if the consumer of this message didn't know what the square and compass logo that accompanied it was, he certainly didn't know what "1" to ask, never mind trying "2B1."

Times have changed, and finding a lodge to join and Masons who will actually talk about the fraternity is easier than ever. In this chapter, I tell you how to pick a lodge, how the petition process works, and what some of the membership benefits are. I also share a few personal observations from Masons, explaining why they joined.

Examining Why Men Become Masons

Men become Freemasons for many reasons, yet you hear a common thread over and over again. It generally leads back to following the example of a relative, co-worker, teacher, or friend the member admired — a man whose conduct or philosophy stood out as especially kind, generous, or honorable.

What's in it for you

When asked about the benefits of their membership in Freemasonry, most members speak of the friendships they make or the spiritual and philosophical growth it has stirred in them. And men receive other benefits from becoming Masons, including the following:

- **A worldwide fraternity:** Masonic Brothers live in almost every country on Earth and come from every social, religious, economic, and ethnic background. Being part of the biggest and the best society of gentlemen brings prestige and honor.

- **Centuries of tradition:** The Masonic degree rituals connect you with 300 years of history, 1,100 years of tradition, and 3,000 years of legend.

- **A network of mutual friendship and aid:** Masons pledge to help, aid, and assist each other in every walk of life.

- **Help for your community:** The charities of Masonry are vast and can be as massive as the Shriners Hospital network, as local as a child identification program, or as simple as shoveling snow from a lodge widow's sidewalk. It can mean the entire lodge raising money for a community cause or one single Brother buying a winter coat for a poor child at the local school. It can mean money or time or the simple act of human kindness.

- **College scholarships:** Many Grand Lodges, and some local lodges as well, offer scholarships for college students. Some of these scholarships are for the children and grandchildren of Masons, while others are offered to the community.

- **Retirement homes:** One of the most extensive Grand Lodge charities and benefits is the Masonic retirement homes. These homes are designed for the members of the fraternity and their relatives. Many of them provide everything from independent-living cottages to intensive-care nursing-home facilities.

- **Spiritual awareness:** Masonry does not desire or attempt to replace a man's religious beliefs. But it does encourage him to study his own religion and strengthen his own faith.

Every Grand Lodge jurisdiction is different and offers its own programs to its members. Most Grand Lodges publish a regular magazine to inform its members of news from around its region. These magazines can often be found online at the Grand Lodges' websites (see Appendix C).

Hearing from Masons themselves

Every Mason has his own reason for joining. Here are a few comments from famous Masons and their feelings about the fraternity.

Freemasonry embraces the highest moral laws and will bear the test of any system of ethics or philosophy ever promulgated for the uplift of man.

—General Douglas MacArthur

We represent a fraternity which believes in justice and truth and honorable action in your community . . . men who are endeavoring to be better citizens . . . [and] to make a great country greater. This is the only institution in the world where we can meet on the level all sorts of people who want to live rightly.

—Harry S. Truman
President of the United States, Past Grand Master of Missouri

One of the things that attracted me so greatly to Masonry . . . was that it really did live up to what we, as a government, are pledged to — of treating each man on his merits as a Man.

—Theodore Roosevelt
President of the United States

The more I come in contact with the work of the Masonic Fraternity, the more impressed I am by the great charitable work and the great practical good which we are carrying out.

—Franklin D. Roosevelt
President of the United States

There is no doubt in my mind that Masonry is the cornerstone of America.

—Dave Thomas
Founder of Wendy's International

When you go into our lodge, on the back of the Tyler's chair are the words 'Know Thyself.' That is important. That is the ultimate message to all Masons: truly know who you are.

—Michael Richards
Actor (Kramer from *Seinfeld*)

Why I joined

Every Mason has his own story, his own reason for seeking membership in Freemasonry. Let me share mine, and then I'll pester you no further.

When I was in my 20s, if someone had told me that, by the time I was 40, I'd be driving a Chrysler with two sets of golf clubs in the trunk and be a member of the Freemasons, I would have laughed in his face. But people change.

I spent a lot of years studying the Freemasons, peripherally at first, in conjunction with research for a novel my wife was writing about modern-day Knights Templar (many years before Dan Brown, author of *The Da Vinci Code,* discovered them). Later, my interest led me into the possible origins of Freemasonry, what they had been, and what their modern role has become. But even then, Masons were a mere curiosity and struck me as nothing more than an aging, middle-class social club that wore funny aprons and exchanged comical handshakes — no more meaningful in my mind than Fred Flintstone and his Water Buffalo Lodge. Then my father-in-law died.

Bob Funcannon was what's known as a local personality. For nearly 30 years, if you attended the Indianapolis Motor Speedway during the month of May on any day but race day, you heard the deep, resonant tones of Bob over the P.A. system. The rest of the year he was a candy salesman. He was a veteran of the Battle of Leyte Gulf, a deacon in the local Presbyterian Church, and a Mason. He never talked about it, but he had been raised in Social Lodge #86 in Terre Haute, Indiana, in 1942. He didn't go to lodge very often in his later years, but he paid his dues and stayed in touch. He was a fixture around Lawrence, Indiana, assisting in the building of one VFW post and a member of yet another. Bob and his wife, Vera, were pretty regular visitors to the dance floor of the local Grotto. He loved nothing more than to sit in a tavern or a post, sip the same beer all afternoon, and tell stories; that deep booming voice coming out of that skinny little man, even when he tried to whisper, carried clear across a crowded room.

In later years, Bob retired to Dallas, Texas, but he still managed to drive back home to Indiana each year in May and announce at the track. And he eventually received his 50-year Mason pin. In Dallas, he never attended a lodge, but he was a mainstay at the VFW posts and was always setting up a library, spinning records at a dance, or just sipping an O'Doul's and passing the time with buddies. He seemed to know everyone in the neighborhood and always knew how to make you smile. No one was a stranger to Bob, and even as his health failed him, his wife passed away, and his private moods became less patient, in public he was always center stage and your instant friend. He always treated me like one of his own sons.

So when he died, we were torn by a dilemma and decided to have his funeral in Texas where he had spent the last 15 years of his life. We saw to it that the biggest funeral chapel was reserved so his many friends could be accommodated. At the last minute, my wife remembered that her dad had been a Mason, and we knew Masons performed a funeral service for departed Brothers. So, late on the Sunday evening before the Monday funeral, we started madly calling every Masonic lodge in Dallas and Fort Worth. At last we found a janitor working late, and he said he would try to contact some of the Brothers. We didn't hold out much hope.

The next day, we discovered to our great dismay that virtually no one had come, and that we should have brought him home to Indiana after all. That cavernous chapel was populated by the four of us in his family, a neighbor, and the three people he lived with. And ten Masons.

Ten men who never knew him, called by a stranger on a Sunday night, dropped what they were doing that morning and came to say goodbye to a Brother they had never met and extend a helping hand to his family. I'm certain that all ten of them had obligations of work and family. But not one was too tired or too busy to be there for a Brother. They performed a memorial service far more moving, comforting, and final than the rented minister who mispronounced Bob's last name every time he said it. And when it was all over, they stayed behind and made it clear that they would help us in any way they possibly could. This was no empty gesture, no hollow recitation of platitudes from strangers. Their offer of aid was sincere, the fulfillment of an obligation they had all sworn to abide by.

That's why I joined.

We, sadly, are surrounded by a society of increasingly cold indifference and isolation, populated by people who have become too afraid or busy or selfish or skeptical or bored to even leave their houses and simply find out the names of their next-door neighbors. Yet Freemasonry survives. It teaches and celebrates commitment, honor, tradition, integrity, truth, responsibility — words and ideas that have fallen out of fashion and become concepts that are foreign to far too many people in this world. When you assist in the learning and passing of Masonic ritual, you become another link in a long, honorable, and ancient chain. The heritage of the United States is populated by Masons who infused the foundations of the country with the intrinsic fundamentals and philosophies they learned from Freemasonry.

I am far from a perfect man. But the very act of putting on one of those aprons that I long ago made fun of, laying my hand on the Bible and the ancient tools of a Craft whose origins are shrouded in antiquity, and obligating myself to a world of Brothers — who are as ready to stand up in a quiet, empty chapel for me and extend their hands in friendship and aid to my own family when I am gone as those ten Brothers did in Dallas that day for Bob — is a duty I feel honored and proud to shoulder.

To Be One, Ask One

With a few exceptions, the Masons aren't going to ask you to join. One of the oldest tenets of the fraternity is that a man must ask "of his own free will and accord." His Masonic friends aren't supposed to pressure him, and he's supposed to knock on the door of the lodge because he has a good opinion of the fraternity, not out of simple curiosity or a desire for social or financial advancement.

Some exceptions to the "don't ask" rule do exist. Many Grand Lodges have altered their rules to allow gentle suggestions these days, to avoid that problem of why Dad never asked his son to join.

Finding a Freemason

The days are long past when everyone knew who and what the Freemasons were. You may not know any Freemasons. But then again, you may very well know a Freemason without realizing it. If your dad or uncles aren't Masons, try your grandfather. Ask around your workplace, too.

Spotting Masons is pretty easy these days. They wear Masonic rings (like the one shown in Figure 16-1), hats, belt buckles, lapel pins, ties, and jackets. Their cars have small, round medallions on the bumper displaying symbols of the lodge or some of the appendant bodies. More than 30 states even issue special license plates for Masons.

Figure 16-1:
Lots of men first notice Freemasons because of their Masonic rings.

Photograph courtesy of Christopher Hodapp

Finding a lodge

If you can't find any Masons to ask, go find a lodge instead. Lodges don't hide themselves in the United States. Most are pretty easy to find — they generally display a square and compass somewhere on the building. The initials *F.&A.M.* (Free and Accepted Masons) or *A.F.&A.M.* (Ancient Free and Accepted Masons) are also a giveaway. If you can't find a lodge, see if your town has a Scottish Rite or Shrine Center — they'll be able to steer you in the right direction. Ask to take a tour while you're there — Masons are pretty proud of their buildings.

Nearly every Grand Lodge has a website with contact information, and many have simplified the process for finding a lodge near your home or business (see Appendix C for addresses, phone numbers, and web addresses for all mainstream and Prince Hall Grand Lodges in the United States and Canada). The majority of local lodges have websites, too.

Walking into a lodge building when you see cars in the parking lot is a lousy way to get the attention of the members. Walking in during a lodge meeting will probably scare the wits out of the *Tyler* (the guard with the sword). He probably won't take a swing at you — that sort of thing hasn't been popular since the Middle Ages — but you never know. Just to make sure that you don't lose a finger or get an eye poked out, see if the lodge has a public event coming up. Lodges frequently have public breakfasts, dinners, open houses, officers' installations, or fundraisers where you can get to know some of the members.

After you find a lodge, you'll probably have plenty of questions to ask. Make sure that you get good answers. You want to enjoy the lodge you join, so be sure that you feel comfortable and welcome there. Masons want new members, and they want to share their lodge experiences with you. They aren't allowed to tell you everything about the ritual ceremonies, but they should be pretty upfront about everything else. Meet with members a couple of times. Ask if the lodge has other members your age, but also be receptive to the fact that you'll be making new friends from other generations. Active members in my own lodges (I belong to two of them) range from 18 into their 90s, and they're all close friends. Don't be put off from joining a lodge because you see a lot of gray hair.

Joining a Lodge

When you find a lodge you'd like to join, you're ready to begin the petitioning process. In the following sections, I fill you in on some basic qualifications you'll need in order to become a Freemason (specific qualifications vary from one lodge to the next, but some general rules apply), and then I walk you through the process from petitioning to becoming a full member.

Qualifying for membership

The qualifications to join a lodge vary from one jurisdiction to another, but some basic qualifications are common to all *regular* Masonic lodges (I discuss the issue of Masonic regularity and recognition in Chapter 5):

- **You must believe in a Supreme Being.** No atheist or "irreligious libertine" may become a Freemason, but your religious beliefs and affiliations are your own business. Masons only care that you believe in God, not where you go to pray to Him.

- **You must be joining of your own free will.** Masonry requires a commitment of time and effort. Don't let your dad, uncle, neighbor, or friend pressure you into joining. Join because you want to.

- **You must be a man.** Regular, mainstream Freemasonry is a male-only institution.

- **You must be "free-born."** Freemasonry does not engage in racial discrimination. The term "free-born" is a holdover from the days when slavery, indentured servitude, and bonding were common. It means that a man must be his own master, and not be bound to another man. That's not a problem these days, but the language is retained because of its antiquity and a desire to retain the heritage of the fraternity.

- **You must be of lawful age.** Depending on the Grand Lodge, this can be anywhere from 18 to 25. The average minimum age in the United States is 21, but many Grand Lodges are lowering it to 18.

- **You must be well recommended.** At least two existing Freemasons from the lodge you're petitioning must recommend you. That's no problem if your friend, relative, or co-worker is bringing you into his lodge. But if you're a stranger to all the members, you'll want to spend a little time getting to know one or two of them.

Masonry doesn't care about your worldly wealth or social position. Both the bank's president and the bank's janitor can apply for membership, and they're considered equally qualified.

You'll be asked other important questions before you'll be allowed to join a lodge:

- **Are you unbiased by friends and uninfluenced by any mercenary motives?** Don't apply for membership if you think you'll be using your membership card to get out of a speeding ticket or to network for your business.

- **Do you have a favorable opinion of Freemasonry?** You should have a desire for knowledge and a sincere wish to be of service to mankind. If you're merely curious about what goes on behind locked doors, read the rest of this book.

> ✔ **Do you agree to follow the rules?** Nothing especially scary here. There are dues to be paid, meetings to attend, and you should avoid inappropriate behavior. Health clubs and city parks have the same requirements.

Petitioning to join the lodge

When you decide on the lodge you want to join, ask for a petition. It's a standard questionnaire that's usually provided by the Grand Lodge for the lodges in its jurisdiction. Answer all the questions completely and truthfully.

All lodges charge annual dues (in Europe, the dues are often monthly payments, or *subscriptions*). Most lodges also charge a petitioning or initiation fee. Be sure that you understand all costs before joining.

After you turn in your petition, the lodge Secretary presents your petition to the members at the next regular business meeting (sometimes called a *stated meeting*). In the United States, the petition is read to all the members, and an investigative committee is appointed by the Worshipful Master to meet with you in an official, investigative capacity.

Being investigated

In the United States, the most common method of investigation is by an investigative committee. The investigative committee is the eyes and ears of the lodge. Because not every lodge member can meet with you, the committee does, and it issues a report. The committee may meet you at the lodge, at a local restaurant, or even in your home, depending on the customs of the lodge. The committee members may meet you as a group or one-on-one. Some may even telephone you for their part of the investigation.

Meeting with the investigative committee is sort of like sitting through a job interview. Use the investigation as an opportunity to get any of your questions answered, in addition to answering the questions they have for you.

The committee reports at the next business meeting. These two meetings — the meeting when the investigative committee is appointed and the meeting at which it reports its findings — are usually a month apart. In some jurisdictions, you have an additional delay because petitions are forwarded to the Grand Lodge for further examination. Be aware that some jurisdictions may also conduct a criminal background check and that felony convictions are not looked upon favorably.

Bear in mind that some lodges have a custom of not meeting, or *going dark,* during summer months. This tradition goes back to the days when farmers needed to be in their fields nonstop during that part of the year. It was also the custom to go dark because of the lack of air conditioning in hot, airless, upstairs lodge rooms. The point is, if you notice a delay of more than a month in the summer, don't think you're being ignored.

Outside the United States, the investigation and interview process can vary widely. Some lodges require the petitioner to write an essay explaining why he wants to join. Some bring the petitioner into the lodge blindfolded and ask him questions. Some post the petition and a photo of the petitioner in the lodge hall for a period of time and allow any Mason who knows anything about him to come forth and report.

Balloting

After the investigative committee reports to the lodge, your petition is voted on. The election (or rejection) of a candidate in a Masonic lodge is a secret ballot, and with few exceptions, must be completely unanimous. One vote against the petitioner generally rejects him.

The Grand Lodge of New York has recently changed its rules to require three negative votes to reject a petitioner. This change was made to account for the possibility of one crazy voter. The thinking is that if a sitting lodge member has a reason why a petitioner should be rejected, he should stand up and tell the lodge why, instead of simply voting in secret.

If a lodge rejects a petitioner, most Grand Lodges have rules that require a waiting period before he can petition that lodge again or try to petition another one. This period is usually one year.

Scheduling your degree ceremonies

After you're elected to receive the degrees of Masonry, the only thing left is for the lodge to schedule your degree ceremonies (see Chapter 6 for details about the degree rituals). Depending on the state or country you're in and the customs of your individual lodge, you may have some options concerning your degree conferral.

Proving your proficiency

Most lodges prefer that you to go through your degrees by yourself, one at a time, with a certain waiting period between them. You'll doubtless have to prove your *proficiency* (knowledge of the degree) before moving to the next one, so a mentor will be assigned to you — possibly one of the men who signed your petition.

The Masonic ballot

To vote in ancient Greece, a little clay ball was given to each voter, and the voter would drop the ball into one of several pots to elect his favorite candidate. The word *ballot* actually comes from the Italian word for a little ball — *ballota*.

In a Masonic lodge, there's no tampering at the polls. The vote in a lodge is taken with a very old, traditional system. The Senior Deacon carries a box around the room and stops at every member. In the box are white and black balls the size of marbles (see the figure). The white ball denotes a *yes* vote, and the black ball is a *no* vote. The member reaches into a large opening in one end of the box, so his hand is hidden from view from other members. Inside, at the other end of the box, is a smaller hole. He chooses the color ball he wants and drops it into the small hole, where it falls into a drawer in the bottom of the box, recording the vote. When everyone has voted, the drawer is opened, the balls can be seen, and the vote is counted.

This voting system is where the term *blackballing* (meaning to be excluded from a group) originated. In some lodges, the black balls have been replaced with cubes to avoid confusion while groping around in the dark ballot box.

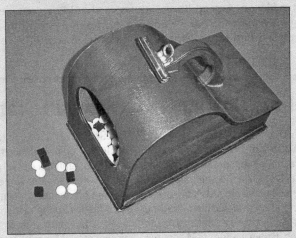

Photograph courtesy of Christopher Hodapp

Masonic proficiency is different from one Grand Lodge to another and even between lodges in the same jurisdiction. Rules govern some of the requirements, while local customs prevail on others. Some jurisdictions require you to commit a series of questions and answers to memory. Others require a research paper on a Masonic topic, read by you in open lodge. Still others may have a study program to teach you about the history and customs of the fraternity. Each jurisdiction has its own differences.

Opting for one-day classes

A few Grand Lodges in the United States offer controversial one-day classes, allowing you to receive all three degrees in one day, with no waiting period. Instead of participating in the degrees, you sit in an audience and witness the degree performed, with one man acting as an *exemplar candidate,* meaning that he represents you and your "classmates."

It is up to you and your lodge to decide if a one-day class suits your situation. These classes are not universally offered, and many jurisdictions have big objections to them.

Being welcomed as a Brother

When you complete your Entered Apprentice, Fellow Craft, and Master Mason degrees, you're a full member. Although the appendant bodies offer other degrees with more exalted titles, higher numbers, and impressive jewelry (see the chapters in Part III), none is more important than becoming a Master Mason. Any additional degrees should be considered optional, and sort of the Masonic equivalent of a continuing-education course. But a 32nd-degree Scottish Rite Mason does not outrank a 3rd-degree Master Mason.

Harry S. Truman: A Masonic Brother

President Harry Truman was a Mason and a Past Grand Master of the Grand Lodge of Missouri before becoming president. While passing through Indiana on the campaign trail, a Navy corpsman who had served as the president's massage therapist told Truman he (the corpsman) was to receive his Master Mason degree in Beech Grove Lodge #694, on the outskirts of Indianapolis. After his campaign stop, the president ditched the press corps, hopped off the train, and took a private car to the lodge with two Secret Service men in tow.

The Secret Service tried to insist on going into the lodge room with him, but the nervous Tyler would not let them pass. Truman assured them that he was far safer in the lodge room than he was on his campaign train. After a search of the Masons in attendance and the lodge room itself, Truman went on in to be present at the raising of his Masonic Brother. Truman insisted that night on being introduced not as President of the United States, but as the Past Grand Master of Missouri.

Part V
The Part of Tens

The 5th Wave   By Rich Tennant

In this part . . .

In this part, you get a quick and fun look at notable people, places, and stories connected to the Freemasons. I'll admit it: Chapter 17 had me flummoxed. It's supposed to be a list of Ten Famous Freemasons, but I couldn't do it. To pick just ten out of millions of men who have been Masons, well, it was just indecent. So I cheated: Chapter 17 is a list of ten *groups* of famous Freemasons. Sue me.

The same was almost true of Chapter 18. So many wild conspiracies, hoaxes, and accusations have been laid on Freemasonry's doorstep that it's hard to keep the list to just ten. In Chapter 18, I give you the ten juiciest ones.

Chapter 19 helps you plan your travel itinerary with ten great Masonic sightseeing spots, from the origins of Freemasonry to a bevy of bodacious buildings.

Chapter 17

Ten Groups of Famous Masons

In This Chapter

▶ Discovering Freemasons who are famous for their achievements

▶ Identifying historical figures who were Masons

*Y*ou could write a list of the ten greatest members from many organizations. However, because such an overwhelming number of the world's best and brightest have been or are Freemasons, a list of ten groups of great members makes more sense. What follows in all ten groups is far from a comprehensive list of the most famous and extraordinary Masons — it's just a sampling.

Founding Fathers

America's most famous Freemason, **George Washington** was initiated in 1752, in Fredericksburg, Virginia. After the Revolutionary War, there was a strong movement to unite the nation's Freemasons under a national Grand Lodge of the United States, and Washington was offered the position of national Grand Master, which he refused. He was elected as Worshipful Master of Alexandria Lodge #22 in 1788. When the new Capitol City that would eventually bear his name was designed under his watchful eye, · Freemasons laid the cornerstone of the new Capitol building in 1793, over which Washington presided in full Masonic regalia.

Other illustrious Freemasons include

- ✔ **Benjamin Franklin:** Inventor, publisher, author, and statesman, Grand Master of Pennsylvania, and member of the Lodge of Nine Sisters in Paris

- ✔ **Paul Revere:** American metalsmith and patriot, famed for his "Midnight ride," and a Grand Master of Massachusetts

- ✔ **Marquis de Lafayette:** French aristocrat who fought with American colonists against the British and was a great friend of George Washington

- **Robert R. Livingston:** Member of the Constitutional Committee that drafted the Declaration of Independence and a Grand Master of New York

- **John Hancock:** President of the Continental Congress from 1775 until 1777 and famous for signing his name large on the Declaration of Independence so that "King George can read it without his spectacles"

- **John Marshall:** Chief Justice of the U.S. Supreme Court from 1801 until 1835

- **John Paul Jones:** Father of the U.S. Navy

- **Aaron Burr:** Revolutionary War colonel and adventurer, Thomas Jefferson's vice-president after a tie vote was decided by Congress, and killed Alexander Hamilton in a famous duel

Explorers and Adventurers

Following are some Freemasons who blazed new trails:

- **Davey Crockett:** American frontiersman from Tennessee

- **Jim Bowie:** American frontiersman and inventor of the Bowie knife, or "Arkansas toothpick"

- **Sam Houston:** The man who avenged the slaughter at the Alamo and defeated Santa Anna at the battle of San Jacinto, becoming the first president of the Republic of Texas

- **Christopher "Kit" Carson:** American frontiersman and Indian fighter

- **William "Buffalo Bill" Cody:** American soldier and showman famous for his Wild West Show

- **Meriwether Lewis** and **William Clark:** Explorers sent by President Thomas Jefferson to the Pacific to chart the unknown western territory of the United States

- **Charles Lindbergh:** American aviation pioneer who made the first non-stop solo flight across the Atlantic in May 1927

- **John Glenn, Gordon Cooper, Virgil "Gus" Grissom, Wally Shirra,** and **Edwin "Buzz" Aldrin:** American astronauts, among them the first American to orbit the earth and the second man to walk on the Moon

- **Admiral Robert Edwin Peary, Matthew Henson, Robert Falcon Scott, Admiral Richard E. Byrd,** and **Sir Ernest Shackleton:** Five of the most well-known arctic explorers

The Masonic presidents

Fourteen U.S. presidents are definitely known to have been Freemasons: George Washington, James Monroe, Andrew Jackson, James Polk, James Buchanan, Andrew Johnson, James Garfield, William McKinley, Theodore Roosevelt, William Taft, Warren Harding, Franklin Roosevelt, Harry Truman, and Gerald Ford.

James Madison was probably a Freemason, but no surviving documentation proves it. Lyndon Johnson took the Entered Apprentice degree in 1937 but never continued to become a Master Mason. In 1988, Ronald Reagan was made an honorary Scottish Rite Mason jointly by the Northern and Southern Masonic Jurisdictions of the Scottish Rite, but he never received the first three degrees of Masonry and had no privileges of Masonic membership. Bill Clinton joined DeMolay as a teenager but never went on to become a Freemason.

Abraham Lincoln applied for membership in a lodge in Springfield, Illinois, shortly after he was nominated for the presidency in 1860. Lincoln withdrew his application because he was concerned that it would be construed as a political ploy to win votes. Lincoln told the lodge that he intended to resubmit his application when he returned to private life.

Pioneers of Science and Medicine

Many Freemasons have played an important role on the scientific and medical frontiers. Among them are these notables:

- ✔ **Edward Jenner:** Discoverer of the cure for smallpox, inventor of the concept of vaccination

- ✔ **Joseph Lister:** Surgeon and scientist, the man who pioneered the concept of antiseptics in medicine

- ✔ **Alexander Fleming:** Scottish bacteriologist who won the Nobel Prize for his discovery of penicillin, opening the golden door of antibiotic therapy for infectious diseases

- ✔ **Vannevar Bush:** Computer pioneer and the man who first envisioned the Internet in 1945

Actors and Entertainers

Movies, music . . . heck, the entire entertainment industry has had its share of Masons, including these men:

- ✔ All seven of the **Ringling Brothers,** of circus fame

- ✔ **Florenz Ziegfeld,** the greatest Broadway showman of all time and creator of the Ziegfeld Follies

- Jazz greats **William "Count" Basie** and **Lionel Hampton**

- Influential movie-studio founders **Louis B. Mayer** (M.G.M.), **Jack L. Warner** (Warner Brothers), **Carl Laemmle** (Universal Studios), and **Darryl F. Zanuck** (20th Century Fox)

- Legendary film directors **Cecil B. DeMille** and **D. W. Griffith**

- Hollywood leading men **Douglas Fairbanks, John Wayne,** and **Clark Gable**

- The immortal American magician, escape artist, and showman **Harry Houdini** (real name Erich Weiss)

- Hollywood comedians **W. C. Fields, Harpo Marx, Red Skelton, Richard Pryor,** and **Bronson Pinchot**

- Actor **Peter Sellers,** best remembered for *Dr. Strangelove* and *Pink Panther* movies

- Character actors **Ernest Borgnine** and **Telly Savalas**

- **Audie Murphy,** an actor who was the most decorated soldier in World War II

- **Mel Blanc,** the voice of all the Looney Tunes characters

- Actor **Michael Richards,** best known as Kramer on *Seinfeld* (Richards joined after discovering his comic idol, **Red Skelton,** was a Mason)

- World-class guitarist and country music star **Brad Paisley**

- **Phil Collins,** solo artist and lead singer of Genesis

Incredible Athletes

Famous athletic Masons include

- **"Sugar Ray" Robinson:** Immortal boxer, five-time World Middleweight boxing champion

- **Jack Dempsey:** The "Manassa Mauler," World Heavyweight boxing champion from 1919 to 1926

- **Joe Frazier:** Heavyweight boxing champion

- **Charlie Conacher:** Ice hockey legend

- **John Elway:** NFL Hall of Fame quarterback for the Denver Broncos

- **Scottie Pippin** and **Shaquille O'Neal:** NBA superstars

- **Sam Hornish, Jr.:** Indy Racing League champion

Military Leaders

Many important military leaders of Europe and the United States have been Freemasons. **Arthur Wellesley, Duke of Wellington,** great English war hero and brilliant tactical soldier, known as the "Iron Duke," the man who defeated Napoleon at Waterloo was a Freemason. Eventually he became Prime Minister of England. Although it has often been speculated that his perennial enemy, Napoleon Bonaparte, may have been a Mason as well, there is no documented proof of it. However, Napoleon re-instated Masonry in France after it was banned in the postrevolutionary years, and all four of his brothers were Masons. Even Napoleon's wife, the **Empress Josephine,** was a member of a Masonic lodge in Paris that allowed women.

Brigadeer General Lewis Armistead, who served with Pickett and Lee at Gettysburg, where he was killed, was a Mason. (**George Pickett** was also a Mason.) Armistead was the nephew of Freemason **Major George Armistead,** whose valiant defense of Fort McHenry against British invasion inspired one witness, Mason **Francis Scott Key,** to write the lyrics to the national anthem, "The Star-Spangled Banner" (which actually is set to the tune of an English song composed by **John Stafford Smith,** yet another Freemason). Even **James McHenry,** the Secretary of War for whom the fort was named, was a Mason.

The following men were also Masons:

- **Eddie Rickenbacker:** World War I flying ace who downed 21 enemy planes
- **General Blackjack Pershing:** Hero of the trenches in World War I
- **Jimmy Doolittle:** Daring aviator, who, after the devastating attack on Pearl Harbor, led a ragtag and courageous group of pilots in a sort of Star Wars–style attack on Tokyo
- **General Douglas MacArthur:** Fought in both World Wars, freed the Philippines in World War II, and then governed postwar Japan, where he is revered as the father of Japanese democracy
- **General Omar Bradley:** Much-admired general of World War II
- **George Marshall:** American army general and U.S. army chief of staff during World War II; later Secretary of State and Secretary of Defense; proposed a humane European recovery plan after WWII later referred to as the *Marshall Plan*

Significant Businessmen

Henry Ford, a titan of American industry, was a Freemason. He was the founder of Ford Motor Company, inventing the concept of the assembly line in order to feed America's insatiable appetite for his Model T Ford. Not always a poster boy for good Masonic conduct, he was a virulent and poisonous anti-Semite, as well as a union buster, who would use any and all tactics to control his workers. However, many of the best ideas of the founders of American industry, including the five-day work week, profit sharing, the shortened average workday, and wages twice the minimum wage, were Henry Ford's ideas first.

Ford shared the ties of Masonic brotherhood with **Walter P. Chrysler, Ransom E. Olds** (father of the Oldsmobile), **Andre Citroen** (known as the Henry Ford of Europe), and **Harry Stutz** (creator of the Stutz-Bearcat).

Other business-minded Masons include 19th-century tycoons **Nathan Meyer Rothschild** and **John Jacob Astor; James C. Penney,** founder of the department store chain; **Charles Hilton,** founder of the Hilton hotel chain; **David Sarnoff,** the "father of American television" and founder of NBC; **Colonel Harland Sanders,** founder of KFC; **Bob Evans,** founder of Bob Evans Restaurants; **Dave Thomas,** founder of Wendy's; **Tim Horton,** Canadian hockey player and founder of Canada's largest coffee and donut chain; and **Steve Wozniak,** cofounder of Apple Computer.

Players in the World of Statecraft

Masons have made great leaders around the world. Among them are

- **Sir Winston Churchill:** Great Britain's greatest Prime Minister
- **J. Edgar Hoover:** Founder of the FBI
- **Fiorello Laguardia:** Three-time mayor of New York City
- **Robert Byrd:** Senator from West Virginia
- **Robert Dole:** Senator from Kansas
- **Trent Lott:** Senator from Mississippi
- **Jack Kemp:** Congressman from New York
- **Hugo L. Black:** U.S. Supreme Court justice
- **Kalakaua:** King of Hawaii
- **John A. MacDonald:** The first prime minister of Canada
- **Benito Juárez:** President of Mexico; national hero for driving out the French occupation under the Emperor Maximilian
- **William IV, Edward VII, Edward VIII, George IV,** and **George VI:** English kings

In England, the post of Grand Master is always offered to a member of the royal family, usually the Prince of Wales. The present Grand Master is **HRH Prince Edward, the Duke of Kent,** cousin to Prince Charles.

U.S. Civil Rights Leaders

Masons who've been active in the quest for equal rights for all citizens of the United States include the following men:

- ✔ **Josiah Henson:** Abolitionist and one-time slave whose flight from slavery in Kentucky inspired Harriet Beecher Stowe to write *Uncle Tom's Cabin*

- ✔ **Booker T. Washington:** Educator and reformer; prime mover behind the Tuskegee Institute, the first normal and technical school for African Americans

- ✔ **W. E. B. DuBois:** American sociologist; one of the founders of the National Association for the Advancement of Colored People (NAACP) and editor of its magazine, *Crisis*

- ✔ **Julian Bond, Benjamin Hooks,** and **Kweisi Mfume:** Other NAACP notables with Masonic membership

- ✔ **Thurgood Marshall:** The first black member of the U.S. Supreme Court, who successfully argued against the doctrine of separate but equal in *Brown v. Board of Education,* the decision that integrated American schools

- ✔ **Medgar Evers:** Martyred civil-rights activist

- ✔ **Jesse Jackson:** Perhaps the most famous civil-rights leader apart from Martin Luther King, Jr.

- ✔ **Al Sharpton:** Activist and political hopeful

- ✔ **Thomas Bradley, Willie Brown, Carl Stokes,** and **Andrew Young:** Mayors of Los Angeles, San Francisco, Cleveland, and Atlanta, respectively

Men of Arts and Letters

The world of art, music, and literature would not be the same if it weren't for the contributions of these famous Masons:

- ✔ **Wolfgang Amadeus Mozart:** Famed classical composer and virtuoso pianist; gave an underlying Masonic theme to one of his operas, *The Magic Flute*

- ✔ **Joseph Haydn:** Classical composer from Austria

- ✔ **Jean Sibelius:** A Finnish composer of the Romantic period

- **Aleksander Pushkin:** Revered Russian poet

- **Jonathan Swift:** Liberal Anglo-Irish writer and satirist; author of *Gulliver's Travels*

- **Alexander Pope:** Poet and satirist

- **Oscar Wilde:** Nineteenth-century Irish playwright and poet; author of *The Importance of Being Earnest* and *The Picture of Dorian Gray*

- **Giovanni Casanova:** Writer, statesman, and free-booting adventurer whose exhausting amorous conquests ran into the hundreds

- **Robert ("Robbie") Burns:** Scotland's national poet; author of the poem "Auld Lang Syne," sung at many Masonic dinners

- **Sir Arthur Conan Doyle:** Creator of Sherlock Holmes

- **Alex Haley:** Author of *The Autobiography of Malcolm X* and the enormously popular *Roots*

- **Sir Walter Scott:** Scottish poet and author of *Ivanhoe*

- **Mark Twain:** Author of *The Adventures of Tom Sawyer, The Adventures of Huckleberry Finn, A Connecticut Yankee in King Arthur's Court,* and many other books, all riddled with biting social commentary disguised as fiction

Rudyard Kipling

Author and poet Rudyard Kipling was born in Bombay, India, December 30, 1865. He was made a Mason at Hope and Perseverance Lodge No. 782 at Lahore Punjab, India. In fact, the same evening that he was raised as a Master Mason, he was elected secretary of his lodge and recorded his own degrees in the minutes of his lodge. His early exposure to the many races and cultures of India, as well as the distinctly British culture of the Raj, left him with a lifelong sense of brotherhood for all mankind, one that he felt was best expressed in Freemasonry.

When he left India for England, he affiliated with Mother Lodge #3861 in London as well as two others, Author's Lodge No. 3456 and Lodge Builders Lodge of the Silent Cities Lodge No. 4948. In 1905, Canongate Kilwinning Lodge No. 2, Edinburgh, Scotland, chose him as poet laureate. In 1925, Kipling wrote:

I was Secretary for some years of Hope and Perseverance Lodge No. 782, E.C. (English Constitution) Lahore, which included Brethren of at least four creeds. I was entered by a member of Bramo Somaj, a Hindu; passed by a Mohammedan; and raised by an Englishman. Our Tyler was an Indian Jew. We met, of course, on the level, and the only difference anyone would notice was that at our banquets, some of the Brethren, who were debarred from eating food not ceremonially prepared, sat over empty plates.

The Indians of Lahore referred to the Masonic Lodge as a "house of magic" because nothing but magic could bring together so many men of different classes, castes, and religions. Kipling's poem "The Mother Lodge" is beautifully illustrative of the special brotherhood that he found in his lodge.

Chapter 18

Ten Amazing Conspiracies, Anti-Masons, and Hoaxes

● ●

In This Chapter

▶ Uncovering cunning con artists

▶ Exposing bogus Masonic malcontents

▶ Debunking dopey and diabolical deceptions

● ●

*O*ver the last three centuries, Freemasonry has been accused of everything from Satan worship and blood sacrifice to political assassination and world domination. Because each of these myths has been reported
throughout the world with breathless excitement, each gets its own exclama-
tion point. (They look more authentic that way.) For many more sensational
stories, see *Conspiracy Theories & Secret Societies For Dummies* by Chris
Hodapp and Alice Von Kannon (Wiley).

Leo Taxil and the Great Hoax!

Gabriel Antoine Jogand-Pagès was born in Marseilles, France, in 1854, and
at a very young age, he fell in love with the life of a con artist and took up
the alias Leo Taxil. At the wise old age of 25, Taxil decided to capitalize on
the wave of anti-Catholic sentiment in France at the time and began writing
a series of satires, pamphlets, and pornographic stories against the Church.
In 1881, he joined a Masonic lodge. After his first degree, he was quickly
expelled for his repeated run-ins with the law over his plagiarism and other
publishing outrages. Taxil needed to find a new and better source of income
and fun. Peeved over being chucked from the lodge, Leo conceived a master-
ful hoax, and this time he took aim at *both* Catholics and Freemasons.

In 1885, he trotted off to a Catholic church and confessed his sins to the local priest. He even threw in a completely fictitious confession to a murder, as a joke to test the confidentiality of the confessional. Next, as a newly minted and "outraged" Catholic, he began writing a series of fictitious exposés of the secret rituals of the Freemasons. Never mind that he had only experienced the first degree. What he didn't know, he made up. In short order, he published *The Three-Point Brothers, The Anti-Christ and the Origin of Masonry, The Cult of the Great Architect,* and *The Masonic Assassins.*

To his great amusement, Taxil became the darling of the Catholic hierarchy and was granted a private audience in Rome with Pope Leo XII. The pope declared himself to be Taxil's biggest fan and wanted more books and more exposés of the Masons, a situation Taxil found to be absolutely hilarious as well as financially lucrative. He was running dry but soon created what would become a story that has long outlived him.

Taxil's most fanciful invention was a version of Freemasonry he claimed was called *Palladism* or *Luciferian High-Masonry.* He wrote that Palladism was created and directed from Charleston, South Carolina, where Albert Pike founded it. According to his increasingly bizarre story, Palladism was a coed version of Masonry that organized sexual orgies and Satan worship among its members. Albert Pike, whom Taxil gave the title Supreme Pontiff of Universal Freemasonry, supposedly directed 23 Supreme Confederated Councils of the World by passing instructions to them through a woman named Diana Vaughan. According to Taxil, Ms. Vaughan was able to blow the whistle on Pike and his unholy band of Satan worshipers when she escaped the fiendish clutches of a Palladian lodge.

His entire absurd and convoluted tale didn't contain a speck of truth, apart from the existence of a real lady named Diana Vaughan who typed Taxil's manuscripts, but the public ate it up. Fortunately for Taxil, Albert Pike had died in 1891, so there wasn't much chance of a slander lawsuit from across the sea. So Taxil could gleefully write that Pike, the "Luciferian Pope," met with Lucifer every Friday at 3 p.m. (We're left to wonder if this was a late-in-the-day, three-martini lunch.) Palladian lodges engaged in devil worship, ritual sex, and any other sacrileges Taxil could think of.

Meanwhile, other people feverishly embroidered Taxil's popular works about nonexistent female Palladian lodges. The Bishop of Grenoble asserted that these female lodges were harems for the male lodges, and Jesuit Bishop Leon Meurin wrote in his book *Synagogue of Satan* that *everything* about Freemasonry was Satanic, including aprons, symbols, signs, and handshakes.

On April 19, 1897, Taxil rented the auditorium of the Paris Geographic Society and filled the hall with a carefully invited guest list of freethinkers, Catholics, and the press. In a long presentation, he dropped the bomb on them all: Everything he had written had been a carefully designed hoax, specifically intended to humiliate the Catholic Church for being so easily manipulated. The gathering erupted in competing clamors of both laughter and anger, depending on whose ox was being gored. His 33-page confession was printed in the papers the following week, and it was the talk of Paris. He had made a fat wad of cash with his books and thumbed his nose at both the Masons and the Church. He left Paris and retired to a very nice country house where he died in 1907.

More than a hundred years after his confession, Taxil's quotes about Luciferian Masonry and his deceitful misquoting of Albert Pike's writings still get trotted out in new anti-Masonic works. Jack Harris, J. Edward Decker, James Holly, Gary H. Kah, William Schnoebelen, Jack Chick, and even Pat Robertson (who *really* should know better, as his own father was a Freemason) have all published anti-Masonic books over the last 25 years that use portions of Taxil's self-confessed lies. Leo the liar is long dead, but his practical joke lives on.

The Illuminati!

The conspiracy version of the butler in mystery novels is the Illuminati. If something goes *too* wrong or *too* right in the world, the conspiracy theorists will notoriously begin shouting "The Illuminati did it!" That knee-jerk accusation has been flying for more than 200 years, yet no one seems to be able to identify just what or who the Illuminati really is or just exactly what they really do. And no one seems to have ever quit the organization and ratted them out.

As I discuss in Chapter 4, Adam Weishaupt conceived the Illuminati in Bavaria in the 1770s. Originally, the little group was based on ideals of the Enlightenment, and the members questioned church teachings and the divine right of kings to keep their jobs. At first, Weishaupt was all about helping society, but he quickly became convinced that churches and governments needed to be toppled to make the world a more perfect place. The Illuminati never attracted more than about 2,000 European members at its height. It was publicly exposed, Weishaupt fled in disgrace, and the Illuminati died out by about 1785.

In 1798 a Scottish pro-monarchist named John Robison wrote *Proofs of a Conspiracy against All the Religions and Governments of Europe, Carried On in the Secret Meetings of Free Masons, Illuminati, and Reading Societies, Collected from Good Authorities* (nobody has snappy titles like these anymore). Meanwhile, a French abbot named Augustin Barruel was working on his own hit four-volume work, *Memoirs Illustrating the History of Jacobinism.* Both of these works put forth the theory that the Illuminati had caused the French Revolution by roaming the countryside, planting the vile seeds of heresy and revolt among happy and contented French peasants. (Barruel's works would later be plagiarized and rewritten as anti-Jewish propaganda, the notorious *Protocols of the Elders of Zion*).

To these toadies of the status quo, the Illuminati and the Freemasons were the same thing. They were in cahoots with each other, and even if the Illuminati had died out, there were still plenty of Masonic lodges all over the countryside to fear and hate. And the dangerous messages of liberty, equality, and brotherhood were being encouraged in them. Thus was born the myth of Freemasonry as a hotbed of revolutionaries and World Takeover Plots.

Over the years, the Illuminati became the general, all-purpose conspiracy theory boogeyman. Hitler figured the Illuminati was a group of Jews and Freemasons. The John Birch Society in the 1950s and 1960s took up the anti-Illuminati banner, but they figured the group to be the founders of worldwide Communism. Depending on who's doing the accusing, the Illuminati are either really creepy conservatives or really creepy liberals.

The latest incarnation of the Illuminati conspiracy theorists is what's been labeled the American neoconservative movement. The Internet is filled with accusations that the U.S. government is now packed with members of the Illuminati who are pro-Israeli Zionists, using their powers of world control to conquer all the sovereign Arabic and Islamic nations of the Middle East and place them under the control of tiny Israel. The saga continues.

Trilats, CFRs, and Bilderbergers, Oh My!

This myth is really a continuation of the Illuminati conspiracy claims. The belief is that there's just *gotta* be a secret group of shadowy world leaders who get together and work out world economies, politics, and events like a really friendly game of Risk with your least-liked relatives. There's just *gotta*. The following three groups are the most commonly named suspects. None is a Masonic organization, despite sinister accusations to the contrary, but facts never kept a good conspiracy theory down.

- ✔ **The Trilateral Commission:** This group (www.trilateral.org) is actually a nongovernment think tank of about 300 members from North America, Europe, and Japan — the dominant areas of democracy in the world. Members are business leaders and former government and United Nations officials. They meet on a regular basis and publish the papers presented at their gatherings, frequently on issues of expanding democracy. If some Freemasons are members, they make up no larger a portion of the commission than they do of society at large. Far from being secret, you're free to contact them for a list of their members.

- ✔ **The Council on Foreign Relations:** The CFR (www.cfr.org) is another think tank made up of U.S. and world leaders dedicated to educating policymakers, journalists, businesspeople, and students about international cultures, economies, policies, and defense issues. Again, it is hardly secret. It publishes *Foreign Affairs* magazine, and its website lists its notable members along with meeting dates and locations. Annual reports on a wide array of topics are available to anyone.

✔ **The Bilderberg Group:** This organization (www.bilderbergmeetings. org) is the oddest of the three. It was created in 1954 by Prince Bernhard in Oosterbeek, Netherlands, and is named after the hotel where they met in that first year. It began at the height of the Cold War to increase understanding between leaders of Europe and the United States. The theory was that World War III could be averted in the future if leaders of the countries involved in the previous World Wars had a chance to meet and get to know each other in an informal setting. Each year, 100 government, economic, and business leaders are invited to meet and talk freely without the interference of the news media (or their own constituents). Some of the notable attendees in the past have been former United States presidents Bill Clinton, George H. W. Bush, and George W. Bush; former prime minister of the United Kingdom Tony Blair; U.S. senators John Kerry and John Edwards; Bill Gates; Henry Kissinger; Donald Rumsfeld; and Steven Spielberg, as well as well-placed European notables. Conspiracy addicts see this regular meeting as an evil plot for one-world government, yet the group proposes no legislation, issues no policy statements, and takes no votes. The participants regard it as an opportunity to chat informally with people who are their international peers, without CNN or the BBC analyzing every offhanded remark ad infinitum. The list of invitees every year is no secret and is made available from its office in the Netherlands.

The Secret 33rd Degree!

I'm a 33rd-degree Mason, so I know all about the double-extra-supersecret Satanic and Luciferian ceremonies that go on in the ultrasecret meetings of the Scottish Rite's 33rd-degree members. That's the claim, anyway, of this particular hoax. The way the theory goes is that just 5 percent of the Freemasons of the world know the *real* secrets of Masonry, and that they alone secretly control the fraternity. Or the world. Or something that's *really* big. The reasons for and the breadth of their evil control get a little hazy from one anti-Masonic accuser to the next.

The 33rd degree is an honor bestowed on Scottish Rite Masons who have served the Scottish Rite or the community in extraordinary ways. It is an award of merit or service. It is *not* secretly conferred. In fact, the recipients of the 33rd degree are regularly listed with their photographs in Masonic magazines. Recipients of the 33rd degree are undeniably proud of their award and are entitled to write *33°* after their signature on Masonic documents. And Freemasons often give them an air of extra dignity, referring to them as "Illustrious 33rds."

Jack the Ripper: A Freemason!

In 1976, Stephen Knight published *Jack the Ripper: The Final Solution,* in which he theorized that the Whitechapel killer of 1888 was, in fact, Dr. William Gull, private physician to Victoria, Queen of England. Knight alleged that Gull was a Freemason and had been ordered by the queen (or the prime minister) to kill five London prostitutes because they knew of a secret marriage between Vicky's grandson, Prince Albert Edward, and a prostitute named Annie Crook. Eddy, as he was known, was in line to the throne after his father, the Prince of Wales, and being married to a hooker was bad enough. Worse was that she was Catholic and, compounding the scandal, she supposedly gave birth to a daughter.

According to the theory, Dr. Gull killed the women who knew about the marriage and the child according to Masonic ritual. He cut them from ear to ear, as described in the Entered Apprentice penalty. He tore open a left breast or two, as in the Fellow Craft penalty. He cut open a torso, removed the organs, and even burned them, as described in the Master Mason penalty.

The other "evidence" was a message scrawled in chalk on a wall near one of the murder scenes: "The Juwes are the men That Will not be Blamed for nothing." (The tagger wasn't exactly a grammarian.) Sir Charles Warren, Commissioner of the Metropolitan Police and a Freemason, ordered the message destroyed because he was afraid that anti-Jewish sentiment would be inflamed and Jews would be blamed for the killings (several near-riots and violence against Jews had already taken place). Knight's version is that Warren erased the words before they could even be photographed, in order to protect Freemasons. Knight believed that the "Juwes" were the attackers of Hiram Abiff in the Master Mason degree, who were named Jubela, Jubelo, and Jubelum. Never mind that no one besides Knight has ever referred to the three ruffians in the ritual as *Juwes.*

Knight's theory hangs on the allegations of Joseph Sickert, who claimed that he had learned the "truth" from his father, Walter Sickert, a well-known eccentric and painter of the period. But in later years, Joseph retracted the entire story, gleefully calling it "a whopping fib" and a hoax. Mystery author Patricia Cornwell's nonfiction book *Jack the Ripper: Portrait of a Killer — Case Closed* actually makes a compelling case that the Ripper was, in fact, none other than Walter Sickert himself.

Nevertheless, Knight went on to write another anti-Masonic book attempting to smear the fraternity even more. When he died in 1985 of a brain tumor after being hit in the head during a cricket match, a fellow anti-Mason named Martin Short (not the comedian) went on the radio and implied that the Masons had used an ultrasound death ray to kill him. No, I didn't make this stuff up — I'm not that good.

No serious researcher believes the William Gull/Freemason theory. The three attackers of Hiram Abiff had been removed from English Masonic ritual 70 years before the Ripper murders took place, and no one has ever called them *Juwes* anyway. The women's bodies were horribly mutilated, but there was no pattern to them to really suggest any connection to Masonic ritual. Sir William Gull was 72 years old with a heart condition and had recently suffered a stroke — hardly a likely man to run down dark alleys after young girls, much less engage in the grueling act of carving them up while they struggled. And the English public would hardly have needed to be protected from the scandals of philandering princes, as they were as common as ragweed. English law forbade a Catholic from ascending to the throne, and it turned out that the real Annie Crook wasn't even a Catholic to begin with. No evidence currently points to any secret marriage between Crook and Prince Albert Edward.

This theory would have died out in the 1980s after Joseph Sickert blew the whistle on himself if it hadn't been for its revival in a graphic novel by Alan Moore and Eddie Campbell called *From Hell*. The novel is considered to be a masterpiece of the graphic novel genre (another term for a very long, sophisticated, and detailed comic book). In 2001, it was made into a film of the same name starring Johnny Depp.

In many ways, a better telling of the story was made in 1979. *Murder by Decree* dramatized the same story as a Sherlock Holmes case, starring Christopher Plummer as Holmes and James Mason as Dr. Watson. Completely untrue, it is still an entertaining yarn — and that's all it is.

The Italian P2 Lodge Scandal!

In 1895, a Masonic lodge called Propaganda Due (pronounced *doo*-ay, Italian for "two") opened in Italy by the authority of the Grand Orient of Italy. Now, it's no secret that government in Italy over the last century had been riddled with corruption, both prior to and since World War II. In the 1970s, the Communist Party gained enormous power in Italian Parliamentary elections, and the country was plagued with violence and terrorism. Italy was in a social mess, and the terrorists and members of the Mafia were having a field day. It was the next best thing to anarchy.

Propaganda Due lodge became filled with unscrupulous businessmen as well as government and military officials, many with Mafia connections. By 1976, it had become so notorious that the Grand Master of the Grand Orient of Italy finally ordered it shut down, pulled its charter, and expelled its members and its Worshipful Master, Lucio Gelli. Gelli collected up the mailing lists of the members and went right back into business. He called the group P2 and still ran it like a Masonic lodge. Never mind that it was illegal, unrecognized, and unsanctioned by any Masonic body.

P2 member Roberto Calvi was a Milanese banker who, along with Michele Sindora, a banker in the employ of the mafia, was secretly smuggling cash out of the country. Sindora was also in charge of managing the investments of the Vatican. Between Calvi and Sindora, they embezzled 80 billion *lire* of Church money (roughly $50 million). Just as Banco Ambrosiano was about to be shut down, Calvi got out of town and disappeared.

In 1981, the scandals hit the newspapers. Enough P2 members were involved in the government that public confidence plummeted, and the government fell in May. Explanations of the difference between real Masons and a rogue lodge of crooks largely fell on deaf ears. The papers loudly decried the Freemasons as thieves and murderers. Masons were accused of assassinating Pope John Paul I, who died that year after just 33 days in office, as well as bombing a train and killing 80 people. Italy had no shortage of wacko antigovernment terrorism at the time, but the Freemasons made a great scapegoat.

Calvi turned up in London in 1982 hanging by a rope under Blackfriars Bridge, his pockets stuffed with bricks and his feet dangling in the Thames River. The bricks were clear proof to the press that the Freemasons had killed him. For more than 20 years, the murder remained unsolved, and the Masons were almost universally blamed. In 2005, new evidence was introduced that led to the prosecution of the real murderers, who had been directed by Mafia boss Pippo Calo — not the Freemasons. Nevertheless, whenever P2 is mentioned today, the word *Freemason* is almost always attached to it.

Washington, D.C., Is Satan's Road Map!

Take a look at a map of Washington, D.C., and look just north and east of the White House. There it is! Massachusetts Avenue, Rhode Island Avenue, Connecticut Avenue, Vermont Avenue, and K Street NW do, indeed, form a five-pointed pentagram! It's occult! It's evil! It's Satanic! And Freemason George Washington put it there!

Here's the boring truth: Washington hired Pierre Charles L'Enfant to create the design of the new federal city, but it was Secretary of State Thomas Jefferson who made the initial recommendations of building and street placement, based on the topography of the land and his own ideas. Andrew Ellicott and Benjamin Bannecker were hired to survey and execute the designs. Of all those men, only Washington and L'Enfant were Freemasons, and apart from choosing the site, Washington had little to do with the design.

Even if a five-pointed star was deliberately included in the design, to buy into this hoax you have to presume that everybody accepts that a five-pointed star is an evil symbol. They don't, despite all those creaky old Peter Cushing movies about devil worship. You also have to presume that including it in the street plan of Washington would somehow influence government. Finally, you have to believe that Freemasons revere the pentagram as a symbol of some sort of unholy worship, which they do not. Masons don't worship symbols. They use them as memory and teaching devices, but the symbols themselves are not venerated. Some Masonic jurisdictions regard the five-pointed star as a representation of God. Some use it as a memory device for the five points of fellowship, a portion of the Master Mason degree. Most don't even refer to it at all. It is a symbol of the Order of the Eastern Star, a group created in the mid-1800s, long after Washington, D.C., was laid out (see Chapter 13).

The world has no shortage of folks who would agree that Washington, D.C., is evil, or at least a bothersome repository of pests, Satanic pentagrams notwithstanding. And anyone who has driven through Washington on a busy day would probably agree that the only explanation for its mazelike traffic patterns is that it had to be designed by the Horned One himself. I can haul out a map of almost any city in the United States and, with squinty eyes and selective dot-connecting, come up with pentagrams. Any city that is laid out in a grid with the occasional diagonal street or two achieves it. Indianapolis looks positively like Beelzebub's Satanic bus route.

By the way, pull out a map of Sandusky, Ohio, sometime. Freemason Hector Kilbourn planned the city in 1818. He used two sets of diagonal streets and some wide-open spaces to duplicate the Masonic square and compass and an open Bible. Cue the eerie organ music.

One website claims the George Washington Masonic Memorial in nearby Alexandria, Virginia, is a beacon for UFOs, and the giant square and compass in front of it is a navigation marker for their landings. That road-map stuff is silly, but I believe *this* is absolutely true. (Yeah, right.)

Aleister Crowley, Satanist and Freemason!

The trouble with Freemasonry is that anyone can stroll around the countryside and claim to be a Mason without many people having the resources to question him. Any oddball can write his own ritual, lock himself in a room, slap a square and compass on his chest, and claim to be practicing Freemasonry. Which brings me to Aleister Crowley.

Crowley was an occult adventurer. He was a mystic, a writer, a poet, a social critic, and a painter. He climbed the Himalayas and studied astrology, chemistry, and the occult. He was also a heroin addict and what we today would call a sexual predator (or, what they called in earlier times, a sick-minded old pervert). He was particularly proud of being referred to in the press as "The Wickedest Man in the World." Even as a child, young Aleister didn't care for his parents' religion, and his mother began to regularly refer to him as "the Beast," from the Book of Revelation, a nickname he wore with pride in later years.

By the time he got to college, Crowley was obsessed with blood, torture, and being sexually "degraded," both by men and "Scarlet women." In 1899, he joined a witch's coven, where he quickly wore out his welcome with appalling attitudes toward women and sexual demands that were considered bizarre even by witch standards. Crowley quit school before graduating, moved to London, and started calling himself Count Vladimir. He joined the Hermetic Order of the Golden Dawn, a mystic group in London, which eventually sued him for publishing its rituals.

Crowley's feelings were hardly hurt. He ate up notoriety and enjoyed his growing reputation as a Satanist and Black Magician. At various times of his life, he would call himself "Baphomet" or associate himself with 666, the biblical number of the Beast. His failed attempts at using "sexual magick" to create a "magical" child were novelized in his book *Moonchild.*

Next, Crowley became obsessed with Egyptology and claimed the spirit of the Egyptian god Horus had divinely dictated his *Book of the Law* to him. The book became the basis for his own religion, *Thelema,* and it contained the primary rule he lived his life by: "Do what thou wilt shall be the whole of the Law." That's not a philosophy; that's an excuse — and it doesn't exactly rank right up there with "Love thy neighbor."

Aleister Crowley was initiated into an irregular Masonic lodge in Mexico City in 1900. He received the 33rd degree from an equally Masonically illegal body. He joined another unrecognized French lodge in Paris in 1904. Eventually, Crowley took over and redefined the rituals of the *Ordo Templi Orientis,* drawing heavily on the rituals of Freemasonry as well as Masonic Templarism. Less generously inclined people would say he stole them. Regardless of the semantics, *Ordo Templi Orientis* rituals are *very* different from those in regular, recognized Freemasonry.

Contrary to books that claim otherwise, and contrary to Crowley's own endlessly fantastic claims, he had virtually no contacts with regular Freemasonry. Crowley was never an active Freemason, was never recognized or claimed as a Freemason by any regular Masonic body, and has had absolutely no impact on Freemasonry. Still, the myth that he was a Mason and that he was somehow part of Freemasonry persists, and photos of Crowley dressed in Masonic regalia frequently appear.

Freemasons Founded the Nazis!

Freemasons were responsible for Nazism? Not even close. In 1912, a group of German believers in the occult formed a fraternity called the *Germanenorden,* based on the writings of Guido von List. List was an Austrian researcher of mysticism who became popular by writing about *runes* (symbols that purportedly had magical, mystical meanings and powers). List was also one of the first to popularize the theories of the Aryan race.

One of the founding members of *Germanenorden* was Rudolf Glandeck von Sebottendorff. Sebottendorff was involved in several mystical, occult groups before and after World War I, and in 1909 he claimed he had joined a pseudo-Masonic Memphis-Mizraim lodge in Turkey. From his own descriptions of it, this particular lodge combined Rosicrucianism, alchemy, astrology, and even Islamic Sufism — not exactly what anyone would accept as regular, recognized Freemasonry.

The *Germanenorden* quickly suffered from internal struggles and split off another group called the German Order Walvater of the Holy Grail, founded by Hermann Pohl. In 1918, Pohl started yet another occult group called *Thule Gesellschaft,* which was a study group for believers of List's philosophies, as well as a nice, harmless-sounding front for stockpiling guns and ammo to attack the growing Communist Party.

A year later, Thule merged with the Committee of Independent Workers and renamed itself the German Workers' Party. Adolf Hitler found a home in this hapless haven of political hobos and became Member #7 in the ragtag group. Hitler quickly took over and chose the swastika as the group's symbol. The next year, he changed its name yet again, this time to the National Socialist German Workers' Party, or the Nazi Party for short. During this period, the only people getting rich were the membership card and stationary printers.

After Hitler became a popular figure and chancellor in the 1930s, Sebottendorff decided to climb on the bandwagon and feather his own cap by claiming in a book that his own "Masonic" influences and the mystical and occult workings of *Thule* had been a big, helpful inspiration to Hitler and the philosophy of Nazism. Hitler preferred to believe that he thought it all up on his own. Sebottendorff's book was banned by the Bavarian secret police, and the Gestapo tossed him into a concentration camp before deporting him to Turkey. No serious historian has ever authenticated Sebottendorff's claims, and no authentic Masonic organization has ever espoused the odd brand of Freemasonry he peddled. The fact that Hitler outlawed Freemasonry everywhere he saw it and executed or threw its members into concentration camps should be argument enough that there was no serious connection between Nazism and Masonry. But the myth persists.

Masonic Cops! Masonic Judges!

There are Freemasons in the police department! There are Freemasons sitting on the judicial bench! There are Freemasons in city hall! And the point is . . . ?

Gallons of ink have been spilled in the British press accusing Freemasonry of being an elite club of upper-class twits who lay secret plans to keep the yobs and lamers out and help each other while trampling over bothersome poor people. If these stories simply remained the sour-grape whine-festivals of editorialists engaging in social-class incitement, they might be nothing more than insulting and ignorant accusations. Unfortunately, in the 1990s, they became far more than that.

In 1997, after a long, windy campaign, a member of Parliament named Chris Mullin finally persuaded the British prime minister, the home secretary, and the House of Commons to allow hearings on the influence of Freemasonry in the criminal justice system. Mullin was convinced that Masonic policemen were giving special privileges to each other and to Masonic criminals and covering up misconduct. In the courts, he accused Masonic judges of going easy on defendants who gave secret Masonic signals from the dock. Despite lots of hysteria in the British press, no patterns of actual abuse, influence, or discrimination were found, but the public perception remained that clannish Freemasons were up to no good.

Throughout Great Britain, laws and local regulations have been passed requiring judges, police officers, government workers, and members of Parliament to publicly divulge their membership in the Freemasons. Curiously, they used to be required to do so, along with most other membership groups, as part of Britain's Unlawful Societies Act, but the act was repealed in 1967 as being obsolete. The difference is that, until 2011, the Freemasons alone were being singled out as something dangerously sneaky. Never mind that fellow members of a country club, business group, or any other association could give equally preferential treatment to their fellow members.

Anti-Masonic laws in both England and Italy have been found by the European Union to be in violation of the EU's constitution, and they were finally repealed in 2009. Nevertheless, suspicions in Europe about Masonic cops and judges still persist.

Many anti-Masons make a lot of noise about the oaths taken by Freemasons. Yes, Masons do promise to help, aid, and assist their Brothers. The part that most of the detractors leave out is that Masons also promise to whisper good counsel in the ear of a Brother and, in the most tender manner possible, remind him of his faults and aid in his reformation. Nowhere does Freemasonry encourage a Masonic cop to ignore a Brother running away from a broken shop window with a television set under his arm.

Chapter 19

Ten Cool Masonic Places

In This Chapter

▶ Checking out U.S. temples, halls, and cathedrals

▶ Discovering Masonic sites worldwide

*1*f you're traveling the globe and going in search of great Masonic sites, the first place to start is usually with the headquarters of a state or country's Grand Lodge. It's usually the largest and most magnificent Masonic building in the area, although that's not always the case.

Pantagraph Printing in Bloomington, Illinois, publishes the indispensable *List of Lodges — Masonic*, which is updated every year to help the confused Masonic traveler in search of lodges in different jurisdictions. Additionally, the two-volume *Freemasonry Universal* by Kent Henderson and Tony Pope is an exhaustive guide to recognized Freemasonry around the world; it includes much in the way of historical background and contact information for the globetrotting Freemason.

But let's say you're just looking for a great photo op as you blast through town. Or you're a non-Mason who can't go to a lodge meeting but you'd still like to peer inside those mysterious buildings. In this chapter, I give you a list of my ten favorite Masonic sites around the world.

George Washington Masonic Memorial (Alexandria, Virginia)

Located in Alexandria, Virginia, atop Shooter's Hill, this 333-foot-tall monument serves two purposes: It's a memorial to the first president and America's most famous Freemason and is also a monument and museum of the Masonic fraternity in the United States. It includes a replica of George Washington's Masonic lodge room. The view is incredible from the observation deck. It's featured in Dan Brown's book *The Lost Symbol* and stood in for the Smithsonian in *National Treasure 2: Book of Secrets*. A symbol of the cooperation of the Freemasons in the United States, a portion of every American Freemason's initiation fee goes to support this magnificent structure. The memorial's website is http://gwmemorial.org.

House of the Temple (Washington, D.C.)

Located at 1733 16th Street, NW, in Washington, D.C., the House of the Temple is the headquarters of the Ancient Accepted Scottish Rite, Southern Jurisdiction (www.srmason-sj.org). This building is so magnificent that it has to be seen to be believed. The imposing sphinxes guarding the entrance make it look exactly like what the headquarters of a secret society is supposed to look like. Its architect was John Russell Pope, who based its design on the Mausoleum at Halicarnassus in Turkey, one of the Seven Wonders of the Ancient World. It is, in fact, the burial place of Albert Pike (see Chapter 11). It contains several museum displays and has the largest Masonic library in North America. It plays a starring role in the exciting climax of Dan Brown's book *The Lost Symbol*.

Freemason's Hall (Philadelphia)

Located at 1 North Broad Street in Philadelphia, this building is the headquarters of the Grand Lodge of Pennsylvania and one of the most incredible Grand Lodge buildings in the world. Dedicated in 1873, it's based on Norman architecture. Its magnificent lodge rooms each have a different theme. You can find out more at its website (www.pagrandlodge.org).

While you're in Philadelphia, be sure to visit Independence Hall. Rumor has it a bunch of Freemasons hung out there.

Masonic Temple (Detroit)

Located at 500 Temple Avenue in Detroit and opened in 1926, the Gothic-style Masonic Temple is unique among the world's Masonic buildings. Containing more than 12 million cubic feet, it was designed to accommodate all of Detroit's Blue Lodges and appendant bodies. The 14-story tower provides a home for 26 lodges, a Scottish Rite consistory, 2 Knight Templar commanderies, 5 Royal Arch chapters, and 1 Cryptic Council. The top floor contains an auditorium that was designed to hold 800 spectators solely for conferring the Master Mason degree, and the Scottish Rite auditorium holds 1,600. One entire floor is a massive drill hall for the Templar's marching drill teams. The main theater (yep, another one) holds 4,400 and is the premiere theatrical venue in Detroit today.

The Shrine dominates the other end of the building, which is another ten-story structure. It was built with ballrooms, a library, a billiard room, a barber shop, a bowling alley, an indoor swimming pool, and a gymnasium, plus 80 hotel rooms — in all, over 1,000 interior rooms.

Freemason Henry Ford contributed generously to the temple's construction, and Detroit's Masons dreamed big before the Great Depression hit —

they even had their own country club. Their website is www.detroit masonic.com.

Grand Lodge of the State of New York (New York City)

Located at 71 West 23rd Street in New York City, the Grand Lodge of the State of New York is an extraordinary building with a wide variety of beautiful lodge rooms. Its website is www.nymasons.org.

Scottish Rite Cathedral (Indianapolis)

This one is my own biased inclusion for the home team. The Scottish Rite Cathedral (www.aasr-indy.org), located at 650 North Meridian Street in Indianapolis, is a Gothic masterpiece. Built in mathematical multiples of 33, it is the largest strictly Scottish Rite building in the world. It was declared "one of the seven most beautiful buildings in the world" by the International Association of Architects.

Freemason Hall (London)

Freemason Hall is the headquarters of the United Grand Lodge of England (www.ugle.org.uk). It's located at 60 Great Queen Street, near Covent Garden, between the Holborn and Covent Garden Tube stations. Freemason Hall contains a memorial to 3,225 English Masons who died in World War I, a vast museum that includes items used by Freemasons to hold secret meetings while they were held as prisoners in World War I and World War II, a library, and a gift shop. The Grand Lodge Room is one of the most spectacular in the world. Foreign Masons who want to visit a lodge meeting should make arrangements through their own Grand Secretary's office.

Be sure to hoist a pint at the Freemason Arms pub and to visit the two Masonic regalia stores across the street. Sadly, the Goose and Gridiron Tavern in the shadow of St. Paul's Cathedral has not survived.

Templar Church (London)

Hidden behind the walls of the Inns of Court in London, just off Fleet Street at Chancery Lane, the Templar Church, with its distinctive circular design and stone effigies of buried Templar knights, is a site every member of the

Knights Templar should visit. (It's also a key player in *The Da Vinci Code* by Dan Brown!) The church can be a devil of a place to find, and its hours are very haphazard. Consult the website (www.templechurch.com) for the latest schedule — it can change at the drop of a hat. It remains a working church, and concerts are often performed there.

After you see the church, walk a few blocks up Chancery Lane and have lunch at the Knights Templar Pub.

Rosslyn Chapel (Roslin, Scotland)

Located in Roslin, Scotland, 6 miles south of Edinburgh's Princes Street, the Rosslyn Chapel is another important site to *Da Vinci Code* fans but very important to Freemasons as well. The St. Clair family built it, and it contains much Templar and Masonic symbolism. Some people believe that the Holy Grail is buried deep within its foundation. The chapel is thought by many to be a physical link between the Knights Templar and the origin of Scottish Freemasonry. Its website is www.rosslynchapel.org.uk.

Grande Loge Nationale Française and Other Masonic Buildings (Paris)

The *Grande Loge Nationale Française* (www.grandelogenationale francaise.com) has a wonderful contemporary headquarters that is very difficult to find at 12 rue Christine de Pisan. It's so secret that most taxi drivers can't seem to figure out where it is. Many Paris lodges, as well as the Grand Lodge, meet in this building.

Don't let recognition and regularity issues keep you from visiting other great Masonic sites. Both the largely unrecognized *Grande Loge de France* (www.gldf.org) and the unrecognized and irregular *Grand Orient de France* (www.museefm.org) also have outstanding buildings with museums. You can find out more at their websites.

Knights Templar will be saddened to know there is no remnant of the Templar Preceptory in Paris, despite many streets and even a Metro stop named after the temple. Napoleon III destroyed the last remains of the temple in the 19th century. However, go and visit the place where Jacques de Molay was put to death (see Chapter 10). It is the tiny park at the western edge of the Isle de la Cité. The south of France has many Templar sites, and Chinon Castle in the Loire Valley contains the tower where de Molay was held under arrest; his graffiti has been preserved.

Part VI

Appendixes

The 5th Wave   By Rich Tennant

"Why would an idiotic organization like the Masons be dumb enough to have a square and compass as its symbol? Well, here's where the square comes in."

In this part . . .

The earliest written record of Freemasonry is a document called the Regius Manuscript, and it lays down the basic structure and rules of the operative stonemason guilds of the middle ages. I let you take a look at it in Appendix A.

Almost four centuries later, Dr. James Anderson published the first Book of Constitutions for the Grand Lodge of England. By contrast, it's the rules and regulations of the first speculative Freemasons, and most Grand Lodges today have adopted the basic rules set down by Anderson. You'll find them in Appendix B.

Appendix C is a listing of the regular, recognized Grand Lodges in the United States and Canada, including Prince Hall Grand Lodges. If you're a Mason who wants to go traveling or a non-Mason interested in finding a lodge to join, this appendix is a good place to start.

Appendix A

The Regius Manuscript

....

*T*he Regius Manuscript was written in about AD 1390. It is the oldest and arguably the most important Masonic document in existence. It is unusual because it is written as a poem, whereas Masonic documents that followed it are in prose. It was also written at a time when Roman Catholicism prevailed in England, and it contains a section on proper behavior in church. It includes much of the legendary "history" of Freemasonry and was most likely interpreted in poetic form by a monk who was inspired by even earlier Masonic writings that no longer exist. It is one of 99 documents of varying ages referred to as the *Gothic Constitutions,* which make up the earliest rules for the stonemason guilds that eventually became the modern fraternity of Freemasonry. Over time, the Gothic Constitutions became less influenced by Trinitarian Christianity, and less secular, but this early document is quite religious in tone.

The original document is written in Old English language that is difficult to understand. The version I include here is a translation by James Halliwell from 1840 (it is sometimes referred to as the *Halliwell Manuscript* for this reason). It is preserved in the British Museum in London and was donated to the museum in 1757 by King George II (which is why it is called *regius,* Latin for "king").

A Poem of Moral Duties

Here begin the constitutions of the art of Geometry according to Euclid.

Whoever will both well read and look
He may find written in old book
Of great lords and also ladies,
That had many children together, certainly;
And had no income to keep them with,
Neither in town nor field nor enclosed wood;
A council together they could them take,
To ordain for these children's sake,

How they might best lead their life
Without great disease, care and strife;
And most for the multitude that was coming
Of their children after great clerks,
To teach them then good works;

And pray we them, for our Lord's sake.
To our children some work to make,
That they might get their living thereby,
Both well and honestly full securely.
In that time, through good geometry,
This honest craft of good masonry
Was ordained and made in this manner,
Counterfeited of these clerks together;
At these lords' prayers they counterfeited geometry,
And gave it the name of masonry,
For the most honest craft of all.
These lords' children thereto did fall,
To learn of him the craft of geometry,
The which he made full curiously;

Through fathers' prayers and mothers' also,
This honest craft he put them to.
He learned best, and was of honesty,
And passed his fellows in curiosity,
If in that craft he did him pass,
He should have more worship than the less,
This great clerk's name was Euclid,
His name it spread full wonder wide.
Yet this great clerk ordained he
To him that was higher in this degree,
That he should teach the simplest of wit
In that honest craft to be perfect;
And so each one shall teach the other,
And love together as sister and brother.

Furthermore yet that ordained he,
Master called so should he be;
So that he were most worshipped,
Then should he be so called;
But masons should never one another call,
Within the craft amongst them all,
Neither subject nor servant, my dear brother,
Though he be not so perfect as is another;
Each shall call other fellows by friendship,
Because they come of ladies' birth.

On this manner, through good wit of geometry,
Began first the craft of masonry;
The clerk Euclid on this wise it found,
This craft of geometry in Egypt land.

In Egypt he taught it full wide,
In divers lands on every side;
Many years afterwards, I understand,
Ere that the craft came into this land.
This craft came into England, as I you say,
In time of good King Athelstane's day;
He made then both hall and even bower,
And high temples of great honour,
To disport him in both day and night,
And to worship his God with all his might.
This good lord loved this craft full well,
And purposed to strengthen it every part,
For divers faults that in the craft he found;
He sent about into the land

After all the masons of the craft,
To come to him full even straight,
For to amend these defaults all
By good counsel, if it might fall.
An assembly then could let make
Of divers lords in their state,
Dukes, earls, and barons also,
Knights, squires and many more,
And the great burgesses of that city,
They were there all in their degree;
They were there each one always,
To ordain for these masons' estate,
There they sought by their wit,
How they might govern it;

Fifteen articles they there sought,
And fifteen points there they wrought,

Here begins the first article.

The first article of this geometry;
The master mason must be full securely
Both steadfast, trusty and true,
It shall him never then rue;
And pay thy fellows after the cost,
As victuals goeth then, well thou knowest;

And pay them truly, upon thy faith,
What they may deserve;
And to their hire take no more,
But what that they may serve for;
And spare neither for love nor dread,

Of neither parties to take no bribe;
Of lord nor fellow, whoever he be,
Of them thou take no manner of fee;
And as a judge stand upright,
And then thou dost to both good right;
And truly do this wheresoever thou goest,
Thy worship, thy profit, it shall be most.

Second article.

The second article of good masonry,
As you must it here hear specially,
That every master, that is a mason,
Must be at the general congregation,
So that he it reasonably be told
Where that the assembly shall be held;

And to that assembly he must needs go,
Unless he have a reasonable excuse,
Or unless he be disobedient to that craft
Or with falsehood is overtaken,
Or else sickness hath him so strong,
That he may not come them among;
That is an excuse good and able,
To that assembly without fable.

Third article.

The third article forsooth it is,
That the master takes to no 'prentice,
Unless he have good assurance to dwell
Seven years with him, as I you tell,
His craft to learn, that is profitable;

Within less he may not be able
To lords' profit, nor to his own
As you may know by good reason.

Fourth article.

The fourth article this must be,
That the master him well besee,
That he no bondman 'prentice make,
Nor for no covetousness do him take;
For the lord that he is bound to,
May fetch the 'prentice wheresoever he go.
If in the lodge he were taken,
Much disease it might there make,
And such case it might befall,
That it might grieve some or all.

For all the masons that be there
Will stand together all together.
If such one in that craft should dwell,
Of divers disease you might tell;
For more ease then, and of honesty,
Take a 'prentice of higher degree.
By old time written I find
That the 'prentice should be of gentle kind;
And so sometime, great lords' blood
Took this geometry that is full good.

Fifth article.

The fifth article is very good,
So that the 'prentice be of lawful blood;
The master shall not, for no advantage,

Make no 'prentice that is deformed;
It is mean, as you may hear
That he have all his limbs whole all together;
To the craft it were great shame,
To make a halt man and a lame,
For an imperfect man of such blood
Should do the craft but little good.
Thus you may know every one,
The craft would have a mighty man;
A maimed man he hath no might,
You must it know long ere night.

Sixth article.

The sixth article you must not miss

That the master do the lord no prejudice,
To take the lord for his 'prentice,
As much as his fellows do, in all wise.
For in that craft they be full perfect,
So is not he, you must see it.
Also it were against good reason,
To take his hire as his fellows do.

This same article in this case,
Judgeth his 'prentice to take less
Than his fellows, that be full perfect.
In divers matters, know requite it,
The master may his 'prentice so inform,
That his hire may increase full soon,

And ere his term come to an end,
His hire may full well amend.

Seventh article.

The seventh article that is now here,
Full well will tell you all together,
That no master for favour nor dread,
Shall no thief neither clothe nor feed.
Thieves he shall harbour never one,
Nor him that hath killed a man,
Nor the same that hath a feeble name,
Lest it would turn the craft to shame.

Eighth article.

The eighth article sheweth you so,
That the master may it well do.
If that he have any man of craft,
And he be not so perfect as he ought,
He may him change soon anon,
And take for him a more perfect man.
Such a man through recklessness,
Might do the craft scant worship.

Ninth article.

The ninth article sheweth full well,
That the master be both wise and strong;
That he no work undertake,
Unless he can both it end and make;
And that it be to the lords' profit also,
And to his craft, wheresoever he go;
And that the ground be well taken,
That it neither flaw nor crack.

Tenth article.

The tenth article is for to know,
Among the craft, to high and low,
There shall no master supplant another,
But be together as sister and brother,
In this curious craft, all and some,
That belongeth to a master mason.
Nor shall he supplant no other man,
That hath taken a work him upon,
In pain thereof that is so strong,

That weigheth no less than ten pounds,
but if that he be guilty found,
That took first the work on hand;
For no man in masonry
Shall not supplant other securely,
But if that it be so wrought,
That in turn the work to nought;
Then may a mason that work crave,
To the lords' profit for it to save
In such a case if it do fall,
There shall no mason meddle withal.
Forsooth he that beginneth the ground,
If he be a mason good and sound,
He hath it securely in his mind

To bring the work to full good end.

Eleventh article.

The eleventh article I tell thee,
That he is both fair and free;
For he teacheth, by his might,
That no mason should work by night,
But if be in practising of wit,
If that I could amend it.

Twelfth article.

The twelfth article is of high honesty
To every mason wheresoever he be,
He shall not his fellows' work deprave,
If that he will his honesty save;
With honest words he it commend,

By the wit God did thee send;
But it amend by all that thou may,
Between you both without doubt.

Thirteenth article.

The thirteenth article, so God me save,
Is if that the master a 'prentice have,
Entirely then that he him tell,
That he the craft ably may know,
Wheresoever he go under the sun.

Fourteenth article.

The fourteenth article by good reason,
Sheweth the master how he shall do;
He shall no 'prentice to him take,
Unless divers cares he have to make,
That he may within his term,
Of him divers points may learn.

Fifteenth article.

The fifteenth article maketh an end,
For to the master he is a friend;
To teach him so, that for no man,
No false maintenance he take him upon,
Nor maintain his fellows in their sin,
For no good that he might win;
Nor no false oath suffer him to make,
For dread of their souls' sake,
Lest it would turn the craft to shame,
And himself to very much blame.

Plural constitutions.

At this assembly were points ordained more,
Of great lords and masters also.
That who will know this craft and come to estate,
He must love well God and holy church always,
And his master also that he is with,

Whersoever he go in field or enclosed wood,
And thy fellows thou love also,
For that thy craft will that thou do.

Second point.

The second point as I you say,
That the mason work upon the work day,
As truly as he can or may,

To deserve his hire for the holy-day,
And truly to labour on his deed,
Well deserve to have his reward.

Third point.

The third point must be severely,
With the 'prentice know it well,
His master's counsel he keep and close,
And his fellows by his good purpose;
The privities of the chamber tell he no man,
Nor in the lodge whatsoever they do;
Whatsoever thou hearest or seest them do,
Tell it no man wheresoever you go;
The counsel of hall, and even of bower,

Keep it well to great honour,
Lest it would turn thyself to blame,
And bring the craft into great shame.

Fourth point.

The fourth point teacheth us also,
That no man to his craft be false;
Error he shall maintain none
Against the craft, but let it go;
Nor no prejudice he shall not do
To his master, nor his fellow also;
And though the 'prentice be under awe,
Yet he would have the same law.

Fifth point.

The fifth point is without doubt,
That when the mason taketh his pay
Of the master, ordained to him,
Full meekly taken so must it be;
Yet must the master by good reason,
Warn him lawfully before noon,

If he will not occupy him no more,
As he hath done there before;
Against this order he may not strive,
If he think well for to thrive.

Sixth point.

The sixth point is full given to know,
Both to high and even low,

For such case it might befall;
Among the masons some or all,
Through envy or deadly hate,
Oft ariseth full great debate.
Then ought the mason if that he may,
Put them both under a day;
But loveday yet shall they make none,
Till that the work-day you must well take
Leisure enough loveday to make,
Hinder their work for such a fray;
To such end then that you them draw.

That they stand well in God's law.

Seventh point.

The seventh point he may well mean,
Of well long life that God us lend,
As it descrieth well openly,
Thou shalt not by thy master's wife lie,
Nor by thy fellows', in no manner wise,
Lest the craft would thee despise;
Nor by thy fellows' concubine,
No more thou wouldst he did by thine.
The pain thereof let it be sure,
That he be 'prentice full seven year,
If he forfeit in any of them
So chastised then must he be;
Full much care might there begin,
For such a foul deadly sin.

Eighth point.

The eighth point, he may be sure,
If thou hast taken any cure,
Under thy master thou be true,
For that point thou shalt never rue;
A true mediator thou must needs be
To thy master, and thy fellows free;

Do truly all that thou might,
To both parties, and that is good right.

Ninth point.

The ninth point we shall him call,
That he be steward of our hall,
If that you be in chamber together,
Each one serve other with mild cheer;
Gentle fellows, you must it know,
For to be stewards all in turn,
Week after week without doubt,
Stewards to be so all in turn about,
Amiably to serve each one other,
As though they were sister and brother;
There shall never one another cost
Free himself to no advantage,
But every man shall be equally free

In that cost, so must it be;
Look that thou pay well every man always,
That thou hast bought any victuals eaten,
That no craving be made to thee,
Nor to thy fellows in no degree,
To man or to woman, whoever he be,
Pay them well and truly, for that will we;
Thereof on thy fellow true record thou take,
For that good pay as thou dost make,
Lest it would thy fellow shame,
And bring thyself into great blame.
Yet good accounts he must make
Of such goods as he hath taken,

Of thy fellows' goods that thou hast spent,
Where and how and to what end;
Such accounts thou must come to,
When thy fellows wish that thou do.

Tenth point.

The tenth point presenteth well good life,
To live without care and strife;
For if the mason live amiss,
And in his work be false I know,

And through such a false excuse
May slander his fellows without reason,
Through false slander of such fame

May make the craft acquire blame.
If he do the craft such villainy,
Do him no favour then securely,
Nor maintain not him in wicked life,
Lest it would turn to care and strife;
But yet him you shall not delay,
Unless that you shall him constrain,
For to appear wheresoever you will,
Where that you will, loud, or still;
To the next assembly you him call,
To appear before his fellows all,
And unless he will before them appear,

The craft he must need forswear;
He shall then be punished after the law
That was founded by old day.

Eleventh point.

The eleventh point is of good discretion,
As you must know by good reason;
A mason, if he this craft well know,
That seeth his fellow hew on a stone,
And is in point to spoil that stone,
Amend it soon if that thou can,
And teach him then it to amend,
That the lords' work be not spoiled,
And teach him easily it to amend,

With fair words, that God thee hath lent;
For his sake that sit above,
With sweet words nourish his love.

Twelfth point.

The twelfth point is of great royalty,
There as the assembly held shall be,
There shall be masters and fellows also,
And other great lords many more;
There shall be the sheriff of that country,
And also the mayor of that city,
Knights and squires there shall be,

And also aldermen, as you shall see;
Such ordinance as thy make there,

They shall maintain it all together
Against that man, whatsoever he be,
That belongeth to the craft both fair and free.
If he any strife against them make,
Into their custody he shall be taken.

Thirteenth point.

The thirteenth point is to us full lief,
He shall swear never to be no thief,
Nor succour him in his false craft,
For no good that he hath bereft,
And thou must it know or sin,
Neither for his good, nor for his kin.

Fourteenth point.

The fourteenth point is full good law
To him that would be under awe;
A good true oath he must there swear
To his master and his fellows that be there;
He must be steadfast and true also
To all this ordinance, wheresoever he go,
And to his liege lord the king,
To be true to him over all thing.
And all these points here before
To them thou must need be sworn,
And all shall swear the same oath
Of the masons, be they lief be they loath.
To all these points here before,

That hath been ordained by full good lore.
And they shall enquire every man
Of his party, as well as he can,
If any man may be found guilty
In any of these points specially;
And who he be, let him be sought,
And to the assembly let him be brought.

Fifteenth point.

The fifteenth point is full good lore,
For them that shall be there sworn,
Such ordinance at the assembly was laid
Of great lords and masters before said;
For the same that be disobedient, I know,

Against the ordinance that there is,
Of these articles that were moved there,
Of great lords and masons all together,
And if they be proved openly
Before that assembly, by and by,
And for their guilt's no amends will make,
Then must they need the craft forsake;
And no masons craft they shall refuse,
And swear it never more to use.
But if that they will amends make,
Again to the craft they shall never take;
And if that they will not do so,
The sheriff shall come them soon to,

And put their bodies in deep prison,
For the trespass that they have done,
And take their goods and their cattle
Into the king's hand, every part,
And let them dwell there full still,
Till it be our liege king's will.

Another ordinance of the art of geometry.

They ordained there an assembly to be hold,
Every year, wheresoever they would,
To amend the defaults, if any were found
Among the craft within the land;
Each year or third year it should be held,

In every place wheresoever they would;
Time and place must be ordained also,
In what place they should assemble to,
All the men of craft there they must be,
And other great lords, as you must see,
To mend the faults the he there spoken,
If that any of them be then broken.

There they shall be all sworn,
That belongeth to this craft's lore,
To keep their statutes every one
That were ordained by King Athelstane;
These statutes that I have here found
I ordain they be held through my land,
For the worship of my royalty,
That I have by my dignity.

Also at every assembly that you hold,
That you come to your liege king bold,
Beseeching him of his grace,
To stand with you in every place,
To confirm the statutes of King Athelstane,
That he ordained to this craft by good reason.

The art of the four crowned ones.

Pray we now to God almighty,
And to his mother Mary bright,

That we may keep these articles here,
And these points well all together,
As did these holy martyrs four,
That in this craft were of great honour;
They were as good masons as on earth shall go,
Gravers and image-makers they were also.
For they were workmen of the best,
The emperor had to them great liking;
He willed of them an image to make
That might be worshipped for his sake;
Such monuments he had in his day,
To turn the people from Christ's law.

But they were steadfast in Christ's law,
And to their craft without doubt;
They loved well God and all his lore,
And were in his service ever more.
True men they were in that day,
And lived well in God's law;
They thought no monuments for to make,
For no good that they might take,
To believe on that monument for their God,
They would not do so, though he was furious;
For they would not forsake their true faith,

And believe on his false law,
The emperor let take them soon anon,
And put them in a deep prison;
The more sorely he punished them in that place,
The more joy was to them of Christ's grace,
Then when he saw no other one,
To death he let them then go;
By the book he might it show
In legend of holy ones,
The names of the four-crowned ones.

Their feast will be without doubt,
After Hallow-e'en eighth day.
You may hear as I do read,
That many years after, for great dread
That Noah's flood was all run,
The tower of Babylon was begun,
As plain work of lime and stone,
As any man should look upon;
So long and broad it was begun,
Seven miles the height shadoweth the sun.

King Nebuchadnezzar let it make
To great strength for man's sake,
Though such a flood again should come,
Over the work it should not take;
For they had so high pride, with strong boast
All that work therefore was lost;
An angel smote them so with divers speech,
That never one knew what the other should tell.

Many years after, the good clerk Euclid
Taught the craft of geometry full wonder wide,
So he did that other time also,
Of divers crafts many more.
Through high grace of Christ in heaven,
He commenced in the sciences seven;

Grammar is the first science I know,
Dialect the second, so I have I bliss,
Rhetoric the third without doubt,
Music is the fourth, as I you say,

Astronomy is the fifth, by my snout,
Arithmetic the sixth, without doubt,
Geometry the seventh maketh an end,
For he is both meek and courteous,
Grammar forsooth is the root,
Whoever will learn on the book;
But art passeth in his degree,
As the fruit doth the root of the tree;

Rhetoric measureth with ornate speech among,
And music it is a sweet song;
Astronomy numbereth, my dear brother,
Arithmetic sheweth one thing that is another,
Geometry the seventh science it is,

That can separate falsehood from truth, I know
These be the sciences seven,
Who useth them well he may have heaven.
Now dear children by your wit
Pride and covetousness that you leave it,
And taketh heed to good discretion,
And to good nurture, wheresoever you come.
Now I pray you take good heed,

For this you must know needs,
But much more you must know,
Than you find here written.
If thee fail thereto wit,
Pray to God to send thee it;
For Christ himself, he teacheth us
That holy church is God's house,
That is made for nothing else
But for to pray in, as the book tells us;
There the people shall gather in,
To pray and weep for their sin.
Look thou come not to church late,
For to speak harlotry by the gate;

Then to church when thou dost fare,
Have in thy mind ever more
To worship thy lord God both day and night,
With all thy wits and even thy might.
To the church door when thou dost come
Of that holy water there some thou take,
For every drop thou feelest there
Quencheth a venial sin, be thou sure.
But first thou must do down thy hood,
For his love that died on the rood.
Into the church when thou dost go,
Pull up thy heart to Christ, anon;

Upon the rood thou look up then,
And kneel down fair upon thy knees,
Then pray to him so here to work,
After the law of holy church,

For to keep the commandments ten,
That God gave to all men;
And pray to him with mild voice
To keep thee from the sins seven,
That thou here may, in this life,

Keep thee well from care and strife;
Furthermore he grant thee grace,
In heaven's bliss to have a place.

In holy church leave trifling words
Of lewd speech and foul jests,
And put away all vanity,
And say thy *pater noster* and thine *ave;*
Look also that thou make no noise,
But always to be in thy prayer;
If thou wilt not thyself pray,
Hinder no other man by no way.
In that place neither sit nor stand,
But kneel fair down on the ground,
And when the Gospel me read shall,

Fairly thou stand up from the wall,
And bless the fare if that thou can,
When *gloria tibi* is begun;
And when the gospel is done,
Again thou might kneel down,
On both knees down thou fall,
For his love that bought us all;
And when thou hearest the bell ring
To that holy sacrament,
Kneel you must both young and old,
And both your hands fair uphold,
And say then in this manner,

Fair and soft without noise;
"Jesu Lord welcome thou be,
In form of bread as I thee see,
Now Jesu for thine holy name,
Shield me from sin and shame;
Shrift and Eucharist thou grant me both,
Ere that I shall hence go,
And very contrition for my sin,
That I never, Lord, die therein;
And as thou were of maid born,
Suffer me never to be lost;
But when I shall hence wend,

Grant me the bliss without end;
Amen! Amen! so mote it be!
Now sweet lady pray for me."
Thus thou might say, or some other thing,
When thou kneelest at the sacrament.
For covetousness after good, spare thou not
To worship him that all hath wrought;

For glad may a man that day be,
That once in the day may him see;
It is so much worth, without doubt,
The virtue thereof no man tell may;
But so much good doth that sight,

That Saint Austin telleth full right,
That day thou seest God's body,
Thou shalt have these full securely:
Meet and drink at thy need,
None that day shalt thou lack;
Idle oaths and words both,
God forgiveth thee also;
Sudden death that same day
Thee dare not dread by no way;
Also that day, I thee plight,
Thou shalt not lose thy eye sight;
And each foot that thou goest then,

That holy sight for to see,
They shall be told to stand instead,
When thou hast thereto great need;
That messenger the angel Gabriel,
Will keep them to thee full well.
From this matter now I may pass,
To tell more benefits of the mass:
To church come yet, if thou may,
And hear the mass each day;
If thou may not come to church,
Where that ever thou dost work,
When thou hearest the mass toll,

Pray to God with heart still,
To give thy part of that service,
That in church there done is.
Furthermore yet, I will you preach
To your fellows, it for to teach,
When thou comest before a lord,
In hall, in bower, or at the board,
Hood or cap that thou off do,
Ere thou come him entirely to;
Twice or thrice, without doubt,
To that lord thou must bow;
With thy right knee let it be done,

Thine own worship thou save so.
Hold off thy cap and hood also,
Till thou have leave it on to put.
All the time thou speakest with him,

Fair and amiably hold up thy chin;
So after the nurture of the book,
In his face kindly thou look.
Foot and hand thou keep full still,
For clawing and tripping, is skill;
From spitting and sniffling keep thee also,
By private expulsion let it go,
And if that thou be wise and discrete,

Thou has great need to govern thee well.
Into the hall when thou dost wend,
Amongst the gentles, good and courteous,
Presume not too high for nothing,
For thine high blood, nor thy cunning,
Neither to sit nor to lean,
That is nurture good and clean.
Let not thy countenance therefore abate,
Forsooth good nurture will save thy state.
Father and mother, whatsoever they be,
Well is the child that well may thee,
In hall, in chamber, where thou dost go;

Good manners make a man.
To the next degree look wisely,
To do them reverence by and by;
Do them yet no reverence all in turn,
Unless that thou do them know.
To the meat when thou art set,
Fair and honestly thou eat it;
First look that thine hands be clean,
And that thy knife be sharp and keen,
And cut thy bread all at thy meat,
Right as it may be there eaten,
If thou sit by a worthier man,

Then thy self thou art one,
Suffer him first to touch the meat,
Ere thyself to it reach.
To the fairest morsel thou might not strike,
Though that thou do it well like;
Keep thine hands fair and well,
From foul smudging of thy towel;
Thereon thou shalt not thy nose blow,
Nor at the meat thy tooth thou pick;
Too deep in cup thou might not sink,
Though thou have good will to drink,
Lest thine eyes would water thereby.

Then were it no courtesy.
Look in thy mouth there be no meat,
When thou begins to drink or speak.
When thou seest any man drinking,
That taketh heed to thy speech,
Soon anon thou cease thy tale,
Whether he drink wine or ale,
Look also thou scorn no man,
In what degree thou seest him gone;
Nor thou shalt no man deprave,
If thou wilt thy worship save;
For such word might there outburst.

That might make thee sit in evil rest.
Close thy hand in thy fist,
And keep thee well from "had I known."
Hold thy tongue and spend thy sight;
Laugh thou not with no great cry,
Nor make no lewd sport and ribaldry.
Play thou not but with thy peers,
Nor tell thou not all that thou hears;
Discover thou not thine own deed,
For no mirth, nor for no reward;
With fair speech thou might have thy will,
With it thou might thy self spoil.

When thou meetest a worthy man,
Cap and hood thou hold not on;
In church, in market, or in the gate,
Do him reverence after his state.
If thou goest with a worthier man
Then thyself thou art one,
Let thy foremost shoulder follow his back,
For that is nurture without lack;

When he doth speak, hold thee still,
When he hath done, say for thy will,
In thy speech that thou be discreet,
And what thou sayest consider thee well;
But deprive thou not him his tale,
Neither at the wine nor at the ale.
Christ then of his high grace,
Save you both wit and space,
Well this book to know and read,
Heaven to have for your reward.
Amen! Amen! so mote it be!
So say we all for charity.

Appendix B

Anderson's Constitutions

● ●

*I*n 1723, Dr. James Anderson and a Grand Lodge committee crafted a new set of rules for Masonic lodges, based on the old laws passed down from the Middle Ages. This document has been adopted today by most Grand Lodges, and nearly every Masonic lodge in the world is required to read these rules, or a version of them, aloud at least once every year. They are sometimes referred to as the Ancient Charges. This version includes the original spelling, punctuation, and capitalization from the edition published in 1723.

The Charges Of A Free Mason

Extracted from The Ancient Records of Lodges beyond the Sea, and of those in England, Scotland, and Ireland, for the use of the Lodges in London:

To be read At The Making Of New Brethren Or When The Master Shall Order It.

The General Heads, viz.:

i. Of God and Religion.

ii. Of the Civil Magistrate Supreme and Subordinate.

iii. Of Lodges.

iv. Of Masters, Wardens, Fellow, and Apprentices.

v. Of the Management of the Craft in Working.

vi. Of Behavior, viz.:

> 1. In the Lodge while constituted.
>
> 2. After the Lodge is over and the Brethren not gone.
>
> 3. When the Brethren meet without Strangers, but not in a Lodge.
>
> 4. In the presence of Strangers not Masons.
>
> 5. At Home and in the Neighborhood.
>
> 6. Towards a strange Brother.

i. Concerning God And Religion

A Mason is oblig'd by his Tenure, to obey the moral law; and if he rightly understands the Art, he will never be a stupid ATHEIST, nor an irreligious LIBERTINE. But though in ancient Times Masons were charged in every Country to be of the Religion of that Country or Nation, whatever it was, yet it is now thought more expedient only to oblige them to that Religion in which all Men agree, leaving their particular Opinions to themselves; that is, to be good Men and true, or Men of Honour and Honesty, by whatever Denominations or Persuasions they may be distinguish'd; whereby Masonry becomes the Center of Union, and the Means of conciliating true Friendship among Persons that must have remain'd at a perpetual Distance.

ii. Of The Civil Magistrate Supreme And Subordinate

A Mason is a Peaceable Subject to the Civil Powers, wherever he resides or works, and is never to be concern'd in Plots and Conspiracies against the Peace and Welfare of the Nation, nor to behave himself undutifully to inferior Magistrates; for as Masonry hath been always injured by War, Bloodshed and Confusion, so ancient Kings and Princes have been much dispos'd to encourage the Craftsmen, because of the Peaceableness and Loyalty, whereby they practically answer'd the Cavils of their Adversaries, and promoted the Honour of the Fraternity, who ever flourish'd in Times of Peace. So that if a Brother should be Rebel against the State, he is not to be countenanc'd in his Rebellion, however he may be pitied as an unhappy Man; and if Convicted of no other Crime, though the loyal Brotherhood must and ought to disown his Rebellion, and give no Umbrage or Ground of Political Jealousy to the Government for the time being, they can not expel him from the Lodge, and his relation to it remains indefeasible.

iii. Of Lodges

A Lodge is a Place where members assemble and work; Hence that Assembly, or duly organiz'd Society of Masons, is call'd a Lodge, and every Brother ought to belong to one, and to be subject to its By-Laws and the General Regulations. It is either particular or general, and will be best understood by attending it, and by the Regulations of the General or Grand Lodge hereunto annex'd. In ancient Times, no Master or Fellow could be absent from it, especially when warn'd to appear at it, with incurring a severe Censure, until it appear'd to the Master and Wardens, that pure Necessity hinder'd him.

The Persons admitted Members of a Lodge must be good and true Men, free-born and of mature and discreet Age, no Bondmen, no Women, no immoral or scandalous Men, but of good Report.

iv. Of Masters, Wardens, Fellows, And Apprentices

All preferment among Masons is grounded upon real Worth and Personal Merit only; that so the Lords may be well served, the Brethren not put to Shame, nor the Royal Craft despis'd: Therefore no Master or Warden is chosen by Seniority, but for his Merit. It is impossible to describe these things in writing, and every Brother must attend in his Place, and learn them in a way peculiar to the Fraternity: Only Candidates may know, that no Master should take on an Apprentice, unless he has sufficient Employment for him, and unless he be a perfect Youth, have no Maim or Defect in his body, that may render him incapable of learning the Art, of serving his Master's Lord, and of being made a Brother, and then a Fellow-Craft in due time, and even after he has served such a Term of Years, as the Custom of the Country directs; and that he should be descended of honest Parents; that so, when otherwise qualify'd, he may arrive to the Honour of being the Warden, and at length the Grand-Master of all the Lodges, according to his Merit.

No Brother can be a Warden until he has pass'd the part of a Fellow-Craft; nor a Master until he has acted as a Warden, nor Grand Warden until he has been a Fellow-Craft before his election, who is also to be nobly-born, or a Gentleman of the best Fashion, or some eminent Scholar, or some curious Architect, or other Artist, descended of honest Parents, and who is of singular great Merit in the Opinion of the Lodges. And for the better, and easier, and more honourable discharge of his Office, the Grand-Master has a Power to chuse his Deputy Grand-Master, who must be then, or must have been formerly, the Master of a particular Lodge, and has the Privilege of acting whatever the Grand-Master, his Principal, should act, unless the said Principal be present, or interpose his Authority by a Letter.

These Rulers and Governors, Supreme and Subordinate, of the ancient Lodge, are to be obey'd in their respective Stations by all the Brethren, according to the Old Charges and Regulations, with all Humility, Reverence, Love and Alacrity.

v. Of The Management Of The Craft In Working

All Masons shall work honestly on working Days, that they may live creditably on Holy Days; and the time appointed by the Law of the Land, or confirm'd by Custom, shall be observ'd.

The most expert of the Fellow-Craftsmen shall be chosen or appointed the Master or Overseer of the Lord's Work; who is to be call'd Master by those that work under him. The Craftsmen are to avoid all ill Language, and to call each other by no disobliging Name, but Brother or Fellow; and to behave themselves courteously within and without the Lodge.

The Master, knowing himself to be able of Cunning, shall undertake the Lord's Work as reasonably as possible, and truly dispend his Goods as if they were his own; nor to give more Wages to any Brother or Apprentice than he really may deserve.

Both the Master and Masons receiving their Wages justly, shall be faithful to the Lord, and honestly finish their Work, whether Task or Journey; nor put the Work to Task that hath been accustom'd to Journey.

None shall discover Envy at the Prosperity of a Brother, nor supplant him, or put him out of his Work, if he be capable to finish the same; for no Man can finish another's Work so much to the Lord's Profit, unless he be thoroughly acquainted with the Designs and Draughts of him that began it.

When a Fellow-Craftsman is chosen Warden of the Work under the Master, he shall be true both to Master and Fellows, shall carefully oversee the Work in the Master's Absence to the Lord's profit; and his Brethren shall obey him.

All Masons employ'd shall meekly receive their Wages without murmuring or Mutiny, and not desert the Master till the Work is finish'd.

A younger Brother shall be instructed in working, to prevent spoiling the Materials for want of Judgement, and for increasing and continuing of Brotherly Love.

All the Tools used in working shall be approved by the Grand Lodge.

No Labourer shall be employ'd in the proper work of Masonry; nor shall Free Masons work with those that are not free, without an urgent Necessity; nor shall they teach Labourers and unaccepted Masons, as they should teach a Brother or Fellow.

vi. Of Behavior

1. In the Lodge while constituted.

You are not to hold private Committees, or separate Conversation, without Leave from the Master, nor to talk of any thing impertinent or unseemly, nor interrupt the Master or Wardens, or any Brother speaking to the Master; nor behave yourself ludicrously or jestingly while the Lodge is engaged in what is serious and solemn; nor use any unbecoming Language upon any Pretence whatsoever; but to pay due Reverence to your Master, Wardens, and Fellows, and put them to worship.

If any Complaint be brought, the Brother found guilty shall stand to the Award and Determination of the Lodge, who are the proper and competent Judges of all such Controversies, (unless you carry it by Appeal to the Grand Lodge,) and to whom they ought to be referr'd unless a Lord's Work be hinder'd the meanwhile, in which case a particular Reference may be made; but you must never go to Law about what concerneth Masonry, without an absolute Necessity apparent to the Lodge.

2. Behaviour after the Lodge is over and the Brethren not gone.

You may enjoy yourselves with innocent Mirth, treating one another according to Ability, but avoiding all Excess, or forcing any Brother to eat or drink beyond his Inclination, or hindering him from going when his Occasions call him, or doing or saying anything offensive, or that may forbid an easy and free Conversation; for that would blast our Harmony, and defeat our Laudable Purposes. Therefore no private Piques or Quarrels must be brought within the Door of the Lodge, far less any Quarrels about Religion, or Nations, or State Policy, we being only, as Masons of the Catholick Religion abovemention'd; we are also of all Nations, Tongues, Kindreds, and Languages, and are resolv'd against all Politicks, as what never yet conduc'd to the Welfare of the Lodge, nor ever will. This charge has been always strictly enjoin'd and observ'd, but especially ever since the Reformation in Britain, or the Dissent and Secession of these Nations from the Communion of Rome.

3. Behaviour when Brethren meet without Strangers, but not in a Lodge form'd.

You are to salute one another in a courteous manner as you will be instructed, calling each other Brother, freely giving mutual Instruction as shall be thought expedient, without being overseen or overheard, and without encroaching upon each other or derogating from that Respect which is due to any Brother, were he not a Mason: For though all Masons are as Brethren upon the same Level, yet Masonry takes no Honour from a Man that he had before; nay rather it adds to his Honour, especially if he has deserv'd well of the Brotherhood, who must give Honour to whom it is due, and avoid ill manners.

4. Behaviour in presence of Strangers not Masons.

You shall be most cautious in your Words and Carriage, that the most penetrating Stranger shall not be able to discover or find out what is not proper to be intimated; and sometimes you shall divert a discourse, and manage it prudently for the Honour of the worshipful Fraternity.

5. Behaviour at Home, and in your Neighbourhood.

You are to act as becomes a moral and wise Man; particularly, not to let your Family, Friends, and Neighbours know the Concerns of the Lodge, &c., but wisely to consult your own Honour, and that of the ancient Brotherhood, for Reasons not be mention'd here. You must also consult your health, by not continuing together too late, or too long from home, after Lodge Hours are past; and by avoiding of Gluttony or Drunkenness, that your Families be not neglected or injured, nor you disabled from working.

6. Behaviour towards a strange Brother.

You are cautiously to examine him, in such a method as prudence shall direct you, that you may not be impos'd upon by an ignorant false Pretender, whom you are to reject with Contempt and Derision, and beware of giving him any Hints of Knowledge.

But if you discover him to be a true and Genuine Brother, you are to respect him accordingly; and if he is in want, you must relieve him if you can, or else direct him how he may be reliev'd. You must employ him some Days, or recommend him to be employ'd. But you are not charged to do beyond your Ability, only to prefer a poor Brother, that is a good Man and true, before any other poor People in the same Circumstances.

Finally, all of these Charges you are to observe, and also those that shall be communicated to you in another way; cultivating Brotherly-Love, the foundation and Cap-stone, the Cement and Glory of this ancient Fraternity, avoiding all Wrangling and Quarreling, all Slander and Backbiting, nor permitting others to slander any honest Brother, but defending his Character, and doing him all good offices, as far as is consistent with your own or his Lodge; and from thence you may appeal to the Grand Lodge at the Quarterly Communication, and from thence to the annual Grand Lodge; as has been the ancient laudable Conduct of our Forefathers in every Nation; never taking a legal Course but when the Case cannot be otherwise decided, and patiently listening to the honest and friendly Advice of Master and Fellows, when they would prevent you from going to Law with Strangers, or would excite you to put a speedy Period to all Lawsuits, that so you may mind the Affair of Masonry with the more Alacrity and Success; but with respect to Brothers or Fellows at Law, the Master and Brethren should kindly offer their Mediation, which ought to be thankfully submitted to by the contending Brethren, and if that submission is impracticable, they must however carry on their Process, or Lawsuit, without Wrath and Rancor (not in the common way), saying or doing nothing which may hinder Brotherly Love, and good Offices to be renew'd and continu'd; that all may see the benign Influence of Masonry, as all true Masons have done from the Beginning of the World, and will do to the End of Time.

Amen so mote it be.

Appendix C
Finding a Lodge

*I*f you're looking for a Grand Lodge, I've got you covered. In this appendix, I provide the contact information for mainstream Grand Lodges and Prince Hall Grand Lodges in the United States and Canada.

Mainstream U.S. Grand Lodges

Grand Lodge of Alabama Free & Accepted Masons
2055 Cobbs Ford Rd., Suite 200
Prattville, AL 36066
Phone 334-272-8961
Website www.alafreemasonry.org

Grand Lodge of Alaska Free & Accepted Masons
P.O. Box 190668
Anchorage, AK 99519
Phone 907-561-1477
Website www.alaska-mason.org

Grand Lodge of Arizona Free & Accepted Masons
345 West Monroe St.
Phoenix, AZ 85003
Phone 602-252-1924
Website www.azmasons.org

Grand Lodge of Arkansas Free & Accepted Masons
700 Scott St.
Little Rock, AR 72201
Phone 501-374-6408

Grand Lodge of California Free & Accepted Masons
1111 California St.
San Francisco, CA 94108
Phone 415-776-7000
Website www.freemason.org

Grand Lodge of Colorado Free & Accepted Masons
1130 Panorama Dr.
Colorado Springs, CO 80904
Phone 800-482-4441 (toll free) or
719-471-9587
Website www.coloradofreemasons.org

Grand Lodge of Connecticut Ancient Free & Accepted Masons
P.O. Box 250
Wallingford, CT 06492
Phone 203-284-3900
Website http://gl.ctfreemasons.net

Grand Lodge of Delaware Ancient Free & Accepted Masons
818 Market St.
Wilmington, DE 19801
Phone 302-652-4614
Website www.masonsindelaware.org

Grand Lodge of the District of Columbia Free & Accepted Masons
5428 MacArthur Blvd. NW
Washington, DC 20016
Phone 202-686-1811
Website http://dcgrandlodge.org

Grand Lodge of Florida Free & Accepted Masons
P.O. Box 1020
Jacksonville, FL 32201
Phone 904-354-2339
Website www.glflamason.org

Grand Lodge of Georgia Free & Accepted Masons
Mailing address:
P.O. Box 4665
Macon, GA 31208
Street address:
811 Mulberry St.
Macon, GA
Phone 912-742-1475
Website www.glofga.org

Grand Lodge of Hawaii Free & Accepted Masons
1227 Makiki St.
Honolulu, HI 96814
Phone 808-949-7809
Website www.hawaiifreemason.org

Grand Loge of Idaho Free & Accepted Masons
219 North 17th St.
Boise, ID 83702
Phone 208-343-4562
Website www.advancedcreation
systems.net/afam2

Grand Lodge of Illinois Ancient Free & Accepted Masons
Mailing address:
P.O. Box 4147
Springfield, IL 62708
Street address:
2866 Via Verde St.
Springfield, IL 62703
Phone 217-529-8900
Website www.ilmason.org

Grand Lodge of Indiana Free & Accepted Masons
Mailing address:
P.O. Box 44210
Indianapolis, IN 46244
Street address:
525 North Illinois St.
Indianapolis, IN 46204
Phone 317-634-7904
Website www.indianafreemasons.com

Grand Lodge of Iowa Ancient Free & Accepted Masons
Mailing address:
P.O. Box 279
Cedar Rapids, IA 52406
Street address:
813 First Ave SE
Cedar Rapids, IA 52402
Phone 319-365-1438
Website www.gl-iowa.org

Grand Lodge of Kansas Ancient Free & Accepted Masons
Mailing address:
P.O. Box 1217
Topeka, KS 66601
Street address:
320 SW Eighth St.
Topeka, KS 66603
Phone 913-234-5518
Website www.kansasmason.org

Grand Lodge of Kentucky Free & Accepted Masons
300 Masonic Home Dr.
Louisville, KY 40041
Phone 502-893-0192
Website www.grandlodgeofkentucky.org

Lodge of Louisiana Free & Accepted Masons
Mailing address:
P.O. Box 12357
Alexandria, LA 71315-
Street address:
5800 Masonic Dr.
Alexandria, LA 71301
Phone 504-523-4382 or 318-443-5610
Website www.la-mason.com

Grand Lodge of Maine Ancient Free & Accepted Masons
Mailing address:
P.O. Box 15058
Portland, ME 04112
Street address:
415 Congress St.
Portland, ME 04101
Phone 207-773-5184
Website www.mainemason.org

Grand Lodge of Maryland Ancient Free & Accepted Masons
304 International Circle
Cockeysville, MD 21030
Phone 410-527-0600
Website www.mdmasons.org

Grand Lodge of Massachusetts Ancient Free & Accepted Masons
186 Tremont St.
Boston, MA 02111
Phone 617-426-6040
Website www.glmasons-mass.org

Grand Lodge of Michigan Free & Accepted Masons
233 East Fulton St.
Grand Rapids, MI 49503
Phone 616-459-2451
Website www.gl-mi.org

Grand Lodge of Minnesota Ancient Free & Accepted Masons
200 East Plato Blvd.
St. Paul, MN 55107
Phone 612-222-6051
Website www.mn-masons.org

Grand Lodge of Mississippi Free & Accepted Masons
Mailing address:
P.O. Box 1030
Meridian, MS 39302
Street address:
2400 23rd Ave.
Meridian, MS 39301
Phone 573-482-2914
Website www.msgrandlodge.org

Grand Lodge of Missouri Ancient Free & Accepted Masons
800 Highway 63 North
Columbia, MO 65201
Phone 314-474-8561
Website www.momason.org

Grand Lodge of Montana Ancient Free & Accepted Masons
Mailing address:
P.O. Box 1158
Helena, MT 59624
Street address:
425 North Park Ave.
Helena, MT 59601
Phone 406-442-7774
Website www.grandlodgemontana.org

Grand Lodge of Nebraska Free & Accepted Masons
1240 North Tenth St.
Lincoln, NE 68508
Phone 402-475-4640
Website www.glne.org

Grand Lodge of Nevada Free & Accepted Masons
40 West First St.
Suite 317
Reno, NV 89501
Phone 775-786-5261
Website www.nvmasons.org

Grand Lodge of New Hampshire Free & Accepted Masons
30 Mont Vernon St.
P.O. Box 486
Milford, NH 03055
Phone 603-668-8744
Website www.nhgrandlodge.org

Grand Lodge of New Jersey Free & Accepted Masons
1114 Oxmead Rd.
Burlington, NJ 08016
Phone 609-239-3950
Website www.newjerseygrandlodge.org

Grand Lodge of New Mexico Ancient Free & Accepted Masons
Mailing address:
P.O. Box 25004
Albuquerque, NM 87125
Street address:
1638 University Blvd. NE
Albuquerque, NM 87102
Phone 505-243-4931
Website http://nmmasons.org

Grand Lodge of New York Free & Accepted Masons
71 West 23rd St.
New York, NY 10010
Phone 212-741-4500 or 212-337-6600
Website www.nymasons.org

Grand Lodge of North Carolina Ancient Free & Accepted Masons
Mailing address:
P.O. Box 6506
Raleigh, NC 27628
Street address:
2921 Glenwood Ave.
Raleigh, NC 27608
Phone 919-787-2021
Website www.grandlodge-nc.org

Grand Lodge of North Dakota Ancient Free & Accepted Masons
201 14th Ave. North
Fargo, ND 58102
Phone 701-235-8321
Website www.glnd.org

Grand Lodge of Ohio Free & Accepted Masons
Mailing address:
P.O. Box 629
Worthington, OH 43085
Street address:
634 High St.
Worthington, OH 43085
Phone 614-885-5318
Website www.freemason.com

Grand Lodge of Oklahoma Ancient Free & Accepted Masons
Mailing address:
P.O. Box 1019
Guthrie, OK 73044
Street address:
102 South Broad St.
Guthrie, OK 73044
Phone 405-282-3212
Website www.gloklahoma.com

Grand Lodge of Oregon Ancient Free & Accepted Masons
Mailing address:
P.O. Box 96
Forest Grove, OR 97116
Street address:
3435 Pacific Ave.
Forest Grove, OR 97116
Phone 503-357-3158
Website www.masonic-oregon.com

Grand Lodge of Pennsylvania Free & Accepted Masons
1 North Broad St.
Philadelphia, PA 19107
Phone 215-988-1900
Website www.pagrandlodge.org

Grand Lodge of Rhode Island Free & Accepted Masons
222 Taunton Ave.
East Providence, RI 02914
Phone 401-435-4650
Website www.rimasons.org

Grand Lodge of South Carolina Ancient Free Masons
1445 Pisgah Church Rd.
Lexington, SC 29072
Phone 803-808-4377
Website www.scgrandlodgeafm.org

Grand Lodge of South Dakota Ancient Free & Accepted Masons
P.O. Box 468
Sioux Falls, SD 57101
Phone 605-332-2051
Website www.mygrandlodge.org

Grand Lodge of Tennessee Free & Accepted Masons
Mailing address:
P.O. Box 24216
Nashville, TN 37202
Street address:
100 Seventh Ave. North
Nashville, TN 37203
Phone 615-255-2625
Website www.grandlodge-tn.org

Grand Lodge of Texas Ancient Free & Accepted Masons
Mailing address:
P.O. Box 446
Waco, TX 76703
Street address:
715 Columbus St.
Waco, TX 76701
Phone 817-753-7395
Website www.grandlodgeoftexas.org

Grand Lodge of Utah Free & Accepted Masons
650 East South Temple St.
Salt Lake City, UT 84102
Phone 801-363-2936
Website www.utahgrandlodge.org

Grand Lodge of Vermont Free & Accepted Masons
East Rd.
RR #3, Box 6742B
Barre, VT 05641
Phone 802-223-1883
Website www.vtfreemasons.org

Grand Lodge of Virginia Ancient Free & Accepted Masons
4115 Nine Mile Rd.
Richmond, VA 23223
Phone 804-222-3110
Website www.grandlodgeofvirginia.org

Grand Lodge of Washington Free & Accepted Masons
47 St. Helens Ave.
Tacoma, WA 98402
Phone 800-628-4732 or 206-272-3263
Website www.freemason-wa.org

Grand Lodge of West Virginia Ancient Free & Accepted Masons
Mailing address:
P.O. Box 2346
Charleston, WV 25328
Street address:
107 Hale St.
Charleston, WV 25301
Phone 304-342-3543
Website www.wvmasons.org

Grand Lodge of Wisconsin Free & Accepted Masons
36274 Sunset Dr.
Dousman, WI 53118
Phone 262-965-2200
Website www.wisc-freemasonry.org

Grand Lodge of Wyoming Ancient Free & Accepted Masons
Mailing address:
P.O. Box 649
Saratoga, WY 82331
Street address:
117 W. Bridge Ave.
Saratoga, WY 82331
Phone 307-326-8346
Website http://wyomingmasons.com

Prince Hall Grand Lodges

Most Worshipful Prince Hall Grand Lodge Free & Accepted Masons of Alabama
1630 North Fourth Ave.
Birmingham, AL 35203
Phone 205-328-9078
Website www.phaglal.org

Most Worshipful Prince Hall Grand Lodge of Alaska Free & Accepted Masons
1200 East Ninth Ave., Suite 101
Anchorage, AK 99501
Phone 907-646-2210
Website www.mwphglak.com

Most Worshipful Prince Hall Grand Lodge of Arizona Free & Accepted Masons
6035 South 24th St.
Phoenix, AZ 85042
Phone 602-268-8511
Website www.azmwphgl.com

Most Worshipful Prince Hall Grand Lodge Jurisdiction of Arkansas, Free & Accepted Masons
119 East Fourth Ave.
Pine Bluff, AR 71601
Phone 870-534-5467
Website http://arkphagrandlodge.com

Most Worshipful Prince Hall Grand Lodge of California, Free & Accepted Masons.
9027 South Figueroa St.
Los Angeles, CA 90003
Phone 323-242-2393
Website www.mwphglcal.org

Most Worshipful Prince Hall Grand Lodge of Colorado, Wyoming, Utah and parts of South Korea
2921 South Vaughn Way
Aurora, CO 80014
Phone 303-671-0046 or 303-884-0055
Website www.mwphglco.com

Most Worshipful Prince Hall Grand Lodge of Connecticut, Inc., Free & Accepted Masons
P.O. Box 4112
66 Montville St.
Hartford, CT 06120
Phone 860-727-8108
Website www.mwphgl-ct.org

Most Worshipful Prince Hall Grand Lodge Free & Accepted Masons of Delaware
623 South Heald St.
Wilmington, DE 19801
Phone 302-652-9283
Website www.mwphglde.org

Most Worshipful Prince Hall Grand Lodge, Free & Accepted Masons, Prince Hall Affiliated, Jurisdiction of the District of Columbia, Inc.
1000 U St. NW
Washington, DC 20001
Phone 202-462-8878 or 202-462-8877
Website http://mwphgldc.com

Most Worshipful Union Grand Lodge, Most Ancient and Honorable Fraternity, Free and Accepted Masons, Prince Hall Affiliated Florida & Belize, Central America, Inc.
410 Broad St.
Jacksonville, FL 32202
Phone 904-354-2368
Website www.mwuglflorida.org

Most Worshipful Prince Hall Grand Lodge Free and Accepted Masons Jurisdiction of Georgia
Mailing address:
P.O. Box 490750
College Park, GA 30349
Street address:
7340 Old National Hwy.
Riverdale, GA 30296
Phone 770-994-1569
Website www.mwphglga.org

Most Worshipful Prince Hall Grand Lodge Free & Accepted Masons of Hawaii and Its Jurisdiction, Inc.
P.O. Box 89-3553
Mililani, HI 96789
Website www.phglofhawaii.org

Note: Prince Hall lodges in Idaho are chartered by Prince Hall Grand Lodges of Oregon and Nevada.

Most Worshipful Prince Hall Grand Lodge Free & Accepted Masons, State of Illinois and Its Jurisdiction
809 East 42nd Place
Chicago, IL 60653
Phone 773-373-2725
Website www.mwphglil.com

Most Worshipful Prince Hall Grand Lodge Free and Accepted Masons of Indiana
5605 East 38th St.
Indianapolis, IN 46218
Phone 317-546-8062
Website www.mwphglin.org

Most Worshipful Prince Hall Grand Lodge of Iowa and Jurisdiction, Inc.
2420 Prospect Rd.
Des Moines, IA 50310

Most Worshipful Prince Hall Grand Lodge Free & Accepted Masons of Kansas and Its Jurisdiction
P.O. Box 300463
Kansas City, MO 64130
Phone 913-621-4300
Website www.phglks.com

Most Worshipful Prince Hall Grand Lodge Free & Accepted Masons of Kentucky, Inc.
1304 South 28th St.
Louisville, KY 40211
Phone 502-776-5560
Website www.phglky.com

Most Worshipful Prince Hall Grand Lodge Free & Accepted Masons for the State of Louisiana and Jurisdiction
Mailing address:
P.O. Box 2974
Baton Rouge, LA 70821
Street address:
1335 North Boulevard, Suite 301
Baton Rouge, LA 70802
Phone 504-387-0996
Website www.mwphglla.com

Note: Prince Hall lodges in Maine are chartered by the Prince Hall Grand Lodge of Massachusetts.

Most Worshipful Prince Hall Grand Lodge Free & Accepted Masons, State of Maryland and Jurisdiction
1307 Eutaw Place
Baltimore, MD 21217
Phone 410-669-4966
Website www.mwphglmd.org

Prince Hall Grand Lodge Free & Accepted Masons Jurisdiction of Massachusetts
Mailing address:
P.O. Box 173
Dorchester, MA 02121
Street address:
24 Washington St.
Dorchester, MA
Phone 617-445-1145
Website www.princehall.org

Most Worshipful Prince Hall Grand Lodge Free & Accepted Masons of Michigan
3100 Gratiot Ave.
Detroit, MI 48207
Phone 313-579-3333
Website www.miphagl.org/new

**Most Worshipful Prince Hall Grand Lodge
of Minnesota and Jurisdiction**
3836 Fourth Ave.
Minneapolis, MN 55409
Phone 612-824-5150
Website www.mwphglmn.net

**Most Worshipful Stringer Grand Lodge
Free & Accepted Masons (Prince Hall
Affiliations) Jurisdiction of Mississippi**
1072 John R. Lynch St.
Jackson, MS 39202
Phone 601-354-1403 or 601-354-1404
Website www.mwstringergl.org

**Most Worshipful Prince Hall Grand Lodge
Free & Accepted Masons of Missouri and
Jurisdiction**
4525 Olive St.
St. Louis, MO 63108
Phone 314-361-3044
Website www.glmopha.org
Note: Prince Hall lodges in Montana are
chartered by the Prince Hall Grand Lodge
of Oregon.

**Most Worshipful Prince Hall Grand Lodge
Free & Accepted Masons of Nebraska and
Its Jurisdiction**
2418 Ames Ave.
Omaha, NE 68111
Phone 402-451-5177
Website http://mwphglne.org

**Most Worshipful Prince Hall Grand
Lodge, Free & Accepted Masons, of
Nevada, Inc.**
Mailing address:
P.O. Box 44227
Las Vegas, NV 89030
Street address:
2700 Colton Ave.
North Las Vegas, NV 89032
Phone 702-647-2095

Note: Prince Hall lodges in New Hampshire
are chartered by the Prince Hall Grand
Lodge of Massachusetts.

**Most Worshipful Prince Hall Grand Lodge
Free & Accepted Masons State of New
Jersey**
180–192 Irvine Turner Blvd.
Newark, NJ 07108
Phone 973-824-6457
Website www.mwphglnj.org

**Most Worshipful Prince Hall Grand Lodge
Free & Accepted Masons of the State of
New Mexico, Inc.**
Mailing address:
P.O. Box 5674
Albuquerque, NM 87185
Street address:
525 San Pedro Dr. Northeast
Albuquerque, NM 87108
Phone 505-268-5823
Website www.mwphglnm.org

**Worshipful Prince Hall Grand Lodge
of the Most Ancient and Honorable
Fraternity of Free & Accepted Masons of
the State of New York**
454 West 155th St.
New York, NY 10032
Phone 212-281-2211
Website www.princehallny.org

**Most Worshipful Prince Hall Grand Lodge
of Free & Accepted Masons of North
Carolina and Jurisdictions, Inc.**
Mailing address:
P.O. Box 1507
Durham, NC 27702
Street address:
315 East Main St.
Durham, NC 27701
Phone 919-683-3147
Website www.mwphglnc.com

Note: Prince Hall lodges in North Dakota
are chartered by the Prince Hall Grand
Lodge of Minnesota.

Most Worshipful Prince Hall Grand Lodge of Ohio Free & Accepted Masons
50 Hamilton Park
Columbus, OH 43203
Phone 614-221-6197 or 614-221-9982
Website www.phaohio.org

Most Worshipful Prince Hall Grand Lodge Free & Accepted Masons Jurisdiction of Oklahoma
Mailing address:
P.O. Box 2348
Muskogee, OK 74402
Street address:
1304 West Broadway St.
Muskogee, OK 74401
Phone 918-683-3123

Most Worshipful Prince Hall Grand Lodge of Ontario Free & Accepted Masons in the Province of Ontario and Jurisdiction, Canada
414 Parent Ave.
Windsor, Ontario N9A 2C1
Canada
Phone 519-258-8350
Website www.princehallonj.org

Most Worshipful Prince Hall Grand Lodge Free & Accepted Masons of Oregon, Inc.
115–118 Northeast Russell St.
Portland, OR 97212
Phone 503-218-2225

Most Worshipful Prince Hall Grand Lodge of Pennsylvania Free & Accepted Masons
4301 North Broad St.
Philadelphia, PA 19140
Phone 215-457-6110
Website www.princehall-pa.org

Most Worshipful Prince Hall Grand Lodge Free & Accepted Masons of the State of Rhode Island
883 Eddy St.
Providence, RI 02905-4705
Phone 401-461-2600

Most Worshipful Prince Hall Grand Lodge of Free & Accepted Masons of the State of South Carolina
2324 Gervais St.
Columbia, SC 29204
Phone 803-254-7210
Website www.mwphglsc.com

Note: Prince Hall lodges in South Dakota are chartered by the Prince Hall Grand Lodge of Kansas.

Worshipful Prince Hall Grand Lodge Free & Accepted Masons of Tennessee
253 South Pkwy.
Memphis, TN 38109
Phone 901-774-7230
Website www.phgltennessee.org

Prince Hall Grand Lodge of Texas
Mailing address:
P.O. Box 1478
Fort Worth, TX 76101
Street address:
3433 Martin Luther King Fwy.
Fort Worth, TX 76119
Website www.mwphglotx.org

Note: Prince Hall lodges in Utah are chartered by the Prince Hall Grand Lodges of Texas and Colorado.
Note: No known Prince Hall lodges exist in Vermont.

Most Worshipful Prince Hall Grand Lodge of Virginia, Inc.
Mailing address:
P.O. Box 14646
Richmond, VA 23221
Street address:
906 North Thompson St.
Richmond, VA 23230
Phone 804-359-1111
Website www.mwphgl-va.org

**Most Worshipful Prince Hall Grand Lodge
Free & Accepted Masons Washington and
Jurisdiction**
306 24th Ave. South
Seattle, WA 98144
Phone 206-323-8835
Website www.mwphglwa.org

**Most Worshipful Prince Hall Grand
Lodge of West Virginia, Free & Accepted
Masons, Inc.**
P.O. Box 233
Whitman, WV 25652
Phone 304-239-2731

**Most Worshipful Prince Hall Grand Lodge
Free & Accepted Masons of Wisconsin, Inc.**
600 West Walnut St.
Milwaukee, WI 53212
Phone 414-265-6555
Website www.princehallmasonic
foundation.com

Note: Prince Hall lodges in Wyoming are
chartered by the Prince Hall Grand Lodge
of Colorado.

Canadian Grand Lodges

Grand Lodge of Alberta
330 12th Ave. SW
Calgary
Alberta T2R OH2
Canada
Phone 403-262-1149
Website www.freemasons.ab.ca

**Grand Lodge of British Columbia and
Yukon, Ancient Free & Accepted Masons**
1495 West 8th Ave.
Vancouver
British Columbia V6H IC9
Canada
Phone 604-736-8941
Website www.freemasonry.bcy.ca

**Grand Lodge Ancient Free & Accepted
Masons in the Province of Ontario**
363 King St. West
Hamilton
Ontario L8P 1B4
Canada
Phone 905-528-8644
Website www.grandlodge.on.ca

Grand Lodge of Manitoba
420 Corydon Ave.
Winnipeg
Manitoba R3L 0N8
Canada
Phone 204-453-7410
Website www.glmb.ca

Grand Lodge of New Brunswick
P.O. Box 6430
Station A
St. John
New Brunswick E2L 4R8
Canada
Phone 506-652-2390
Website www.glnb.org

**Grand Lodge of Newfoundland and
Labrador, Ancient Free & Accepted
Masons**
P.O. Box 23018
St. John's
Newfoundland A1B 4J9
Canada
Phone 709-754-6520
Website www.glnl.ca

Grand Lodge of Nova Scotia. Ancient Free & Accepted Masons
1533 Barrington St.
Halifax
Nova Scotia B3J 1Z4
Canada
Phone 902-423-6149
Website www.grandlodgens.org

Worshipful Grand Lodge of Ancient Free & Accepted Masons of Prince Edward Island
P.O. Box 337
Charlottetown
Prince Edward Island C1A 7K7
Canada
Phone 902-629-1265
Website www.freemasonry.pe.ca

La Grande Loge du Québec de Maçons Anciens, Francs et Acceptés
2295, rue Saint-Marc
Montréal, Québec H3H 2G9
Canada
Phone 514-933-6739
Website www.glquebec.org

Grand Lodge of Saskatchewan, Ancient Free & Accepted Masons
1930 Lorne St.
Regina
Saskatchewan S4P 2M1
Canada
Phone 306-522-5686
Website www.saskmasons.ca

Index

• A •

acacia (symbol), 148–149

admitted/accepted Masons, 22, 28–29

advertising and promotion, 13, 53–54, 262

A.F.&A.M. (Ancient Free and Accepted Masons), 273

African Americans. *See* Prince Hall Masonry; racism/racial discrimination; slaves/slavery

Age of Enlightenment, 36–37, 80–81, 119

Age of Reason, 28–29

Ahiman Rezon [*A Help to a Brother*] (Dermott), 34

alchemy (magick), 61, 140, 149, 156–157, 177–178, 214, 299. *See also* sexual "magick"/perversions

alcohol, 50, 265

Aldrin, Buzz (Mason, astronaut), 52

All Saints Day, 141

allegory, 62, 119, 141. *See also* symbolism/symbols

Allied Masonic Degrees (York Rite), 166, 168, 199–200

All-Seeing Eye, 132, 139, 144, 153–155

American Federation of the Human Rights *(Le Droit Humain)*, 20, 112

American Indians, 39, 85–86

American neoconservative movement, 292

American Revolution, 38–39, 80, 85–86

American Rite. *See* York Rite

ample form ritual shortcuts, 106

anagram, 213

anchor and the ark (symbols), 139

Ancient Accepted Scottish Rite. *See* Scottish Rite

Ancient and Primitive Rite of Memphis-Misraim, 112

Ancient Arabic Nobles of the Mystic Shrine. *See* Shriners International

Ancient Charges, 6, 13, 33, 329–334

Ancient Craft Masonry. *See also* Freemasonry
about the history, 22
ceremonies and rituals, 93, 115–116
defined/described, 16
neutrality toward religion, 64–65, 69
origins of the Blue Lodge, 131

Ancient Egyptian Order of SCIOTS, 166, 171, 244

Ancient Free and Accepted Masons (A.F.&A.M.), 273

Ancient Order of Foresters, 48

Anderson, James (Mason, minister), 33, 329

Angels and Demons (Brown), 54, 259

animal lodges, 172–173

Annihilation of Freemasonry through the Revelation of Its Secrets (Ludendorff), 83

Annuit Coeptis ("He had favored our undertakings"), 154

anti-Catholic rhetoric, 79, 158, 289–290

The Anti-Christ and the Origin of Masonry (Taxil), 290

Antient Grand Lodge (Ireland), 34

Antients and the Moderns controversy, 34, 36, 43–44, 122, 184

anti-Masonic efforts. *See also* conspiracy theories
Catholic Church, 43, 182
divulging Masonic secrecy, 2
fundamentalist Christianity and, 71–72
German post-WWI propaganda, 83
Italian purges, 84
modern day restrictions, 299–300
Protocols of the Learned Elders of Zion, 74
secrecy and the Morgan Affair, 45–47
writings by Albert Pike, 159–161, 215
writings by Leo Taxil, 158–159, 289–291

anti-Semitism, 51, 152–153

Apollonian Society for the Lovers of Music and Architecture, 119
appendant bodies. *See also* concordant groups; *specific body*
  about the family of, 5, 16, 165–166
  additional degrees, 128, 278
  collective list of, 19–20
  defined/described, 167–168
  increasing popularity and growth, 48–50
  membership decline, 238
  regularity/recognition of, 109
  relationship to Freemasonry, 166
apron. *See* lambskin apron
architecture, geometry and, 23–24, 29
Armstrong, Neil (astronaut), 11
ashlars (symbol), 147
Ashmole, Elias (Mason), 29
assassination, 12
at-sight membership, 106
atheism, 37, 64–65, 113, 155, 274, 330

• *B* •

Baby Boomers, 52–53
Baden-Powell, Robert (creator of Cub Scouts), 241
balloting, 276, 277
Baphomet, 157–158, 196, 197
Beard, Daniel Carter (creator of Boy Scouts), 241
beehive (symbol), 141
Benevolent and Protective Order of Elks (BPOE), 48, 173
Bessel, Paul M. (Mason, researcher), 248
Bible. *See* Masonic bible; Volume of Sacred Law
Bilderberg Group, 293
blackballing, 277
Blue Lodge, 16, 106, 131. *See also* Masonic lodge
Boaz and Jachin (pillars), 147–148
Bolivar, Simón (Mason, political leader), 43, 68, 82
Bonaparte, Napoleon (emperor of France), 43, 82
Book of Constitutions (Anderson), 33, 329–334

Book of the Law (Crowley), 298
Born in Blood (Robinson), 30–31
Boston Tea Party, 39, 175
Bowling Alone (Putnam), 253
Boy Scouts of America, 241
Bradley, Omar (Mason, general), 51
Brant, Joseph (Mason), 85–86
brotherhood of man
  about, 144–145
  ancient charges of Masonry, 77, 330, 333
  as basic principle, 59
  Boy Scouts education, 241
  creation of Shriners, 222–223
  Freemasonry and, 255–256, 288
  French Revolutionary motto, 41
  Illuminati conspiracy and, 292
  Masonic education, 58
  overcoming barriers to, 266
  symbolism of letter *G*, 143
  during times of war, 85–88
brotherly love
  as basic principle, 13, 56–57, 256
  bridging political divides, 84–85
  bridging religious divides, 75
  overcoming war and conflicts, 85
  Pythrianism and, 176
  Square and Compass as symbol, 11, 137
  trowel as symbol, 146
"brought to light," Fellow Craft, 127
Brown, Dan (writer), 7, 54, 197, 259, 270, 304

• *C* •

cable-tow, 124
Canadian Grand Lodges, 344–345
Capitular Rite. *See* York Rite
caput mortuum (skull, symbol), 149
Catholic Church
  adaptation of pagan feasts, 141
  anti-Catholic writing of Taxil, 158
  clergy as Masons, 81
  connections to Knights Templar, 30–31
  developments during Renaissance, 25–26
  Knights of Columbus, 48, 176–177
  Protestant reformation, 27–28

relationship to Freemasonry, 43, 48, 66–71, 132, 182, 259

supremacy in French politics, 80–81

Cedars of Lebanon, 134

ceremonies. *See* Masonic ritual

Chaplain, 102, 123

charity/charities. *See also* relief (charity toward others); Shriners Hospitals

changing Masonry focus, 19, 47, 50, 262

Freemasonry is not a, 2

the Grotto, 244

misunderstandings about, 152

non-Masonic fraternal groups, 172–173

Order of the Eastern Star, 236

Scottish Rite bodies, 219

service clubs, 173–174

Social Order of the Beauceant, 239

Tall Cedars of Lebanon, 245

York Rite bodies, 202

Chevalier Bienfaisant de Cite Saint (the Rectified Rite), 200

Chick, Jack (anti-Masonic writer), 291

Chinon Parchment, 197

chisel (symbol), 149

Chivalric degrees/orders, 168, 184, 190–192. *See also* Crusades/Crusader Knights; Knights Templar

Christianity

fundamentalist Christians, 71–72

Masonic principles and, 56

membership requirements, 65

Scottish Rite requirements, 182

Templar origins, 30–31, 193–198

York Rite requirements, 182

Church of England, 27–28, 141

Church of the Latter Day Saints (Mormon Church), 116

Churchill, Winston (Mason, British prime minister), 12, 51, 83

cipher books/rituals/codes, 121, 122

circumabulating, 125

Civil War, 48, 87, 176

clandestine Masons, 110, 111, 204

Clarke, Arthur C. (historian), 61

Clemens, Samuel (Mason, a.k.a. Mark Twain), 48

Clinton, Bill (DeMolay, U.S. president), 240

Clinton, Dewitt (Mason, governor), 46

Cochrane, Robert (Master Mason, Earl of Mar), 26

co-ed bodies (co-Masonry), 20, 112, 113, 290

coffin (symbol), 148–149

Coil's Masonic Encyclopedia, 131

Collectanea (journal), 169

College for the Promoting Physico-Mathematical Experimental Learning. *See* Royal Society

commemorative jewelry, 106–107

Commemorative Order of St. Thomas of Acon, 201

community service. *See* service club/clubs

concordant groups. *See also* appendant bodies, *specific body*

Scottish Rite, 205–208

York Rite, 182–185

Conference of Grand Masters of North America, 248

Confucianism, 56, 65, 155

conspiracy theories. *See also* legends/mythology; world domination

American neoconservatives, 292

Bilderberg Group, 293

Council on Foreign Relations, 292

Freemasonry and, 1, 12

French Revolution, 82

Illuminati movement, 291–292

Jewish world domination, 51

Protocols of the Learned Elders of Zion, 74

secret control of government, 299–300

Trilateral Commission, 292

Conspiracy Theories & Secret Societies For Dummies (Hodapp and Von Kannon), 152

The Constitutions of the Free-Masons (Anderson), 33, 329–334

convocation (communication), 105

cornerstone ceremonies, 16–17

Council on Foreign Relations (CFR), 292

craft guilds, 15

craft/Craft Lodge, defined/described, 16

Crocker, Hannah Mather (Worshipful Master), 20

Cromwell, Oliver (English ruler), 27–28, 66

Cronkite, Walter (DeMolay, newscaster), 240

Cross, Jeremy (Mason), 137

Crowley, Aleister (professional pervert), 177–178

Crusades/Crusader Knights, 30, 78, 192, 193. *See also* Chivalric degrees/orders

Cryptic Council Royal & Select Masters, 166

Cryptic Rite Masons (York Rite)
about the origins, 19, 34–35, 188–189
charity/foundation, 202
defined/described, 168
degrees conferred, 189
early American adaptation, 44–45
governing councils, 184
symbols, 188

The Cult of the Great Architect (Taxil), 290

cults, 4, 64, 213

The Da Vinci Code (Brown), 53, 54, 198, 259, 270, 304

Dalco, Frederick (Mason, doctor), 210

Dan Brown effect, 54, 197, 259

Daughters of the Nile (Shrine), 166, 171, 228

de Molay, Jacques (Grand Master), 196

Deacon (Junior/Senior), 98–99

Decker, J. Edward (anti-Masonic writer), 291

Declaration of Independence, 12

degrees. *See* Masonic degrees

DeMolay International (the Order of DeMolay), 19–20, 166, 172, 202, 239–240

Dermott, Laurence (Mason), 34

Desaguliers, Jean T. (Mason, doctor), 29

Disney, Walt (DeMolay, businessman), 240

Dogme et Rituel de la Haute Magie [Dogma and Ritual of High Magic] (Levi), 157, 214–215

dues
cost of joining a lodge, 275
Masonic history, 25, 40, 49
origin of low dues payments, 171
results of low dues, 262–263

• **E** •

Eagles. *See* Fraternal Order of Eagles

"the editorial without words," 225

education
applying new technologies to, 265–266
Masonic degrees, 127, 128, 278
Masonic principles, 56, 58, 147
scholarships, 50, 57, 202, 246, 268
Scottish Rite, 208
Traditional Observance lodges, 53–54
York Rite, 199

Elements (Euclid of Alexandria), 138

Elks. *See* Benevolent and Protective Order of Elks

Empire State Twin Towers Grand Lodge, 179–180

Entered Apprentice (degree), 15, 25, 55, 117–118, 123–126

equality and tolerance. *See also* racism/racial discrimination
American Revolution, 44
as basic principle, 13–14, 60, 257–258
Deism, 37
French Revolution, 41, 80–81
Illuminati movement, 79, 81, 291–292
level as symbol of, 142–143
lodge officers, 95
overcoming class distinctions, 33
Protestant reformation, 27–28
religion, 65, 66, 73

Euclid of Alexandria (Greek mathematician), 138

Eulogian Club, 178

European Concept lodges, 53–54, 264

eye. *See* All-Seeing Eye

• **F** •

F.&A.M. (Free and Accepted Masons), 273

faith (beyond specific religion)
in the Age of Enlightenment, 36–37
in the Age of Reason, 28

as basic principle, 59
survival in the face of no "rulz," 5, 252
symbolism, 139, 141, 143, 147
tolerance toward differences, 257–258, 263
Fellow Craft (degree), 15, 25, 118–119, 127
festive boards, 14–15, 54, 94, 264
fez, 50, 76, 223–224, 225, 244
five-pointed star (symbol), 145, 233–235, 296–297
Flavius Josephus (Jewish historian), 134, 135
Fleming, Walter (Mason, doctor), 223
Florence, Billy (Mason, actor), 223
Ford, Gerald (Mason, U.S. president), 52
4th–32nd degrees (Scottish Rite), 166, 170, 216–219
47th Problem of Euclid, 104, 138
Frale, Barbara (historian), 197
Francken, Henry (Mason), 210
Franklin, Benjamin (Mason, American statesman), 36, 39, 154
Fraternal Order of Eagles (FOE), 173
fraternal organization(s). *See also* non-Masonic groups
anti-Masonic movement and, 46–47
cost of joining, 49
formation of competing groups, 47–48
Freemasonry as, 1
insurance societies, 49
legend of riding a goat, 153
origins of degree ritual, 116
post-WWII growth, 51–52
relevancy in modern society, 251–254
Free and Accepted Masons (F.&A.M.), 273
Free Masons/Freestone masons (stonecutters). *See* operative Masons
Freemason Hall (London), 303
Freemasonry. *See also* Ancient Craft Masonry; appendant bodies; concordant groups; Masonic history
about the origins, 23, 61
applying new technologies to, 265–266
assumptions about you and, 3–4
Dan Brown effect, 54, 197, 259
declining membership, 52–53, 259–261
defined/described, 13–14
facing the future, 259–263

finding the value of, 263–265
maintaining membership, 264
mystic bond of, 61–62
negative reactions to, 11–12
patron saints, 118
relationship to religion, 33, 64–65, 69
relevancy in modern society, 251–254
role in modern society, 254–258
as substitute for religion, 65
ultrasound death ray of, 294
what it is/is not, 2, 4
women, membership, 20
Freemasonry, Its World View, Organization and Policies (Schwarz), 83
Freemason's Hall (Philadelphia, PA), 302
Freemason's Monitor (Webb), 44, 47, 119, 137
French Revolution, 36, 41, 73, 74, 80–82. *See also* Masonic history in France
Funcannon, Bob (Mason), 270–271
funeral services, 17, 271

• *G* •

G (letter, symbol), 143–145
Garibaldi, Giuseppe (Mason, Italian politician), 68, 82
General Grand Chapter of Royal Arch Masons, 202
General Grand Council of Royal and Select Masters, 202
Geneva Bible, 148
"gentlemen" Masons, 22, 28–29
geometry
Gothic architecture, 23–24
Masonic mysticism and, 61
Pythagorean theorem, 104, 138
symbolism of letter *G*, 144–145
George VI (Mason, king of England), 51
George Washington Masonic Memorial (Alexandria, VA), 297, 301
George-Washington Union (co-Masonic group), 20
Germany, 27, 37, 73, 298–299. *See also* Hitler, Adolph; Nazism
Glenn, John (Mason, astronaut), 52

God
  3, symbolism of number, 132
  Ancient Charges of Masonry, 330
  concept of Deism, 37
  Freemasonry beliefs, 13
  G and the All-Seeing Eye, 144–145
  as Grand Architect, 13, 33, 64, 153
  Tetragammaton, 188–189, 213
going dark, 276
Golden Rule, 56–57
Good, Weldon (Mason), 219
Goodnow, David (DeMolay, newscaster), 240
Gothic architecture, 23–24
Grand Architect, 13, 64, 144–145, 153
Grand College of Rites of the USA, 169
Grand Encampment of the Knights
    Templar, 202
Grand Lodge. *See also* Masonic lodge;
    Prince Hall Masonry
  about the role and functions, 14, 91, 105
  advertising/promotion, 13, 53–54, 262
  avoiding irregular groups, 179–180
  commemorative jewelry, 107
  contact information, 335–339
  contacting/finding a, 273
  creation in colonial America, 38–39
  female (irregular) lodges, 112
  identifying irregular lodges, 111–114
  identifying mainstream lodges, 108–111
  maintaining membership, 264–265
  one-day classes, 261–262, 278
  recognition of Prince Hall Lodges, 53
  research lodges, 248
  rules options and shortcuts, 106
Grand Lodge of All England (York; *Totius
    Angliae*), 34, 183
Grand Lodge of England (London), 31–32,
    34, 40–41, 66, 111
Grand Lodge of India, 111
Grand Lodge of Iran, 84
Grand Lodge of Ireland, 34
Grand Lodge of Israel, 75
Grand Lodge of Massachusetts, 40–41, 111
Grand Lodge of Missouri, 278
Grand Lodge of New York, 111
Grand Lodge of Paris, 36

Grand Lodge of Russia, 85, 258
Grand Lodge of Saint John of Scotland, 34
Grand Lodge of Scotland, 111
Grand Lodge of the State of New York, 303
Grand Lodge Symbolic of Memphis-
    Misraïm (co-Masonic group), 20
Grand Master, 14, 32, 105–106
Grand Orient lodges
  about, 113
  Grand Orient of France, 36, 65, 69, 81,
      112, 155–156
  Grande Oriente d'Italia, 84, 111, 295–296
Grand Secretary, 110
Grande Loge de France, 304
Grande Loge Féminine de France, 20
Grande Loge Nationale Française (Paris),
    111, 113, 304
Grange (National Grange of the Order of
    Patrons of Husbandry), 48
Great Seal of the United States, 154
grips (handshakes), 17–18, 25, 117, 146.
    See also Masonic secrecy
Grissom, Gus (Mason, astronaut), 52
Grotto (Mystic Order of the Veiled
    Prophets of the Enchanted Realm
    of North America), 19, 166, 170–171,
    243–244
Guillotine, Joseph (Mason, inventor), 81
Gull, William (doctor, alleged Jack the
    Ripper), 294–295

• *H* •

Hall, Manley (Mason, writer), 61
Hall, Prince (Mason), 40–41
Halliwell, James (translator), 307
hammer/gavel (symbol), 150
Hancock, John (Mason), 39
handshakes. *See* grips (handshakes)
Harding, Warren G. (Mason, U.S. president),
    42, 50
Harris, Jack (anti-Masonic writer), 291
Hebrew Bible, 65
Heirloom Bible Publishers, 155
From Hell (Moore and Campbell), 53,
    260, 295

A Help to a Brother [*Ahiman Rezon*]
    (Dermott), 34
Hermes Trismigestes, 61
Hermetic Order of the Golden Dawn, 178, 298
High Twelve International, 166, 171, 246
Hinduism, 57, 65, 155
Hiram Abiff, legend of, 120, 122, 127,
    189, 202, 294
Hitler, Adolph (German leader), 12, 51,
    74, 82–83, 292. *See also* Germany
Hodapp, Christopher (author)
    Conspiracy Theories & Secret Societies For
        Dummies (Wiley), 152
    The Templar Code For Dummies
        (Wiley), 193
Holly, James (anti-Masonic writer), 291
Holy and Noble Knights of Labor, 48
Holy Royal Arch degree (York Rite), 188
Holy Royal Arch Knight Templar Priests,
    166, 168, 200
Holy Saints John, 118, 141
Honourable Fraternity of Antient
    Free-Masons, 20, 112
hoodwinked, 124
Hortman, Al (Shriner), 225
House of the Temple (Scottish Rite),
    219, 302
how-to become a Mason. *See* Mason,
    becoming a
Humanitarian Foundation of the Supreme
    Council (MOVPER), 244

fees/costs, 49, 262, 275, 301
Fellow Craft, 127
one-day classes, 261–262
other fraternal groups, 48, 177, 219, 223
presentation of the lambskin, 17, 125
riding the goat, 153
Shriners, 224, 226
insurance-benefit societies, 49, 173
International Modern and Free Accepted
    Masons, 179–180
International Order of Job's Daughters.
    See Job's Daughters International
International Order of the Rainbow for
    Girls, 19–20, 166, 172, 242
international organization/governance,
    6, 14. *See also* world domination
Internet, connecting Masons via, 53, 266
irregular Masonic groups, 179–180. *See*
    also non-Masonic groups
irregular/unrecognized lodges, 111–113.
    See also Grande Orient lodges;
    regularity/recognition
Islam
    concept of the golden rule, 57
    Illuminati conspiracy, 292
    Jewish conspiracy theory, 74
    Knights Templar and, 196
    Koran, 65, 155
    relationship to Masonry, 75–76, 82, 84
    Solomon's Temple, 136
Italy, 67–68, 79, 84, 111–112, 295–296

• I •

Illuminati (Order of Perfectibilists), 79,
    81–82, 291–292
"Illustrations of Freemasonry" (Preston),
    119, 137
Illustrious Order of the Red Cross, 191
Improved Order of Red Men, 47, 175–176
Independent Order of Odd Fellows
    (IOOF), 47, 175
initiation. *See also* Masonic degrees
    about the ritual, 115–116
    appendant bodies, 238–240
    derived from medieval guilds, 25
    Entered Apprentice, 117, 123–126

• J •

Jachin and Boaz (pillars), 147–148
Jack the Ripper, Masonry and, 294–295
Jacobites/Jacobins, 35–36, 78, 81, 209
Jacob's Ladder (symbol), 139
Jerusalem. *See* King Solomon's Temple;
    Knights Templar
jewelry (badges, medals, pins,
    ribbons), 106–107
jewels of the office. *See also* symbolism/
    symbols
    apron designs, 107
    Chaplain, 102
    Junior Deacon, 99

jewels of the office *(continued)*
  Junior Warden, 98
  Past Master, 104
  Secretary, 102
  Senior Deacon, 99
  Senior Warden, 97
  Steward (Junior/Senior), 100
  Treasurer, 101
  Worshipful Master, 96
The Jewish War (Flavius Josephus), 135
Jews/Judaism. *See also Protocols of the
    Learned Elders of Zion*; Zionism
  anti-Semitism, 51, 152–153
  concept of the golden rule, 57
  construction of the Temple, 134–135
  destruction of the Temple, 135–136
  German post-WWI propaganda, 83
  Holocaust, 51
  Masonic lodges in Israel, 75, 134
  Masonry open to, 33
  relationship to Freemasonry, 72–73
  role in French Revolution, 82
Job's Daughters International, 19–20, 166,
    172, 242–243
Jogand-Pagès, Gabriel. *See* Taxil, Leo
John, Holy Saints, 118, 141, 197
John Wiley and Sons
  *Conspiracy Theories & Secret Societies
    For Dummies* (Hodapp and Von
    Kannon), 152
  The Templar Code For Dummies (Hodapp
    and Von Kannon), 193
joining Masons. *See* Mason, becoming a
Journal of the Masonic Society, 248
journeyman. *See* Fellow Craft
Juarez, Benito (Mason, Mexican
    president), 68, 82
Junior Deacon, 99
Junior Warden, 97–98, 142

● *K* ●

Kabbalism (Jewish mysticism), 61, 156,
    212–213
Kah, Gary H. (anti-Masonic writer), 291
Key of Solomon (ancient grimoire), 61

Kilwinning Lodge ("Mother Lodge of
    Scotland"), 26
King James Bible, 65, 75, 155, 160–161
King Solomon Grand Lodge, 179–180
King Solomon's Temple
  about, 92–93
  about the symbolism of, 134–136
  basis of degree ritual, 123
  building of, 22
  Fellow Craft lecture, 127
  legend of Hiram Abiff, 120, 122, 127, 189,
    202, 294
  pillars (Jachin and Boaz), 147–148
  sanctum sanctorum, 22, 135, 140
Kingdom of Heaven (movie, 2005), 195
Kipling, Rudyard (Mason, writer), 260, 288
Kiwanis International, 174
Knigge, Adolph (Mason, Baron), 79
Knight, Stephen (anti-Masonic writer),
    294–295
Knight Masons, 166, 168, 199
Knights of Columbus, 48, 71, 176–177
Knights of Eulogia, 178–179
Knights of Pythias, 48
Knights of Saint Andrew, 166, 219
Knights Templar (Poor Knights of Christ
    and the Temple of Solomon). *See also*
    Chivalric degrees/orders
  charity/charities, 202, 239
  early American adaptation, 44–45
  Freemasonry connections to, 19, 34–35
  historical origins, 30–31, 193–197
  legends of hidden wealth, 197–198
  relationship to Christianity, 65
  relationship to Freemasonry, 166
  symbols, 190, 192
  The Templar Code For Dummies
    (Wiley), 193
Koran (Islam), 65, 155
Ku Klux Klan, 116, 214

● *L* ●

lambskin apron, 17, 106–107, 125, 139–140
Land, Frank S. (Mason, DeMolay
    founder), 240

Le Droit Humain (co-Masonic group), 20, 112

The League of Extraordinary Gentlemen (Moore and O'Neill), 53, 260

legends/mythology. *See also* conspiracy theories; Masonic ritual; Masonic secrecy

about, 1, 4, 151–153

All-Seeing Eye on the $1 bill, 153–155

building of King Solomon's Temple, 22

character of Baphomet, 157–158

Hiram Abiff, 120, 122, 127, 189, 202, 294

illegal activities, 162

Jack the Ripper murders, 294–295

learning the facts behind, 7

length of the cable-tow, 124

Masonic bible, 155–156

meetings as act of "worship," 155–156

Nazism connections, 298–299

riding the goat, 153

Satanic design of Washington, DC, 296–297

secret society, 161–162

"squaring the lodge," 125

world domination, 161–162

L'Enfant, Pierre Charles (Mason, architect and engineer), 296

Leopold I (Mason, king of Belgium), 43

level (symbol), 142–143

Levi, Eliphas (French mystic), 156–157, 197, 214–215

Lincoln, Abraham, 176

Lions Clubs International, 174

Livingston, Robert (Mason, American statesman), 39, 42

lodge. *See* Blue Lodge; European Concept lodges; Grand Lodge; Masonic lodge; Traditional Observance lodges

The Lost Symbol (Brown), 7, 54, 153, 259, 301–302

Loyal Order of Moose, 48, 172–173

Lucifer (Prince of Darkness). *See* Satanism

Luciferian High-Masonry (a.k.a. Palladism), 158–159, 290–291

• *M* •

MacArthur, Douglas (Mason, general), 51, 269

Mackey, Albert (Mason, writer), 61

magick (alchemy), 61, 140, 149, 156–157, 177–178, 214, 299. *See also* sexual "magick"/perversions

The Man Who Would Be King (movie, 1975), 260

Mark Twain (Mason, a.k.a. Samuel Clemens), 48

Marshall, George (Mason, general), 51

Mason, becoming a

benefits (what's in it for you), 267–269

finding a Mason to talk to, 272–273

finding and joining a lodge, 273–278, 335–345

reasons for joining, 269–271

Mason, famous people, 281–288

The Masonic Assassins (Taxil), 290

Masonic bible, 64–65, 155–156. *See also* King James Bible; Volume of Sacred Law

Masonic degrees. *See also* concordant groups; Entered Apprentice; Fellow Craft degree; initiation; Master Mason

about the meaning and characteristics, 15–16, 115–116

Ancient Charges of Masonry, 331–332

Antients and Moderns controversy, 34, 36, 43–44

appendant bodies, 167

becoming a Brother by way of, 278

changes for the future, 53

concordant groups, 168–170

eligibility for joining Shriners, 52

irregular/unrecognized lodges, 114

membership "at sight," 106

oath/obligation, 65

one-day classes, 261–262, 278

performing rituals, 121–123

proficiency, demonstrating, 15, 126, 128, 276–277

relationship to appendant bodies, 166

Masonic degrees *(continued)*
  Scottish Rite system, 19, 48–49, 205–208
  standardized ritual handbook, 44
  York Rite system, 182–185
Masonic family. *See* appendant bodies;
    concordant groups
Masonic history
  about, 4, 6
  during Age of Enlightenment, 36–37, 80–81
  Ancient Charges of Masonry, 329–334
  Antients and the Moderns controversy,
    34, 36, 43–44, 122, 184
  appearance of women's groups, 231–232
  architecture and geometry in, 23–24
  connection to Knights Templar,
    30–31, 34–35
  creation of the *Regius Manuscript*, 25
  divisions within Christendom, 27–28
  during the Age of Enlightenment, 36–37
  during the Renaissance era, 25–26
  formation of first Grand Lodges, 31–32, 34
  guild system of operative Masons, 21–23
  modern day anti-Masonic
    restrictions, 84–85
  relationship to religion, 63–66
  relationship with Catholicism, 66–71
  relationship with Islam, 75–76
  relationship with Judaism, 72–75
  relationship with Protestantism, 71–72
  worldwide spread of Freemasonry, 42–43
  writing of *Book of Constitutions*, 33–34
Masonic history in America
  arrival in colonial America, 38
  Boston Tea Party, 39
  Civil War, 87
  historical origins of Scottish Rite, 210
  increasing popularity and growth, 44–45
  Morgan affair and anti-Masonic
    movement, 45–47, 50
  Revolutionary period, 38–39, 80, 85–86
  rise of appendant bodies, 48–50
  War of 1812, 86–87
  World War II, 87–88
  early 1900s, social concerns, 50
  1930–50s, pre/post-WWII issues, 51–52
  1960–90s, membership decline, 52–53

2000s, connecting with the millennial
    generation, 53–54
Masonic history in Europe
  arrival from England, 77–78
  connections to Nazism, 298–299
  formation of Illuminati, 79
  modern-day anti-Masonic restrictions,
    84–85, 299–300
  totalitarian persecution, 82–84
Masonic history in France. *See also*
    French Revolution
  growth of Freemasonry, 43
  historical origins of Scottish Rite, 209
  Jacobite controversy, 35–36
  modern day anti-Masonic restrictions,
    84–85
  origins of Templar Theory, 34–35, 78
  persecution following the Revolution, 41
Masonic history in Russia, 43, 51, 73–74,
    82, 85, 258
Masonic lodge. *See also* Blue Lodge;
    Grand Lodge
  about the meaning of, 92
  about the workings and symbols, 4
  Ancient Charges of Masonry, 330–334
  appearance of the temple, 45
  awarding optional degrees, 187
  defined/described, 15–16
  degree ceremonies, 94
  details/description, lodge room, 92–94
  growth of speculative Masons, 28–29
  how-to find, 272–273
  meetings as act of "worship," 155–156
  "Mother Lodge of Scotland," 26
  stated communications, 94, 275
  survival, finding ways, 263–266
Masonic officers (appointed), 101–104
Masonic officers (elected), 96–100
Masonic philosophy, 55–60, 65
Masonic Research Societies, 246–248
Masonic Restoration Foundation, 53–54, 264
Masonic ritual. *See also* legends/
    mythology; *Regius Manuscript*
  about the secret elements, 2, 115–116
  ample form shortcuts, 106
  applying new technologies to, 265–266

cipher books/rituals/codes, 121, 122
demonstrating proficiency, 15, 126, 128, 276–277
development from the guilds, 116–119
irregular/unrecognized lodges, 114
performance in lodge, 121–123
role of Albert Pike, 210–215
tracing boards, 125, 132–134
Traditional Observance lodges, 53–54
Masonic secrecy. *See also* legends/
    mythology
about, 2, 115–116
aura and renewed interest, 53
exposure, 122
guild system origins, 25
initiatory ritual ceremony, 117
modes of recognition, 17–81
Morgan affair and anti-Masonic
    movement, 45–47
oath/obligation, 124
overcoming the myths of, 152
violations/punishments for, 107, 126
Masonic Service Association, 50
Masonic Society, 248
Masonic Temple of Detroit, MI, 302–303
Master Mason (3rd-degree)
about the meaning, 15
origins of the ritual, 119
performing the ritual for, 127–128
rank of, 205, 278
role in the guild system, 25
McKinley, William (Mason, U.S. president),
    50, 87
McKinstry, John (Mason), 86
Mecca Temple (Shriners), 223
meetings
about the functions of, 14–15
ample form shortcuts, 106
arrangement of the lodge, 93
degree ceremonies, 94
going dark, 276
"squaring the lodge," 125
stated communications, 275
Mein Kampf [*My Struggle*] (Hitler), 51, 83
membership qualifications, 273–275
*Memoirs Illustrating the History of
    Jacobinism* (Barruel), 291

memorization
appendant bodies, 187
cipher books, 121
demonstrating proficiency, 15, 126,
    128, 276–277
derived from medieval guilds, 117
symbols as memory devices, 130,
    137–150, 297
metaphysics, 61
Mick, Ethel T. Mead (founder of Job's
    Daughters), 242
Minstrel's Guild, 118
Mitchell, John (Mason), 210
Mohammed [Muhammad] (Prophet),
    136, 197
Moose. *See* Loyal Order of Moose
morality and code of conduct
about the basic principle of, 55, 58–60
Ancient Charges, 33, 329–334
degrees as lessons in, 65, 120, 127, 217
Illuminati movement, 79
Jewish conspiracy theory, 74
Job's Daughters lessons, 242
lessons from appendant bodies, 165
Masonry as system of, 13–14, 255–258
papal infallibility, 68
Regius Manuscript, 25, 307–327
ritual as lessons in, 121, 226
Scottish Rite lessons, 208
Shriners activities, 229
square and compass as symbol, 11, 137
survival in face of no "rulz," 5, 252, 255
symbolism, 62, 92–93, 149
Morals and Dogma (Pike), 155–156,
    159–160, 161, 213–215
Moray, Robert (Mason), 29
Morgan, William (Mason), 45–46
Morin, Etienne (Mason), 210
Mormon Church, 116
Morris, Rob (Mason), 232
"Mother Lodge of Scotland" (Kilwinning
    Lodge), 26
Mount Moriah, 92, 134, 188
Murder by Decree (movie, 1979), 260, 295
Muslims. *See* Islam
Mystery Schools of Egypt, 61
mystery/miracle plays, 118, 119

Mystic Order of the Veiled Prophets of the Enchanted Realm of North America. *See* Grotto
Mystic Tie Grand Lodge, 179–180
mysticism, 61–62, 156
myths. *See* legends/mythology

• N •

naked heart and sword (symbol), 145
National Heritage Museum (Lexington, MA), 219
National Sojourners, 166, 171, 245
National Treasure (movie, 2004), 153, 259–260
Nazism, 51, 87–88, 129, 148, 298–299. *See also* Germany; Hitler, Adolph
"new order of the ages" (Novus Ordo Seclorum), 154
New World Order (Novus Ordo Mundi), 60, 79, 154. *See also* world domination
Noah (Biblical patriarch), 118, 119, 120, 188, 242
non-Christians, Freemasonry and, 33
non-Masonic groups, 172–179. *See also* fraternal organization/s; irregular Masonic groups

• O •

oath/obligation
Entered Apprentice, 117, 124–125
Fellow Craft, 127
Masonic degrees, 15
Order of the Eastern Star, 233
penalties for breaking, 107, 126
Scottish Rite, 208
occult
all-seeing eye of God, 153–155
five-pointed pentagram, 296–297
Kabbalah (Jewish mysticism), 212–213
Masonic connection, 61, 64, 156, 214–215
Masonic symbols as, 130
Nazism connections to, 298–299

non-Masonic groups, 177–179
odd-ball practitioners, 297–298
one-day classes, 261–262, 278
operative Masons, 21–24
Operatives (Worshipful Society of Free Masons), 201–202
Order of DeMolay. *See* DeMolay International
Order of Good Templars, 48
Order of Good Things, 173
Order of Job's Daughters. *See* Job's Daughters International
Order of King David Hebrew Grand Lodge, 179–180
Order of Knights of the York Cross of Honour, 166, 168, 201
Order of Malta, 191
Order of Perfectibilists. *See* Illuminati
Order of the Amaranth, 19–20, 166, 171, 236–237
Order of the Ancient, Free and Accepted Masons for Men and Women, 20
Order of the Arrow (Boy Scouts), 241
Order of the Eastern Star (OES)
about the origins, 48, 232–233
as appendant body, 19–20, 112
five-pointed star, 233–235, 297
governance and organization, 235–236
membership requirements, 233
relationship to Freemasonry, 166, 171
Order of the Knights of Pythias, 176
Order of the Rainbow for Girls. *See* International Order of the Rainbow for Girls
Order of the Red Cross of Constantine, 166, 168, 201
Order of the Star-Spangled Banner, 47–48
Order of the Temple, 191
Order of Women's Free-Masons, 20
Ordo Templi Orientis (Order of the Oriental Templars), 177–178
Ordo Templi Orientis (Crowley redefinition), 298
orphans and widows, 50

• P •

pagan rites/paganism, 61, 141, 156
pageants/pageant wagons, 118
Palladism (a.k.a. Luciferian High-Masonry),
    158–159, 290–291
Paradise Lost (Milton), 160–161
parallel lines (symbol), 140–141
Parsons, Samuel H. (Mason, general), 86
"passing," Fellow Craft, 127
passwords, 17–18, 25, 117. *See also*
    Masonic secrecy
Past Master, 104, 186
Patrick, M. (Mason, general), 50
patron saints, 118, 141
pencil (symbol), 149
Pershing, John J. ["Blackjack"] (Mason,
    general), 50
petition for membership, 275–276
Philalethes Society, 247
Philo Musicae et Architecturae Societas
    Apollini, 119
philosophy, Freemasonry as, 13–14
Phylaxis Society, 247
Pike, Albert (Mason, writer), 48, 61, 155,
    203, 210–215, 290
pillars (symbol), 147–148
plumb (symbol), 142
point within a circle (symbol), 140–141
politics
    about Freemasonry and, 2, 63
    anti-Masonic movement and, 43, 46–47
    exclusion from lodge, 34, 60, 77, 110
    legends about world domination, 161–162
    lodge officers, 95–96
    Order of the Eastern Star, 233
    other fraternal groups, 175
    world domination, 161–162, 292–293
Poor Knights of Christ and the Temple of
    Solomon. *See* Knights Templar
pot of incense (symbol), 141
Preston, William (Mason), 119, 137
Prince Hall Eastern Star, 236
Prince Hall Grand Lodges, 340–344

Prince Hall Masonry. *See also* Grand Lodge
    about the origins, 40–41
    bogus (irregular) lodges, 114
    contacting/finding a lodge, 273
    Grand Lodge jurisdiction, 111
    recognition by white lodges, 53
    recognition of Grand Lodges, 108–109
profanes (non-Masons), 132
proficiency, demonstrating, 15, 126, 128,
    276–277
progressive line (going through
    the line), 95–96
Proofs of a Conspiracy . . . (Robinson), 291
Protestant reformation, 27–28
Protestantism, 71–72, 80, 132
Protocols of the Learned Elders of Zion,
    51, 74, 291. *See also* Jews/Judaism;
    Zionism
public ceremonies, Masonic
    participation, 16–17
pyramid (symbol), 144, 153–155
Pythagorean theorem, 104, 138

• Q •

Quaturo Coronati Lodge No. 2076, 247

• R •

racism/racial discrimination, 40, 71–72,
    83, 252, 298–299. *See also* equality
    and tolerance; slaves/slavery
Rainbow. *See* International Order of the
    Rainbow for Girls
Ramsay, Andrew Michael (Chevalier
    Ramsay), 30–31, 34–35, 78, 190,
    193, 209
Rectified Rite (Chevalier Bienfaisant
    de Cite Saint), 200
Regius Manuscript, 6, 25, 307–327. *See also*
    Masonic ritual
regularity/recognition, 105, 108–111,
    179–180. *See also* irregular/
    unrecognized lodges

relief (charity toward others). *See also*
    charity/charities
  as basic principle, 39, 56–57, 58, 85
  creating opportunities for, 255–256, 268
  incorporation into symbols, 139
  initiatory education, 123, 125
  York Rite principles, 186
religion. *See also* equality and tolerance;
    Satanism; *specific religion*
  about Freemasonry and, 2, 13, 63–64
  Ancient Charges of Masonry, 330
  concept of Deism, 37
  impact of scientific method on, 28
  Masonry as act of "worship," 156–157
  Masonry descendence from, 61
  Masonry open to all, 33
  persecution and intolerance in the
    name of, 66
  persecution of Freemasonry, 12
  practicing tolerance, 257–258
  prohibition of Masonic membership, 48
Revere, Paul (Mason), 39
Revised Standard Pike Ritual
    (York Rite), 216
Richards, Michael (Mason, actor), 269
Rickenbacker, Eddie (Mason, pilot), 50
Rite of Perfection (Scottish Rite), 209–210
RiteCare clinics/programs, 219
Robertson, Pat (anti-Masonic writer), 291
Robinson, John (anti-Masonic writer),
    30–31, 291
Roosevelt, Franklin D. (Mason, U.S.
    president), 51, 83, 269
Roosevelt, Theodore (Mason, U.S.
    president), 50, 59, 269
Rosicrucian Society, 178
Rosslyn Chapel (Scotland), 198, 304
Rotary International, 70, 174
rough and smooth ashlars (symbol), 147
Royal Antediluvian Order of Buffaloes, 173
Royal Arch Masons (York Rite)
  about the origins, 19
  Antients and Moderns controversy,
    43–44, 184
  defined/described, 168
  degrees conferred, 185–188

early American adaptation, 44–45
governing chapters, 184–185
origins of the degree, 34–35
relationship to Freemasonry, 166
symbols, 185
Royal Arch Research Assistance, 202
Royal Society of London for Improving
    Natural Knowledge, 29
ruler/24-inch gauge (symbol), 150
Russia. *See* Masonic history in Russia

• *S* •

Sacred Congregation for the Doctrine
    of the Faith (formerly Office of the
    Inquisition). *See* Spanish Inquisition
sanctum sanctorum ("holy of holies"),
    22, 135, 140
Satanism, 157–161, 290–291, 297–298
Sayer, Anthony (first Grand Master), 32
scandals. *See also* conspiracy theories;
    legends/mythology
  Italian P2 lodge, 295–296
  secret 33rd Degree, 293
  writings and acts of Aleister Crowley,
    297–298
  writings by Leo Taxil, 289–291
Schnoebelen, William (anti-Masonic
    writer), 291
scholarships. *See* education
science, Freemasonry beliefs, 14
scientific method, 28
scimitar (sword), 223
Scotland, 26, 30
Scott, Walter (Mason, author), 48
Scottish Rite (Ancient Accepted
    Scottish Rite)
  4th–32nd degrees, 48–49, 166, 170
  32nd degree, 19, 28, 169
  33rd degree, 19, 128, 166, 169
  about, 19–20, 169–170, 203, 205
  Albert Pike's role in creating, 210–215
  arrival in U.S., 35, 169, 210
  charities, 219
  degrees, 65, 169–170, 183
  early American adaptation, 44–45

historical origins, 208–210
influence of Kabbalah, 212–213
jurisdictions, 170, 204–205, 207, 210–212, 215–219, 248, 302
membership requirements, 206–207
one-day classes, 261–262
presentation of degrees, 208
relationship to Freemasonry, 165–166
symbols, 204
Scottish Rite, divisions
about, 205
Chapter of the Rose Croix, 206, 217, 218
Consistory, 206, 217, 218–219
Council of Kadosh, 206, 217
Council Princes of Jerusalem, 206, 218
Lodge of Perfection, 206, 216–217, 218
Supreme Council, 206, 217, 219
Scottish Rite Cathedral of Indianapolis, 49, 303
Scottish Rite Research Society, 248
scythe and hourglass (symbol), 138
secret ballot, 276, 277
secret society, 1, 13–14, 161–162, 259–260. *See also* Masonic secrecy
Secretary, 101–102
Senior Deacon, 98–99, 125
Senior Warden, 96–97, 142
Sertoma (Service to Mankind), 174
service club/clubs, 2, 70, 173–174
setting maul (symbol), 148–149
Sexson, William Mark (founder of Rainbow), 242
sexual "magick"/perversions, 158, 177–178, 290, 297–298. *See also* magick (alchemy)
shovel (symbol), 148–149
Shriners Hospitals, 19, 50, 224–226, 229
Shriners International (formerly Ancient Arabic Nobles of the Mystic Shrine)
about, 50, 221
Daughters of the Nile, 166, 171, 228
defined/described, 19, 222
disapproval by Muslims, 76
forming units and fundraising, 227–228
historical origins, 222–224
initiation and temple gatherings, 226–227

membership requirements, 168, 222
one-day classes, 261–262
post-WWII growth, 51–52
relationship to Masonry, 166, 170–171
role in the future of Masonry, 229
signs (gestures), 17–18, 86, 117, 208. *See also* Masonic secrecy
The Simpsons (TV program), 260
skerrit/string (symbol), 149
Skull and Bones (non-Masonic group), 178–179
skull and bones (symbol), 148–149, 192
slaves/slavery, 40–41, 117, 214, 257, 274, 287. *See also* racism/racial discrimination
slipper/slipshod (shoe, symbol), 140
social groups (appendant bodies), 166, 171–172
Social Order of the Beauceant, 166, 171, 239
Societas Rosicruciana in Civitatibus Foerderatis (York Rite), 166, 200
Solomon (prophet and king of Israel), 22, 32, 134. *See also* King Solomon's Temple
Some of Our Business Society (SOOB), 239
Sons of Honor, 48
Sons of Liberty, 175
Southern California Research Lodge (SCRL), 248
Soviet Union. *See* Masonic history in Russia
Spanish Inquisition, 68, 70
speculative Masons
about the origins, 21–22
development of ritual, 119
formation of the Grand Lodge, 31–32, 34
growth during Renaissance, 25–26
rise during Age of Reason, 28–29
square and compass
about the origins, 11–12
Grand Lodge of Israel adaptation, 75
identification of Masons, 22
symbolism, 136–137
"squaring the lodge," 125
St. John's Bible, 42
St. Paul's Cathedral (London), 31

Stafford, Tom (Mason, astronaut), 52
Stalin, Joseph (Soviet leader), 12
Statute of Apprenticeship, 117
Steward (Junior/Senior), 100
Strader, Robert (Mason), 87–88
Stretton, Clement Edwin (Mason,
    engineer), 202
Sun, Moon, and stars (symbols), 139
Supreme Being. *See* God
swastika (symbol), 129
Symbolic Lodge, 16
symbolism/symbols. *See also* allegory;
    jewels of the office
  about the meaning, 62, 129–131
  acacia, 148–149
  All-Seeing Eye, 132, 139, 144, 153–155
  applying new technology to, 265–266
  beehive, 141
  chisel, 149
  Cryptic Rite, 188
  double-headed eagle, 204
  five-pointed Eastern Star, 233–235
  five-pointed star, 145, 233–235, 296–297
  Jacob's Ladder, 139
  King Solomon's Temple, 134–136
  Knights Templar, 190, 192
  lambskin apron, 139–140
  letter *G*, 143–145
  level, 142–143
  naked heart and sword, 145
  number 3, 131–132
  parallel lines, 140–141
  pencil, 149
  pillars/Pillars of the Porch, 147–148
  plumb, 142
  point within a circle, 140–141
  pot of incense, 141
  pyramid, 144, 153–155
  Pythagorean theorem, 104, 138
  rough and smooth ashlars, 147
  Royal Arch, 185
  ruler and hammer, 150
  scimitar, 223
  scythe and hourglass, 138
  shovel, setting maul, coffin, skull, 148–149
  skerrit (string), 149
  slipper (shoe), 140
  square and compass, 11–12, 136–137
  Tetragammaton, 188–189
  tracing boards, 132–134
  trowel, 146
  Tyler's Sword and Book, 146
  White Shrine of Jerusalem, 238
Synagogue of Satan (Meurin), 290

● *T* ●

Taft, William H. (Mason, U.S. president), 50
Tales of the Arabian Nights, 76
Tall Cedars of Lebanon, 19–20, 166, 171,
    244–245
Tanach (Hebrew Bible), 65, 155
Tarkenton, Fran (DeMolay, athlete), 240
Taxil, Leo (anti-Masonic author), 158–159,
    289–291
Templar Church (London), 194, 303–304
The Templar Code For Dummies (Hodapp
    and Von Kannon), 193
temple. *See* Masonic lodge
Temple of King Solomon. *See* King
    Solomon's Temple
Tetragammaton, name of God, 188–189, 213
3, symbolism of number, 131–132
3rd-degree Master Mason, 15, 25, 119,
    127–128, 205, 278
32nd-degree Mason (Scottish Rite)
  about the meaning of, 16, 169
  additional degrees, 128
  as appendant body, 19
  awarding of the degrees, 206–208
  Knights of Saint Andrew, 219
33rd-degree Mason (Scottish Rite)
  about the meaning of, 16, 169
  additional degrees, 128
  as appendant body, 19
  awarding of the degree, 206–208
  relationship to Freemasonry, 166
  Satanic connections, 293
Thomas, Dave (Mason, businessman), 269
tolerance. *See* equality and tolerance
Torrigiani, Domizio (Grand Master), 84
tracing boards, 125, 132–134

Traditional Observance lodges, 53–54, 264
Treasurer, 101
trestle board, 134
Trilateral Commission, 292
trowel (symbol), 146
The True Masonic Chart and Hieroglyphic Monitor (Cross), 137
Truman, Harry S (Mason, U.S. president), 51, 269, 278
truth
    as basic principle, 56–58, 271
    initiatory education, 123
    Rotary "Four Way Test" of ethics, 174
    symbolism, 11, 142, 175
    teachings and ritual, 217
24-inch gauge (symbol), 150
29 degrees (Scottish Rite), 19
Tyler (Tiler), 103, 123, 146

• *U* •

United Grand Lodge of England, 34, 43–44, 106, 112, 113
urban legend. *See* legends/mythology
U.S. $1 bill, 153–155
U.S. Constitution, 39
U.S. government
    Great Seal of the United States, 154
    Illuminati conspiracy and, 292
    influence of Masonry on, 39
    Masonic principles as foundation, 12
    Satanic design of Washington, DC, 296–297
    takeover, 161
    Washington as first president, 42

• *V* •

Vatican. *See* Catholic Church
Vedas (Hindu), 65, 155
visitors, lodge, 98–99, 101, 103, 110
Voltaire (author and philosopher), 12, 36
Volume of Sacred Law, 59, 93, 102, 113, 124.
    See also Masonic bible

Von Kannon, Alice (author)
    Conspiracy Theories & Secret Societies For Dummies (Wiley), 152
    The Templar Code For Dummies (Wiley), 193

• *W* •

Waite, Edward (Mason, writer), 61, 178
Warden (Junior/Senior), 96–98
warrants (charters), 105
Washington, George (Mason, U.S. president), 12, 42, 217, 281, 283, 296
Wayne, John (DeMolay, actor), 240
Webb, Thomas Smith (Mason), 44, 47, 119, 137
Weishaupt, Adam ["Spartacus"] (founder of Illuminati), 79, 291
white leather apron. *See* lambskin apron
White Shrine of Jerusalem, 19–20, 166, 238
Wiley. *See* John Wiley and Sons
Wirt, William (anti-Masonic political candidate), 46
witchcraft, 16, 23, 153
Wolcott Foundation, Inc., 246
women
    appendant bodies, 19–20, 171
    female (irregular) lodges, 112, 113
    Jack the Ripper murders, 294–295
    Masonic membership, 20
    Order of the Eastern Star, 48
    Palladian lodges, 290
Women's Grand Lodge of Belgium, 20, 112
Woodmen of the World, 177
world domination. *See also* conspiracy theories; international organization/ governance
    Freemasonry and, 12, 60, 91, 161–162
    Illuminati and, 79, 292
    Jewish conspiracy theory, 51
    Masonic governing bodies and, 14
World War I, 50
World War II, 51–52, 87–88
Worshipful Master, 96, 123

Worshipful Society of Free Masons, Rough Masons, Wallers, Slaters, Paviors, Plaisterers and Bricklayers (the Operatives), 201–202
Wright, Bobbi Jo (crippled child), 225

● Y ●

York Rite
  about the groups, 19–20, 168, 181–182
  additional bodies, 198–202
  arrival in U.S., 35
  charities, 202
  commemorative jewelry, 107
  degrees, 34–35, 65, 168, 183–185
  early American adaptation, 44–45

one-day classes, 261–262
relationship to Freemasonry, 165–166
York Rite, Chivalric orders, 191. *See also* Knights Templar
York Rite, Cryptic Rite degrees, 189
York Rite, Royal Arch degrees, 185–188
York Rite College, 166, 168, 199
youth groups. *See* DeMolay International; International Order of the Rainbow; Job's Daughters International

● Z ●

Zionism, 74, 76, 228, 292. *See also* Jews/ Judaism
Zoroastrianism, 65, 155, 156

pple & Mac

ad 2 For Dummies,
d Edition
8-1-118-17679-5

hone 4S For Dummies,
h Edition
8-1-118-03671-6

od touch For Dummies,
d Edition
8-1-118-12960-9

ac OS X Lion
r Dummies
8-1-118-02205-4

ogging & Social Media

tyVille For Dummies
8-1-118-08337-6

cebook For Dummies,
h Edition
8-1-118-09562-1

m Blogging
r Dummies
8-1-118-03843-7

itter For Dummies,
d Edition
8-0-470-76879-2

rdPress For Dummies,
Edition
8-1-118-07342-1

siness

sh Flow For Dummies
8-1-118-01850-7

esting For Dummies,
Edition
8-0-470-90545-6

Job Searching with Social
Media For Dummies
978-0-470-93072-4

QuickBooks 2012
For Dummies
978-1-118-09120-3

Resumes For Dummies,
6th Edition
978-0-470-87361-8

Starting an Etsy Business
For Dummies
978-0-470-93067-0

Cooking & Entertaining

Cooking Basics
For Dummies, 4th Edition
978-0-470-91388-8

Wine For Dummies,
4th Edition
978-0-470-04579-4

Diet & Nutrition

Kettlebells For Dummies
978-0-470-59929-7

Nutrition For Dummies,
5th Edition
978-0-470-93231-5

Restaurant Calorie Counter
For Dummies,
2nd Edition
978-0-470-64405-8

Digital Photography

Digital SLR Cameras &
Photography For Dummies,
4th Edition
978-1-118-14489-3

Digital SLR Settings
& Shortcuts
For Dummies
978-0-470-91763-3

Photoshop Elements 10
For Dummies
978-1-118-10742-3

Gardening

Gardening Basics
For Dummies
978-0-470-03749-2

Vegetable Gardening
For Dummies,
2nd Edition
978-0-470-49870-5

Green/Sustainable

Raising Chickens
For Dummies
978-0-470-46544-8

Green Cleaning
For Dummies
978-0-470-39106-8

Health

Diabetes For Dummies,
3rd Edition
978-0-470-27086-8

Food Allergies
For Dummies
978-0-470-09584-3

Living Gluten-Free
For Dummies,
2nd Edition
978-0-470-58589-4

Hobbies

Beekeeping
For Dummies,
2nd Edition
978-0-470-43065-1

Chess For Dummies,
3rd Edition
978-1-118-01695-4

Drawing For Dummies,
2nd Edition
978-0-470-61842-4

eBay For Dummies,
7th Edition
978-1-118-09806-6

Knitting For Dummies,
2nd Edition
978-0-470-28747-7

Language &
Foreign Language

English Grammar
For Dummies,
2nd Edition
978-0-470-54664-2

French For Dummies,
2nd Edition
978-1-118-00464-7

German For Dummies,
2nd Edition
978-0-470-90101-4

Spanish Essentials
For Dummies
978-0-470-63751-7

Spanish For Dummies,
2nd Edition
978-0-470-87855-2

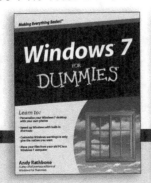

ilable wherever books are sold. For more information or to order direct: U.S. customers visit www.dummies.com or call 1-877-762-2974.
U.K. customers visit www.wileyeurope.com or call (0) 1243 843291. Canadian customers visit www.wiley.ca or call 1-800-567-4797.

Connect with us online at www.facebook.com/fordummies or @fordummies

Math & Science

Algebra I For Dummies,
2nd Edition
978-0-470-55964-2

Biology For Dummies,
2nd Edition
978-0-470-59875-7

Chemistry For Dummies,
2nd Edition
978-1-1180-0730-3

Geometry For Dummies,
2nd Edition
978-0-470-08946-0

Pre-Algebra Essentials
For Dummies
978-0-470-61838-7

Microsoft Office

Excel 2010 For Dummies
978-0-470-48953-6

Office 2010 All-in-One
For Dummies
978-0-470-49748-7

Office 2011 for Mac
For Dummies
978-0-470-87869-9

Word 2010
For Dummies
978-0-470-48772-3

Music

Guitar For Dummies,
2nd Edition
978-0-7645-9904-0

Clarinet For Dummies
978-0-470-58477-4

iPod & iTunes
For Dummies,
9th Edition
978-1-118-13060-5

Pets

Cats For Dummies,
2nd Edition
978-0-7645-5275-5

Dogs All-in One
For Dummies
978-0470-52978-2

Saltwater Aquariums
For Dummies
978-0-470-06805-2

Religion & Inspiration

The Bible For Dummies
978-0-7645-5296-0

Catholicism For Dummies,
2nd Edition
978-1-118-07778-8

Spirituality For Dummies,
2nd Edition
978-0-470-19142-2

Self-Help & Relationships

Happiness For Dummies
978-0-470-28171-0

Overcoming Anxiety
For Dummies,
2nd Edition
978-0-470-57441-6

Seniors

Crosswords For Seniors
For Dummies
978-0-470-49157-7

iPad 2 For Seniors
For Dummies, 3rd Edition
978-1-118-17678-8

Laptops & Tablets
For Seniors For Dummies,
2nd Edition
978-1-118-09596-6

Smartphones & Tablets

BlackBerry For Dummies,
5th Edition
978-1-118-10035-6

Droid X2 For Dummies
978-1-118-14864-8

HTC ThunderBolt
For Dummies
978-1-118-07601-9

MOTOROLA XOOM
For Dummies
978-1-118-08835-7

Sports

Basketball For Dummies,
3rd Edition
978-1-118-07374-2

Football For Dummies,
2nd Edition
978-1-118-01261-1

Golf For Dummies,
4th Edition
978-0-470-88279-5

Test Prep

ACT For Dummies,
5th Edition
978-1-118-01259-8

ASVAB For Dummies,
3rd Edition
978-0-470-63760-9

The GRE Test For
Dummies, 7th Edition
978-0-470-00919-2

Police Officer Exam
For Dummies
978-0-470-88724-0

Series 7 Exam
For Dummies
978-0-470-09932-2

Web Development

HTML, CSS, & XHTML
For Dummies, 7th Edition
978-0-470-91659-9

Drupal For Dummies,
2nd Edition
978-1-118-08348-2

Windows 7

Windows 7
For Dummies
978-0-470-49743-2

Windows 7
For Dummies,
Book + DVD Bundle
978-0-470-52398-8

Windows 7 All-in-One
For Dummies
978-0-470-48763-1

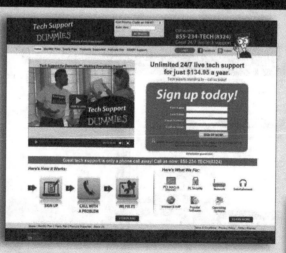